THE CENTURY PSYCHOLOGY SERIES

Richard M. Elliott, *Editor*

Kenneth MacCorquodale *and* Gardner Lindzey, *Assistant Editors*

Projective Techniques

and

Cross-Cultural Research

GARDNER LINDZEY
UNIVERSITY OF MINNESOTA

Projective Techniques
and
Cross-Cultural Research

New York

APPLETON-CENTURY-CROFTS, INC.

PRINTED IN THE UNITED STATES OF AMERICA

To ANDREA

Preface

THIS MONOGRAPH FOCUSES on problems and contributions generated by extensive use of projective techniques in cross-cultural research. Although some topics, such as the definition of projective techniques and their relation to psychological theory, are treated more comprehensively here than elsewhere in the literature, the volume is not intended primarily for the specialist in projective testing. Rather, it is written for the person who is interested in applying these instruments in anthropological research. The problems encountered in such research are by no means unique, however, and many of the issues discussed here are relevant to the use of projective techniques in other areas, including the clinical setting.

The original impetus for this volume was an invitation from the former Committee on Social Behavior of the Social Science Research Council. The committee at the time of our initial discussion consisted of Donald G. Marquis, Chairman, Leonard S. Cottrell, Leon Festinger, Irving L. Janis, Horace M. Minor, Robert R. Sears, William H. Sewell, M. Brewster Smith, Staff Representative, and Robin Williams. Most of the members of this group have made important suggestions, both at the original conference and after reading drafts of various chapters, and the counsel and encouragement of Professor Smith have been indispensable throughout. In addition, I have gained from conversations with Pendleton Herring, Eleanor C. Isbell, and Paul Webbink.

The list of other individuals who have contributed to the monograph by their suggestions and comments is distressingly long. Considering the number of distinguished social scientists whose aid I acknowledge, the reader might anticipate a volume far more substantial than the one to follow. To be honest, however, I must report having benefited from generous advice from: Theodora M. Abel, Gordon W. Allport, John W. Atkinson, Donald T. Campbell, William Caudill, George A. DeVos, Cora DuBois, James L. Gibbs, Thomas Gladwin, Jules Henry, William E. Henry, Adam Hoebel, Robert R.

Holt, John J. Honigmann, Bert Kaplan, the late Clyde Kluckhohn, Henry A. Murray, the late David Rapaport, Ephraim Rosen, Seymour B. Sarason, David Schneider, George D. Spindler, Melford E. Spiro, Murray A. Straus, Evon Z. Vogt, Anthony F. C. Wallace, and Robert D. Wirt. In final preparation of the manuscript, Mrs. Jean Bradford, Mrs. Judith Lucking, and Miss Sara L. Jorvik provided essential assistance.

Preparation of the volume was facilitated by financial support from the Social Science Research Council, the Ford Foundation, and Grant M-1949 from the National Institute of Mental Health of the National Institutes of Health, Public Health Service. A pleasant and productive interlude at the Center for Advanced Study in the Behavioral Sciences played an essential role in the successful completion of this work. I am profoundly grateful to Dr. Ralph Tyler and all of his staff for this unusual opportunity to retreat into scholarship and conviviality.

G. L.

Contents

Contents

Projective Techniques

and

Cross-Cultural Research

1. The Introduction of Projective Techniques in Anthropological Research

THERE IS NO DOUBT that during the past decade and a half individuals trained in each of the traditional social science disciplines have shown impatience with limiting themselves to the methods, problems, and theories assigned to them by convention. A number of these scholars have set out earnestly either to educate members of one of the other behavioral disciplines or else to seek education from them. As a consequence we have had a hasty and stimulating exchange of missionaries moving from one set of values, techniques, problems, and beliefs to a new set of theories, methods, and questions. There is no clearer illustration of this interdisciplinary movement than the application of projective techniques in anthropological research.

Projective techniques, by origin as well as by convention, are tools of the clinician. They are used primarily by the person who is assessing individual personalities, usually with a therapeutic or diagnostic intent. At present, however, they are beginning to be employed extensively to provide insight into a variety of problems that traditionally have been the concern of the anthropologist, sociologist, and social psychologist. Although this trend is observable in a variety of settings, the most extensive application has been in the hands of the cultural anthropologist. Of all the instruments for assessing personality the psychologist has devised, it is only projective techniques that seem to have aroused much interest on the part of the anthropologist, and the study of personality in cross-cultural settings has proceeded in recent years with extensive utilization of results provided by these instruments.

1

The present volume is intended to examine and appraise the use of projective techniques in this unusual setting. In the chapters to follow I shall attempt to examine the nature of the applications that have been made of these techniques in anthropology and to point out some of the difficulties that have arisen as a result of these applications. I shall pose the kinds of questions that the individual who is considering this kind of research should, it seems to me, have in the forefront of his mind. Where existing evidence and theory provide relevant material, I shall also provide tentative answers to these questions. It is my belief that projective techniques offer real and tangible empirical fruits for the individual who employs them wisely. I am equally convinced, however, that they have often been used injudiciously so that their contribution to the investigator on occasion has been slight or even negative. In this connection, I shall have something to say about the circumstances under which it is not advisable to use such techniques.

Our venture, then, will have a little of the flavor of a survey, as I shall summarize a good deal of research that has been conducted employing projective techniques to investigate cross-cultural phenomena. It will also be something of a critique, however, as I shall attempt to identify misuse of these techniques where it has occurred, as well as the special difficulties that beset the investigator working in this area. Finally, it will be a bit of a cookbook for I shall try to provide for the nonspecialist some of the information he should have in order to proceed with such investigation or decide to abandon it.

In the present chapter I shall consider some evidence indicating that there is, in fact, a trend toward applying projective techniques in cross-cultural research, and I shall also try to indicate some of the main sources of influence that have stimulated or facilitated such research. I shall discuss some of the early and typical studies in this area, and in a final section I shall make clear that these developments have not been considered an unmixed blessing by all observers.

EVIDENCE OF INTEREST IN THE USE OF PROJECTIVE TECHNIQUES IN ANTHROPOLOGY

Let us consider for a moment this trend toward application of projective techniques in the hands of anthropologists. The detailed documentation of just how much use has been made of these instruments in anthropology must be left to subsequent chapters that will summarize or refer to the bulk of relevant investigation. Here, however, we may consider some of the public statements that have been made by competent observers concerning the contribution of projective techniques to anthropology.

One anthropologist who has contributed notably to the area of culture and personality is the late Clyde Kluckhohn, who reasoned that projective tests play a crucial role in anthropological research.

Projective techniques, however, can now be regarded as almost indispensable to fineness of interpretation at the personological level. Especially for those fairly well adjusted in their society, the communal and role components of the personality tend to constitute disguises. Just as the outer body screens the viscera from view and clothing the genitals, so the "public" facets of personality shield the private personality from the curious and conformity-demanding world of other persons. . . . Often only projective techniques will bring out what the individual does not want to tell about himself and what he himself does not know. (Kluckhohn, 1949, pp. 81-82)

A. Irving Hallowell, a cultural anthropologist who has pioneered in the introduction of the Rorschach test in anthropological studies, concurs with Kluckhohn's judgment:

Information derived from the Rorschach and other projective techniques, therefore, cannot be ignored by the anthropologist if he is interested in joining forces with the psychologist in the pursuit of a common goal—a thorough understanding of *all* factors that enter into the determination of the behavior of man and the functioning of human societies through cultural instrumentalities. From this point of view, the information obtainable from Rorschach data may be just as significant, at the personality level, in validating the anthropologist's interpretation of the functioning of cultures, as a consideration of cultural data has proved of value to the psychologist in gaining a more comprehensive knowledge of the determinants relevant to the functioning of individuals. (Hallowell, 1955, p. 63)

S. F. Nadel comments upon the increasing use of projective tests by anthropologists:

A new kind of routine seems to be emerging whereby anthropologists, before setting out for the field, pack into their kitbag a set of Rorschach cards and TAT much as they do cameras, a compass, or a copy of *Notes and Queries*. (Nadel, 1955, p. 247)

Henry and Spiro, introducing a summary of the use of projective techniques by anthropologists, conclude that of all psychological tests the projective techniques are most commonly used by anthropologists:

The psychological techniques that have been used by anthropologists to study the mental and emotional functioning of peoples outside occidental culture are numerous. . . . In this paper we have limited ourselves almost exclusively to *projective tests*, for it is these that, at the present time, are in widest use by anthropologists interested in the field of personality and culture. (Henry & Spiro, 1953, p. 419)

To these individual statements can be added the observation that the *American Anthropologist*, official publication of the American Anthropological Association, has during recent years published a long article dealing with a comparison of direct observation and psychological tests in the field setting (Mensh & Henry, 1953), and has also published a symposium devoted to appraising critically the use of projective techniques in anthropological investigation (Henry, 1955; Nadel, 1955, etc.).

All in all, there seems little doubt that projective techniques have been seized upon with enthusiasm by many cultural anthropologists and applied extensively in cross-cultural settings. Let us now consider some of the factors that may have played a role in the emergence of this trend.

SOME DETERMINANTS OF INTEREST IN PROJECTIVE TECHNIQUES AMONG ANTHROPOLOGISTS

An attempt to answer the question of just why it is that individuals have become interested in studying cultural phenomena with the aid of projective techniques is subject to all the dangers that beset any effort to answer an historical question. A multitude of factors have had some effect upon this development and at best we can hope to capture only a portion of these. Although it is difficult to be wise and insightful concerning events in the immediate past, there are nevertheless some influences so profound that their role is clear even from the short perspective of a mere ten or twenty years.

Easily the most important single factor promoting an interest in the application of projective techniques outside of clinical settings is the pervasive and powerful impact of *psychoanalytic theory*. Freud and his theory have become a commonplace in almost every corner of the social sciences. Social psychology, social anthropology, sociology, even history and political science have been shaped and modified to some degree by the creations of Freud's seminal mind. The central nature and extent of Freud's contributions in the social sciences have been amply documented elsewhere (Hall & Lindzey, 1954; Hilgard, 1952; Pumpian-Mindlin, 1952) and Kluckhohn (1944, 1954) has made evident the general impact of Freudian thought upon anthropology. All in all it seems safe for us to accept the sizable influence of psychoanalysis upon anthropology and to consider how such a development may have served to heighten interest in projective techniques.

It is clear that anyone seriously interested in psychoanalytic theory must develop a concomitant interest in unconscious motivation since these forces are assigned a position of key importance in psychoanalytic formulation. If an investigator develops an interest in latent or unconscious determinants of behavior, it is easy to see why he should wish to use projective techniques in his research, for one of the most salient characteristics of these instruments is their purported sensitivity to determinants of behavior of which the subject himself is unaware. Not only does psychoanalytic theory imply an interest in covert or latent measures of personality but also it is particularly at home with just the variety of rich and multiform data typically obtained by projective techniques. Psychoanalysis developed in intimate relation with the data provided by free association, dreaming, and clinical interviews so that there is every reason to expect that the theory and its concepts should apply with unusual relevance to projective technique data. Thus, the psychoanalytically oriented investigator is likely to be interested in projective techniques both because of their presumed sensitivity to unconscious or covert motives and because they provide a class of data similar to that with which psychoanalysis traditionally has dealt.

A second theoretical emphasis that has had some influence upon cultural anthropology and has contributed to the concern with projective techniques is *holism*. The distinctive feature of this position is an emphasis upon the importance of studying behavior in a full context, with little or no attempt to analyze it into small elements and component parts. Actually, the general holistic position can be divided into two special points of view that may be labelled respectively *field* and *organismic*. Field theory places primary emphasis upon studying behavior in a full environmental context while organismic theory is more concerned with the essential unity of the individual and all of his actions. In field theory the observer is admonished not to attempt to understand a given behavioral event without examining in detail the situational, cultural, and physical setting within which the event occurs. The organismic position emphasizes that the understanding of one behavioral event without a full consideration of all other aspects of the individual, including his other behavior and physiological functioning, is likely to be fruitless. One or both of these emphases have been present in the writings of a number of influential anthropologists, including Ruth Benedict, Franz Boas, A. I. Hallowell, Clyde Kluckhohn, Alfred Kroeber, and Bronislaw Malinowski, among others.

Once the investigator has accepted the importance of studying behavior in a full context, relating each item of behavior to all other relevant behavior, as well as to its situational and cultural context, it becomes extremely difficult for him to use typical objective instruments for personality measurement. Such instruments usually provide a means of measuring, in relative isolation, a small number of personality dimensions that have been given prior definition. In contrast, the investigator may use projective techniques without committing himself to one or a limited number of explicit dimensions and, further, he may hope to secure by means of the instrument a variety of information concerning the internal relations between those variables he eventually selects as appropriate. Thus, what might in some contexts appear to be a lack of specificity and precision in projective techniques is an appealing attribute for the individual strongly influenced by holistic theory.

The motivation of many persons who seize upon projective techniques is deftly outlined by Marguerite Hertz, well-known champion of the Rorschach test. As she makes clear, this motivation is often linked with holistic theory:

The atomistic conception of personality had met with challenge. Personality as a bundle of characteristics, each subject to identification, segregation, and measurement and together forming a whole which was merely the sum of its parts, encountered resistance. The newer disciplines—Gestalt psychology, Phychoanalysis, Typology, Psychodiagnostics, and the Psychology of *Verstehen,* postulated personality as more than the sum total of assembled static qualities and rather as a living, functioning whole, a dynamic synthesis.

Thus was formulated a new approach to the study of personality. The problems of how to study a synthesis rather than a conglomeration of isolated parts still remained, for both research and practice had made it clear that personality possessed aspects which eluded the stereotyped and conventionalized paper-and-pencil tests, the questionnaires, the rating scales, and laboratory techniques of measurements.

There ensued a quest for the elusive which opened new avenues and forged new tools. Projective techniques were developed so that today many students of personality no longer rely exclusively upon answers to questions or on minute reactions elicited in the laboratory routine. Nor do they judge the individual solely by comparing him with his fellows.

They prefer to place the individual in a specific situation, presenting him with words, unfinished sentences, plastic materials, puppets, pictures, or ink-blots, and study what he does. Conduct in specific situations now dominates the attention of these students of personality. They evaluate the individual in terms of himself, knowing that mental, emotional, and experiential equipment and background will lead him to react in his unique way. His reactions will yield an insight into his mental processes, fantasy life, desires, emotionality, talents, and the like and thus permit us, by their revelations and projections, to reconstruct his personality. (Hertz, 1942, pp. 529-530)

The emphasis upon studying behavior holistically not only created resistance to the use of ordinary dimensional measures of personality but also contributed to the development of an interest in personality variables on the part of investigators who previously had shown little concern for them. The individual who was concerned with the operation of some aggregate institution, such as religion or government, could easily restrict his analysis to a set of variables that completely overlooked psychological dimensions of the problem. Acceptance of the importance of studying such phenomena in full context, however, led in many cases to an expanded conception including personality variables of individual actors. In other words, if the investigator accepts the importance of a full context of investigation, it is much more likely that he will find personality attributes relevant to his problem than if he adopts some less inclusive conception of the event at question. Thus, holism has produced an interest in psychological dimensions on the part of many social scientists who might otherwise have ignored this domain and at the same time has made projective techniques seem particularly attractive as a means of appraising psychological factors because they are relatively free from the demands of molecular and segmental analysis.

Related to the holistic position is the emergence of a point of view sometimes identified with *phenomenology,* or at least with the importance of the phenomenal world. This viewpoint places heavy emphasis on the essential importance of measuring and understanding the *environment as it is perceived* by the actor or subject. The person responds not to an objective world but rather to a phenomenal world that he constructs out of the world of reality. An interest in this "internal frame of reference" has not only been characteristic of many well-known psychologists but also it has been associated with projective techniques for many years. These devices have often been presented as uniquely sensitive means of representing or capturing the inner world of subjects or respondents (Frank, 1939). Moreover, there are within anthropology a number of influential figures, including Irving Hallowell, Dorothy Lee, and Benjamin Whorf, who have consistently emphasized the crucial importance of securing information concerning the psychological or subjective reality of informants.

The general point to be made here is simply that projective techniques have often been represented as unusually effective means of assessing the phenomenal world of the subject and within contemporary anthropology there are a sizable number of advocates of this emphasis upon subjective reality. It is not surprising that among the latter there have been some or many who have shown a distinct interest in the cross-cultural use of projective techniques.

So much for theoretical developments that seem to have had some role in advancing the use of projective techniques in anthropology. A further consideration is the establishment and extension of special empirical fields concerned with questions to which projective techniques seem especially relevant. These empirical developments are, of course, intimately related to the theoretical emphases we have just discussed.

A field of great contemporary interest that has been heavily influenced by psychoanalytic theory and importantly, although less manifestly, shaped by holistic theory is the study of *culture and personality*. For various reasons, projective techniques have appeared to many observers to offer more possibility for cross-cultural application than most other personality instruments, which often display a heavy dependence upon a given language and specific cultural content or experience. Consequently, as the empirical study of various problems concerned with the relation between cultural variables on the one hand and personality variables on the other has expanded, there have been increasing demands upon projective techniques to fill the need for an instrument that can make meaningful statements concerning personalities from a variety of cultures.

Related to culture and personality study is the more specialized field of *national character*. This enterprise has focussed upon the attempt to find personality or characterological qualities of an entire nation or culture. Again it is clear that to approach the end goal of this type of study one must have measuring instruments that will permit the assessment of personality and, further, that these instruments should provide for cross-cultural comparability. Thus, many investigators in this area have turned to projective devices for assistance in their efforts to extract valid general descriptions of national groups. It is pertinent to observe that many of these individuals were heavily influenced by psychoanalytic theory and that the relation between psychoanalytic theory and projective techniques, which we have already mentioned, increased the tendency to favor projective techniques over other available instruments.

One investigative area of great interest in contemporary social science is the assessment of the relation between *infant experience and adult behavior*. The so-called genetic propositions of psychoanalysis, with their detailed implications for the relation between events of infancy and adulthood, undoubtedly bear some responsibility for this development. There are now, however, many investigators with an interest in this topic of investigation who owe little specifically to psychoanalytic theory. It is clear that there is great difficulty in testing predictions concerning relations between infantile events and adult events, at least with human subjects. One of the most hopeful alternatives is to identify groups of adults who can be depended upon to have had widely different kinds of childhood experience and then to compare them in terms of adult personality.

The variation in child training and adult behavior commonly observed between different societies makes cross-cultural study an appealing approach to this problem. Again, there is the task, however, of assessing the adult personality, and again, we find that projective techniques have on occasion been called upon for this purpose.

A recent trend that has done a great deal to promote the application of projective techniques in anthropology has been an increased interest in the *socialization* process. Anthropologists and psychologists today are intensely interested in the process whereby the individual assumes the characteristic motives, values, and attitudes of his society. As this process came to be analyzed more carefully and studied in detail, it was inevitable that investigators would seek to devise or borrow techniques that would permit the assessment of personality in a reasonably manifold and complete manner. For many reasons the cross-cultural study of socialization has proven to be attractive and fruitful. In this cross-cultural perspective many of the traditional methods used by psychologists to study personality have proven manifestly infeasible. Projective techniques, on the other hand, seem to offer at least some possibility of cross-cultural applicability and consequently have been employed frequently.

A further influence, neither theoretical nor related to the development of an empirical domain, pertains to the characteristic approach of the cultural anthropologist to the study of behavior. Typically the ethnologist has been a *naturalistic observer* with a heavy commitment to representing the world of reality fully and vividly. Moreover, most cultural anthropologists in the field have had extensive and intimate contacts with their informants and have developed considerable clinical skill in understanding and generalizing concerning these individual cases. This exposure to complex human behavior under revealing conditions obviously prepares such an investigator for responding more enthusiastically to data that bear some resemblance to the full richness of the intensive interview than to data that take the form of a sparse number of scores or a highly analytic description limited to a few specified variables. In other words, projective techniques produce data and are accompanied by general principles of interpretation that are relatively congruent with the characteristic manner in which cultural anthropologists have approached and interpreted behavior. There is indeed a kind of professional affinity between the highly skilled clinician and the seasoned anthropologist that manifests itself in many ways, including the readiness of many cultural anthropologists to appreciate and accept the potential utility of projective techniques.

Our brief discussion has pointed to a number of factors that may have played a role in contributing to the popularity of projective techniques in cross-cultural settings. It seems likely that the most important of these has been the widening impact of psychoanalytic theory and holistic theory, coupled with the popular conception that projective techniques are particularly consistent with these positions, the general postwar expansion of the field of culture and personality, and the congruence between the cultural anthropologist's customary data and the data provided by projective techniques. Let us turn now to a rapid examination of some early and significant investigations that have utilized projective techniques in cultural settings.

SOME EARLY STUDIES ILLUSTRATING THE APPLICATION OF PROJECTIVE TECHNIQUES IN CULTURAL ANTHROPOLOGY

In the next chapter we shall return to the question of defining projective techniques more precisely. Here, let us simply agree that there is a class of personality instruments, conventionally referred to as projective tests, typified by the Rorschach test and the Thematic Apperception Test but including many other techniques. Given this crude designation our concern for the moment is to examine some early instances in which these instruments, traditionally the exclusive property of the clinician, have been applied to problems of the anthropologist.

This section is intended to give the reader some historical context and a general appreciation for the kinds of studies that initiated this field of investigation. It is not an exhaustive survey but rather an attempt to identify those influential studies that clearly preceded the general trend that exists today. I have also sought to include investigations that show some heterogeneity in the empirical problem they approach, or novelty in their approach to the problem. These studies may be considered to qualify under the "grandfather clause" and consequently they are presented with little or no attempt to underline their weaknesses or flaws, although in one or two instances we shall return to consider a study critically and in more detail in a subsequent chapter.

Perhaps the first publication dealing directly with the use of projective techniques in cultural research is Hermann Rorschach's own monograph in which he introduced his now famous instrument. Under the heading of "Comparative Researches in Experience Type," Rorschach suggests that his test can be used fruitfully to compare a variety of different groups and even provides preliminary results from one such investigation. He suggests the utility of comparing the sexes in their performance on the test and reports that females tend to produce fewer Whole responses and more Color responses than males. Finally, he reasons:

The experience type should be different in various peoples and races. The average experience type of the forty-year old Englishman is very probably quite different from that of the Russian, German, etc., of the same age. This difference should be even greater if the difference in race were greater. . . . The test itself is technically so simple—it can be done through an interpreter—that it may be done with the most primitive Negro as easily as with a cultured European. (Rorschach, 1921, pp. 96-97)

Thus, at the literal introduction of the test we find a strong endorsement by its creator of its utility for cross-cultural investigation. Needless to say, not everything that Rorschach has said about this issue would sit well today with the trained ethnologist. Still, he did envision the potential usefulness of his instrument in this type of investigation, and if he overlooked some of the difficulties and minimized others, this is no more than would be expected from someone as committed to the test and as untrained in ethnology as he was.

Not only does Rorschach recommend his test for cross-cultural research but he actually gives an informal report of a study in which he compared the Bernese and Appenzeller, individuals coming from two different Swiss cantons. He indicates that the Bernese tend to be introversive while the Appenzeller tend to be extraversive. The Bernese also show a tendency to provide more Movement responses. These test differences are consonant with general stereotypes concerning individuals from these two regions, according to Rorschach, and also correspond to typical differences in the form of schizophrenia in the two areas.

Another early cross-cultural study employing the Rorschach test is reported in an article by Bleuler and Bleuler (1935) comparing the Rorschach performance of Moroccans and Europeans. The

Rorschach was administered to 29 adult male and female Moroccans, simply described as farmers living in a single locality but having come originally from various parts of Morocco. There is no description of the European sample with which these North Africans were compared but it appears to consist of the subjects in Switzerland and Germany that the authors had tested in connection with their professional practice.

The results are based upon the investigators' impressions as to group differences. In general, they conclude that there is little difference between the Moroccan and European groups in Form, Movement, and Color responses; in Popular and Original responses; in incidence of Animal responses; or in number of responses and latency of response. The principal observed difference has to do with the relative frequency of Small Detail responses. The Bleulers report that normal Moroccans provide a frequency of Small Detail responses that in a European subject would suggest schizophrenia. Not only are Whole responses relatively infrequent among the Moroccans, but when they do provide such responses, it is usually as a result of combining a number of Detail responses which is in marked contrast to the more abstract method of arriving at Whole responses that characterizes the European subject.

In interpreting this propensity for Small Detail responses, the Bleulers admit there are cultural factors that would undoubtedly influence this type of response even if there were not underlying personality differences. Most important of these is the fact that the Moroccans are not used to looking at pictures. This lack of skill in examining and interpreting pictures might be expected to lead to difficulty in understanding the "whole" of a picture and consequently result in a tendency to provide small, detailed responses rather than general, integrating responses. The Bleulers reason that if they interpret this characteristic in terms of customary Rorschach principles, and if this interpretation fits with what they have independently observed in the Moroccans, this will argue for the existence of real and important psychological factors which determine both the high incidence of Small Detail responses and also the tendency to avoid pictures even when they are, to some degree, available. Further this psychological description seems to fit well with the impressions the Bleulers formed from their individual contacts with the Moroccans, as well as certain general tendencies that can be observed in the customs and art forms of the Moroccans. In the last analysis they ascribe this tendency to fix upon small details to a "deep-seated racial characteristic" which also has determined their lack of interest in pictorial representation.

In this study one of the authors performed the interpretation of the Rorschach while the other compared the interpretations with the individual subjects with whom he was very familiar. The results of this comparison led the investigators to the conclusion that the test was about as sensitive or diagnostic in this novel cultural setting as it had been in a European setting.

In spite of the manifold empirical shortcomings of this study, it is interesting to note that the investigators show an early concern over problems involved in the use of the projective test in an alien culture by someone not thoroughly familiar with the culture. They indicate that familiarity with the language and the culture was prerequisite to successful completion of their study.

The investigations of A. Irving Hallowell have played a more important role than those of any other individual in bringing the Rorschach test to the serious attention of anthropologists as a tool for personality study. The first of a number of papers concerned with various aspects of Berens River Salteaux Indians was published in 1940. By this time, Hallowell had collected one hundred protocols from individuals of both sexes in this society ranging in age from 13 to 80. Examination of the protocols led him to the conclusion that with a few changes in administration, the Rorschach test could be used effectively in the study of primitive subjects. He reasoned that results could be obtained which were, in general, comparable to those obtained with European and American subjects, although for certain categories accurate interpretation might depend upon normative data from the primitive group being studied. The further analysis and interpretation of these Salteaux Rorschach protocols provided the basis for a number of important papers in which Hallowell explores such topics as acculturation, popular responses in different cultures, psychosexual adjustment, and perception.

For the present let us limit our interest to the earliest of these studies, the attempt by Hallowell to find personality differences by means of the Rorschach between two Salteaux Indian groups differing distinctly in their acculturation to the dominant white society. The highly acculturated were called the *Lakeside Indians,* and members of the relatively unacculturated group were called the *Inland Indians.* Rorschach test results for 35 men and 23 women of the Lakeside group were compared with equivalent results for 31 men and 13 women of the Inland group. Although there were many similarities between the groups, there were also marked differences. Perhaps the most striking difference was the much faster reaction time displayed by the highly acculturated Indians. Hallowell considered the relative slowness of the Inland group a reflection of their greater caution, which in turn stemmed from anxieties and inhibitions derived from the native culture. As the acculturation process proceeded, these inhibitions lessened, and the Indians were able to respond more directly and rapidly to the test. Related to this change was the fact that the Lakeside group was more extratensive (had a lower ratio of Color to Movement responses) than the Inland group. This observation was in turn interpreted as implying that they were more outgoing in their typical adjustment and in freer contact with objects and persons in the outer world.

When subjects were rated in terms of personal adjustment on the basis of Rorschach protocols, Hallowell found that the very well-adjusted and the very poorly adjusted both tended to be in the highly acculturated group. This suggested to him that the change in culture offered the possibility of a superior adjustment, but at the same time, individuals who failed to meet the demands of the new culture might end up more poorly adjusted than they were prior to acculturation. The findings also suggested that women, as a group, made a better adjustment in the acculturated state than did the men, and Hallowell provides some ethnographic details to make this finding seem reasonable. In conclusion, the author reasons that the Rorschach has played an important, if not indispensable, role in permitting him to explore the relation between acculturation and personality.

The first report of an interdisciplinary study of a nonliterate society using the Rorschach test was published by Anna Hartoch Schachtel with Jules and Zunia Henry (1942). The Henrys collected Rorschach protocols from a group of Pilaga children and then turned the records over to Anna Schachtel for interpretation. The tests had been administered individually, without the aid of an interpreter, and the psychologist knew nothing of the culture of this Argentinian, nonliterate society, other than a "slight description" of one of the subjects. The results consist of a comparison of the blind interpretation of the Rorschach with the field notes of the anthropologists for three boys and three girls, and also a general characterization of the Pilaga child based upon a total of ten test protocols.

The Rorschach interpretations of Schachtel and the field notes of Henry as summarized in the article show a general correspondence which leads the authors to the conclusion that "In spite of occasional differences in emphasis there is a close correspondence between the Rorschach findings and the ethnological facts" (p. 680).

The Rorschach scores for the entire group of ten children permit a rough comparison with the kind of performance that might be expected of children in our own society. The most significant difference between the reaction of the Pilaga children and our own children has to do with the concreteness of the percepts reported by the Pilaga. Members of our society are more likely to report the blot as similar to some object or to give a hypothetical or "as if" status to the percept they report. The Pilaga children show a higher incidence of Detail and Small Detail responses and a lower incidence of Whole responses than children of our culture. They also avoid the use of Movement and Shading responses which distinguishes them from the children of our society, as does their very low incidence of Color responses. All of these differences, as well as other, more subtle, differentiating features, are discussed in terms of the cultural differences between the two societies.

Although the investigators reach no general conclusions concerning the merit of the Rorschach Test in a nonliterate society, the confidence with which they present their personality findings coupled with the reported congruence between the test results and the findings of the field observers lend the impression that they consider the technique to have merit in this setting.

David M. Levy (1939), a child psychoanalyst, presented an early endorsement of his doll-play technique for the study of sibling rivalry as better adapted for cross-cultural research than most psychological tests. In order to illustrate the utility of the technique he presented several case histories drawn from a set of data he and a collaborator collected among the Quekchi Indians of Guatemala and a similar set of data collected by Jules and Zunia Henry among the Pilaga Indians of Argentina. Levy concluded from a detailed analysis of the responses of the native children to the doll-play situation that there were components to sibling rivalry that seemed much the same in these two nonliterate societies and in our own society, but that there were also differences in sibling rivalry that must be attributed to the culture.

Application of the Thematic Apperception Test in anthropological research came long after such studies had been initiated with the Rorschach. The first report of a cross-cultural study employing the Thematic Apperception Test was made by Henry (1947), who in connection with a program of Research on Indian Education, studied Hopi and Navaho children by means of a variety of techniques. His primary goal was to assess the utility of the TAT as an instrument in anthropological research. He used a modification of the TAT which was administered individually to Hopi and Navaho children. For each subject there was available also a great deal of additional information including a life-history record, Rorschach test results, and a free-drawing test. This latter material was collected and analyzed independently of the TAT data.

After preliminary studies provided Henry with encouraging results regarding the utility of the test in this setting, he proceeded to conduct several specific validity studies. The first of these inquired into the extent to which TAT personality descriptions of the individual children applied accurately to the child whose record was being interpreted and not to other children, whereas the second compared personality inferences derived from the TAT with comparable inferences secured from the other personality data sources. The results of both studies provided strongly supportive evidence for the usefulness of the TAT as an instrument to assess the individual personalities of these subjects. In a further investigation Henry explored the validity of the TAT inferences concerning the Hopi and Navaho as a group, and again he arrived at the conclusion that the results of the TAT analysis were congruent with evidence from other quarters. Consequently, Henry arrived at the generalization that in this cross-cultural setting TAT results were psychologically and culturally meaningful and, thus, the instrument represented a valuable addition to the instruments available for use by the cross-cultural investigator.

The studies we have just reviewed provide a rather general picture of the manner in which projective techniques were first applied in anthropological research. They suggest a surprisingly early linkage between cross-cultural research and projective techniques and indicate a clear enthusiasm concerning the potential contributions of these devices in this setting.

SOME SIGNS OF UNREST

We have seen that the past decade or two has witnessed an extensive application of projective techniques in cultural anthropology. The relative recency of these studies and the considerable enthusiasm with which they have been greeted on many sides might suggest that there is little in the way of critical reservation concerning their merit. This, however, is by no means the case. Many distinguished psychologists, as well as anthropologists, have displayed serious doubts concerning the potential contribution of projective techniques and something should be said about these reservations before proceeding further.

Projective techniques have never been full-fledged members of the psychologist's measurement array. Their origin in the clinic, their rich and complex response data, their relative lack of standardization, and their compatibility with psychoanalytic theory, all make them stand out from the traditional tests, scales, and ratings of the psychologist. The tough resistance to objectifying these instruments that many projective testers have shown has added to this distinctiveness and has served to increase the doubts of many psychologists.

The Rorschach test, which in most respects stands as the prototype of the projective technique, was introduced by a small cohesive group that maintained a separate identity from the main body of psychology. Inevitably this led to the development of special hostilities and stereotypes on the part of both psychology and the "Rorschachers." Even today many psychologists tend to consider projective testers as an esoteric and somewhat mystical special group within psychology, at home neither with psychological theory nor the accepted tenets of psychological measurement. Such a viewpoint is clearly revealed in the following statements by Thurstone (1948), undoubtedly one of America's most distinguished contributors to the field of psychological measurement:

There was serious study of the logic of the Binet tests and there was serious effort to relate it to the psychological concepts that were current. As a result, psychologists generally took part in deliberations about the underlying theory of the Binet tests. At present we have relatively little of such effort with regard to the Rorschach tests. Such discussion seems to be confined to a cultish group that has adopted its own jargon without relation to current experimental and theoretical work in psychological science. It would be fortunate if the Rorschach test would be removed from its isolation from the rest of the psychological profession. . . . The burden of proof is on them to show that they have not only a useful trick with a particular set of ink blots but that they also have some important ideas that psychologists should learn about. (pp. 471-472) . . . It would be fortunate if students of the Rorschach test would proceed to qualify themselves for membership in the psychological profession by insisting on experimental evidence under reasonably controlled conditions for the various interpretations that they make of the responses to a set of ink blots. There is justification for the belief that the projective test method . . . has great possibilities, and it seems plausible that a set of ink blots may be one of these fruitful test methods. Rorschach students are not making any worthwhile contribution to psychological science as long as they remain in their state of gullible and uncritical acceptance of fanciful interpretations of the responses to a single set of ink blots. (p. 474)

. . . I have attempted to show why it is that the Rorschach test has not been accepted by the psychological profession, and why it is that most students of this test do not have recognition or status in psychological science. (p. 475)

A textbook concerned with contemporary psychological measurement arrives at the following cautious conclusion concerning the present state of projective tests:

During the past 20 years, the invention, exploration, and development of projective tests of personality has been for many psychologists the most exciting adventure in personality evaluation. The tests have many ardent supporters and many severe critics. A sound appraisal of their contribution to our understanding of the individual is difficult to arrive at at the present time. Both claims and results are conflicting.

A great many of the procedures have received very little by way of rigorous and critical test and are supported only by the faith and enthusiasm of their backers. In those few cases, most notably that of the *Rorschach,* where a good deal of critical work has been done, results are varied and there is much inconsistency in the research picture. Modest reliability is usually found, but consistent evidence of validity is harder to come by. (Thorndike & Hagen, 1955, p. 417-418)

A recent survey of the field of personality, included in the *Annual Review of Psychology*, makes the following caustic comment about projective techniques in general and the Rorschach in particular:

The reader may note a scarcity of references in this review to studies based on projective techniques. In the writer's judgment the standard projective techniques *qua* projective techniques have been a failure methodologically and substantively in personality research. . . . The Rorschach in particular has been worthless as a research instrument. Though claiming for decades to be the method *par excellance* for studying personality, the Rorschach method has nothing to show for its applications in the personality field. After more than thirty years of research, the vast bulk of Rorschach studies are still attempts to demonstrate some kind of validity of this test. In view of this poor showing, the hopes and claims that continue to be professed by the adherents of these methods are indeed cause for wonder. (Jensen, 1958, p. 296)

As these statements show, the individual from an allied area who wishes to find fault with the application of projective techniques in his discipline can find a rich harvest of criticism, stemming, for the most part, from individuals who were trained in the laboratory or psychometric traditions of psychology.

From quite another professional background comes Jules Henry, a cultural anthropologist who has had extensive experience with the use of projective techniques, including the Rorschach and play technique, and yet shows little enthusiasm over the use of the Rorschach in primitive cultures:

Were I to go into the field tomorrow to study such a culture I would not use the Rorschach test. Since there is no category of the Rorschach test which is not in hot debate at the present time in clinical psychology, since there are many knotty statistical problems still to be ironed out, and since it is not possible to use the protocols without creating contamination effects, I would not know what I had once I had a batch of Rorschach responses. Furthermore—let us face it—I *personally* am opposed to anything that places an instrument between me and a responding human being. (Henry, 1955, p. 245)

A well-known anthropologist, the late S. F. Nadel, suggests that there are grave difficulties that attend the use of projective techniques in the field:

If there is a profit, it is neither an immediate one nor one easily gained. The projective techniques certainly do not provide anything in the nature of a shortcut. They are wholly additional to field observation and relieve the anthropologist of none of his usual (and lengthy) tasks, such as the collection of life histories or the day-to-day observation of family life.... The reliance of these tests on subtleties of linguistic expression is such that protocols obtained with the help of interpreters can never be satisfactory. ... Granting that the utility of projective techniques for the anthropolgist lies in their promise to provide information of a kind not procurable by direct observation, we may still ask how far the techniques now current fulfill this promise. No very satisfactory answer can be given, partly because the relevant discussions are so often wrongly focused, on the agreement or nonagreement of test results and observation. Nor have we really solved the crucial problem of the cross-cultural validity of the Rorschach and TAT. Adaptation to different cultural conditions, such as in the various modified TAT's which have recently come in use, does not help; all it does, at least at the present stage, is to reduce the comparability of standard and adapted tests. Finally, from the anthropologist's point of view, both the Rorschach and TAT have certain inherent defects. In the Rorschach it is the high generality of the findings, which makes it difficult if not impossible to relate them to the motivations, aims, and values current in social life. The TAT has the opposite weakness, the stimuli corresponding so closely to actual social situations that they rarely provoke more than an expression of current motivations and value judgments. (Nadel, 1955, pp. 247-250)

Mensh and Henry, representing a union of psychology and anthropology, suggest that use of the Rorschach may impose unhealthy restrictions upon the observer:

One of the obvious results of the use of instruments for the study of the universe is that we perceive only what the inherent design of the instrument permits it to transmit.... An instrument is always a mixed blessing. When we come to the use of psychological tests, however, we deal with phenomena of much greater complexity than binoculars ... a projective test like the Rorschach has an interpretive system structured in definite categories, in terms of which personality *must* be perceived. It is as if looking through a pair of binoculars one *had* to see the universe in terms of either the wave or the corpuscular theory of light. Now, since the Rorschach categories are organized in a special way, it means that as long as we use the test we will perceive people in terms of Rorschach theory.... In this way we build for our minds a prison out of the very instruments that were designed to set them free. (p. 465)

A recent publication of the applied anthropologists' professional society includes a discussion of some of the problems involved in the use of these tests under the title "The Battle Over Projective Techniques." This article cautions:

In borrowing the tests, anthropologists inherited some of the arguments of the clinical psychologists, and then added some of their own. The pros and cons are still being heard. The general issue seems to revolve around whether projective tests yield material little different than what is found in other ways. . . . Specific issues involved are: (1) questions about the validity of tests themselves; (2) the accusation that anthropologists have used uncritically, as psychologically acceptable, tests not accepted by the psychologists; (3) the wastefulness of such tests from the standpoint of time consumed in gathering protocols; (4) the allegation that protocols were usually unpublished and, at any rate, relatively valueless as material on the culture, whereas interviewing provided both cultural content and personality information; (5) whether the tests did or did not provide a technique by which the psychologically untrained could bring back psychologically valid material; (6) types of modifications which [were] needed and could be made in test procedure so that they could be used with members of quite different cultures; (7) the level of the personality tapped by the test in relation to the actual social functioning of the individual—such as the findings of the psychosocial study by Frances Macgregor *et al*... where the social functioning of the individual was dramatically altered and projective tests showed little change; (8) the poor predictive record of projective tests during World War II in predicting successful adjustment in the Armed forces; and (9) the preponderantly verbal character of the responses that made it difficult to assess either the actual imagery involved or the relationships to behavior. (Anonymous, 1955, p. 14)

It seems evident that the application of projective techniques in anthropology has not been accomplished without creating serious reservations in the minds of many observers. Although in some quarters we have found intense enthusiasm concerning the potential contribution of projective techniques to anthropological research, we have found also that these positive sentiments must be weighed against powerful negative reactions from other quarters. There are some who feel that these instruments have made no contribution to understanding human behavior in any setting. Others have reservations only concerning the nonclinical use of these tests. Still others see definite merit even in the cross-cultural application of these devices. All three of these groups should welcome a sober appraisal of the use and misuse of projective techniques in anthropological research. The goal of this volume is to provide such an appraisal.

REFERENCES

ANONYMOUS. The battle over projective techniques. *Human Organization Clearinghouse Bull.*, 1955, 3, 14-19.

BLEULER, M., & BLEULER, R. Rorschach's ink-blot test and racial psychology: mental peculiarities of Moroccans. *Character and Pers.*, 1935, 4, 97-114.

FRANK, L. K. Projective methods for the study of personality. *J. Psychol.*, 1939, 8, 389-413.

HALL, C. S., & LINDZEY, G. Psychoanalytic theory and its application in the social sciences. In G. Lindzey (Ed.), *Handbook of social psychology*. Vol. 1. Cambridge, Mass.: Addison-Wesley, 1954. Pp. 143-180.

HALLOWELL, A. I. Rorschach as an aid in the study of personalities in primitive societies. *Rorschach Res. Exch.*, 1940, 4, 106.

HALLOWELL, A. I. Acculturation processes and personality changes as indicated by the Rorschach technique. *Rorschach Res. Exch.*, 1942, 6, 42-50.

HALLOWELL, A. I. "Popular" responses and cultural differences: an analysis based on frequencies in a group of American Indian subjects. *Rorschach Res. Exch.*, 1945, 9, 153-168.

HALLOWELL, A. I. Psychosexual adjustment, personality and the good life in a nonliterate culture. In P. H. Hoch & J. Zubin (Eds.), *Psychosexual development in health and disease*. New York: Grune & Stratton, 1949. Pp. 102-123.

HALLOWELL, A. I. The use of projective techniques in the study of the sociopsychological aspects of acculturation. *J. proj. Tech.*, 1951a, 15, 26-44.

HALLOWELL, A. I. Cultural factors in the structuralization of perception. In J. H. Rohrer & M. Sherif (Eds.), *Social psychology at the crossroads*. New York: Harper, 1951b. Pp. 164-195.

HALLOWELL, A. I. *Culture and experience*. Philadelphia: Univer. of Pennsylvania Press, 1955.

HENRY, J. Symposium: Projective testing in ethnography. *Am. Anthrop.*, 1955, 57, 245-247, 264-269.

HENRY, J., & SPIRO, M. E. Psychological techniques: Projective tests in field work. In A. I. Kroeber (Ed.), *Anthropology today*. Chicago: Univer. of Chicago Press, 1953. Pp. 417-429.

HENRY, W. E. The Thematic Apperception Technique in the study of culture-personality relations. *Genet. Psychol. Monogr.*, 1947, 35, 3-135.

HERTZ, Marguerite R. Rorschach: twenty years after. *Psychol. Bull.*, 1942, 39, 529-572.

HILGARD, E. R. Experimental approaches to psychoanalysis. In E. Pumpian-Mindlin (Ed.), *Psychoanalysis as science.* Stanford, Calif.: Stanford Univer. Press, 1952. Pp. 3-45.

JENSEN, A. R. Personality. In P. R. Farnsworth & Q. McNemar (Eds.), *Annual review of psychology.* Vol. 9. Palo Alto: Annual Reviews, 1958. Pp. 295-322.

KLUCKHOHN, C. The influence of psychiatry on anthropology in America during the past one hundred years. In J. K. Hall, G. Zilboorg, & H. A. Bunker (Eds.), *One hundred years of American psychiatry.* New York: Columbia Univer. Press, 1944. Pp. 589-618.

KLUCKHOHN, C. Needed refinements in the biographical approach. In S. S. Sargent & M. W. Smith (Eds.), *Culture and personality.* New York: Viking Fund, 1949. Pp. 75-89.

KLUCKHOHN, C. Culture and behavior. In G. Lindzey (Ed.), *Handbook of social psychology.* Vol. II. Cambridge, Mass.; Addison-Wesley, 1954. Pp. 921-976.

LEVY, D. M. Sibling rivalry studies in children of primitive groups. *Am. J. Orthopsychiat.*, 1939, 9, 205-214.

MENSH, I., & HENRY, J. Direct observation and psychological tests in anthropological field work. *Am. Anthropol.*, 1953, 55, 461-480.

NADEL, S. F. Symposium: Projective testing in ethnography. *Am. Anthropol.*, 1955, 57, 247-250.

PUMPIAN-MINDLIN, E. The position of psychoanalysis in relation to the biological and social sciences. In E. Pumpian-Mindlin (Ed.), *Psychoanalysis as science.* Stanford, Calif.: Stanford Univer. Press, 1952. Pp. 129-158.

RORSCHACH, H. *Psychodiagnostics: A diagnostic test based on perception.* (4th ed.) New York: Grune & Stratton, 1942. (Originally published in 1921)

SCHACHTEL, Anna H., HENRY, J., & HENRY, Zunia. Rorschach analysis of Pilaga Indian children. *Am. J. Orthopsychiat.*, 1942, 12, 679-712.

THORNDIKE, R. L., & HAGEN, Elizabeth. *Measurement and evaluation in psychology and education.* New York: Wiley, 1955. Reprinted with permission of John Wiley & Sons, Inc.

THURSTONE, L. L. The Rorschach in psychological science. *J. abn. soc. Psychol.*, 1948, 43, 471-475.

2. What Is a Projective Technique?

BEFORE GOING FURTHER it seems only reasonable to specify the nature of projective techniques. Those readers who are familiar with these instruments and the publications dealing with them will not be surprised to learn that we shall approach this goal somewhat circuitously. Although there are a host of available definitions of projective tests, none of these provides an unambiguous set of criteria that effectively discriminate the group of tests we wish to include in the present discussion from other personality measures in conventional use. One solution to this problem of definition is simply to point to what we mean, and we shall certainly rely upon this device among others. However, we shall postpone until the next chapter, the simple enumeration and description of these instruments and concentrate our efforts here upon providing a set of more general specifications.

Before approaching directly the question of what is a projective test, it seems wise to ask: What is *projection?* In attempting to answer this question, we shall examine briefly the origin and meaning of the term projection and then outline the path that has led to the development of the major projective techniques and to their being labelled projective tests. Next, we shall inspect a representative cluster of definitions that have been suggested for projective techniques, and, in conclusion, we shall propose a specific definition for this volume.

THE NATURE OF PROJECTION

It is well known that the term *projection* came into existence in the psychological literature as one of the central constructs in psycho-

25

analytic theory. Most readers will also be aware that projection is one of the defense mechanisms that was early identified and defined within Freud's own writings. Many will remember that when Freud developed his influential theory of the origin of paranoid delusions in connection with the famous Schreber case, he employed projection as one of the central theoretical terms in his account. Somewhat less well known is the fact that Freud had introduced the construct in his writings as early as 1895. In a paper entitled, "The justification for detaching from neurasthenia a particular syndrome: the anxiety-neurosis," he alludes, in a single brief statement, to a process whereby inner stimulation is projected into the outer world. A brief year later, Freud (1896) dealt again with this same process and this time applied the label *projection* to the mechanism whereby the paranoid avoids recognition of self-reproach or self-distrust by directing these tendencies upon others.

Freud employed the concept in a number of subsequent papers, but it is in the interpretation of the Schreber case that he made his most detailed and explicit statements concerning this process:

> The mechanism of symptom-formation in paranoia requires that internal perceptions—feelings—shall be replaced by external perceptions. Consequently the proposition "I hate him" becomes transformed by *projection* into another one: "*He hates* (persecutes) *me*, which will justify me in hating him." And thus the impelling unconscious feeling makes its appearance as though it were the consequence of an external perception "I do not *love* him—I *hate* him, because HE PERSECUTES ME." (Freud, 1911, p. 63)

> The most striking characteristic of symptom-formation in paranoia is the process which deserves the name of *projection*. An internal perception is suppressed, and, instead, its content, after undergoing a certain degree of distortion, enters consciousness in the form of an external perception. In delusions of persecution the distortion consists in a transformation of affect; what should have been felt internally as love is perceived externally as hate. We should feel tempted to regard this remarkable process as . . . being absolutely pathognomic . . . if we were not opportunely reminded (that) . . . it makes its appearance not only in paranoia but under other psychological conditions as well, and in fact it has a regular share assigned to it in our attitude toward the external world. For when we refer the causes of certain sensations to the external world, instead of looking for them (as we do in the case of the others) inside ourselves, this normal proceeding, too, deserves to be called projection. (Freud, 1911, p. 66)

The core of projection as defined within orthodox psychoanalytic theory is clearly outlined in this passage—the disturbed individual, confronted with unacceptable impulses or attributes within himself, defends against these (reduces conflict or avoids anxiety) by displacing them into the outer world upon another person. This passage reveals also that Freud began very early to use this term to refer to a normal process whereby the individual's perceptions of the outer world are influenced by inner states.

In Freud's (1913) excursion into the realm of anthropology, the mechanism of projection was assigned a central role in accounting for various cultural phenomena, particularly the development of taboos. In this volume he suggests that the taboos enforced by primitives in connection with death derive from projection of the negative feelings felt toward individuals who have died. After death the inevitable ambivalence (love versus hate), that characterizes the relatives' feelings for the individual who has died, is resolved by means of projecting the hate upon the deceased. Thus, instead of the living hating the dead, the dead hate the living, and therefore must be guarded against and appeased by the living; with the result that taboos become necessary. Freud compares the primitive's reaction to death with the reactions to death he has frequently observed in obsessional neurotics but goes on to remark that:

> ... this hostility, distressingly felt in the unconscious as satisfaction over the death, is differently dealt with among primitive peoples. The defence against it takes the form of displacing it on to the object of the hostility, on to the dead themselves. This defensive procedure, which is a common one both in normal and in pathological mental life, is known as a *"projection."* The survivor thus denies that he has ever harboured any hostile feelings against the dead loved one; the soul of the dead harbours them instead and seeks to put them into action during the whole period of mourning. (p. 61)

Both of the two sets of feelings (the affectionate and the hostile), which, as we have good reason to believe, exist towards the dead person, seek to take effect at the time of the bereavement, as mourning and as satisfaction. There is bound to be a conflict between these two contrary feelings. ... The hostility, of which the survivors know nothing and moreover wish to know nothing, is ejected from internal perception into the external world, and thus detached from them and pushed on to someone else. It is no longer true that they are rejoicing to be rid of the dead man; on the contrary, they are mourning for him; but, strange to say, *he* has turned into a wicked demon ready to gloat over their misfortunes and eager to kill them. It then becomes necessary for them, the survivors, to defend themselves against this evil enemy; they are relieved of pressure from within, but have only exchanged it for oppression from without. (p. 63)

The fact that projection is not solely a mechanism of defense to be observed among neurotic and psychotic patients, or in situations of intense conflict, is referred to again by Freud in the following passage:

... projection was not created for the purpose of defence; it also occurs where there is no conflict. The projection outwards of internal perceptions is a primitive mechanism, to which, for instance, our sense perceptions are subject, and which therefore normally plays a very large part in determining the form taken by our external world. Under conditions whose nature has not yet been sufficiently established, internal perceptions of emotional and thought processes can be projected outwards in the same way as sense perceptions; they are thus employed for building up the external world, though they should by rights remain part of the *internal* world. (p. 64)

It is evident that Freud conceived of projection as a mechanism that was important both in normal and in pathological development. Furthermore, he realized almost from the outset that this mechanism could play an important part in the creative process; that in the process of constructing a story or a painting, the artist unwittingly would strive to secure some expression for those unconscious impulses that were denied expression in his everyday existence. It is this assumption, of course, that lies at the base of so much current thinking concerning projective techniques.

Consistent with this position is Freud's analysis of a novel called *Gradiva*, (Freud, 1907), in which he points to certain important parallels between the process of interpreting dreams, as engaged in by the psychoanalyst, and the construction of a literary work by a novelist. In *Totem and Taboo* this congruence is again alluded to:

The projected creations of primitive men resemble the personifications constructed by creative writers; for the latter externalize in the form of separate individuals the opposing instinctual impulses struggling within them. (Freud, 1913, p. 65)

There have been a number of attempts to refine the concept of projection and to differentiate types of projection. For example, Murray (1933) suggested the important distinction between *supplementary projection*, which occurs when the individual projects his own impulse or attribute directly upon another, for example, the fearful perceiver sees people about him as more fearful than they actually are; and *complementary projection*, where the individual perceives his environment in such a manner as to make it congruent with his own impulses, for example, the fearful person perceives people about him as more hostile than they are, thus complementing or serving to justify his fears. Murray (1951) has also briefly alluded to *contrast projection*, in which the individual perceives others as more dissimilar to him than they really are, for example, the individual who is very depressed or very ambitious tends to perceive others as happier than they really are or as less ambitious than they really are. Thus, in the case of supplementary projection, the perceiver sees others as *more* like him than they are in actuality, whereas under the influence of contrast projection, others are seen as *less* like the perceiver than they really are.

In a general discussion of the concept of projection, both within psychoanalysis and in application to projective techniques, Bellak (1950) suggests abandoning the broad use of the term *projection* in favor of the more inclusive term *apperceptive distortion.* Included within the general category of apperceptive distortion is a variety of mechanisms that Bellak labels projection, inverted projection, simple projection, sensitization, and externalization. He recommends reserving the term *projection* for the process involving the largest degree of distortion, where the individual actually misperceives others through assigning to them self-characteristics that are so unacceptable to him that he could come to recognize them only through prolonged therapy. He suggests the label *inverted projection* when a defensive maneuver, called reaction formation, is applied to the unacceptable impulse prior to its being projected onto the outer world. The typical instance of inverted projection is the case of the paranoid where it is hypothesized that his initial formulation of "I love you" becomes reversed into "I hate him," before the process of projection converts it into "He hates me." *Simple projection* is used to refer to the normal process whereby the individual misperceives the outer world as a result of inner states. This differs from projection, both in the relative ease with which the misperception can be removed and in the extent to which projected attributes of the perceiver are unconscious. The term *sensitization* is used to refer to the well-known tendency of an individual to pay particular attention to those real stimuli in the external world that are relevant to and fit with his inner states. Bellak suggests the term *externalization* for the process whereby the individual consciously attributes to the outer world characteristics of himself, as in the case where the individual tells a story in response to a projective technique with full awareness that the characters in the story represent himself and figures from his life. The fact that Freud employed the term *projection* to refer to a normal as well as a pathological process is also noted by Bellak.

A recent paper by Murstein (1959) distinguishes between *classical projection*, which is defined in a manner equivalent to Bellak's restricted use of the term *projection; rationalized projection*, which is equivalent to Murray's concept of complementary projection; *attributive projection*, which can be equated to Bellak's concept of simple projection; and *autistic projection*, which seems to be a special case of attributive projection involving a marked influence by needs upon perception.

These suggested modifications, in sum, have had rather limited impact, and the general status of the concept of projection within contemporary psychology is probably little different than it was over twenty years ago when Anna Freud identified projection as one of the nine mechanisms of defense outlined in her father's writings. More significant is the fact that in spite of the existence in Freud's own writings of assertions that projection should be considered both a pathological means of resolving conflict and a normal process which occurs in the absence of conflict, the typical use of this term has been to describe a defense against the anxiety aroused by unconscious conflict. The essence of this conservative view is captured very well by Murray, who suggests that an orthodox definition of projection implies: (*a*) an actual misperception in which the individual believes something that is manifestly false concerning another; (*b*) this misperception involves attributing to the other person a tendency directed toward either the perceiver or toward a third person; (*c*) the tendency is an important part of the perceiver's own personality; (*d*) the tendency is unacceptable to the perceiver and he is unaware of its existence in his own make-up; (*e*) the function of the process is to maintain self-esteem, or to escape from anxiety. (Murray, 1951, p. xii)

It is evident from our discussion that the term *projection* has been used in two important senses. The first of these, which might be called *classic projection,* refers to an unconscious and pathological process whereby the individual defends against unacceptable impulses or qualities in himself by inaccurately ascribing them to individuals or objects in the outer world. The second usage, which might be called *generalized projection,* refers to a normal process whereby the individual's inner states or qualities influence his perception and interpretation of the outer world. Although it is customary to assume that Freud used the term to refer only to classic projection, we have found clear evidence in his writings that he used the term in both senses.

Let us now turn to some early events in the development of projective techniques and, in particular, examine the circumstances surrounding the labelling of these devices as projective techniques.

THE ORIGIN OF PROJECTIVE TECHNIQUES

A full treatment of the history of all of the techniques we shall be concerned with in this volume is clearly beyond the scope of the present chapter. What we can hope to do realistically is to examine briefly the circumstances under which the most important of these instruments were created and some of the conditions accompanying their early development. This casual scrutiny should give us some idea of the events preceding the point where the Freudian concept of projection and this class of personality instruments came to be joined, at least in name. Before turning to the specific instance, let us take a brief glance at the general climate that surrounded these developments.

In our discussion of factors that facilitated the application of projective techniques in social research, we have already mentioned several considerations that played a crucial role in the general development of projective techniques. In particular, we referred to psychoanalytic theory and holistic theory as stimulating agents. During the first four decades of this century, these two systematic positions evolved from obscurity to the brink of supremacy, and projective techniques showed an almost parallel development. Although one may question the logical necessity of this association between instrument and theory, there seems to be no question that individuals strongly influenced by psychoanalysis and holism have shown a distinct preference for projective techniques over other instruments. Intimately related to these theoretical movements was the development of a clinical tradition concerned with the study of human behavior. This tradition centered about the careful, detailed study of individual subjects, frequently disturbed individuals, and developed predominantly within medical settings, although it drew heavily upon academic knowledge. For the most part, as we shall see, projective techniques developed within clinical settings, and it is thus not surprising that they have been, in general, the favored instrument of individuals influenced by the clinical tradition.

At roughly the same time, there was a parallel development taking place solidly within academic psychology—the psychometric tradition. The contributions of Binet, Terman, Thorndike, and Thurstone led to a series of instruments that permitted the standardized measurement of intelligence, social attitudes, aptitudes, and other dimensions of behavior. Further, the movement led to the development of objective personality measures which typically were inventories, questionnaires, or rating scales. These instruments were characterized by an emphasis upon careful quantification, repeatability, efficiency, and exact specification. In contrast, the clinical instruments were less developed as instruments of precise measurement although their defenders maintained that they dealt with more significant areas of behavior.

Thus, by the end of the 1930's there were two traditions of psychological measurement, each concerned with the use of rather diverse instruments and each, according to its advocates, possessing unique strengths not possessed by the other. Since then, there have been important steps toward integrating these two traditions, although even now the void between them is more manifest than the efforts to bridge it. So much for the general background against which projective techniques developed. Let us look briefly at the origins of some of the most prominent of these devices.

There is no exact time at which we can state with assurance that projective techniques began. However, if we decide arbitrarily to seize upon a single incident as marking the modern beginnings of this development, there would probably be wide agreement that this honor belongs to Freud's *The Interpretation of Dreams* (1900). This volume not only outlines the new technique of dream analysis developed by Freud but also includes the statement of a general theory that has provided the background from which emerged many other projective techniques. Freud himself referred to dream interpretation as "the royal road to the unconscious" and consistently identified *The Interpretation of Dreams* as his most significant work. Although he published a number of subsequent papers on the interpretation of dreams (1916, 1933), his original volume contains the essence of his method, even as it is employed today. In general, psychoanalysts have been reluctant to alter Freud's techniques, and psychologists have been slow to turn to the study of dreams, perhaps because of the traditional use of dreams in the hands of charlatans and mystics.

The most immediate outcome of Freud's conceptions and technique took place as a result of the synthesis of academic association-psychology of this era with psychoanalytic theory. At the famous Burghozli psychiatric clinic in Zurich, then directed by Bleuler, one of the most distinguished contributors to European psychiatry of this era, a young psychiatrist named Carl Jung was just beginning to establish himself as a significant figure. Both Jung and Bleuler showed a profound interest in Freud's theories long before they were generally fashionable, and they were particularly interested in applying his technique to the most severe mental disorders, the psychoses. Freud himself had been limited almost altogether to the study of neurotics by the circumstance of private practice. Early in this century, Jung (1906, 1907, 1910, 1918) made the brilliant discovery that *word association* techniques, long fashionable among academic psychologists for the study of normal cognitive structure (Cattell, 1887; Galton, 1879), and already used by Kraepelin in psychiatric research (1892), could be used to identify what he called complexes, important areas of unconscious conflict. Only a little later, and with no indication of any direct influence by Jung, Kent and Rosanoff (1910*a*, 1910*b*) published the results of an extensive study of word association in normal and disturbed subjects. These studies showed that there were marked differences between the associations of normal and mentally disordered subjects. They also provided a standard against which the responses of other groups of subjects could be compared. These psychiatric studies employing the word association technique resulted in a steady flow of applications of the device in clinical settings and, more recently, have led to extensive application by psychologists in personality research.

The next significant development was to involve the use of ink blots. Just as academic psychologists had long made use of association measures, so too, they had used ink blots in their study of normal mental functions (Tulchin, 1940). In fact, Whipple (1910) had prepared a manual of mental tests at the suggestion of Titchener, archconservative of American psychology, which included the report of a number of studies that had used ink blots as stimulus material. However, it remained for Hermann Rorschach, a young Swiss psychiatrist, to develop the possibility of using the blots for personality diagnosis.

The line of descent from Freud and *The Interpretation of Dreams* remains manifest, for Rorschach received his introduction to psychiatry at the Burghozli clinic during the period when Jung and Bleuler were deeply interested in psychoanalytic theory and at a time when Jung was developing his word association technique (Ellenberger, 1954). Further evidence of the influence of psychoanalysis upon Rorschach is provided by the fact that when he began the practice of psychiatry, he employed psychoanalytic technique and also published several minor papers in psychoanalytic journals. His use of the ink blots was, in many respects, similar to the use to which Jung had put words, and it seems likely that Rorschach was directly influenced by his knowledge of Jung's technique. In spite of Rorschach's involvement in the psychoanalytic movement and the fact that early users of the test, such as Oberholzer, were psychoanalysts, this connection became increasingly remote with the passage of time. During the three decades following the publication of Rorschach's *Psychodiagnostik* (1921), the test became enormously popular, far outstripping all other projective techniques in the extensiveness of its use. Yet many of the most prominent figures in the group were no longer openly identified with psychoanalysis. In fact, many users of the test manifested overt hostility toward psychoanalytic theory and practice. This trend has now, however, been considerably modified and there are important signs of a growing rapprochement between the Rorschach test and psychoanalysis (Klopfer, 1955; Schafer, 1954). The present popularity of the test is such that it must be considered one of the two or three best known of all psychological measuring instruments.

Another projective technique of general interest is the sentence completion test, where for the first time we find no intimate historical link with psychoanalysis. Again, however, there was a history of prior application in the hands of academic psychologists studying intellectual functions. As a measure of emotional factors, the test was first employed by Tendler (1930). His stated intent of assessing ". . . trends, fixed attitudes, attachments to persons, conflicting desires, satisfactions and annoyances . . ." (p. 122) differs little from the aims of Freud, Jung, and Rorschach. Nevertheless, aside from the author's familiarity with the word association techniques in general and the Kent-Rosanoff Word List in particular, there is little evidence that his technique derived from, or was influenced by, the developments we have already mentioned. Jung's theory is alluded to in a single sentence, but there is no reason to believe Tendler's endeavor was influenced importantly by it. Sentence completion measures developed slowly during the thirties, but because of the pressures of war and the demands of group personality assessment, many investigators developed an interest in the technique, with the result that there is now a considerable literature dealing with the test and its application.

A further major development involved a technique in which the subject was asked to create or originate rather than associate or complete. This was the Thematic Apperception Test which required the subject to construct stories, each of which was congruent with a specific picture. It is highly appropriate that the key figure in the development of this technique should be Henry A. Murray, an individual trained in psychoanalysis who has displayed a deep and enduring interest in literary creation. There were a number of forerunners of the TAT, including studies by Brittain (1907), Clark (1926), Libby (1908), and Schwartz (1932). It is also reported by Van Lennep (1951) that he began to use the Four-Picture Test, which involves story construction, as early as 1930. However, the most important development in this area was the publication by Morgan and Murray (1935) of a brief article describing the Thematic Apperception Test, followed by a more detailed report of the test and its application in Murray's *Explorations in Personality* (1938). Not only are the ties to psychoanalysis implied by the training in psycholoanalysis that both Christiana Morgan and Murray had received, but also by the recommendations for interpretation of the test (Murray, 1943), which lean heavily upon psychoanalytic principles. This device proved so useful in clinical and research settings that within a short period it came to be employed more extensively than any other projective technique aside from the Rorschach.

At this point, even overlooking a number of additional techniques that had made their appearance, there was an array of five major personality measures, all enjoying a moderately extensive application, and all possessing certain qualities in common. This communality was particularly marked when such devices were compared with the questionnaires and ratings scales in common use among psychologists of the late thirties. It remained only for some observer to note these similarities and to provide a label and the projective test movement was under way. It is generally agreed that this observer was L. K. Frank (1939), a student of human behavior already heavily identified with the holistic point of view in the study of personality. However, the term *projective technique* was used earlier in a publication by Horowitz and Murphy (1938), although they credit Frank with origination of the label. More significant is the fact that the term *projection test* appeared in *Explorations in Personality* (Murray, 1938) in the absence of any prior influence from Frank. Thus, it seems clear that historical priority for linking the concept of projection to these personality measures belongs rightfully to Henry A. Murray.

On the other hand, there is no doubt that it was Frank's influential paper (1939) that led to the popularization of the term *projective technique*. In this paper Frank places heavy emphasis upon the importance of measuring personality in such a manner as to give adequate representation to man's individuality, his personal or phenomenal world, and the field in which he exists. Further, Frank suggests that the term *projective method* be applied to the techniques we have just discussed, and he defends this class of instruments as of paramount importance in the study of human behavior. He suggests that projective methods are attempts to answer "the problem of how we can reveal the way an individual personality organizes experience, in order to disclose or at least gain insight into the individual's *private world* of meanings, significances, patterns, and feelings" (p. 402). He also indicates their utility for assessing the covert aspects of personality, suggesting that they may be used to "obtain from the subject, 'what he cannot or will not say,' frequently because he does not know himself and is not aware what he is revealing about himself through his projections" (p. 404). His general conception of the projective techniques is outlined in the following passage:

... we may approach the personality and induce the individual to reveal his way of organizing experience by giving him a field (objects, materials, experiences) with relatively little structure and cultural patterning so that the personality can project upon that plastic field his way of seeing life, his meanings, significances, patterns, and especially his feelings. Thus we elicit a projection of the individual personality's *private world* because he has to organize the field, interpret the material and react affectively to it. More specifically, a projection method for study of personality involves the presentation of a stimulus-situation designed or chosen because it will mean to the subject, not what the experimenter has arbitrarily decided it should mean (as in most psychological experiments using standardized stimuli in order to be "objective") but rather whatever it must mean to the personality who gives it, or imposes upon it, his private, idiosyncratic meaning and organization. The subject then will respond to *his* meaning of the presented stimulus-situation by some form of action and feeling that is expressive of his personality. (pp. 402-403)

A careful examination of Frank's paper reveals an interesting paradox. Although contemporary users of projective techniques have shown considerable interest in the relation between the process underlying their techniques and the mechanism of projection as outlined in psychoanalytic writing, there is no evidence to suggest that Frank was concerned with this relation. He undoubtedly was familiar with the psychoanalytic mechanisms of defense but there is no specific reference to Freud's writings in this paper, even in its very extensive bibliography. Moreover, his actual introduction of the label, including the passage quoted above, implies that he is using the term in a rough spatial analogy (a projection extends outward) simply to refer to the general tendency of an individual to reveal significant portions of his own personality when he is freely structuring objects in the outer world. Thus, one might reason that when contemporary authors argue that this or that device meets, or fails to meet, the criteria of Freudian projection—for example, Anderson, 1951; Cattell, 1951; & Murray, 1951—they are introducing a quite different meaning to the term projective technique from that which Frank intended.

Not only may one maintain that arguments about whether a given test involves projection are introducing a significant change in the definition originally presented, but also, if we remember what has already been said about the dual use of the term projection in the hands of Freud, it becomes clear that the broader usage, what we have called generalized projection, is apparently the same as the process that Frank had in mind. This usage would embrace virtually all of the tests that are commonly considered to be projective devices. Consequently, on historical grounds alone, there appears to be no basis for insisting that our definition of projective techniques involve a process identical with, or very similar, to that involved in classic projection.

We have now examined the meaning of the term projection within psychological theory and have witnessed briefly some of the major developments preceding the linkage of the term projective technique to the instruments in which we are interested. Our remaining task is to provide an acceptable definition of this group of instruments.

SOME TYPICAL DEFINITIONS OF
PROJECTIVE TECHNIQUES

Let us inspect for a moment some of the many definitions that have been proposed for projective techniques in the hope that they may disclose attributes that will serve to distinguish those tests from other personality instruments.

> The general idea behind these methods is to confront the subject with an unstructured, ambiguous situation . . . and ask him to do something with it. The subject is thus given several degrees of freedom to organize a plastic medium in his own way, and since little external aid is provided from conventional patterns he is all but obliged to give expression to the most readily available forces within himself. It is further characteristic of projective methods that the subject does not know what kind of inferences the experimenter intends to make. (White, 1944, p. 215)

This definition emphasizes the ambiguity of the stimulus material presented to the subject, the considerable freedom permitted in responding to the stimulus, and the fact that the subject is ordinarily unaware of the intent of the examiner.

> There are some common characteristics (to these tests) . . . presentation of a stimulus to a subject which does not make manifest, or only par-

tially makes manifest, the real purpose of the examiner in requesting a response . . . they sample individual behavior in a structured event of sufficient brevity to be clinically practicable and of sufficient stimulation to call forth a wide range of individual responses . . . projective techniques . . . regard the recorded behavior, as well as the personality that produces it, as an organized totality. (Bell, 1948, pp. 4-6)

Here again, we find mention of the subject's lack of understanding of the purpose of the test, with the addition of reasonable brevity and the capacity to evoke a wide variety of different responses, as distinguishing characteristics. Further, it is suggested that these tests are regularly accompanied by a holistic view of behavior.

The projective test uses a stimulus even more unstructured than the situational test—if possible, one so novel that the subject can bring to it no specific knowledge of how to respond. . . . Projective tests come nearer to grasping "the whole person" at once than any other testing technique. (Cronbach, 1949, p. 433)

In this passage, we find the ambiguity or lack of structure of the stimulus material mentioned again, and, in addition, it is specified that the stimulus should be outside of the usual experience of the subject so that he cannot employ habitual responses in reacting to the test. The conviction that projective techniques permit a "whole" view of the subject is referred to again.

. . . indirect methods for studying the inner life of an individual. The basic theory underlying all these devices is that each person unconsciously "projects" his private feelings and attitudes into his dealings with the everyday situations of the external world and that his actions thus have a symbolic as well as a literal reference . . . plastic materials (are employed) that permit a wide variety of symbolic structuralization. (Goodenough, 1950, p. 562)

This description points to the fact that the subject reveals himself in responding to the projective technique without being aware of it and emphasizes again the fact that the stimulus material can be responded to in many different ways by the subject. It also alludes to the possibility that responses may have important symbolic meanings.

The typical psychological test deals with one variable or function and attempts to provide a means of placing all tested individuals on a continuum with respect to that function. The fact that a few tests deal with several variables and several continua at once does not change the essential basis of the approach. Projective techniques such as the Rorschach deal with *n* functions or variables and attempt to describe the individual in terms of a dynamic pattern of interrelated functions or variables. This multiplicity of interrelated and interdependent variables constitutes the most important differences between projective techniques and other types of psychological tests. . . . (Ainsworth, 1954, p. 410)

This author points to the multiplicity of variables that can be dealt with by projective techniques and the tendency to treat these variables simultaneously and in relation to one another as characteristic of projective techniques.

In such tests, the subject is given a relatively "unstructured" task which permits wide latitude in its solution. The assumption underlying such methods is that the individual will "project" his characteristic modes of response into such a task. Like the performance and situational tests, projective techniques are more or less disguised in their purpose, thereby reducing the chance that the subject can deliberately create a desired impression (p. 17) . . . projective techniques are likewise characterized by a *global* approach to the appraisal of personality. (Anastasi, 1955, p. 598)

Here, we find the lack of structure, the large number of response alternatives, the concealment from the subject of the real purpose of the test and the holistic view of the individual's personality, all identified as distinguishing features of projective techniques.

The test stimulus is made as unstructured, loose, ambiguous, "meaningless" as possible (ink-blots, vague pictures, half-heard sounds, drawings made with minimal directives, etc.), and the subject is asked to tell what it might mean or somehow to take focused action. The meaning and focus are thus introduced by the subject. His unguided choice provides the material used by the examiner in interpretation. . . . Successful interpretation depends upon appreciation of the *pattern* of the subject's reaction to the test stimuli in infinite variety. No two subjects are exactly the same, as no two daisies are alike; no single test element carries a specific meaning. (Munroe, 1955, p. 45)

In this definition the observer comments upon the ambiguity of the stimulus material, the relative freedom permitted the subject in determining how he will respond, and the importance of considering many aspects of the test response simultaneously in the process of interpretation. In general this definition links projective techniques firmly with holistic analysis and the idiographic method.

By now the reader will have recognized that although there are important differences between these definitions, there is, nevertheless, a basic similarity in the view they present of these techniques. In particular we find proposed, usually repeatedly, the following distinguishing characteristics: *(a)* ambiguity or lack of structure in the stimulus material, *(b)* encouragement of a holistic treatment of personality, *(c)* lack of awareness on the part of the subject as to the purpose of the test, *(d)* wide individual latitude in responding to the test, *(e)* measurement of an unlimited number of variables and their interrelationships, *(f)* reasonable brevity, *(g)* removal from everyday behavior and habitual response.

Are all of these definitional criteria equally useful and appropriate? I think not. In particular, one may question the utility of proposing brevity and removal from everyday behavior as distinguishing features. Clearly, projective techniques are not brief when compared to most other psychological instruments. In addition, many projective techniques make a serious effort to establish continuity between the task or activity involved in the test and activities involved in everyday life. Further, not all of the remaining criteria are of equal importance.

At this point, let us take some of the characteristics that have been proposed, add whatever other qualities seem vital, and see if we can arrive at a useful, general characterization of these techniques.

THE ESSENTIAL FEATURES OF PROJECTIVE TECHNIQUES

In suggesting criteria for the differential identification of projective techniques, it seems desirable to distinguish between two types of attributes. The first includes the most critical differentiating features, whereas the second includes features derived from the first or of relatively minor significance in distinguishing these tests from other instruments.

Primary Criteria

Perhaps the most distinctive feature of projective techniques is their *sensitivity to unconscious or latent aspects of personality*. These devices, as a class, are presumed to provide the most efficient means of gaining access to those attributes of the person most difficult to view —those of which the individual himself is unaware. When we consider the historical ties between psychoanalytic theory and projective techniques, it is, of course, not surprising that these devices should be considered a particularly efficient means of getting at domains of behavior which are of unique importance within psychoanalytic theory. In any case, the capacity of these devices to intercept the private, covert, latent, unconscious components of the individual personality distinguishes them from most other psychological instruments.

One may lament the fact that this essential property of projective techniques lacks an appropriate degree of easy objectivity. That is, unlike some of the other properties of these tests that we shall discuss, this is not an attribute that inheres directly in the test itself. Rather it is a functional outcome of the test in application, and in most cases the question of how successfully the test displays this property must remain at least partly a matter of conjecture. In spite of this projective tests are distinguished by their frequent use to infer covert aspects of personality, and individuals closely associated with projective techniques agree completely that sensitivity to unconscious or latent aspects of personality is the most unusual feature of these tests.

A second consideration of major importance is the *multiplicity of response* permitted the subject by most projective techniques. In contrast to the typical questionnaire or inventory, projective tests ordinarily permit the subject to select the particular responses that he wishes to make from a theoretically unlimited number of response alternatives. It is clear that in story construction, as well as in many of the completion techniques, the individual responding to the test is bound only by the restrictions of his own language and psychological make-up. Even in the association techniques, the range of response is very great. The limitation of the subject's response to one of three or four categories, as in the typical personality inventory, provides a striking contrast to the projective technique.

A further distinctive feature is the *multidimensionality* of these devices. Many projective techniques are presented with no effort whatsoever to specify a particular set of dimensions that they are appropriate to assess. Those that suggest such a list of variables ordinarily make clear that the instrument may be used, in addition, for the measurement of many other personality variables. The history of projective techniques in application makes clear that these devices have been employed for the most diverse and distinctive empirical purposes, and it is hard to conceive of a psychological variable that some investigator has not attempted to assess by means of a projective technique.

A fourth feature of these tests that distinguishes them from some other psychological instruments is the *lack of subject awareness of the purpose of the test.* None of the projective techniques, as ordinarily employed, involves a full understanding by the subject of what the examiner is attempting to assess. Although the subject may know something about the general goal of the investigator, for example, that he is interested in measuring personality, the details of this intent, including the variables to be used in the analysis of the protocols, are routinely kept from the subject. In the usual case the subject is not only unaware of what the psychological variable is that the examiner wishes to measure, but he is also uninformed of the aspects of his test response that will be of interest to the examiner.

A fifth distinguishing feature of projective techniques is the *profusion and richness of the response data they elicit.* Ordinarily, projective-test responses far exceed in sheer amount or quantity the typical product of an inventory or rating scale. Not only are the response data numerous, they also tend to be very multiform or varied. Thus, in both quantity and complexity of response, these devices seem distinguished from conventional personality instruments.

Secondary Criteria

One of the most frequently proposed qualities for distinguishing projective techniques from other tests is the *ambiguity of the stimulus presented to the subject.* It is true that as a class these tests appear to involve more ambiguous stimuli than most other psychological instruments, although this property is present to a variable degree among projective tests. Some, for example, present stimuli that are perfectly meaningful and easy to identify, and even the most ambiguous are capable of exact identification given an appropriate set. For example, an ink blot is easy to identify as an ink blot. It is only when the subject is asked to say "what this might be" that the stimulus becomes ambiguous. Even if we were to accept ambiguity as a primary quality and attempt to identify its relative existence, it is almost inevitable that we would fall back on a response definition of ambiguity. This suggests that the degree of ambiguity is defined not simply by the stimulus but by the stimulus in conjunction with the particular set of instructions that are given to the subject, and the outcome of this interaction is measured by the responses evoked. In other words, the important aspect of ambiguity is represented by the diversity of response elicited from the subject, and we have already included this among our essential criteria. For our purposes, then, we can freely admit the relative ambiguity of the stimuli used in projective techniques but maintain that this feature of the test is adequately subsumed under the criterion, multiplicity of response permitted or encouraged in the subject.

A further distinctive feature of projective tests that is often mentioned is their appropriateness for *holistic analysis.* Sometimes this is referred to as their sensitivity to the "total person"; at other times, the user may point to the necessity of considering patterns and profiles rather than individual scores. In any case, it implies that a simple variable-by-variable analysis of the individual is not appropriate to the technique. Here it seems safe to agree that many more users of projective techniques have chosen to employ what might be called a "holistic" analysis than would be true of users of objective tests of personality. This, however, is not a property of the test but of the individuals who characteristically employ it. There are, it is true, attributes of the test that make this kind of analysis more appropriate here than with other tests, but these have already been identified as the multidimensionality of the test and the richness and profuseness of the data elicited. Consequently, the ease with which projective test protocols can be subjected to holistic analysis is an important property of these instruments, but this feature can be accounted for by means of criteria we have already listed.

A third characteristic that applies to most projective techniques has to do with their tendency to evoke *fantasy responses* from the subject. A high proportion of these techniques ask the subject to take an "as if" set, to respond without reality restriction, to imagine or to invent. Even though the responses themselves may be closely linked to realistic situations, the subject is encouraged to respond without concern for the sanctions of the real world, to respond imaginatively.

Closely related to the fantasy aspects of these responses is the fact that the subject's responses have *no right or wrong status*. Thus, as the subject is instructed, there is ordinarily no "correct" or "true" response to the test. The individual is to respond in whatever manner seems most natural and appropriate with the assurance that there is no criterion of correctness against which his responses can be arrayed and scored.

It is evident that by no means all of these criteria are differentially characteristic of projective techniques. Many of the "objective" measures of personality would meet one or more of these requirements, even though we could secure complete consensus among psychologists that they were not projective techniques. This is not a serious matter, however, if the entire complex of criteria succeeds in distinguishing the projective technique from other tests, and this is indeed the case. Although there are individual projective techniques that do not fulfill all of these criteria, and there are nonprojective techniques that meet one or more of these requirements, the vast majority of projective techniques will fulfill many more of these requirements than will nonprojective measures of personality.

A DEFINITION

For our purposes, then, *a projective technique is an instrument that is considered especially sensitive to covert or unconscious aspects of behavior, it permits or encourages a wide variety of subject responses, is highly multidimensional, and it evokes unusually rich or profuse response data with a minimum of subject awareness concerning the purpose of the test.* Further, it is very often true that *the stimulus material presented by the projective test is ambiguous, interpreters of the test depend upon holistic analysis, the test evokes fantasy responses, and there are no correct or incorrect responses to the test.*

This relatively abstract statement will be unsatisfactory to some readers. Fortunately, in the chapter to follow, the reader will find a more concrete and substantive discussion of what projective techniques are as well as a brief consideration of the variety of ways in which projective techniques can be subdivided or classified. The present chapter has provided an overview of projective techniques within which we can approach efficiently the task of discussing the individual techniques.

REFERENCES

AINSWORTH, M. D. Problems of validation. In B. Klopfer *et al.*, *Developments in the Rorschach Technique: technique and theory*. Vol. 1. New York: Harcourt, Brace & World, 1954. Pp. 405-500.

ANASTASI, Anne. *Psychological testing*. New York: Macmillan, 1955.

ANDERSON, H. H. Human behavior and personality growth. In H. H. Anderson & Gladys L. Anderson (Eds.), *An introduction to projective techniques*. Englewood Cliffs, N. J.: Prentice-Hall, 1951. Pp. 3-25.

BELL, J. *Projective techniques*. New York: Longmans, Green, 1948.

BELLAK, L. On the problems of the concept of projection. In L. E. Abt & L. Bellak (Eds.), *Projective psychology:* Clinical approaches to the total personality. New York: Knopf, 1950. Pp. 7-32.

BRITTAIN, H. L. A study in imagination. *Pedagog. Sem.*, 1907, 14, 137-207.

CATTELL, J. McK. Experiments on the association of ideas. *Mind*, 1887, 12, 68-74.

CATTELL, R. B. Principles of design in "projective" or misperception tests of personality. In H. H. Anderson & Gladys L. Anderson (Eds.), *An introduction to projective techniques*. Englewood Cliffs, N. J.: Prentice-Hall, 1951. Pp. 55-98.

CLARK, L. P. The phantasy method of analyzing narcissistic neuroses. *Med. J. and Record*, 1926, 123, 154-158.

CRONBACH, L. J. *Essentials of psychological testing*. New York: Harper, 1949.

ELLENBERGER, H. The life and work of Hermann Rorschach. *Bull. Menninger Clinic*, 1954, 18, 173-219.

FRANK, L. K. Projective methods for the study of personality. *J. Psychol.*, 1939, 8, 389-413.

FREUD, Anna. *The ego and the mechanisms of defence*. London: Hogarth, 1937. (Originally published in 1936.)

FREUD, S. The justification for detaching from neurasthenia a particular syndrome: the anxiety-neurosis. In S. Freud, *Collected papers*. Vol. 1. London: Hogarth, 1924. Pp. 76-106. (Originally published in 1895.)

FREUD, S. Further remarks on the defence neuro-psychoses. In S. Freud, *Collected papers*. Vol. 1. London: Hogarth, 1924. Pp. 155-182. (Originally published in 1896.)

FREUD, S. The interpretation of dreams. In J. Strachey (Ed.), *The complete psychological works of Sigmund Freud*. Vols. 4 & 5. London: Hogarth, 1953. (Originally published in 1900.)

FREUD, S. Delusions and dreams in Jensen's 'Gradiva.' In J. Strachey (Ed.), *The complete psychological works of Sigmund Freud*. Vol. 9. London: Hogarth, 1959, pp. 7-95. (Originally published in 1907.)

FREUD, S. Psychoanalytic notes on an autobiographical account of a case of paranoia (dementia paranoides). In J. Strachey (Ed.), *The complete psychological works of Sigmund Freud*. Vol. 12. London: Hogarth, 1958, pp. 9-82. (Originally published in 1911.)

FREUD, S. Totem and taboo. In J. Strachey (Ed.), *The complete psychological works of Sigmund Freud*. Vol. 13. London: Hogarth for Routledge Kegan Paul, 1955, pp. 1-161. (Originally published in 1913.)

FREUD, S. A metapsychological supplement to the theory of dreams. In J. Strachey (Ed.), *The complete psychological works of Sigmund Freud*. Vol. 14. London: Hogarth, 1957, pp. 217-235. (Originally published in 1916.)

FREUD, S. *New introductory lectures on psychoanalysis*. New York: Norton, 1933.

GALTON, F. Psychometric experiments. *Brain*, 1879, 2, 149-162.

GOODENOUGH, Florence L. *Mental testing*. New York: Holt, Rinehart & Winston, 1949.

HOROWITZ, Ruth, & MURPHY, Lois B. Projective methods in the psychological study of children. *J. exp. Educ.*, 1938, 7, 133-140.

JUNG, C. G. Diagnostiche Assoziationsstudien. *J. f. Psychol. u. Neur.*, 1906, 8, 25-60.

JUNG, C. G. Diagnostiche Assoziationsstudien. *J. f. Psychol. u. Neur.*, 1907, 9, 188-197.

JUNG, C. G. The association method. *Am. J. Psychol.*, 1910, 21, 219-269.

JUNG, C. G. *Studies in word association*. New York: Dodd, Mead, 1918.

KENT, Grace H., & ROSANOFF, A. J. A study of association in insanity: Part 1. Association in normal subjects. *Am. J. Insanity*, 1910a, 67, 37-96.

KENT, Grace H. A study of association in insanity: Part II. Association in insane subjects. *Am. J. Insanity*, 1910b, 67, 317-390.

KLOPFER, B. Rorschach hypotheses and ego psychology. In B. Klopfer *et al.*,

Developments in the Rorschach Technique: technique and theory. Vol. 1. New York: Harcourt, Brace & World, 1954. Pp. 561-600.

KRAEPELIN, E. *Ueber die Beinflussing einfacher psychischer Vorgange durch Arzneimittel: experimentelle Unterschungen.* Jena: G. Fischer, 1892.

LIBBY, W. The imagination of adolescents. *Am. J. Psychol.*, 1908, 19, 249-252.

MORGAN, Christiana D., & MURRAY, H. A. A method for investigating fantasies: the Thematic Apperception Test. *Arch. Neurol. Psychiat.*, 1935, 34, 289-306.

MURSTEIN, B. I., & PRYER, R. S. The concept of projection: a review. *Psychol. Bull.*, 1959, 56, 353-374.

MUNROE, Ruth L. *Schools of psychoanalytic thought.* New York: Holt, Rinehart & Winston, 1955.

MURRAY, H. A. The effect of fear upon estimates of the maliciousness of other personalities. *J. soc. Psychol.*, 1933, 4, 310-339.

MURRAY, H. A. *Explorations in personality.* New York: Oxford, 1938.

MURRAY, H. A. *Thematic Apperception Text Manual.* Cambridge, Mass.: Harvard Univer. Press, 1943.

MURRAY, H. A. Foreword. In H. H. Anderson & Gladys L. Anderson (Eds)., *An introduction to projective techniques.* Englewood Cliffs, N. J.: Prentice-Hall, 1951. Pp. xi-xiv.

RORSCHACH, H. *Psychodiagnostics: A diagnostic test based on perception.* (4th ed.) New York: Grune & Stratton, 1942. (Originally published in 1921.)

SCHAFER, Roy. *Psychoanalytic interpretation in Rorschach testing: theory and application.* New York: Grune & Stratton, 1954.

SCHWARTZ, L. A. Social-situation pictures in the psychiatric interview. *Am. J. Orthopsychiat.*, 1932, 2, 124-133.

TENDLER, A. D. A preliminary report on a test for emotional insight. *J. appl. Psychol.*, 1930, 14, 122-136.

TULCHIN, S. H. The pre-Rorschach use of ink blot tests. *Rorschach Res. Exch.*, 1940, 4, 1-7.

VAN LENNEP, D. J. The Four-picture Test. In H. H. Anderson & Gladys L. Anderson (Eds.), *An introduction to projective techniques.* Englewood Cliffs, N. J.: Prentice-Hall, 1951. Pp. 149-180.

WHIPPLE, G. M. *Manual of mental and physical tests.* Baltimore, Md.: Warwick & York, 1910.

WHITE, R. W. Interpretation of imaginative productions. In J. McV. Hunt (Ed.), *Personality and the behavior disorders.* Vol. 1. New York: Ronald, 1944. Pp. 214-251.

3. What Are the Varieties of Projective Techniques?

WE HAVE NOW SEEN some of the circumstances that played a role in the development of projective techniques, we have considered a variety of factors that contributed to the application of these devices in cross-cultural research, and, in broad terms, we have agreed upon the attributes that typify or distinguish projective techniques. It seems high time to take a detailed and specific look at these instruments we have discussed in such general terms. This is, indeed, the major purpose of the present chapter. Before proceeding to this enumeration, however, let us pause to consider the problem of how projective techniques can be classified, for out of this exercise will come a modest system that we can use to organize our subsequent descriptive efforts.

A number of prior observers have suggested ways in which projective techniques can be clustered or grouped together (Campbell, 1950, 1957; Cattell, 1951; Frank, 1939, 1948; Sargent, 1945), and these various classificatory efforts have been summarized in a recent paper (Lindzey, 1959). In this analysis of the problem of classification, I suggested that these various approaches can themselves be categorized in terms of the particular attribute or aspect of the test they focus upon. First, there are distinctions based upon *attributes that inhere in the test material itself.* Here we are concerned with variation in the stimulus material, for example, structured stimuli versus unstructured stimuli or auditory stimuli versus visual stimuli. Second, we may classify the tests in terms of the *manner in which the technique was devised* or constructed, for example, the distinction between tests derived from theory or rational considerations as opposed to tests justified solely in terms of

49

a particular set of empirical findings. Third, we may distinguish between these devices on the basis of the *manner in which test is interpreted,* for example, tests emphasizing formal analysis versus tests emphasizing content analysis. Fourth, we might propose a classification that is based upon the *purpose of the test,* for example, the assessment of conflict as opposed to the measurement of motives, or the diagnosis of psychosexual fixation as opposed to the estimation of neuroticism. Fifth, we might propose a set of categories concerned with *differences in the administration of the test,* for example, group technique as opposed to individual technique. Sixth, we can distinguish between the instruments on the basis of the *type of response they elicit* from the subject, for example, story construction as opposed to association.

All of these distinctions have some usefulness and something can be said in favor of each of them as providing the best means for classifying projective techniques. In spite of this, I have argued that the final type of classification, the one based upon differences in type of response, is easily the most important and the one that should be emphasized. The essential consideration here is that this classification seems most likely to be closely related to underlying psychological processes involved in the various tests, for it is this classification that points to what the subject is actually doing. Insofar as these tests are distinctive and to be treated as uniquely different, it seems likely that the major determinant of this distinctiveness will be the nature of the subject's response. It is also worth noting that a number of the other types of classifications are more or less directly specified by distinctions based upon type of response, for example, if the technique elicits choice response, we know a good deal about whether it will emphasize formal or content analysis, whether it is likely to be suitable for group administration, and whether it will be structured or not.

Even if we agree that the most important distinctions between projective techniques are based upon variation in the type of response elicited, there is still the task of arriving at just the proper array of such distinctions. For present purposes it seems sufficient to think in terms of five general types of response. These are (a) association; (b) construction; (c) completion; (d) choice or ordering; and (e) expression. Obviously, not every test can be fitted neatly into only one of these categories. The world of reality provides its customary overlap and ambiguity. However, with very little effort, it is possible to classify virtually every projective technique as involving predominantly one of these types of response. More significant is the fact that when projective techniques are classified on this basis, we find that the techniques brought into the same category have a general congruence and psychological consistency that makes it reasonable to conceive of similar underlying psychological processes.

In discussing the various projective techniques we shall attempt to: (*a*) indicate what the test consists of and how it is administered; (*b*) consider in broad terms how it is scored and interpreted; (*c*) specify the range of variables or dimensions that it is particularly appropriate to assess; (*d*) estimate the frequency with which the test has been used; (*e*) describe the amount of standardization to which the test has been subjected; (*f*) identify the major modifications of the instrument; (*g*) enumerate the principal advantages and difficulties in the use of the test; and (*h*) suggest the major references that the reader can consult for further information concerning the test. Not all of these matters are relevant to each of the tests we shall discuss, for many of them are so new, or so poorly explored, as to offer little information under certain of these headings. However, where available, we shall try to present information relevant to each of these topics.

ASSOCIATION TECHNIQUES

Here the subject is set to respond to some stimulus presented by the examiner with the first word, image, or percept that occurs to him. Such devices minimize ideation and emphasize immediacy. The subject is not to reflect or reason but rather to respond with whatever concept or word, however unreasonable, first rises to consciousness.

These techniques, in certain respects, represent a bridge between experimental psychology and the clinical setting, for in both areas there has been intense interest in what happens when an individual is asked to respond to some stimulus with the first association that comes to his mind. It was natural that students of the normal, conscious human mind should use this device as a means of mapping or laying bare the structure of mental events. Further, once Freud had devised the method of free association, this appeared to be an important means of gaining insight into the subterranean reaches of the mind. It is not surprising, therefore, that a number of important techniques embodying this response set have been developed, the most popular of which are the word association test and the Rorschach test.

Word Association Technique

This test consists of a list of stimulus words that are presented to the subject, usually by means of an examiner who reads the words one at a time. The subject is instructed to respond with the first word that occurs to him after hearing the stimulus word. Typically the examiner records both the word with which the subject responds and the latency of response, the duration of time between the stimulus word and the elicited response. There are many different lists of stimulus words in existence, although the two encountered most commonly are the early list provided by Kent and Rosanoff (1910a, 1910b) consisting of 100 words and the more recent list of 60 words proposed by Rapaport (1946). Actually it is quite common in research for the word list to be constructed on an ad hoc basis with the intention of developing particular sensitivity for one or more specific variables.

Scoring of the test typically involves a content analysis in which the stimulus words and responses are grouped in terms of the particular motives or psychlogical processes they reflect or with which they seem to be associated. In some instances the subject's responses may be compared further with responses that have been observed already in groups of defined subjects. In addition to the content of the response, the length of time taken in responding is considered a relevant dimension and various kinds of temporal deviation are used as evidence of conflict or tension in the area represented by the stimulus word. In general, either an unusually quick or a very slow response is believed to indicate disturbance.

The interpretation of test results is obviously linked directly to the principles that have guided the original selection of stimulus words and to the various reference groups whose responses are available for comparison. Thus, if the words have been selected in such a manner that a number of them bear upon the variable of dominance, the responses to these items will be examined to provide a measure of the strength of dominance needs or of conflict and disturbance centering about this area. Or, if the typical performance of neurotic and normal groups on these words is available for comparison with the subject's pattern of response, it may be possible to arrive at a judgment concerning the likelihood that the subject is either normal or neurotic by comparing his responses to those reported for the two reference groups.

Illustrative of the aspects of the word association test that are focussed upon in interpretation are the four classes of disturbance indicators outlined by Rapaport (1946). First, there are *close reactions,* typified by repetition of the stimulus word or a definition of the word. Second are *distant reactions,* where the association has little or no apparent relation to the stimulus word. Third are the *content disturbances,* which may involve either the stimulus word or the association. In the former case the subject may indicate that he is unfamiliar with the word, or he may misunderstand it. In the latter case there are a variety of possibilities, the most prominent of which are vulgar responses and personal names. Fourth are *disturbances in reproduction of response,* which usually involve a failure to respond or a long delay in responding.

Although the test has been used very widely in research, its clinical application has been less frequent than that of the most popular projective devices. It has been employed only occasionally in cross-cultural settings (Carstairs, 1957; DuBois, 1944). Perhaps the most frequent application of the instrument has been in the hands of the personality investigator.

The variable that the test has been used to assess most frequently is general adjustment or neuroticism. However, there is no clear restriction upon the variables with which the test can be linked; for, depending upon the particular stimulus words employed, the investigator can derive an index to appraise almost any conceivable dimension. Suitable investigation is, of course, necessary before the investigator can be confident that his intentions are mirrored in the actual performance of the instrument.

Although the test has been modified frequently, the comparatively simple mode of administration, coupled with the relatively specific response data, has led to more standardization than is typical of projective techniques. The directions for administration are simple and usually adhered to relatively consistently so that there is considerable uniformity in the collection of this kind of response data. Further, a number of studies, beginning with the initial investigation by Kent and Rosanoff (1910*a*, 1910*b*), have provided summaries of the patterns of response of subjects of varying characteristics. In general, there is more information concerning the content of response than there is on the latency of response, presumably because it is somewhat more difficult to record, classify, and report the temporal data.

One of the frequently encountered modifications of the test has consisted of securing certain additional measures while the subject is responding to the stimulus word. Typically these have been physiological, although in at least one instance (Luria, 1932), the additional measure was motoric. It is well known that the electrical conductance of the skin changes during various emotional states, and a common measure of emotionality is the Galvanic Skin Response which is a measure of this variation in conductance. This measure has often been coupled with the word association test in an effort to identify areas of difficulty or disturbance. Actually, the various lie detector instruments usually operate on this principle (Burtt, 1950), and frequently involve the use of word association lists (Crosland, 1929) as well as direct questions concerning the crime. Goodenough (1946) originated an ingenious device which presented graphic homophones (words that are written and pronounced in identical manner) as stimulus words. Thus, each stimulus word can be reacted to in terms of either of two meanings, for example, yarn can be related to knitting or to the telling of stories, and depending on the meaning selected by the subject, the association will vary markedly. There have also been measures (Davids, 1956) where the subject is encouraged to respond with not only the first word that occurs to him but also with as many other words as come to mind within a particular time interval, thus providing a chain of association. Such a procedure can provide a productivity index crudely related to the latency measure that is lost under the usual circumstances of group administration.

In comparison to many projective techniques, the word association technique possesses the delightful qualities of easy, objective administration combined with simple, readily scored response data. We have already commented that the administration of the test has been more standard than most projective techniques and, further, that there has been more usable normative material collected in connection with this test than in connection with most. A further advantage is that the instrument can be adapted readily to almost any variable that the investigator may wish to measure. Objective scoring systems are no more difficult to devise for this test than for other personality instruments.

On the negative side we find, first of all, that the limited response data of the instrument fail to provide much of the information that is often expected from a projective technique. For example, there is little information here concerning the internal frame of reference or the subject's characteristic way of viewing the world. The detailed content of the individual's subjective world is strikingly absent from the customary results of this test. Further, the test is closely linked to a particular linguistic structure so that cross-cultural studies face all the problems intrinsic in the many structural and lexical differences between languages. Although response time provides an intriguing quantitative index, there is by no means complete agreement concerning just how this type of data should be used.

In the last analysis, the most important shortcoming of this instrument seems to be that the scores readily derived from the test do not satisfy the needs of the personality investigator for discovering new facets of the subject under scrutiny. Although the test is demonstrably sensitive to unconscious motives, it tends to provide only an indication of "disturbed" or "not disturbed" or perhaps a single score on a disturbance continuum. These data, useful though they may be under many circumstances, are too sparse to please the individual who is most likely to turn to projective techniques for assistance.

There are a number of general treatments of the word association technique, the most important of which are by Bell (1948), Rapaport, Schafer, & Gill (1946), and Rotter (1951). The interested reader will also want to examine the pioneer studies of Jung (1910, 1918) and Kent and Rosanoff (1910*a*, 1910*b*).

The Rorschach Test

Perhaps no psychological instrument has piqued the public's interest more than Hermann Rorschach's set of ink blots. In the minds of many people, this esoteric and somewhat mysterious instrument has come to typify the kind of activity in which the modern psychologist engages. Although administering and interpreting the Rorschach is far from typical of the daily activities of all psychologists, this instrument has become remarkably widespread in application. Of all the instruments used for individual personality diagnosis, it is by far the most popular, and its use in research is almost as frequent as its clinical application. There is little question but that for better or worse this test has had a profound impact upon developments within psychology during the past two decades.

The Rorschach test consists of ten plates that depict symmetrical ink blots of the sort that might be produced by folding a sheet of paper over a drop of ink. Half the blots are gray and black on a white background, whereas the remaining half involve color. Two of the latter include gray and black, but the other three are multicolored with virtually no gray elements. Typically the test is administered by an examiner, seated slightly to the rear of the subject, who presents the cards individually and in a standardized order with the request that the subject report what he sees or what the figures resemble or suggest to him. During the first stage of the administration, the examiner merely makes a verbatim record of the responses or associations and the latency of response of the subject to each of the ten cards, with as little comment as possible. He also notes the total time taken by the subject on each card and the position(s) in which the card is held. During the inquiry or second stage of the administration, the subject is encouraged to examine the cards again together with his associations and to report just what characteristic of the cards determined or contributed to his associations. It is essential that the examiner secure sufficient information to permit him to score each response, and consequently he must be fully acquainted with the details of scoring Rorschach responses.

The scoring of the Rorschach test is highly complex and individualized. There is no single system that has gained exclusive acceptance among clinical psychologists. On the other hand, there are certain similarities among all the scoring systems and familiarity with the work of Rorschach (1921), Beck (1944, 1945, 1952) and Klopfer (1956; Klopfer, Ainsworth, Klopfer, and Holt, 1954) provides the student with sufficient background to be able to understand any of the variant systems with little difficulty. In fact, when compared with other projective techniques, there is considerably more consistency in common practice here than is typically the case.

One of the congruences among the different systems has to do with the scoring of each response for location, determinant, and content. In scoring *location* it is normal to record each response as referring to the whole blot (W) or to a detail of the blot. Furthermore, Detail responses are divided into those that are normal details (D) and those that are small (Dd) or rare and unusual (Dr). A separate score is typically employed if the subject responds to a white space in the blot (S). In scoring for *determinants* the examiner must decide whether the association was determined primarily by the form or shape of the portion of the blot linked with the response (F); by movement that was seen or perceived in the blot (M, FM, m);by shading, where variations in blackness and whiteness, texture, or shading of the blot determines the response (c, K, k); or whether color determined the response (C). All of these determinants can be subjected to various refinements, the most important of which are the distinction between good Form (F+) and poor Form (F−) responses, and the distinction between movement which is attributed to human figures (M), animal figures (FM), and inanimate objects (m). The responses can also derive from a combination of determinants such as color and form with color playing the dominant role (CF) or with form playing the dominant role (FC). The scoring for *content* of responses varies from simple to highly elaborate and complex, but it is conventional to score at least for Human (H), Human Detail (Hd), Animal (A), Animal Detail (Ad), Nature (N), and Abstract responses (Abs). Responses are also scored as *Original* (O) or *Popular* (P) on the basis of the frequency with which other subjects have provided such responses to the same blot. The rough standard for a Popular response is that it occur at least as often as a third or a sixth of the time with normal subjects, whereas an Original response is presumed to occur no more often than once in a hundred protocols.

The scores for the above categories, in addition to various refinements that are provided by the particular scoring convention employed, together with the number of responses (R) and the reaction time (RT) to each card, provide the basic scoring information which is typically summarized in a *psychogram*. This summary not only presents the results of the scoring graphically but also contains a record of various ratios of scores considered essential to the process of interpretation.

Interpretation of the instrument begins with the psychogram and the scores summarized therein, but it also employs sequence analysis (emphasizing the order in which the responses are given) and the detailed content of the responses, coupled with the general clinical skill and experience of the interpreter. The process can best be described as semistandardized. There are a number of specific and objective scores that play a crucial role in the interpretive process, and there are also a large number of empirical generalizations relating scores or ratios and particular personality attributes. On the other hand, it is a matter of firm principle among clinicians that the test cannot be adequately interpreted by someone capable only of slavishly finding similarities between a given set of scores and specific generalizations. One of the points emphasized by almost all users of the test is that no single score has meaning independent of the other scores. Although the various ratios take into consideration some degree of interrelatedness, they themselves must be conditioned by what is found in the rest of the subject's record. In general, the interpreter of the test should indeed be familiar with the relatively objective method of scoring test responses, and ideally he should also know something about the kinds of relations that have been hypothesized or demonstrated between elements of this scoring system and personality characteristics. For the clinical use of the test, however, it is usually suggested that he must in addition have had considerable experience with the test (100 subjects is often proposed as a minimum number to be tested before an interpretation can be considered adequately based), and, moreover, he is presumed to be familiar with personality theory and to be a shrewd observer of human behavior. These somewhat ideal requirements for the adequate interpretation of the test are mentioned here not with the implication that the test is, or should be, used only when these requirements are fulfilled but simply to make clear the conditions specified by those who have worked most extensively with the test in clinical settings.

Following Beck (1951), let us examine some of the objective elements of test response that are utilized in providing inferences concerning several important domains of behavior. The reader should remember that the generalizations to follow are by no means all firmly established on the basis of well-controlled empirical data.

One of the most important contributions of the Rorschach is believed to be the insight it provides into *intellectual functioning*. Of great importance here is the $F+$ per cent or the proportion of the subject's Form-determined responses that present clear, accurate perceptions. This proportion presumably represents the degree to which the individual is able to perceive accurately and to organize in terms of known concepts and objects. A second measure relevant to the understanding of intellectual functioning is the *W* per cent, the proportion of responses linked to the entire blot, which is considered an index of the subject's abstracting ability. Also important is the sequence of responses, that is, whether on each card the subject tends to move in an orderly fashion from Detail and Whole responses or from Whole responses to Detail responses or whether his approach is haphazard and varied from card to card. According to convention, this index provides evidence concerning the extent to which intellectual abilities are rationally controlled and available for adaptive utilization. An unusually high incidence of Animal responses (A) is typically indicative of a shallow, ineffective intellect, whereas a high incidence of Popular responses (P) suggests the possibility that the subject is overly conventional and conforming in his thinking. On the other hand, a high incidence of Original responses (O) suggests richness of the intellect, and a large number of responses (R) suggests that the individual is likely to be able to devote considerable energy to intellectual productions. A final favorable sign for intellectual richness is a high incidence of human Movement responses (M).

If we are primarily concerned with the affective or *emotional life* of the subject rather than his intellectual functioning, we would ordinarily center our attention upon Color and Shading responses. In general the higher the frequency of responses solely or largely determined by color, without the moderating influence of form, the more direct, uninhibited, and primitive is the emotional life of the subject. A large number of pure Color responses (C) would be expected in the typical case only on a psychotic protocol. When color serves as a determinant that is subordinate to form (FC), emotional expression is permitted but in a socially acceptable fashion. A complete absence of any Color response suggests an impoverishment of emotional life with little or no development of channels for the expression of these tensions. A high incidence of Shading responses is believed to indicate the existence of unpleasant emotions such as anxiety. The nature of the Shading response, that is, whether it is a Vista response in which the subject sees the blot in three dimensions with distance as part of the percept, or whether the subject simply responds to differences between the blackness or whiteness of the blots, or whether he responds to what he perceives as the texture of the blot, provides information concerning the particular kind of anxiety that is being reflected.

The above paragraphs are intended only to suggest the abundance of factors entering into the Rorschach interpretation of personality attributes. In a clinical setting the interpretation may be considerably more complex than that implied by our discussion, but in many investigations only one or a small number of indices may be used.

There have been two principle types of modification of this test. The first has involved developing new stimuli and is exemplified by the Levy blots (Levy, 1946; Zubin & Young, 1948) which were designed especially to elicit movement, and the Behn-Rorschach (Zulliger, 1952) and Howard (1953) sets of blots, which can be used as alternate forms of the test. Considerable attention has been paid also to modifying procedure, particularly so that the test can be given in group settings, and a variety of group tests have been proposed (Harrower & Steiner, 1945). Some of these elicit free responses to a blot presented simultaneously to members of a group, whereas a more controversial variant presents the subjects with multiple choice alternatives for each blot. There has also been some variation in the administration of the test with many examiners introducing a "testing the limits" phase to the test procedure (Hutt & Shor, 1946; Klopfer & Kelley, 1942) and some actually employing an association phase (Janis & Janis, 1946) in which the subject associates to his original responses. The major general modification in scoring is Munroe's (1950) inspection technique, an approach permitting the interpreter, by attending to certain highlights in the protocols, to make general or gross interpretations very rapidly and thus to employ the test in settings that permit little time for scoring individual protocols.

One of the most salient features of the Rorschach test is the large number of variables that it has been used to measure. In fact, Beck (1951), one of the important contributors to the development of the test, actually characterizes it in his writing as a "multidimensional test of personality." Thus, there is almost no variable of personality that the test could not conceivably be used to assess. On the other hand, there is little doubt that the test has been used most often to provide evidence bearing upon what is often referred to as the "structural aspects of personality." These variables are presumed to refer to the general organization of personality or the characteristic manner in which the individual relates to himself and others, rather than to specific motives or conflicts. The use of the experience balance (C/M) to provide evidence of whether the individual is introversive or extratensive is a typical instance. The descriptive statement says nothing about the particular kinds of impulses or behavioral tendencies that the individual will display, but rather it says something about whether the individual is primarily oriented toward the inner world or the outer.

Although the test typically has not been considered most efficient as an index of specific motives, it has nevertheless been used in this manner, and a number of indices have been proposed for inferring from Rorschach responses such variables as aggression (Elizur, 1949), anxiety (Elizur, 1949), homosexuality (Davids, Joelson & McArthur, 1956; Wheeler, 1949), impulsiveness (Holtzman, 1950*b*), intelligence (Altus & Thompson, 1949; Vernon, 1933), and shyness (Holtzman, 1950*a*).

If success is measured by popularity, there is no question but that the Rorschach is the most successful of all projective techniques. The test has been widely used in the most varied settings. In the psychiatric domain it is considered by far the most indispensable of instruments for assessing personality and in cross-cultural settings it has been used more extensively than any other projective technique (for example, Abel & Calabresi, 1951; DuBois, 1944; Gladwin & Sarason, 1953; Henry & Spiro, 1953; Spindler, 1955).

Although the popularity of the Rorschach cannot be questioned, its validity can, and we have seen concrete evidence of this in the first chapter of this volume. As will become increasingly clear in our subsequent discussion, questions of validity of projective techniques are never easy to dispose of. A detailed attempt to assess the validity of the Rorschach would necessitate more space than we are able to devote to our general discussion of all projective techniques (c.f., Ainsworth, 1951). Perhaps the best that we can say here is that a careful scrutiny of the existing literature is likely to leave the neutral observer with the impression that the test is neither so infallible as many of its advocates have claimed, nor is it so devoid of any utility as many critics have asserted. There are many studies, some of them replicated, indicating that the Rorschach effectively serves psychodiagnostic or personality description needs. There are many other studies that leave little doubt that, in particular settings, the test has failed to function as advertised.

In spite of vigorous objections on the part of most clinical psychologists to the suggestion that projective techniques should be standardized, the Rorschach has been subjected to a good deal of standardization. Administration was relatively well structured initially, and there was sufficient objectivity in the original scoring system to permit the casual collection of a good deal of normative data concerning the test and its patterns of response. At the present there are normative findings for a variety of special groups in addition to findings for several normal groups of subjects. In general, then, administration of the test is relatively standard, and there is a fair supply of normative findings for various identified groups. The actual interpretation of the test, however, has typically been considered to involve more than objective scores, and consequently the interpretative process is deliberately poorly standardized, once we venture beyond the psychogram.

Perhaps the most important advantage of this technique is the extensiveness with which it has been employed. No other projective technique has been used so often and in such a variety of situations. There are well over 2,000 published books and articles dealing with the instrument. This wealth of application means that a great deal is known about the instrument, that there are many individuals familiar with the technique who can assist in its application, and that particular findings can often be examined against the background of related results obtained by other investigators. Another advantage for many purposes is the existence of a relatively well-structured system of scoring with a set of general interpretative principles attached to the results of the scoring principles. Thus, unlike many projective techniques, the investigator is not left completely on his own with the task of devising an ad hoc scoring system to obtain the inferences that interest him. The relatively content-less nature of the stimulus material makes it possible to use the technique with groups differing widely in education, social milieu, and cultural background without great difficulties in administration and with no greater problems in interpretation than those involved with other techniques.

One of the objections that is sometimes raised to the Rorschach test is that as a sample of behavioral response it provides a relatively sparse record—often no more than 10 or 15 associations. In comparison with many other projective techniques, this is a small sample of the subject's repertoire of responses and may be considered a somewhat inadequate basis for the very large number of personality inferences that are often derived from the responses. Although the Rorschach scoring technique produces numerical scores quite readily, there are a number of special problems adhering to these scores which make it difficult to employ them in conventional statistical analysis without the risk of grave distortion or error in the results (Cronbach, 1949). Related to the sparcity of the response record is the implication that the test reveals relatively little concerning the content of personality—that is, the specific motives, conflicts, affects, and experiences which play an important role in the subject's life are only dimly outlined or alluded to by this instrument. In the end, the most serious criticism that is raised against this test is the accusation that it lacks satisfactory validity. We have already agreed that a detailed evaluation of this criticism is beyond our present scope. Consequently the most we can say is that an expert, unbiased, and exhaustive survey of the relevant findings would probably disappoint both the devotee and the arch enemy of the Rorschach.

The vast literature dealing with this instrument is largely identified in a bibliography assembled by Klopfer (1956). Probably the most important sources for those concerned with using this instrument are Klopfer's volumes dealing with the details of administering, scoring, and interpreting (Klopfer, Ainsworth, Klopfer & Holt, 1954) and the applications of tests in special settings (Klopfer, 1956). In addition the reader should acquaint himself with Hermann Rorschach's (1921) remarkable monograph which has had a definitive influence on the manner in which this technique has developed. Beck's (1944, 1945, 1952) three volumes provide insight into a rather different approach to the test than that employed by Klopfer, and together these two authors provide a balanced and sophisticated picture of current theory and practice in this area. A volume by Schafer (1954) is certain to be of great interest to anyone concerned with the technique who is also interested in psychoanalytic theory. It is also recommended to all potential users of the test because of its excellent treatment of the testing situation and the interaction between subject and examiner. Finally, Cronbach's (1949) paper dealing with some of the quantitative problems encountered in attempts to use this device in research is an important aid for anyone considering the use of the Rorschach in investigation.

Cloud Pictures

An often mentioned but seldom used projective technique is the cloud-picture method, developed by Struve (1932) working with William Stern (1938). Stern, as one of psychology's leading holistic theorists, was naturally drawn to techniques for appraising personality that permitted the user to avoid aspective or dimensional approaches to understanding his subject. His experience with the Rorschach test led him to the conclusion that it might be useful in the study of psychopathology, but that it was limited in its utility for the study of normal imagination because of the symmetry of the blots and the sharp outlines of the patterns, which led to serious restrictions on the kinds of responses that normal subjects could make. In an attempt to avoid this shortcoming, he and Struve developed a set of three pictures of clouds, which varied in their distinctness, but which were judged to be appreciably more indistinct than the standard Rorschach ink blots. This approach presumably was suggested by the common game played by children in which actual clouds are likened to objects in the physical world. The technique was developed primarily for use with children, although there is no reason in principle why it could not be employed with adults as well.

The test is administered by giving each subject, one at a time, copies of a cloud picture upon which he is asked to outline the objects he perceives together with a label or identification in the margin of the picture. The examiner also records the speech of the subject during the examination as well as his overt behavior. Further, Stern has recommended the introduction of a "suggestion phase" in which the subject is told that some people see certain objects in the clouds, and he is asked whether he can see them. There is no systematic basis for interpretation of the test, although Stern suggests that the responses may be evaluated in terms of the following broad categories: content of imagination, mode of interpretation, drawing task, and suggestions.

Stern reports that when both the Rorschach and the cloud pictures were used with the same subjects, his technique produced more varied associations and also resulted in less fatigue. He suggests that in addition to being useful for the study of imagination, it may be used to study suggestibility, developmental factors, and "racial groups." Such studies remain to be executed. It should be clear to the reader that although the cloud method may have some features to recommend it, as William Stern believed, these features have not led to the utilization of the techniques by other psychologists. Consequently, if the instrument is to be used at present, it must be with almost no guidance from past experience and with little in the way of prescription or generalization to aid in the interpretation of responses.

It is evident that this device remains in the embryonic stage of development with none of the systematic investigation necessary to permit an estimate of the utility of the method. It is possible that the instrument, in spite of its brevity, or perhaps with the addition of more stimuli, might prove to be a useful tool; but at present there seems little other than novelty, and the recommendation of a distinguished psychologist, to suggest a preference for this device.

Auditory Projective Techniques

In view of the glittering success of a device based upon associations to meaningless visual stimuli, it was only natural that there should be attempts to develop projective tests utilizing auditory stimuli. Several such techniques have been suggested, but as yet none of them has met with spectacular success. The best known instrument of this type is Skinner's Verbal Summator (1936) which is a record consisting of a number of vowel combinations. Subjects are told that the record reproduces the speech of a man and that they are to identify what he is saying, even though this will be difficult. The device was modified somewhat by Shakow and Rosenzweig (1940), working in a psychiatric setting, and labelled the Tautophone.

The instrument appears to have had very limited use in either clinical settings or in research. It was employed routinely at the Worcester State Hospital for a number of years during the period when Shakow and Rosenzweig were staff members, and there have been a small number of investigations utilizing it (Grings, 1942; Trussell, 1939). The results of these studies provide little evidence for the superiority of the instrument over other more widely used devices.

Several attempts have been made to develop *auditory apperceptive techniques,* and these are mentioned in our discussion of the

Thematic Apperception Test. Recently Davids and Murray (1955) have developed a projective technique that involves the auditory presentation of a large amount of unconnected or incoherent material relevant to eight different dispositions: pessimism, distrust, anxiety, resentment, egocentricity, optimism, trust, and sociocentricity. After hearing passages that contain much more material than he can possibly retain, the subject is asked to recall the ideas he has heard and also to indicate which ideas he considers to be the major and which the minor ideas. Scores can be obtained for the eight dispositions by computing the proportion of material recalled that is relevant to the disposition. Preliminary findings for a group of twenty subjects indicate that the ratings derived from the test are significantly correlated with independent clinical judgments, as well as equivalent scores derived from the sentence completion test and the word association test. Thus, although this device is the most recently developed of this type, it is already associated with more empirical findings relevant to its evaluation than the Verbal Summator, which has existed for many more years.

There are certain circumstances where the use of an auditory projective technique may seem essential, such as working with the blind or with subjects who for some reason won't respond to visual stimulation, but aside from these cases there seems little reason at present to use the techniques just described. The Verbal Summator was developed over twenty years ago, and yet today we know almost nothing about its functioning. The little we do know provides no basis for choosing it over other instruments. The device developed by Davids and Murray seems somewhat more promising, but even here a vast amount of further application and investigation is necessary before any reasonable judgment can be made concerning its actual utility.

CONSTRUCTION TECHNIQUES

Here we find a group of instruments that require the subject to create or construct a product which is typically an art form such as a story or picture. A minimum of restriction is placed upon the subject's responses, and in some cases, such as the blank card of the Thematic Apperception Test, even the original stimulus is not under control of the examiner.

The focus of this type of instrument is upon the outcome or product constructed by the subject and not upon his behavior or style in the process of creating or responding. The subject is set to provide a product that is meaningful and relevant to the test stimuli. The response process may begin with simple association, but the requirements of these tests force the subject to modify and elaborate the original association so as to satisfy normative requirements of what constitutes a story or other art form. Unlike the associative techniques, these instruments require the subject to engage in complex, cognitive activities that go far beyond mere association.

Thematic Apperception Test

This instrument has now achieved that comfortable status where it is commonly assumed that any clinical psychologist or personality investigator will be familiar with it. In little more than twenty years the Thematic Apperception Test has become, next to the Rorschach, the most widely used of all projective techniques.

The TAT consists of a set of 20 cards, the nature of which is varied somewhat depending upon whether the subject is male or female, child or adult (Murray, 1943). In each case 19 of the 20 cards present pictures of varying content and degree of ambiguity and the remaining card is blank. The cards are presented to the subject individually with the request that he create a story about the picture that describes what is going on in the pictured scene, what the people are thinking and feeling, what led up to this scene, and what will be the outcome. The subject is encouraged to spend approximately five minutes in telling each story and the examiner records the story as nearly verbatim as possible with a minimum of intervention after the initial structuring.

The analysis of TAT stories is far from standardized at present. The original method of analysis proposed by Murray (1943) depended upon an initial identification of a hero figure in each story and then an analysis of needs displayed by the hero in the story as well as press (environmental forces) that acted upon the hero. This method of scoring TAT stories is still probably the most popular of the various schemes used, but there is little restriction upon the interpreter of the TAT and he may use any system of content analysis that strikes his fancy. A number of specific scoring systems have been proposed (Aron, 1949; Bellak, 1947; Fry, 1953; Fine, 1955; Henry, 1956; Stein, 1955; Tomkins, 1947), and many of these systems can be examined together as they are applied to a single case (Shneidman, 1951).

In general, there are certain important distinctions that can be made between the TAT variables that have been employed. First, it is important to distinguish between *content and formal variables.* Most of the variables that have been used focus upon the kind of behavior that takes place in the story, the content of what the hero is doing or experiencing. Certain other variables (adjective/verb ratio, compliance with test instructions, verbal productivity) are scored without any concern for what has actually transpired in the stories. These variables are usually referred to as formal variables. The methods of analysis also show considerable difference in the *unit of analysis* employed. Some of them utilize a broad unit, such as a story, or even a series of stories, and others focus upon a single act or even an individual word. The more popular scoring schemes have tended to employ molar units of analysis. Further, there is variation in the directness, or the *amount of inference* required of the scorer, in analyzing the protocols. Some scoring systems depend solely upon explicit and manifest evidence within the stories, whereas other systems require that the individual scoring the test engage in rather complex reconstructions or inferences. Most investigators using the TAT have attempted to minimize the amount of complex inference required in scoring.

As used clinically, TAT interpretation has not typically rested upon a set of objective scores for specified variables. Much more customary has been the use of the stories as additional behavioral data which could be examined in connection with other information concerning the individual case, and with a background of general experience with the test, in the attempt to identify evidence for new interpretations of the patient's conduct or to support generalizations that had already been advanced.

When interpretation derives originally from some system of objective content analysis, as is customary in investigation, the root assumption is usually that there is a kind of psychological isomorphy between the tendencies felt or expressed on the part of a hero in the story and the tendencies that exist within the storyteller. Thus, dispositions frequently and intensely revealed in the stories are believed to play an important role in determining the behavior of the subject.

There are a number of further assumptions that complicate matters somewhat, such as the conventional acceptance of the fact that if the subject avoids representing certain themes or conflicts in his stories, even though the stimulus material seems naturally to evoke it, and other subjects typically provide such material, this is also evidence for the importance of this area in his behavior. However, the bulk of the interpretations depends on the assumption of a close kinship between the action in the stories created by the subject and the inner life of the subject.

A general statement of the interpretative assumptions commonly employed in the use of this test has been provided by Lindzey (1952), and we shall examine a related set of assumptions in the next chapter.

Although this instrument has not been captured by any single system of analysis, a number of scoring systems for specific variables have been reported. Illustrative of these is the work of McClelland, Atkinson, Clark, and Lowell (1953) on the achievement motive; Atkinson, Heyns, and Veroff (1954) and Shipley and Veroff (1952) on the affiliation motive; Veroff (1957) on the power motives; Clark (1952), and Clark and Sensibar (1955) on the sexual motive. A number of additional investigations bear upon the analysis of such variables as anxiety (Lindzey & Newburg, 1954), castration anxiety (Schwartz, 1955, 1956), homosexuality (Davids, Joelson, & McArthur, 1956; Lindzey, Tejessy, & Zamansky, 1958), and aggression (Lindzey & Tejessy, 1956; Mussen & Naylor, 1954).

It is generally considered that when compared to the Rorschach the TAT is best designed to describe the content of personality rather than its structure. This may seem a somewhat empty statement since the point where structure leaves off and content begins is by no means clear. Furthermore, both instruments are used for both kinds of analysis, no matter where the distinction is established. The generalization has an element of validity, however, in the dependence of Rorschach analysis and interpretation upon formal variables that provide information concerning the organization of personality or very general characteristics that operate regardless of the specific motive or conflict. The TAT, on the other hand, is typically used because of the rich content it provides, which permits specific inferences concerning the nature of particular conflicts and dispositions. The multiform data elicited by the TAT makes it possible to employ the test to assess virtually any variable in which the investigator may be interested.

We have already seen that there is very little standardization in the interpretation of this test. The conditions surrounding the administration of the test, however, are relatively constant. Although there have been some variants, the general practice has been to stay quite close to the instructions outlined in Murray's (1943) manual. A number of the scoring systems that have been developed appear to show relatively satisfactory rater reliability. However, very little progress has been made in the development of norms, first because it is a slow, tedious and unromantic job and second because there is little agreement as to what should be observed or counted in the process of building norms. Some interesting although fragmentary beginnings have been made by Eron (1950), Rosenzweig (1949a), and Rosenzweig & Fleming (1949).

There have been numerous modifications of the TAT in regard to administration, stimulus material, and mode of response. The most important modification has been the development of the group procedure which has typically involved the subject writing his own stories to a picture projected on a screen. This method has been used extensively in research—perhaps more than the individual technique —and the two studies that have inquired into the adequacy of the method (Eron & Ritter, 1951; Lindzey & Heinemann, 1955) suggest that the group technique, at least for research purposes, is as useful as the individual technique. Another variation that is roughly standard in the group administration and is occasionally used with individual technique also, is the practice of exposing the stimulus material prior to the actual storytelling for a short interval only. In many cases this practice appears to keep the subject from limiting himself to stimulus description with no invention or plot creation.

A variety of investigators have created special sets of pictures for particular groups. Best known of these is the Thompson (1949a, 1949b) modification of the TAT for use with Negroes, which has been widely studied and usually found wanting (Korchin & Mitchell, 1950; Riess, Schwartz, & Cottingham, 1950; Schwartz, Riess, & Cottingham, 1951) and the Children's Apperception Test (Bellak, 1954). Other TAT series have been established for children (Hartwell et al., 1951), American Indians (Alexander & Anderson, 1957; Henry, 1947), adolescents (Symonds, 1949), South African natives (Lee,

1953; Sherwood, 1957); Pacific Islanders (Lessa & Spiegelman, 1954); and interacting groups (Henry & Guetzkow, 1951; Horwitz & Cartwright, 1953). New sets of pictures or modified versions have been developed in the attempt to assess particular variables such as achievement (McClelland *et al.*, 1953), affiliation (Atkinson, Heyns, & Veroff, 1954), dominance (Veroff, 1957), and group cohesiveness (Libo, 1953). A new series of TAT cards has also been presented for general use by Phillipson (1956) under the title of The Object Relations Test. Several multiple-choice forms of the TAT have been provided for use in group administration (Clark, 1944; Goodstein, 1954; Hurley, 1955; Johnston, 1955). A final modification of the test has been suggested by a number of investigators (Ball & Bernardoni, 1953; Stone, 1950; Wilmer & Husni, 1953) who have developed sets of auditory stimuli which the subject is asked to incorporate in a story. The general problem of devising alternative sets of pictures for special purposes has been considered by Symonds (1939) and Sherwood (1957), and these authors have attempted to devise principles to guide the investigator interested in an ad hoc instrument. The principles do little to resolve the many ambiguities facing the individual who attempts such a modification, but they serve to make explicit many of the issues that will confront him.

Two close relatives of the TAT that have attracted considerable attention are the Make-A-Picture-Story Test (Shneidman, 1948, 1951) and the Four Picture Test (van Lennep, 1948, 1951). In the M-A-P-S technique the subject is presented with a number of background scenes, together with a large number of human and animal figures, from which he selects those he wishes to include in each scene. Having arranged the figures on the background, the subject is asked to construct a story incorporating the depicted event, in the same manner as the TAT. Interpretation of the test protocols proceeds in the same fashion as the TAT except that there is an additional dimension of response represented by the choice of figures to include in each picture.

Van Lennep's Four Picture Test involves four colored pictures presented simultaneously to the subject with the request that he incorporate them into a story. The pictures represent two persons interacting, a group setting, and two situations involving a single person. Again the interpretation proceeds as in the case of the TAT, except that an additional dimension is introduced by the order or arrangement which the subject makes in constructing his story. The other major difference from the TAT is that only a single story is elicited rather than 10 or 20.

One of the advantages of the TAT is that it can be administered with only a modicum of special training, and, unlike the Rorschach, the examiner need not be intimately familiar with the technique of analysis to be employed subsequently. The richness of the response data elicited provides a relatively satisfactory basis for a wide variety of different kinds of analysis. The thematic material contained in the stories permits the interpreter to make inferences concerning many different dispositions and conflicts, and a great deal can be learned concerning the subject's psychological world and his relations with others, as well as with his physical world. Furthermore, the widespread use of this technique, in addition to the special forms that have been developed, makes clear that a good deal is known about its operation in a number of special settings. The test has been used extensively in cross-cultural settings (for example, Gladwin & Sarason, 1953; Henry, 1947, 1956; Lessa & Spiegelman, 1954).

The test appears to be sensitive to depth or unconscious factors, but at the same time it clearly reflects conscious factors and situational determinants, so that under appropriate circumstances it may provide information concerning all of these types of variables. The test activity is a relatively natural one for almost all subjects, and thus it is usually easy to explain and to elicit co-operation. The absence of a single, widely accepted, objective scoring system has led to a healthy approach to the instrument, in which the method of analysis employed is not acepted as God-given and beyond criticism and furthermore it is usually constructed in such a manner as to maximize the interests of the particular investigator.

On the other hand, the data collected by the instrument are ponderous and difficult to subject to analysis. Furthermore, the absence of a simple, objective scoring system means that the individual employing the instrument often spends dozens of hours in analysis for every hour spent in the collection of data. The fact that the instrument is responsive to dispositional, situational, and fleeting personal determinants means that it is difficult for the interpreter to be certain whether a given test characteristic reflects an enduring personal characteristic or a transient state. The entire test procedure rests upon complex linguistic skills so that for subjects who, because of education or intelligence, find it difficult to manipulate verbal symbols the test is relatively inappropriate. When individuals from a different culture are studied, it is difficult to interpret their stories with confidence because of the differences in the language which they employ. Furthermore, the standard pictures involve content specific to Western European culture and consequently cannot be used confidently in many other cultural settings. On the other hand, introduction of pictures appropriate to the culture being studied raises many problems, some of which we shall return to later.

The best introduction to this instrument is Murray's *TAT Manual* (1943). In addition to this there are several books concerned with the technique (Bellak, 1954; Henry, 1956; Stein, 1955; Tomkins, 1947) and a variety of chapters that provide general discussions of the test (Bellak, 1950, 1952; Holt, 1951; Wyatt & Veroff, 1956). A reasonably complete bibliography for the test is to be found in the volume by Henry, which also considers a number of problems particularly relevant to the cross-cultural investigator.

The Blacky Pictures

This descendant of the TAT was devised by Gerald Blum (1949, 1950*a*). It involves story construction in response to pictures as its central feature but adds preference for the stimulus material and a series of objective questions concerning each of the pictures. The pictures are twelve cartoons concerned with experiences in the life of a dog named Blacky. In addition to Blacky, the various cartoons include Mama, Papa, and Tippy, a sibling whose sex is not specified. The name Blacky was deliberately selected so that depending upon the sex of the subject, the puppy could be introduced as a son or as a daughter. Likewise the name Tippy was selected as sufficiently neutral for the subject to consider the puppy as belonging to either sex. The twelve cartoons were designed to bear specifically upon important psychological variables. Thus they represent scenes intimately related to the activation of these variables, for example, the card intended to measure sibling rivalry pictures Blacky watching from a distance as Mama and Papa affectionately lick Tippy. The cards were drawn to include animals rather than humans on the assumption that the typical subject would be less threatened by the scenes pictured because of their relative remoteness from him and thus better able to present his underlying impulses and conflicts in these areas.

The test is administered by first requesting the subject to create a story about each of the cartoons. Each picture is presented with a brief identification, for example, "Here is Blacky with Mama." When the stories have been completed, the subject is asked a number of questions, most of them multiple-choice, concerning each of the cartoons. After the inquiry the subject is asked to sort the cartoons into two piles, the ones he likes and the ones he doesn't like, and then to select the single picture he likes most and the single picture he dislikes most. Any spontaneous remarks made during the test administration, particularly those bearing upon the subject's reaction to the cartoons, are recorded.

The test is interpreted by bringing these four sources of data to bear upon the eleven psychoanalytic variables which the test is designed to assess. It is possible to achieve some degree of quantification by rating each variable as strong or weak for the particular sample, and scoring samples are provided in the manual to aid in the process. Blum, however, places much more emphasis upon the use of the materials to provide a full qualitative description of the relevance of each dimension for the psychological make-up of the subject. He emphasizes the importance of making certain that the interpretation successfully encompasses all of the data from the spontaneous stories, the inquiry, and the cartoon preferences.

As we have already indicated, this test is designed to investigate eleven specifically designated psychoanalytic variables: oral eroticism, oral sadism, and expulsiveness, anal retentiveness, oedipal intensity, masturbation guilt, castration anxiety (penis envy), positive identification, sibling rivalry, guilt feeling, positive ego ideal, and love object (narcissistic or anaclitic). In addition Blum has developed a Defense Preference Inquiry (Blum, 1956a; Cohen, 1956) a modification of the test based on the subject's choice of alternative responses for each card. This procedure permits the investigator to measure the subject's tendency to employ various mechanisms of defense such as projection, regression, reaction formation, and avoidance.

In spite of their recency, the Blacky Pictures have been used in a wide variety of settings. This very high incidence of research application is due largely to the activity of Blum and the students who have worked with him. Within several years after publication of the test, in a summary of evidence bearing upon the test's validity, Blum and Hunt (1952) were able to cite eight separate investigations already published or in press which had utilized the Blacky Test in a central fashion. By now this number has been increased many times. Although there have been some inquiries that question the merit of the test (Blum, 1950*b*; Seward, 1950), the majority of the studies point to the utility of the instrument.

The administration of the technique is adequately standardized, but in the published instructions for scoring and interpretation a good deal of discretionary power is left to the interpreter (Beck, 1956). The relatively high degree of specification of variables, combined with the evident relation between variables and areas of response, makes it clear that there is no reason why highly objective scoring techniques should not eventually be developed.

The Blacky Pictures have an attractive array of virtues. The test is relatively easy to administer, it deals with a clearly delineated set of psychological variables, it elicits a rich variety of response data, it has been used in a variety of research settings, it can be administered in a group setting, and it can be administered to both children and adults. Inevitably these virtues entail certain shortcomings. The test is of little or no use to the investigator who is not prepared to subscribe to psychoanalytic theory wholeheartedly. The scoring and interpretation of the test still fall short of the optimum in objectivity and exactness. The extent to which the test is disguised seems questionable, at least for dealing with sophisticated subjects familiar with psychoanalytic theory and techniques. Further, it is somewhat unfortunate that so much of the published research dealing with the instrument has been carried out by the originator and his students.

Additional information concerning the test may be found in the introductory publications of Blum (1949, 1950*a*) and the brief literature survey by Blum and Hunt (1952).

COMPLETION TECHNIQUES

These measures provide the subject with some type of incomplete product and require that he complete it in any manner he wishes. They differ from the associative techniques in that both stimulus and response are typically more complex and thus the response is less immediate. Furthermore, the completed product is usually expected to meet certain external standards of good form or rationality; for example there are rules about what constitutes a sentence or a story, and they presumably operate to determine the subject's completions.

The Sentence Completion Test

Easily the best known of the completion techniques is the sentence completion test, which in a relatively brief interval has become a standard tool for both clinician and personality investigator. This device is sometimes considered a variant of the word association test. However, it seems better to consider this instrument separately from the association techniques because the eliciting stimulus is customarily longer and more complex than a single word, the subject is asked to respond not with a single word but with a sentence completion, and latency of response does not play an important role in interpretation. The type of scoring employed and the customary inferences that clinicians glean from the sentence completion test both suggest the close kinship of this test to the TAT. This relation has already been commented upon by Rotter (1951).

The instrument typically consists of a number of stems or stubs, consisting of one or more words, which the subject is instructed to combine with other words of his own choosing to make a sentence. The subject is told that he will find a number of incomplete sentences and is asked to complete them with the first words that come to his mind. In some cases the emphasis is primarily upon speed, and in other cases users of the test have emphasized the importance of completing the sentences so as to reveal the subject's own feelings accurately. The second type of instruction seems somewhat undesirable since it orients the subject toward self-report and thus might be expected to reduce the operation of latent or covert determinants of behavior. The number of items included on such a test usually ranges from 30 to 40 to as many as a hundred. A test consisting of a hundred items can be completed by most well-educated subjects in an hour or less.

The test is sometimes used to order subjects in terms of a single variable; in other instances the test may be constructed to assess a large number of relatively independent variables. Illustrative of an instrument designed to measure a single variable is the sentence completion test originally reported by Rotter and Willerman (1947) and subsequently modified and published by Rotter and Rafferty (1950) as the Rotter Incomplete Sentences Blank. This device is designed to provide a single score or index of personal adjustment or emotional stability. The test consists of 40 incomplete sentences, and the responses to each of the stems is rated on a scale ranging from +3 to —3 with the aid of a relatively specific scoring manual. The cumulation of the scores for the individual items provides a total score which represents an estimate of the subject's emotional stability. This measure is reported to attain reasonable inter-rater and split-half reliability and to correlate satisfactorily with independent measures of adjustment (Rotter & Rafferty, 1950; Rotter, Rafferty, & Schachtitz, 1949).

A more typical procedure is to assemble a number of separate items that bear upon a set of personality variables and then to score the responses of these items in some manner so as to give a score for each of these personality dimensions. An example of such an instrument is the Sacks Sentence Completion Test (Sacks & Levy, 1950) which consists of 60 items designed to tap fifteen different personality variables. Included in the test are four stems designed to elicit responses relevant to each of the following variables: attitude toward mother, father, and family unit, attitudes toward women and toward heterosexual relations, attitudes toward friends, superiors at work or school, people supervised, and colleagues at work or school, fears, guilt feelings, attitude toward own abilities, the past and the future, and goals. The scoring system recommended provides that the four responses bearing upon each of the variables be examined simultaneously and a rating on disturbance in this area be assigned. This procedure differs from most scoring systems which involve individual scoring of items, as in the Rotter Test, and their cumulation to give a total score for each variable.

The test is generally considered to be most efficient in assessing attitudes, motives, and conflicts (the content of personality) rather than general structure or organization of personality. Moreover it is often claimed that it provides information concerning motives and values at a somewhat more conscious or manifest level than do other projective devices such as the TAT or Rorschach. However, within these limits the device seems freely adaptable to the needs of almost any examiner with sufficient ingenuity to create a set of items that are able to evoke responses relevant to the variable in which he is interested. It may even be used to study thinking or cognitive processes as in Cameron's (1938*a*, 1938*b*) well-known studies of schizophrenic thought.

We have already pointed out that during the past decade and

a half the test has come to be used very widely and undoubtedly is now used more often than all but two or three of the other projective techniques. Unfortunately, it is used in such a variety of forms and settings that there is little standardization in scoring and administration and very little in the way of norms that might aid the individual with the problem of making inferences from particular test protocols. The chief exception is the Rotter Test which is relatively well standardized and is accompanied by relatively adequate norms for certain special populations.

It is difficult to talk of modifications of a test that has known such great variation and so little constancy. It is relatively clear that the beginnings of the sentence completion technique as a device for measuring personality variables lie with Tendler (1930) and the subsequent modification of Rohde and Hildreth (Rohde, 1946), but from this point on the device has proliferated into a large number of highly individualized forms, each of which has been designed to meet some special need of a particular investigator. There have, however, been some general variations in the form of the technique, the most important of which has to do with whether the stem is stated in the first or third person. Stein (1947) appears to be the first to have introduced this variation deliberately, followed by Sacks (1949), although the most revealing work in this area has been done by Hanfmann and Getzels (1953). The latter studies found that items in the first person were more revealing of conscious or manifest aspects of the person, whereas the third person items assessed deeper layers. On at least one occasion (Carter, 1947) the sentence completion test has been combined with a physiological measure in the form of the psychogalvanometer, although without notable success.

One interesting, although relatively undeveloped, variant of the sentence completion test, is the story completion technique. This instrument presents the subject with stimulus material somewhat more complex than that of the sentence completion test and requires a somewhat lengthier and more complex response. Use of the test dates back at least to Murray's *Explorations in Personality* in 1938, but the best known example of this instrument is Sargent's (1944, 1953) *The Insight Test*. This test consists of a series of "armatures" or descriptions of human situations, and the subject is asked to tell what the central character does and why and how he feels. The subject is given to understand that the test measures his understanding of others.

There are a number of features to recommend the sentence completion test, the most important of which are its flexibility and the relative economy of time and effort involved in collecting and analyzing the response data. The test is habitually given in a group setting and requires no special training of the administrator, so that in comparison to the individual TAT or Rorschach, it is enormously efficient. Even the analysis of the responses can be accomplished much more readily than the scoring of the voluminous TAT records or the highly refined analysis of the Rorschach. Furthermore, at least where the device is being scored objectively for research purposes, a much lower degree of training is required than would be necessitated for the analysis of many other projective techniques. The test is suitable for almost all subjects who can read and write with reasonable facility, and for those who cannot it can be administered individually by reading the stems and recording the responses. There is now a considerable body of research which is of value to users of the test, although as yet there is very little normative data.

Perhaps the strongest objections to this instrument expressed by experienced users of projective techniques derive from the belief that the purpose of the test is so poorly disguised that the resultant information is often that which is most public or overt in the subject's psychological make-up. Related to this is the relative ease with which the subject can censor or distort his responses to the test. Although administration of the test is roughly standard, there is little that is constant so far as specific content or principles of scoring and interpretation are concerned. There is a strong tendency for each worker who employs the test to devise just those incomplete sentences that he feels will best fit his needs and also to devise a particular scoring system that suits his fancy. The test seems relatively inefficient for providing information concerning structural characteristics of personality. Like the TAT the test is completely imbedded in the linguistic structure of the society within which it is given, so that it is heavily culture bound.

There are several chapters that have been written about this technique (Bell, 1948; Rotter, 1951; Sacks & Levy, 1950) as well as a recent book by Rohde (1957). The most important sources of information concerning the instrument, however, remain the individual articles and monographs, many of which have already been referred to in this chapter.

The Picture-Frustration Study

A logical combination of qualities of the word association technique and the Thematic Apperception Test is contained in Rosenzweig's Picture-Frustration Study (Rosenzweig, 1945). This paper and pencil technique requires that the subject present an association to a variety of stimuli, but in this case each stimulus consists of a line drawing of two persons interacting and includes a verbal response directed from one person to the other. Each of the drawings represents some kind of frustrating situation, and the task of the subject is to provide a verbal response for the depicted subject who has been frustrated. Thus, although the response is associative, the stimulus material is more complex than that of the word association technique and the response is both more complex and more structured. There are 24 situations in all and the subject is instructed to insert the first appropriate reply that occurs to him after examining the picture.

The instrument is designed to provide scores for a number of variables that describe the individual's characteristic mode of dealing with frustration. Each response is scored with the aid of specific scoring samples (Rosenzweig, Clarke, & Garfield, 1946; Rosenzweig, Fleming, & Clarke, 1947) for the direction of the response (extrapunitive, intrapunitive, impunitive) as well as for the type or mode of response (obstacle dominant, ego defensive, need persistive). Combining the two categories provides nine different classifications to which each response can be assigned, such as extrapunitive-need persistive; impunitive-obstacle dominant; intrapunitive-ego defensive. By totaling the number of responses assigned to each of the general or specific categories, it is possible to arrive at an over-all score representing the general tendency for the subject to employ each mode of response. It is also customary to score each response in terms of a Group Conformity Rating, an index of how conventional or usual are the responses of the subject.

Interpretation of the results typically depends heavily upon the scores for the specific variables, although this quantitative evidence can be supplemented by interpretations based upon the content of specific responses as well as upon the sequence of responses (Rosenzweig & Mirmow, 1950). The inferences that can be made from the subject's preference for particular modes of response are strengthened through the use of various normative findings (Rosenzweig, 1945, 1950*b*). It is generally felt that the aspects of behavior reflected by the P-F study are somewhat closer to what Rosenzweig (1950*a*) refers to as Level II behavior (behavior as reported by a neutral observer) than they are to unconscious or covert aspects of behavior, and there is some slight evidence to support this (Lindzey & Goldwyn, 1954). In comparison to other projective techniques, it is clear that the range of variables the instrument is appropriate to assess is both more limited and better specified.

The instrument has been used widely both in clinical settings and in research (Lindzey & Goldwyn, 1954; Mirmow, 1952), but as yet there is only a limited amount of published normative material available. The administration of the test is highly standard and clearly specified. There have been two major modifications of the test, one designed to adapt it for use with children (Rosenzweig, Fleming, & Rosenzweig, 1948) and the other intended to make it appropriate to assess attitudes toward minority group members (Brown, 1947; Sommer, 1954).

The principal strengths of this instrument are its relative ease of administration and interpretation and its clearly specified range of appropriateness. The test can be administered readily in a group setting and provides objective scores for a variety of variables relevant to frustration and its derivatives. Thus, for the investigator interested in characterizing subjects' reactions to frustration, the device provides an attractive alternative. It requires relatively little training to administer and interpret the test, and there is a fairly extensive body of relevant investigations that can be used to attach meaning or significance to new findings. The test is easy to administer to subjects with any degree of verbal fluency, and even where illiteracy intervenes it is possible to use the test individually.

The general utility of the Picture-Frustration Study is somewhat limited by the highly specific set of variables for which it is appropriate. Furthermore, the relative overtness of the tendencies it provides information concerning decreases its appeal for many individuals interested in projective tests. The purpose of the test is only moderately difficult for the subject to infer, and consequently it seems likely that test responses can be altered to create the impression the subject intends. There is some evidence (Silverstein, 1957) to support this contention. When compared to an instrument such as the TAT, or even the sentence completion test, the response data provided by this test are relatively meager. Although problems of education and verbal fluency are not unusually severe in this test, it is clear that it would have to be extensively modified in order to be applicable to another culture.

Perhaps the best single introduction to this test is Rosenzweig's own volume on psychological diagnosis (Rosenzweig, 1949b) but in addition there are several chapters about the technique (Bell, 1948; Clarke, 1951; Mirmow, 1952). Another valuable source is the article in which Rosenzweig first presented a general description of the instrument (1945).

CHOICE OR ORDERING TECHNIQUES

These instruments resemble the associative measures in the simplicity of the response set provided for the subjects. Here the respondent merely chooses from a number of alternatives the item or arrangement that fits some specified criterion such as correctness, relevance, attractiveness, or repugnance. In some cases, such as the multiple-choice Rorschach and TAT, these devices mirror other techniques except that the subject is asked not to produce an association or a construction but rather to select from a number of hypothetical responses the one that seems most appropriate to him.

The Szondi Test

Easily the best known and most widely employed of the projective techniques requiring subjects to choose or order stimulus material is the Szondi Test. Devised in the late 1930's by a Hungarian psychiatrist (Szondi, 1944, 1952), the test has been made popular in this country largely through the efforts of one of Szondi's students, Susan Deri.

The test material consists of 48 photographs that represent the faces of individuals drawn from eight diagnostic categories: homosexuality, sadism, epilepsy, hysteria, catatonic schizophrenia, paranoid schizophrenia, manic-depression (depressed), manic-depression (manic). There are six photographs representing each of the categories, and the pictures are presented to the subject in standard order in sets of eight, with each set including one picture from each of the diagnostic categories. The subject is asked to look at the eight pictures and select the two that he likes the most and the two that he likes the least. Thus, at the end of the administration the examiner has a total of 12 pictures that were selected as "most liked" and an equivalent set of 12 pictures that were selected as the "most disliked." At this point the subject is asked to select from the "liked" pile the four pictures that he likes most and from the other pile the four pictures that he likes least. It is customary to administer the test repeatedly with at least a day interval between each testing. Deri (1949) reports that the results are relatively meaningless unless the test is administered at least six different times, and ideally there should be ten individual administrations.

The basic scoring of the test is very simple and consists merely of recording on a graph each of the choices according to the diagnostic category represented by the picture chosen. The score sheet is divided in half by a horizontal line, and positive choices are recorded above the line and negative choices are recorded below the line. Thus, for each of the variables represented by the diagnostic categories there is a record of how many times the subject selected as "most liked" or "most disliked" the cards representing this category. The results are further simplified by assigning to each of the variables a rating that summarizes the individual responses to the relevant pictures. If the subject chose relevant pictures positively two or more times and never chose them as "least liked," the variable is classified as *positive*. If the reverse is true, that is, if the pictures are rejected two or more times and there are no positive choices, the variable is classified as *negative*. If there are four or more choices that are approximately evenly divided between choice and rejection, the variable is classified as *ambivalent,* and if there are no more than two choices evenly divided between positive and negative, the variable is classified as *open*.

Szondi reasons that when a variable is selected positively this is evidence of tension in this area and that the individual accepts the operation of this drive in his make-up. A negative score indicates tension in the area but suggests that the individual denies or is unable to accept the operation of this drive in himself. An ambivalent score is indicative of conflicting tension or opposing motives in this area, whereas an open score suggests that there is no tension in this area as the individual is either very low in the strength of this drive or is able to find adequate means of reducing his drive whatever its level of intensity.

We have seen that this test consists of eight different types of pictures corresponding to eight different pathological classifications. Each of these types of pictures is believed sensitive to or resonant with a specific drive, and these eight drives are considered related to four vectors. The vectors and their drives are as follows: *S-Vector* (sexual) which includes the homosexual and sadistic drives, *P-Vector* (paroxysmal-surprise) which includes the epileptic and hysterical factor, *Sch-Vector* (self) which includes the catatonic and paranoid factors, *C-Vector* (contact drive) which includes the depressive and manic factors. Each of these variables is given a moderately detailed definition in Deri's (1949) treatment of the test.

The interpretation of the instrument involves not only the individual scores for each variable of positive, negative, ambivalent, and open; the interpreter must also examine a profile of results over a period of six or more administrations. By observing those factors that are constant and those that are relatively variable, the interpreter is able to make judgments concerning which components of the subject's personality are important and enduring and which are fleeting and unstable. However, extremes in variability often point specifically to forms of pathology.

Application of the Szondi Test on a large scale in this country commenced shortly after the last war, when enthusiasm for projective techniques was at a high pitch. The test was immediately adopted in many quarters, a considerable amount of investigation appeared in very short order (Borstelmann & Klopfer, 1953), and the test was employed widely in clinical settings. More recently there has been less evidence of extensive application of the test, although it remains one of the better known projective techniques. In general the instrument has been used much as Szondi and Deri have suggested, although not infrequently their demands for repeated administration are overlooked. Deri (1949) has also suggested using the pictures as stimuli for a storytelling procedure, but this recommendation does not seem to have been employed extensively. There is very little normative material for the test, and interpretation ordinarily proceeds without recourse to results for normative groups.

There are a number of appealing features to the Szondi Test and these were undoubtedly responsible for the quick enthusiasm that greeted the introduction of the instrument in this country. First of all, the response data is exact and easy to score. Further, the colorful profile analysis is a relatively objective procedure for arriving at inferences concerning a number of defined variables, and most important, the scoring procedure makes it easy to judge whether the variable is readily expressed in overt behavior or not. The test is quick and easy to administer and very little skill is required of the examiner. Furthermore, the test procedure is intrinsically interesting to most subjects—at least for the first administration. The general intent, and the variables to be assessed, are concealed very effectively from the subject, and consequently it is a test that would be very difficult to fake. There is less dependence upon educational and verbal skills than in almost any other projective technique.

Although Szondi (1944, 1952) has presented an elaborate theoretical rationale which rests upon a complex set of assumptions concerning the effects of recessive genes upon behavior, this theory has never been given serious consideration in this country. Moreover, this explicit link between the test procedures and a theory which is considered at best bizarre by most American psychologists has led many observers to a rather suspicious view of the instrument. The fact that the test employs numbers or quantities heavily in the interpretative process and yet is accompanied by very few normative findings adds to this suspicion. The standard requirement that the test be administered between six and ten times to each subject presents a formidable obstacle to many test users, since it is difficult to see their subjects that often. Furthermore, the technique is limited in terms of the variables for which it can supply specific information. Thus, if an investigator is interested in a psychological variable that is not a close fit to one of Szondi's eight factors, the test would be of little use to him. The pictures used in the test limit its cultural generality; indeed there has been some question concerning their appropriateness for our own time and culture. Although there is a growing body of investigations concerning this test, their number and relevance is much less than in the case of the best known projective techniques. Moreover, many have produced results discouraging for the utility of this test. Finally there is a relatively meager set of response data elicited by the test.

The best single source for learning more about this test is Deri's (1949) volume. There is also a brief introductory chapter by Rabin (1951) and a survey of the relevant research literature prior to 1952 by Borstelmann and Klopfer (1953). The recent volume by Szondi, Moser, and Webb (1959) provides a strongly partisan description of the technique and its rationale.

The Picture Arrangement Test

This device represents an intriguing combination of the features of many other projective techniques together with some of the qualities ordinarily found only among psychometric tools. Silvan Tomkins and Daniel Horn, who originated the instrument (Tomkins, 1952) first developed their interest in the test through experience with the TAT, but it was the Picture Arrangement subtest of the Wechsler-Bellevue Intelligence Scale that suggested the specific form of the test. Moreover, the cartoon-like stimulus material employed in the test is highly reminiscent of the Picture-Frustration Study. The possibility of machine scoring results, in addition to extensive and varied normative findings (Tomkins & Miner, 1955, 1957, 1959) that can be used in interpreting the test, suggest a close kinship to typical objective questionnaires or tests of aptitudes and abilities.

The test consists of 25 plates, each of which contains three line drawings that depict the same figure involved in three different but related activities. The subject is asked to indicate the order in which these activities took place and is also required to provide a sentence indicating what is going on in the picture. Thus, there are two types of response that can be used in arriving at interpretative statements: the order in which the pictures are arranged and the descriptive statements that are attached to each picture. Although the authors (Tomkins & Miner, 1957) provide some suggestions as to how the descriptive statements may be used clinically to distinguish normal from abnormal subjects, the bulk of their efforts have been devoted to attempts to develop objective methods for dealing with the arrangements selected by each subject.

The basic premise on which interpretation of the test rests is that only those responses that are relatively rare in occurence can be interpreted unambiguously. Consequently, what the authors have done is to secure a large and representative sample of responses and then to identify those patterns of response that are observed infrequently. Further, only those patterns are used in interpretation that offer a ready possibility for interpretation, for example, if the particular pattern of response suggests avoidance of people, hypochondriasis or unhappiness, it would be used, but if the meaning of the pattern is not easy to interpret, it would be overlooked. Thus, to begin with, the interpreter is presented with a series of patterns that occur in less than 5 per cent of normal subjects and that possess a priori significance. Within each of these general patterns or "scales" the authors then proceed to distinguish various subscales that are even more infrequent in occurrence, although they involve some combination of the responses included in the major scale. Thus, the interpretation of the results for an individual subject consists of identifying in his responses patterns that correspond to those encountered only rarely among normal subjects and then determining the rational meaning of these patterns, as well as comparing them with the responses of abnormal or disturbed groups of subjects.

Because of the easy administration of the instrument it was possible for the authors, through the services of the Gallup Poll, to secure a nationwide, representative sample of 1,500 respondents. In addition, a group of slightly more than 1,500 abnormal subjects were tested and about half of these cases were matched on age, intelligence, and education with normal subjects for purposes of comparison.

The existence of an objective technique for scoring the test, in addition to the identification of a large number of rare patterns of responses for normal subjects, coupled with the demonstration of certain distinct differences in the performance of normal and disturbed subjects, makes clear that this instrument possesses objective and normative properties that are encountered nowhere else in the domain of projective techniques. Thus, there seems little doubt that this instrument possesses more of the attractive qualities of an objective instrument than any other projective measure. It is also easy to administer and when used on a large scale, machine scoring can be employed to ease the burden of the interpreter. On the other hand, the data that are collected are sharply delimited, and the process of demonstrating that the results are sensitive or useful has only just begun. Further, the stimulus material is primarily relevant to our own or a highly similar culture, so that the use of the instrument in other social settings is seriously inhibited. Perhaps the most serious shortcoming of this instrument at present is the very limited application the test has had in the hands of anyone other than the authors.

The volumes by Tomkins and Miner (1957, 1959) contain a detailed presentation of the development and rationale of this test as well as extensive normative material, elaborate recommendations for scoring and interpretation, and illustrative case histories.

EXPRESSIVE TECHNIQUES

As a class these techniques represent a bridge between the diagnostic and therapeutic for all of them play an active role in current therapeutic practice. It is presumed that the subject not only *reveals* himself in these measures but also that he *expresses* himself in such a manner as to influence his personal economy or adjustment. Typically, these instruments, as in the case of the constructive techniques, require the subject to combine or incorporate stimuli into some kind of a novel production. Unlike the constructive techniques, however, there is as much emphasis upon the manner or style in which the product is created as upon the production itself. In other words, the chief distinction between these measures and constructive devices is the assumption of therapeutic efficacy and the greater emphasis upon the style or manner in which the constructive process is carried out.

Play Technique

Most of the projective tests we have considered thus far were initially used with adults, although some of them were subsequently modified so as to apply to children. This path of development, logically enough, was reversed in the case of measures that utilize toys or dolls. As might be expected, these measures were initiated in connection with child study and treatment, and in only a few cases have they been used with adult subjects.

The use of play techniques is intimately linked with current methods of child therapy, however, these devices have also been used for many years to diagnose or measure personality. The early work of Barker, Dembo, and Lewin (1941), Erikson (1938, 1940), and Levy (1933, 1936, 1937) made clear that the technique was useful in inferring specific personality dimensions. In particular, Levy's studies of sibling rivalry (1936, 1937) showed that this technique could be used fruitfully, in a relatively standardized manner, to gain further understanding of the determinants and mode of functioning of an important domain of personality. More recently the numerous studies carried out by Robert Sears and his colleagues and students at Iowa and Harvard (Bach, 1945; Phillips, 1945; Pintler, 1945; Pintler, Phillips, & Sears, 1946; Sears, 1950; Sears, Pintler, & Sears, 1946; Sears, Whiting, Nowlis, & Sears, 1953) have shown a number of technical problems involved in the research use of this instrument and moreover have provided a model for the systematic development of a personality measure with simultaneous application of the technique to problems of empirical and theoretical interest.

All of these approaches involve presenting the subject with an array of objects which he is encouraged to employ in some manner. In some instances the subject is presented with a relatively structured situation, as in Levy's studies (1936, 1943), where the subject is presented with a mother doll feeding a baby doll and then asked what the little boy or girl doll is going to do. Other investigators have attempted to make the situation as unstructured and permissive as possible, as in the World Test. This instrument, which was developed by Lowenfeld (1939), presents the subject with an extensive array of varied toys (150 or more pieces) which the subject is encouraged to select from and employ in any manner he desires.

Typically the examiner is responsible for recording as much of the subject's behavior as possible, including his choice of toys and subsequent arrangement of them, his accompanying verbal comments, and his expressive behavior. If the test is structured, this may not be an unduly difficult chore. For example, with Levy's procedure there is typically a single thematic response to each presentation of the mother feeding the baby, and Levy simply classifies this response in terms of the mechanism for dealing with aggression that is revealed. If the test is unstructured, however, the recording of responses may become inordinately difficult, and even result in the necessity of using photographs in order to preserve a faithful record of the treatment of the test materials. With the exception of the measures employed by Sears and his colleagues, there is relatively little specification of just how the process of interpretation shall take place. In most instances it is assumed that the experienced clinician will be able to recognize important motives and conflicts without needing a set of objective prescriptions. Aside from the work carried out by Sears, which has centered upon aggression and dependency, there has been very little in the way of standardization. The device has been used in many research studies on an ad hoc basis, but it is difficult to cumulate the findings of most of these studies and many of them are vague in regard to just how the reported findings were secured. In general, the clinical use of the test, both therapeutic and diagnostic, far exceeds the investigative use, although in recent years there have been increased signs of research interest.

The various play techniques possess an obvious advantage in the hands of the investigator interested in studying children, for they capitalize upon a response area of great natural interest to the subject. Thus, they not only evoke considerable spontaneous interest and enthusiasm, but they tap a wide variety of available response tendencies. The technique is sufficiently adaptable to permit the ingenious user to focus it upon almost any kind of psychological variable, and it typically elicits a rich array of response data. The test makes only minimal demands upon intelligence and language facility and can be used readily with children in a wide variety of settings, as several investigations conducted in nonliterate societies testify (Henry & Henry, 1944; Levy, 1939).

Although the test has been used with adults, it is not ordinarily appropriate for subjects much beyond eight or ten years of age. Most versions of the test are relatively unstructured in regard to both scoring and interpretation, and even the recording of responses is difficult and time consuming. Generally speaking, if dependable and sensitive results are to be secured from this instrument, the examiner must be unusually well trained and alert. If we except a small number of variables that have been studied carefully, there is virtually no normative material and very little agreement as to just how the interpreter should go about extracting inferences from test material. The test cannot ordinarily be given in a group setting and is generally quite time consuming.

A general discussion of play techniques for the diagnosis of personality is provided by Bell (1948), and Woltmann (1952) outlines briefly some of the contributions in this area. A discussion of some of the procedural problems facing any investigator using this technique is presented by Sears (1947). A detailed discussion of the World Test is provided by Bolgar and Fischer (1947) and Buhler and Kelley (1941).

Drawing and Painting Techniques

The use of art forms to provide information concerning the personality of the creator has been practiced for many years, and yet there is little in the way of structure and firm empirical findings in this area of psychological appraisal. The variety of such approaches to personality assessment is very great, but the two most popular revolve around the use of finger paints and the drawing of persons.

The drawing techniques have derived chiefly from the early use of the drawing of persons as a means of assessing intelligence. This measure was included in a number of intelligence scales, in particular the Stanford-Binet, and Florence Goodenough dealt extensively with this approach to the measurement of intelligence in a number of publications, most noticeably her *Measurement of Intelligence by Drawings* (1926). In the process of using the Draw-A-Person technique to estimate intelligence, a number of clinicians noticed what appeared to them to be variations in performance unrelated to ability but intimately linked to personality factors. Out of this observation grew a number of personality measures that centered about the drawing of the human figure, the most publicized of which have been Buck's (1948*a*, 1948*b*, 1949) and Machover's (1948, 1951) tests. Buck's device, which is commonly referred to as the H-T-P Technique, requires the subject to draw a house, a tree, and a person; whereas Machover's test simply requires the subject to draw a person, and after a single person has been drawn, the subject is told to draw a person of the opposite sex. In both tests the subjects are presented with standard drawing equipment, are observed closely while they draw (if the test is administered individually), and any verbal responses, blocking, or unusual approaches to the task are recorded.

Although it was the ingenuity of Ruth Shaw (1934), an educator, which led to the development of finger painting as a therapeutic and diagnostic technique, it has been primarily the recent work of Napoli (1946, 1947, 1951) that has led to interest in this technique as a projective technique. The materials presented to the subject are standard, and he is instructed in such a manner as to give him a maximum of freedom in what he decides to paint and the manner in which he approaches the activity. The examiner is required to record the manner or style of painting as well as any verbalizations. It is considered advisable to secure a series of paintings rather than rest the interpretation upon a single painting.

The interpretation of both drawing and painting techniques is similar in that it involves utilizing the actual art product, the behavior surrounding the production of the painting, and any verbal associations that may have been provided, as well as inquiry results, if one has been conducted. Further, the interpretation generally proceeds on the basis of a large number of specific empirical rules relating particular modes of response to personality characteristics. These rules have to do with both formal qualities of the productions (thickness of lines, placement of picture on page, symmetry, color employed, size) and the content of the picture. A number of these empirical generalizations have been summarized by Bell (1948, pp. 362-387).

Although most of the techniques in this area have relatively standard conditions for administration, the process of interpretation is considerably less precise. In some cases, the interpretation appears to depend largely upon general clinical wisdom, coupled with a knowledge of some specific rules or generalizations. In other cases, there is a relatively specific set of scoring and interpretative rules, but these rules have not as yet been subjected to any well-controlled efforts at validation.

One of the most attractive features of this projective measure is the near universality of drawing and painting. It is easy to administer such instruments with reasonable standardization in a wide variety of age and cultural groups. The fact that the response is not mediated by language suggests that the techniques may be less subject to cultural and age limitations than many of the other projective techniques we have discussed. The test can be administered individually or in group settings, and depending upon the number of creations that are sought, it may be administered in a very brief period of time. The purpose of the test is well cloaked from all but the most sophisticated subjects, and consequently it is not easy for the subject to dissemble or create a desired impression. The instrument has received relatively wide cross-cultural application (Anastasi, 1938; Anastasi & Foley, 1936; DuBois, 1944; Manuel & Hughes, 1932; Schubert, 1930) although most such applications have not centered about personality inferences. Margaret Mead (1954) considers this technique an efficient device for the cross-cultural study of children's personality.

The strongest negative feature of this instrument is the relative paucity of objective methods of interpretation and the lack of general confidence in those systems of interpretation that do exist. For example, an extensive survey of reported research dealing with the Draw-A-Person Test led Swensen (1957) to conclude "... hypotheses concerning the D-A-P have seldom been supported by the research reported in the literature in the past eight years" (Swensen, 1957, p. 463). The number and nature of psychological variables that can reasonably be assessed by these techniques is somewhat restricted, particularly if only one or two drawings are available for analysis.

There are a number of general discussions on the use of painting and drawing as a basis for personality diagnosis, including books by Machover (1948) and Vernier (1952) and chapters by Bell (1948), Levy (1950), and Machover (1951). The most extensive treatment of drawings as a projective device is a recent volume edited by Hammer (1958). A chapter by Brown (1952) deals with finger painting and drawing techniques and in addition a chapter by Kadis (1950) and Napoli's (1946) monograph provide a separate treatment of finger-painting.

Psychodrama and Role-Playing

The vast majority of applications of these techniques are concerned with therapy or social training. In the hands of the psychotherapist, the practitioner of action research, and the industrial psychologist, these techniques have been used to implement a variety of desired personal changes. In addition, however, they have on occasion been used to shed light upon personality variables. These instruments derived originally from Moreno (1946) and Haas and Moreno (1951) and in Moreno's hands have been used for both therapeutic and diagnostic purposes. The approach has been specifically recommended as a projective technique by Del Torto and Corneytz (1944) who consider it to possess many superiorities in comparison with other projective techniques.

There is a wide variety of different devices included under this heading but all require the subject to act out, in a more or less public setting, some kind of personally relevant drama or personal inter-action. In some cases the subject participates in selecting the incident or event to be dramatized, but in other cases this may be standard-ized and he may be told just what role he is to play. The subject may interact with other subjects, or he may be confronted with trained actors who present him with a roughly standard stimulus situation to which he must respond. Where the technique is being used thera-peutically, the events enacted are likely to be drawn from the sub-ject's own experience. When personality appraisal is the purpose of the instrument, the subject is more likely to be placed in standard role-playing situations that are presumed to bear upon particular variables or domains of personality.

Interpretation of the subject's response is usually completely qualitative and there is little in the way of objective guideposts for the investigator. The instrument has not seen wide application in either clinical or research settings when compared to the most popu-lar of projective techniques. In fact, in the hands of social scientists it has probably been used far more often as a training instrument (French, 1945; Lippitt, 1943; Maier, Solem, & Maier, 1957) than as a device for assessing personality. The potential utility of the device for cross-cultural and survey research has been pointed to by the results of at least one investigation (Stanton, Back, & Litwak, 1956).

As a technique for assessing personality, role-playing offers cer-tain interesting qualities. It involves interaction with others more centrally than any other projective technique and involves response at a level that is closer to ordinary behavior than any other projective technique. On the other hand, the device is not accompanied by the degree of objectivity of scoring and interpretation that is customary, even among projective techniques. Further, the collection of this type of data is inefficient and time consuming. At this time it is not clear just what advantages adhere to this approach. The future may well reveal such qualities, but for the present there seems little basis for preference of role-playing techniques in comparison to other measures that are more economical and better studied.

This completes our brief survey of projective techniques. Having adopted a classification that divided these instruments according to whether their mode of response emphasized association, construction, completion, choice, or expression, we proceeded to describe the most important examples of each type of instrument and to examine their respective strengths and weaknesses.

Before leaving this topic it may be helpful to suggest some general sources where, in a single volume, the reader can gain additional introductory information about projective techniques. The most useful books of this kind are those by Abt and Bellak (1950), Anderson and Anderson (1951), and Bell (1948). A volume entitled *Progress in Clinical Psychology* (Brower & Abt, 1952, 1956), which appears at irregular intervals, frequently contains survey chapters of interest to anyone concerned with projective techniques. Finally, any individual contemplating the use of projective techniques would probably do well to see them in a critical context against the background of alternative measurement devices, and here the best sources are volumes by Anastasi (1958) and Cronbach (1960).

The reader has undoubtedly noted the diversity of the measures we have been discussing. Even the broad definition of projective techniques developed in the previous chapter is strained by the extreme heterogeneity of these instruments. In spite of this, we will find it possible, and indeed necessary, to talk about these techniques in general terms in the following chapters that deal with the theoretical foundations of projective techniques and the process of interpreting these tests.

REFERENCES

ABEL, Theodora, & CALABRESI, Renata A. The people (Tepoztecans) from their Rorschach tests. In O. Lewis (Ed.), *Life in a Mexican village: Tepotzlan restudied.* Urbana, Ill.: Univ. of Illinois Press, 1951. Pp. 306-318, 463-490.

ABT, L. E., & BELLAK, L., (Eds.) *Projective psychology: clinical approaches to the total personality.* New York: Knopf, 1950.

ALEXANDER, T., & ANDERSON, R. Children in a society under stress. *Behavioral Sci.*, 1957, 2, 46-55.

ALTUS, W. D., & THOMPSON, G. M. The Rorschach as a measure of intelligence. *J. consult. Psychol.*, 1949, 13, 341-347.

ANASTASI, Anne. *Psychological testing*, 3rd ed. New York: Macmillan, 1958.

ANASTASI, Anne, & FOLEY, J. P. An analysis of spontaneous drawings by children in different cultures. *J. appl. Psychol.*, 1936, 20, 689-726.

ANASTASI, Anne, & FOLEY, J. P. A study of animal drawings by Indian children of the North Pacific Coast. *J. soc. Psychol.*, 1938, 9, 363-374.

ANDERSON, H. H., & ANDERSON, Gladys L., (Eds.) *An introduction to projective techniques.* New York: Prentice-Hall, 1951.

ARON, Betty. *A manual for analysis of the Thematic Apperception Test.* Berkeley, Calif.: Berg, 1949.

ATKINSON, J. W., HEYNS, R. W., & VEROFF, J. The effect of experimental arousal of the affiliation motive on thematic apperception. *J. abn. soc. Psychol.*, 1954, 49, 405-410.

BACH, G. R. Young children's play fantasies. *Psychol. Monogr.*, 1945, 59, No. 2 (Whole No. 272).

BALL, T. B., & BERNARDONI, L. C. The application of an auditory apperception test to clinical diagnosis. *J. clin. Psychol.*, 1953, 9, 54-58.

BARKER, R. G., DEMBO, Tamara, & LEWIN, K. Frustration and regression: an experiment with young children. University of Iowa Studies in Child Welfare, 1941, 18, No. 1.

BECK, S. J. *Rorschach's Test.* Vol. 1. *Basic processes.* New York: Grune & Stratton, 1944.

BECK, S. J. *Rorschach's Test.* Vol. II. *A variety of personality pictures.* New York: Grune & Stratton, 1945.

BECK, S. J. The Rorschach Test: A multi-dimensional test of personality. In H. H. Anderson & Gladys L. Anderson (Eds.), *An introduction to projective techniques.* New York: Prentice-Hall, 1951. Pp. 101-122.

BECK, S. J. *Rorschach's Test.* Vol. III. *Advances in interpretation.* New York: Grune & Stratton, 1952.

BECK, S. J. A review of the Blacky pictures. *J. consult. Psychol.*, 1956, 20, 487-488.

BELL, J. E. *Projective techniques: a dynamic approach to the study of personality.* New York: Longmans, Green, 1948. By permission of Longmans, Green & Co., Inc.

BELLAK, L. *A guide to the interpretation of the Thematic Apperception Test.* New York: Psychological Corp., 1947.

BELLAK, L. The Thematic Apperception Test in clinical use. In L. E. Abt & L. Bellak (Eds.), *Projective psychology: clinical approaches to the total personality.* New York: Knopf, 1950. Pp. 185-229.

BELLAK, L. *The Thematic Apperception Test and the Children's Apperception Test in clinical use.* New York: Grune & Stratton, 1954.

BELLAK, L., & ORT, Eileen. Thematic Apperception Test and other apperceptive methods. In D. Brower & L. E. Abt (Eds.), *Progress in clinical psychology.* New York: Grune & Stratton, 1952. Pp. 149-172.

BLUM, G. S. A study of the psychoanalytic theory of psychosexual development. *Genet. Psychol. Monogr.*, 1949, 39, 3-99.

BLUM, G. S. *The Blacky Pictures: manual of instructions.* New York: Psychological Corp., 1950*a*.

BLUM, G. S. A reply to Seward's "Psychoanalysis, deductive method, and the Blacky Test." *J. abn. soc. Psychol.*, 1950*b*., 45, 536-537.

BLUM, G. S. Defense preferences in four countries. *J. proj. Tech.*, 1956, 20, 33-41.

BLUM, G. S., & HUNT, H. F. The validity of the Blacky pictures. *Psychol. Bull.*, 1952, 49, 238-250.

BOLGAR, H., & FISCHER, L. K. Personality projection in the World Test. *Am. J. Orthopsychiat.*, 1947, 17, 117-128.

BORSTELMANN, L. J., & KLOPFER, W. G. The Szondi Test: a review and critical evaluation. *Psychol. Bull.*, 1953, 50, 112-132.

BROWER, D., & ABT, L. E. (Eds.), *Progress in clinical psychology:* Vol. 1: Sec. 1 & 2. New York: Grune & Stratton, 1952.

BROWER, D., & ABT, L. E. (Eds.), *Progress in clinical psychology:* Vol. II. New York: Grune & Stratton, 1956.

BROWN, F. House-tree-person and human figure drawings. In D. Brower & L. E. Abt (Eds.), *Progress in clinical psychology.* New York: Grune & Stratton, 1952. Pp. 173-184.

BROWN, J. F. A modification of the Rosenzweig Picture Frustration Test to study hostile interracial attitudes. *J. Psychol.*, 1947, 24, 247-272.

BUCK, J. N. The H-T-P test. *J. clin. Psychol.*, 1948*a*, 4, 151-159.

BUCK, J. N. The H-T-P technique: a qualitative and quantitative scoring manual. Part One. *J. clin. Psychol.*, 1948*b*, 4, 319-396.

BUCK, J. N. The H-T-P technique: a qualitative and quantitative scoring manual. Part Two. *J. clin. Psychol.*, 1949, 5, 37-76.

BUHLER, Charlotte, & KELLEY, G. *The World Test: a measurement of emotional disturbance.* New York: Psychological Corp., 1941.

BURTT, H. E. Examination of offenders. In D. H. Fryer & E. R. Henry (eds.), *Handbook of applied psychology.* Vol. 2. New York: Rinehart, 1950. Pp. 555-561.

CAMERON, N. Reasoning, regression and communication in schizophrenia. *Psychol. Monogr.*, 1938*a*, 50, 1-34.

CAMERON, N. A study of thinking in senile deterioration and schizophrenic disorganization. *Am. J. Psychol.*, 1938*b*, 51, 650-664.

CAMPBELL, D. T. The indirect assessment of social attitudes. *Psychol. Bull.*, 1950, 47, 15-38.

CAMPBELL, D .T. A typology of tests, projective and otherwise. *J. consult. Psychol.*, 1957, 21, 207-210.

CARSTAIRS, G. M. *The twice born: a study of a community of high-caste Hindus.* London: Hogarth, 1957.

CARTER, H. L. J. A combined projective and psychogalvanic response technique for investigating certain affective processes. *J. consult. Psychol.,* 1947, 11, 270-275.

CATTELL, R. B. Principles of design in "projective" or misperception tests of personality. In H. H. Anderson & Gladys L. Anderson (Eds.), *An Introduction to projective techniques.* New York: Prentice-Hall, 1951. Pp. 55-98.

CLARK, R. A. The projective measurement of experimentally induced levels of sexual motivation. *J. exp. Psychol.,* 1952, 44, 391-399.

CLARK, R. A., & SENSIBAR, Minda R. The relationship between symbolic and manifest projections of sexuality with some incidental correlates. *J. abn. soc. Psychol.,* 1955, 50, 327-334.

CLARK, Ruth M. A method of administering and evaluating the Thematic Apperception Test in group situations. *Genet. Psychol. Monogr.,* 1944, 30, 3-55.

CLARKE, Helen J. The Rosenzweig Picture-Frustration Study. In H. H. Anderson & Gladys L. Anderson (Eds.), *An introduction to projective techniques.* New York: Prentice-Hall, 1951. Pp. 312-323.

COHEN, A. R. Experimental effects of ego-defense preference on interpersonal relations. *J. abn. soc. Psychol.,* 1956, 52, 19-27.

CRONBACH, L. J. Statistical methods applied to Rorschach scores: a review. *Psychol. Bull.,* 1949, 46, 393-429.

CRONBACH, L. J. *Essentials of psychological testing.* (Rev. ed.) New York: Harper, 1960.

CROSLAND, H. R. *The psychological methods of word-association and reaction-time as tests of deception.* Eugene: Univer. of Oregon Press, 1929.

DAVIDS, A. Personality dispositions, word frequency, and word association. *J. Pers.* 1956, 24, 328-338.

DAVIDS, A., JOELSON, M., & McARTHUR, C. Rorschach and TAT indices of homosexuality in overt homosexuals, neurotics, and normal males. *J. abn. soc. Psychol.,* 1956, 53, 161-172.

DAVIDS, A., & MURRAY, H. A. Preliminary appraisal of an auditory projective technique for studying personality and cognition. *Am. J. Orthopsychiat.,* 1955, 25, 543-554.

DEL TORTO, J., & CORNEYTZ, P. Psychodrama as expressive and projective technique. *Sociometry,* 1944, 8, 356-375.

DERI, Susan. *Introduction to the Szondi Test: theory and practice.* New York: Grune & Stratton, 1949.

DU BOIS, Cora. *The people of Alor: a socio-psychological study of an East Indian island.* Minneapolis: Univer. of Minnesota Press, 1944.

ELIZUR, A. Content analysis of the Rorschach with regard to anxiety and hostility. *Rorschach Res. Exch.,* 1949, 13, 247-284.

ERIKSON, E. H. Dramatic productions test. In H. A. Murray, *et al., Explorations in personality.* New York: Oxford, 1938.

ERIKSON, E. H. Studies in the interpretation of play. I. Clinical observation of play disruption in young children. *Genet. Psychol. Monogr.,* 1940, 22, 557-671.

ERON, L. D. A normative study of the Thematic Apperception Test. *Psychol. Monogr.,* 1950, 64, No. 9.

ERON, L. D., & RITTER, Anne M. A comparison of two methods of administration of the Thematic Apperception Test. *J. consult. Psychol.,* 1951, 15, 55-61.

FINE, R. A scoring scheme and manual for the TAT and other verbal projective techniques. *J. proj. Tech.,* 1955, 19, 306-309.

FRANK, L. K. Projective methods for the study of personality. *J. Psychol.,* 1939, 8, 389-413.

FRANK, L. K. *Projective methods.* Springfield, Ill.: Thomas, 1948.

FRENCH, J. R. P. Role-playing as a method of training foremen. *Sociometry,* 1945, 8, 410-425.

FRY, R. D. Manual for scoring the Thematic Apperception Test. *J. Psychol.,* 1953, 35, 181-195.

GLADWIN, T., & SARASON, S. B. *Truk: man in paradise.* New York: Wenner-Gren Foundation, 1953.

GOODENOUGH, Florence L. *Measurement of intelligence by drawings.* New York: Harcourt, Brace & World, 1926.

GOODENOUGH, Florence L. Semantic choice and personality structure. *Science,* 1946, 104, 451-456.

GOODSTEIN, L. D. Interrelationships among several measures of anxiety and hostility. *J. consult. Psychol.,* 1954, 18, 35-39.

GRINGS, W. W. The Verbal Summator Technique and abnormal mental states. *J. abn. soc. Psychol.,* 1942, 37, 529-545.

HAAS, R. B., & MORENO, J. L. Psychodrama as a projective technique. In H. H. Anderson & Gladys L. Anderson (Eds.), *An introduction to projective techniques.* New York: Prentice-Hall, 1951. Pp. 662-675.

HAMMER, E. F. (Ed.) *The clinical application of projective drawings.* Springfield, Ill.: Thomas, 1958.

HANFMANN, Eugenia, & GETZELS, J. W. Studies of the Sentence Completion Test. *J. proj. Tech.,* 1953, 17, 280-294.

HARROWER, Mary R., & STEINER, Matilda E. *Large-scale Rorschach Techniques.* Springfield, Ill.: Thomas, 1945.

HARTWELL, S .W., HUTT, M. L., ANDREW, Gwen, & WALTON, R. E. The Michigan Picture Test: Diagnostic and therapeutic possibilities of a new projective test for children. *Am. J. Orthopsychiat.,* 1951, 21, 124-137.

HENRY, J., & HENRY, Zunia. The doll play of Pilaga Indian children. *Am. J. Orthopsychiat.*, Research Monogr., 1944, No. 4.

HENRY, J., & SPIRO, M. E. Psychological techniques: projective tests in field work. In A. I. Kroeber (Ed.), *Anthropology today*. Chicago: University of Chicago Press, 1953. Pp. 417-429.

HENRY, W. E. The Thematic Apperception Technique in the study of culture-personality relations. *Genet. Psychol. Monogr.*, 1947, 35, 3-315.

HENRY, W. E. *The analysis of fantasy: the Thematic Apperception Technique in the study of personality*. New York: Wiley, 1956.

HENRY, W. E., & GUETZKOW, H. Group projection sketches for the study of small groups. *J. soc. Psychol.*, 1951, 33, 77-102.

HOLT, R. R. The Thematic Apperception Test. In H. H. Anderson & Gladys L. Anderson (Eds.), *An introduction to projective techniques*. New York: Prentice-Hall, 1951. Pp. 181-229.

HOLTZMAN, W. H. Validation studies of the Rorschach test: shyness and gregariousness in the normal superior adult. *J. clin. Psychol.*, 1950a, 6, 343-347.

HOLTZMAN, W. H. Validation studies of the Rorschach test: impulsiveness in the normal superior adult. *J. clin. Psychol.*, 1950b, 6, 348-351.

HORWITZ, M., & CARTWRIGHT, D. A projective method for the diagnosis of group properties. *Hum. Relat.*, 1953, 6, 397-410.

HOWARD, J. W. The Howard Ink Blot Test. *J. clin. Psychol.*, 1953, 9, 209-255.

HURLEY, J. R. The Iowa Picture Interpretation Test: a multiple-choice variation of the TAT. *J. consult. Psychol.*, 1955, 19, 372-376.

HUTT, M. L., & SHOR, J. Rationale for routine Rorschach "testing-the-limits." *Rorschach Res. Exch.*, 1946, 10, 70-76.

JANIS, Marjorie G., & JANIS, I. L. A supplementary test based on free associations to Rorschach responses. *Rorschach Res. Exch.*, 1946, 10, 1-19.

JOHNSTON, R. A. The effects of achievement imagery on maze-learning performance. *J. Pers.*, 1955, 24, 145-152.

JUNG, C. G. The association method. *Am. J. Psychol.*, 1910, 21, 219-269.

JUNG, C. G. *Studies in word association*. New York: Dodd, Mead, 1918.

KADIS, Asya L. Finger-painting as a projective technique. In L. E. Abt & L. Bellak (Eds.), *Projective psychology: clinical approaches to the total personality*. New York: Knopf, 1950. Pp. 403-431.

KENT, Grace H., & ROSANOFF, A. J. A study of association in insanity. *Am. J. Insanity*, 1910a, 67, 37-96.

KENT, Grace H., & ROSANOFF, A. J. A study of association in insanity. *Am. J. Insanity*, 1910b, 67, 317-390.

KLOPFER, B. *Developments in the Rorschach Technique*. Vol. II. *Fields of application*. New York: Harcourt, Brace & World, 1956.

KLOPFER, B., AINSWORTH, Mary D., KLOPFER, W. G., & HOLT, R. R. *Developments in the Rorschach Technique.* Vol. I. *Technique and theory.* New York: Harcourt, Brace & World, 1954.

KLOPFER, B., & KELLEY, D. M. *The Rorschach Technique.* New York: Harcourt, Brace & World, 1942.

KORCHIN, S. J., MITCHELL, H. E., & MELTZOFF, J. A critical evaluation of the Thompson Thematic Apperception Test. *J. proj. Tech.*, 1950, 14, 445-452.

LEE, S. G. *Manual of a Thematic Apperception Test for African subjects.* Pietermaritzburg, South Africa: Univer. of Natal Press, 1953.

LESSA, W., & SPIEGELMAN, M. Ulithian personality as soon through ethnological materials and thematic test analysis. *University of California Publications in Culture and Society*, 1954, 2, 243-301.

LEVY, D. M. Use of play technique as experimental procedure. *Am. J. Orthopsychiat.*, 1933, 3, 266-277.

LEVY, D. M. Hostility patterns in sibling rivalry experiments. *Am. J. Orthopsychiat.*, 1936, 6, 183-257.

LEVY, D. M. Studies in sibling rivalry. *Res. Monogr. Am. Orthopsychiat. Assn.*, 1937, No. 2.

LEVY, D. M. Sibling rivalry studies in children of primitive groups. *Am. J. Orthopsychiat.*, 1939, 9, 205-214.

LEVY, D. M. Hostility patterns. *Am. J. Orthopsychiat.*, 1943, 13, 441-461.

LEVY, D. M. The German anti-Nazi: A case study. *Am. J. Orthopsychiat.*, 1946, 16, 507-515.

LEVY, S. Figure drawing as a projective test. In L. E. Abt & L. Bellak (Eds.), *Projective psychology: clinical approaches to the total personality.* New York: Knopf, 1950. Pp. 257-297.

LIBO, L. M. *Measuring group cohesiveness.* Ann Arbor: Institute for Social Research, Univer. of Michigan, 1953.

LINDZEY, G. Thematic Apperception Test: interpretative assumptions and related empirical evidence. *Psychol. Bull.*, 1952, 49, 1-25.

LINDZEY, G. On the classification of projective techniques. *Psychol. Bull.*, 1959, 56, 158-168.

LINDZEY, G., & GOLDBERG, M. Motivational differences between male and female as measured by the Thematic Apperception Test. *J. Pers.*, 1953, 22, 101-117.

LINDZEY, G., & GOLDWYN, R. M. Validity of the Rosenzweig Picture-Frustration Study. *J. Pers.*, 1954, 22, 519-547.

LINDZEY, G., & HEINEMANN, Shirley H. Thematic Apperception Test: individual and group administration. *J. Pers.*, 1955, 24, 34-55.

LINDZEY, G., & NEWBURG, A. S. Thematic Apperception Test: A tentative appraisal of some "signs" of anxiety. *J. consult. Psychol.*, 1954, 18, 389-395.

LINDZEY, G., & TEJESSY, Charlotte. Thematic Apperception Test: Indices of aggression in relation to measures of overt and covert behavior. *Am. J. Orthopsychiat.*, 1956, 26, 567-576.

LINDZEY, G., TEJESSY, Charlotte, & ZAMANSKY, H. Thematic Apperception Test: An empirical examination of some indices of homosexuality. *J. abnorm soc. Psychol.*, 1958, 57, 67-75.

LIPPITT, R. The psychodrama in leadership training. *Sociometry*, 1943, 6, 286-292.

LOWENFELD, Margaret. The world pictures of children: a method of recording and studying them. *Brit. J. Med. Psychol.*, 1939, 18, 65-101.

LURIA, A. R. *The nature of human conflicts, or emotions, conflict, and will.* New York: Liveright, 1932.

MACHOVER, Karen. *Personality projection in the drawing of the human figure.* Springfield, Ill.: Thomas, 1948.

MACHOVER, Karen. Drawing of the human figure: a method of personality investigation. In H. H. Anderson & Gladys L. Anderson (Eds.), *An introduction to projective techniques.* Englewood Cliffs, N. J.: Prentice-Hall, 1951. Pp. 341-369.

MAIER, N. R. F., SOLEM, A. R., & MAIER, A. A. *Supervisory and executive development: a manual for role playing.* New York: Wiley, 1957.

MANUEL, H., & HUGHES, Lois S. The intelligence and drawing ability of young Mexican children. *J. appl. Psychol.*, 1932, 16, 382-387.

McCLELLAND, D. C., ATKINSON, J. W., CLARK, R. A., & LOWELL, E. L. *The achievement motive.* New York: Appleton-Century-Crofts, 1953.

MEAD, Margaret. Research on primitive children. In L. E. Carmichael (Ed.), *Handbook of child psychology.* New York: Wiley, 1954. Pp. 735-780.

MIRMOW, Esther. The Rosenzweig Picture-Frustration Study. In D. Brower & L. E. Abt (Eds.), *Progress in clinical psychology.* Englewood Cliffs, N. J.: Prentice-Hall, 1952. Pp. 209-221.

MORENO, J. L. *Psychodrama.* Vol. I. New York: Beacon House, 1946.

MUNROE, Ruth L. The inspection technique for the Rorschach protocol. In L. E. Abt & L. Bellak (Eds.), *Projective psychology: clinical approaches to the total personality.* New York: Knopf, 1950. Pp. 91-145.

MURRAY, H. A. *Explorations in personality.* New York: Oxford, 1938.

MURRAY, H. A. *Thematic Apperception Test manual.* Cambridge, Mass.: Harvard Univer. Press, 1943.

MUSSEN, P. H., & NAYLOR, H. K. The relationships between overt and fantasy aggression. *J. abn. soc. Psychol.*, 1954, 49, 235-240.

NAPOLI, P. J. Finger-painting and personality diagnosis. *Genet. Psychol. Monogr.*, 1946, 34, 129-230.

NAPOLI, P. J. Interpretative aspects of finger-painting. *J. Psychol.*, 1947, 23, 93-132.

NAPOLI, P. J. Finger painting. In H. H. Anderson & Gladys L. Anderson (Eds.), *An introduction to projective techniques.* Englewood Cliffs, N. J.: Prentice-Hall, 1951. Pp. 386-415.

PHILLIPS, R. Doll play as a function of the realism of the materials and the length of the experimental session. *Child Develpm.*, 1945, 16, 123-143.

PHILLIPSON, H. *The Object Relations Technique.* Chicago, Ill.: Free Press, 1955.

PINTLER, Margaret H. Doll play as a function of experimenter-child interaction and initial organization of materials. *Child Develpm.*, 1945, 16, 145-166.

PINTLER, Margaret H., PHILLIPS, Ruth, & SEARS, R. R. Sex differences in the projective doll play of pre-school children. *J. psychol.*, 1946, 21, 73-80.

RABIN, A. I. The Szondi Test. In H. H. Anderson & Gladys L. Anderson (Eds.), *An introduction to projective techniques.* Englewood Cliffs, N. J.: Prentice-Hall, 1951. Pp. 498-512.

RAPAPORT, D., SCHAFER, R., & GILL, M. *Diagnostic psychological testing.* Vol. I & Vol. II. Chicago, Ill.: Year Book Publishers, 1946.

RIESS, B. F., SCHWARTZ, E. K., & COTTINGHAM, Alice. An experimental critique of assumptions underlying the Negro version of the TAT. *J. abn. soc. Psychol.*, 1950, 45, 700-709.

ROHDE, Amanda R. Explorations in personality by the sentence completion method. *J. appl. Psychol.*, 1946, 30, 169-181.

ROHDE, Amanda R. *Sentence completion method: its diagnostic and clinical application to mental disorders.* New York: Ronald, 1957.

RORSCHACH, H. *Psychodiagnostics: a diagnostic test based on perception.* New York: Grune & Stratton, 1942. (Originally published in 1921.)

ROSENZWEIG, S. The picture-association method and its application in a study of reactions to frustration. *J. Pers.*, 1945, 14, 3-23.

ROSENZWEIG, S. Apperceptive norms for the Thematic Apperception Test: I. The problems of norms in projective methods. *J. Pers.*, 1949a, 17, 475-482.

ROSENZWEIG, S. *Psychodiagnosis.* New York: Grune & Stratton, 1949b.

ROSENZWEIG, S. Levels of behavior in psychodiagnosis with special reference to the Picture-Frustration Study. *Am. J. Orthopsychiat.*, 1950a, 20, 63-72.

ROSENZWEIG, S. Revised norms for the Adult Form of the Rosenzweig Picture-Frustration Study. *J. Pers.*, 1950b, 18, 344-346.

ROSENZWEIG, S., CLARKE, Helen J., GARFIELD, Marjorie S., & LEHNDORFF,

Annemarie. Scoring samples for the Rosenzweig Picture-Frustration Study. *J. Psychol.*, 1946, 21, 45-72.

ROSENZWEIG, S., & FLEMING, Edith. Apperceptive norms for the Thematic Apperception Test: II. An empirical investigation. *J. Pers.*, 1949, 17, 483-503.

ROSENZWEIG, S., FLEMING, Edith E., & CLARKE, Helen J. Revised scoring manual for the Rosenzweig Picture-Frustration Study. *J. Psychol.*, 1947, 24, 165-208.

ROSENZWEIG, S., FLEMING, Edith E., & ROSENZWEIG, Louise. The children's form of the Rosenzweig Picture-Frustration Study. *J. Psychol.*, 1948, 26, 141-191.

ROSENZWEIG, S., & MIRMOW, Esther L. The validation of trends in the Children's Form of the Picture-Frustration Study. *J. Pers.*, 1950, 18, 306-314.

ROTTER, J. B. Word association and completion methods. In H. H. Anderson & Gladys L. Anderson (Eds.), *An introduction to projective techniques.* Englewood Cliffs, N. J.: Prentice-Hall, 1951. Pp. 279-311.

ROTTER, J. B., & RAFFERTY, Janet E. *Manual for the Rotter Incomplete Sentences Blank, College Form.* New York: Psychological Corp., 1950.

ROTTER, J. B., & SCHACHTITZ, Eva. Validation of the Rotter Incomplete Sentences Blank for college screening. *J. consult. Psychol.*, 1949, 13, 348-356.

ROTTER, J. B., & WILLERMAN, B. The Incomplete Sentences Test as a method of studying personality. *J. consult. Psychol.*, 1947, 11, 43-48.

SACKS, J. M. Effect upon projective responses of stimuli referring to the subject and to others. *J. consult. Psychol.*, 1949, 13, 12-20.

SACKS, J. M., & LEVY, S. The sentence completion test. In the L. E. Abt & L. Bellak (Eds.), *Projective psychology: clinical approaches to the total personality.* New York: Knopf, 1950. Pp. 357-402.

SARGENT, Helen D. An experimental application of projective principles to a paper and pencil personality test. *Psychol. Monogr.*, 1944, 57, No. 5.

SARGENT, Helen D. Projective methods: their origins, theory, and application in personality research. *Psychol. Bull.*, 1945, 42, 257-293.

SARGENT, Helen D. *The insight test: a verbal projective test for personality study.* New York: Grune & Stratton, 1953.

SCHAFER, R. *Psychoanalytic interpretation in Rorschach testing.* New York: Grune & Stratton, 1954.

SCHUBERT, Anna. Drawings of Orotchen children and young people. *J. genet. Psychol.*, 1930, 37, 23, 2-244.

SCHWARTZ, B. J. The measurement of castration anxiety and anxiety over loss of love. *J. Pers.*, 1955, 24, 204-219.

SCHWARTZ, B. J. An empirical test of two Freudian hypotheses concerning castration anxiety. *J. Pers.*, 1956, 24, 318-327.

Schwartz, E. K., Riess, B. F., & Cottingham, Alice. Further critical evaluation of the Negro version of the TAT. *J. proj. Tech.*, 1951, 15, 394-400.

Sears, R. R. Influence of methodological factors on doll play performance. *Child Develpm.*, 1947, 18, 190-197.

Sears, R. R. Relation of fantasy aggression to interpersonal aggression. *Child Develpm.*, 1950, 21, 5-6.

Sears, R. R., Pintler, Margaret H., & Sears, Pauline S. Effect of father separation on preschool children's doll play aggression. *Child Develpm.*, 1946, 17, 219-243.

Sears, R. R., Whiting, J. W. M., Nowlis, V., & Sears, Pauline S. Some child-rearing antecedents of aggression and dependency in young children. *Genet. Psychol. Monogr.*, 1953, 47, 135-236.

Seward, J. P. Psychoanalysis, deductive method, and the Blacky Test. *J. abn. soc. Psychol.*, 1950, 45, 529-535.

Shakow, D., & Rosenzweig, S. The use of the Tautophone ("Verbal Summator") as an auditory apperceptive test for the study of personality. *Char. & Pers.*, 1940, 8, 216-226.

Shaw, Ruth F. *Finger Painting.* Boston: Little, Brown, 1934.

Sherwood, E. T. On the designing of TAT pictures, with special reference to a set for an African people assimilating Western culture. *J. soc. Psychol.*, 1957, 45, 161-190.

Shipley, T. E., & Veroff, J. A projective measure of need for affiliation. *J. exp. Psychol.*, 1952, 43, 349-356.

Shneidman, E. S. Schizophrenia and the MAPS test: a study of certain formal psychosocial aspects of fantasy production in schizophrenia as revealed by performance on the Make a Picture Story (MAPS) Test. *Genet. Psychol. Monogr.*, 1948, 38, 145-224.

Shneidman, E. S. *Thematic test analysis.* New York: Grune & Stratton, 1951.

Silverstein, A. B., Faking on the Rosenzweig Picture-Frustration Study. *J. appl. Psychol.*, 1957, 41, 192-194.

Skinner, B. F. The Verbal Summator and a method for the study of latent speech. *J. Psychol.*, 1936, 2, 71-107.

Sommer, R. On the Brown Adaptation of the Rosenzweig P-F for assessing social attitudes. *J. abn. soc. Psychol.*, 1954, 49, 125-128.

Spindler, G. D. Sociocultural and psychological processes in Menomini acculturation. *University of California Publications in Culture and Society*, 1955, 5.

Stanton, H., Back, K. W., & Litwak, E. Role-playing in survey research. *Am. J. Sociol.*, 1956, 62, 172-176.

Stein, M. I. The use of a sentence completion test for the diagnosis of personality. *J. clin. Psychol.*, 1947, 3, 47-56.

STEIN, M. I. *The Thematic Apperception Test: an introductory manual for its clinical use with adults.* (Rev. ed.) Cambridge, Mass.: Addison-Wesley, 1955.

STERN, W. Cloud pictures: a new method for testing imagination. *Char. & Pers.*, 1938, 6, 132-146.

STONE, D. R. A recorded auditory apperception test as new projective technique. *J. Psychol.*, 1950, 29, 349-353.

STRUVE, K. Typische Ablaufsformen des Deutens bei 14-15 jahrigen Schulkindern. *Zsch. f. angew. Psychol.*, 1932, 37, 204-274.

SWENSEN, C. H. Empirical evaluations of human figure drawings. *Psychol. Bull.*, 1957, 54, 431-466.

SYMONDS, P. M. Criteria for the selection of pictures for the investigation of adolescent phantasies. *J. abn. soc. Psychol.*, 1939, 34, 271-274.

SYMONDS, P. M. *Adolescent fantasy: an investigation of the picture-story method of personality study.* New York: Columbia Univer. Press, 1949.

SZONDI, L. *Schicksalsanalyse.* Basel: Benno Schwabe, 1944.

SZONDI, L. *Experimental diagnostics of drives.* New York: Grune & Stratton, 1952. (Published originally in 1947.)

SZONDI, L., MOSER, U., & WEBB, M. W. *The Szondi Test: in diagnosis, prognosis and treatment.* Philadelphia: Lippincott, 1959.

TENDLER, A. D., A preliminary report on a test for emotional insight. *J. appl. Psychol.*, 1930, 14, 123-136.

THOMPSON, C. E. The Thompson modification of the Thematic Apperception Test. *J. proj. Tech.*, 1949a, 13, 469-478.

THOMPSON, C. E. *Thompson modification of the Thematic Apperception Test.* Cambridge, Mass.: Harvard Univer. Press, 1949b.

TOMKINS, S. S. *The Thematic Apperception Test.* New York: Grune & Stratton, 1947.

TOMKINS, S. S. The Tomkins-Horn Picture Arrangement Test. *Trans. N. Y. Acad. Sci.*, 1952, 15, 46-50.

TOMKINS, S. S., & MINER, J. B. Contributions to the standardization of the Tomkins-Horn Picture Arrangement Test: plate norms. *J. Psychol.*, 1955, 39, 199-214.

TOMKINS, S. S. *The Tomkins-Horn Picture Arrangement Test.* New York: Springer, 1957.

TOMKINS, S. S. *PAT interpretation.* New York: Springer, 1959.

TRUSSELL, M. A. The diagnostic value of the verbal summator. *J. abn. soc. Psychol.*, 1939, 34, 533-538.

VAN LENNEP, D. J. *Four-Picture Test.* The Hague: Marinus Nijhoff, 1948.

VAN LENNEP, D. J. The Four-Picture Test. In H. H. Anderson & Gladys L. Anderson (Eds.), *An introduction to projective techniques.* Englewood Cliffs, N. J.: Prentice-Hall, 1951. Pp. 149-180.

VERNIER, Claire M. *Projective test productions: I. Projective drawings.* New York: Grune & Stratton, 1952.

VERNON, P. E. The Rorschach Inkblot Test, II. *Brit. J. med. Psychol.*, 1933, 13, 179-200.

VEROFF, J. Development and validation of a projective measure of power motivation. *J. abn. soc. Psychol.*, 1957, 54, 1-8.

WHEELER, W. M. An analysis of Rorschach indices of male homosexuality. *J. proj. Tech.*, 1949, 13, 97-126.

WILMER, H. A., & HUSNI, May. The use of sounds in a projective test. *J. consult. Psychol.*, 1953, 17, 377-383.

WOLTMANN, A. G. Play and related techniques. In D. Brower & L. E. Abt (Eds.), *Progress in clinical psychology.* New York: Grune & Stratton, 1952. Pp. 278-289.

WYATT, F., & VEROFF, Joanne B. Thematic apperception and fantasy tests. In D. Brower & L. E. Abt (Eds.), *Progress in clinical psychology.* New York: Grune & Stratton, 1956. Pp. 32-57.

ZUBIN, J., & YOUNG, K. M. *Manual of projective and cognate techniques.* Madison, Wisc.: College Typing Co., 1948.

ZULLIGER, H. *Der Behn-Rorschach Test. I. Band: Text.* Bern: Verlag Hans Huber, 1952.

4. What Are the Theoretical Foundations of Projective Techniques?

THERE ARE MANY DIFFERENT reasons for displaying an interest in theory. For the person concerned with the potential utility of projective techniques, a leading motive is likely to be the search for reassurance in regard to just how firmly embedded are these devices in general psychology. Our examination of the relation between theory and technique is intended to answer this question and at the same time to tell us something about the particular theoretical approaches to these tests that seem most promising. Further, an examination of the assumptions ordinarily involved in the use of projective techniques should give the interested observer some independent basis for estimating the reasonableness or attractiveness of these instruments.

Before we begin this analysis, it may be wise to remind the reader that most work with projective techniques has been carried out with little serious attention to psychological theory. Moreover, many of those who have attempted to introduce psychological theory in this area have been individuals either deficient in their understanding of psychological theory or else lacking in sophistication and knowledge concerning projective techniques. There is not even unanimity among users of projective techniques concerning how, or whether, to integrate theory and technique. Consistent with this view is Holzberg's suggestion that psychologists hold three general attitudes in regard to projective techniques and theory:

One attitude is that projective techniques are without any roots whatsoever in any psychological theory. A second attitude is that current psychological theory is inadequate as a base for projective techniques and that the projective technique movement must develop its own theoretical substructure. The third attitude is that projective techniques are embedded in all of psychological theory although the concern of those adopting this attitude is similar to that of all psychologists—the absence of a unifying theory of behavior competent to explain personality in all of its diversity and complexity. (Holzberg, 1954, p. 419)

The most typical efforts toward integration of theory and projective techniques have consisted of attempts to *relate major bodies of existing psychological theory to projective techniques*. The chief targets for this variety of synthesis are, not surprisingly, stimulus-response theory and psychoanalytic theory. A somewhat different approach to this problem has been the attempt to *relate projective testing to a particular body of empirical findings and formulation* which lacks the status of a general theory of behavior. The clearest illustrations of this type of effort are attempts to demonstrate the continuity between projective testing and perceptual theory and research. A third type of analysis has attempted to develop *miniature theories* to account for particular findings or classes of findings involving projective techniques. This avenue is illustrated by efforts to account for results showing the relation between fantasy aggression and overt or behavioral aggression, as well as attempts to understand the Movement response of the Rorschach test. A fourth tack involves the attempt to develop a theory specific to projective techniques by explicitly stating the *assumptions underlying current practice*. Although these assumptions may resemble those in other areas of psychological theory, the emphasis here is upon the specific relevance of each assumption to projective-technique interpretation rather than the link between projective techniques and some independent system or body of theory.

In the pages to follow, I shall examine these approaches in turn and provide a brief description and evaluation of representative examples of each. In a final section an attempt will be made to arrive at some over-all conclusions concerning the continuities and discontinuities between psychological theory and projective techniques. The reader who is primarily interested in problems of applying projective techniques and has only a routine or general interest in the projective techniques themselves may find it advisable to turn directly to the final section of this chapter where the outcomes of our detailed discussion are presented.

PROJECTIVE TECHNIQUES AND SYSTEMATIC THEORY

As we have already indicated, the two major theoretical positions that have been employed extensively in explicit attempts to provide a theoretical underpinning for projective tests are stimulus-response theory and psychoanalytic theory. There is nothing remarkable about this state of affairs for it accurately mirrors the position of these two theories in general psychology. There have been, of course, isolated attempts to apply other viewpoints such as field theory (Deutsch, 1954), organismic theory (Hanfmann, 1952), Murray's personology (Holt, 1954), or adaptation-level theory (George & Bonney, 1956; Murstein, 1959) to the phenomena of projective testing, but these have had relatively little enduring impact upon either investigation or clinical practice.

One reason that these two positions attract the majority of interested observers has to do with their theoretical polarity. On the one hand, psychoanalysis, as we have seen, is closely linked historically with the development of projective techniques. Moreover, the kinds of data from which this theory has evolved, and in application to which it is most at home, are closely similar to the kinds of data elicited by projective techniques. Thus, those interested in projective techniques who are closely identified with clinical psychology are likely to view psychoanalysis as the theory of choice. Stimulus-response theory, on the other hand, is essentially a theory derived from the laboratory and represents a conception of theory-building that is most popular among those who are closely identified with psychology as a natural science. Thus, investigators whose principal identification is with experimental science are likely to be drawn to this theory. The plight of the moderate is always precarious and given these two vigorous extremes it is rather difficult for a mid-way position to secure adherents.

Stimulus-Response Theory

The possibility of applying Hull's reinforcement theory to the kinds of data and empirical relations characteristic of the field of projective testing has long been accepted, but it is only in recent years that there has been any serious attempt to carry out the necessary bridging operations. Perhaps the first focussed effort is contained in a paper by Auld (1954) in which he examines the contributions of "behavior theory" to the understanding of projective-technique responses.

Auld limits his attention in this paper to the TAT and presents a single case as illustrative of his approach. Initially he suggests that it is important to distinguish three situations: origin situation, test situation, and criterion situation. Furthermore, the link between these three situations is provided by *emotional habits,* which were learned in the origin situation, appear in the test situation, and will determine behavior, to some degree, in the criterion situation. The psychologist employs the projective test to discover something about the emotional habits learned in the situation of origin, in order to improve his predictions of what will occur in the criterion situation. The extent to which the habits learned in the situation of origin appear in the test and criterion situations represents the degree of *generalization.* In order to make accurate statements concerning the generalization of a habit, it is necessary for the observer to know something about the *strength of the habit* and also something about the amount of *conflict* that it arouses. Auld also discusses some of the problems involved in measuring habit strength and conflict and suggests some types of indices that may be useful in this connection.

In general, this particular expedition provides us with little evidence for the potential fruitfulness of stimulus-response theory either as a means of generating new ideas or as a means of ordering what is already known. Auld essentially limits himself to suggesting that there are important concepts within reinforcement theory that can be interpreted in terms of data secured through the avenue of projective tests. Thus, although he identifies certain congruences between projective techniques and s-r theory, he does little to promote the systematic linking of these two domains.

McClelland and Atkinson (Atkinson, 1954; McClelland, Atkinson, Clark, & Lowell, 1953) have done a good deal of implicit theorizing that has followed the general paradigm of s-r analysis. This work has focussed upon thematic projective techniques but the primary intent has not been to provide a theoretical formulation to account for projective techniques but rather to develop a general theory of motivation that will interact empirically with at least this class of projective-technique responses. Although these authors employ an s-r paradigm, their formulations show little congruence with reinforcement theory but rather represent a form of expectancy theory.

Atkinson (1954, 1958*b*) defines a motive as an anticipatory goal state aroused by cues associated with past experiences of positive and negative affect. Not only is the motive aroused by specifiable cues related to particular affective states but also it leads to the activation of a set of responses that have been involved in these past experiences of positive and negative affect. In Atkinson's words: "The arousal of a motive, then, *mediates* the arousal of perceptual and instrumental response dispositions corresponding to various aspects of behavioral sequences which in the past have been instrumental in producing the same goal state" (1954, p. 86). There are a variety of cues in the projective test (in this case, the TAT) that serve to activate or arouse motives. Among these are cues derived from the normal environment or inner thoughts of the subject, cues deliberately introduced by the experimenter, and cues contained in the stimuli presented by the investigator. If the investigator is interested in assessing individual differences in motives, he holds these cues constant so far as possible and observes the variation in subjects' response.

By further assuming that "picture cues can arouse motives and performance expectancies in much the same manner as cues of real-life situations" (1954, p. 89) and that this tendency to be aroused by picture cues has come out of past learning situations of just the sort involved in the normal learning of a motive, the investigator is able to look upon differences in subjects' imaginative productions as reflecting stable motivational differences. In general, then, Atkinson and McClelland assume that projective-test stimuli activate motives, and these activated motives in turn lead the subject to emit responses derived from past experiences involving these motives. This line of reasoning is by no means unsupported by empirical evidence as a large amount of corroborating research has been reported in a variety of publications (Atkinson, 1954, 1958*a*; McClelland, 1955; McClelland, Atkinson, Clark, & Lowell, 1953).

The unique strength of these formulations derives precisely from this sizable amount of related research. The principle weakness of this work, from our limited perspective, is its focus upon one particular kind of projective technique and the limited interest these investigators have shown in customary interpretive practices even in connection with this instrument. Thus, most of their work has been deliberately designed to provide enlightenment concerning general motivational processes rather than the processes involved in typical projective techniques.

The most painstaking stimulus-response analysis of projective techniques has been carried out by Goss and Brownell. In their treatment the authors first apply s-r concepts to the stimuli presented as part of the projective-test situation and then to the process of interpreting projective-technique productions. They begin their analysis of the stimulus component by suggesting (Goss and Brownell, 1957) a distinction between *external environmental stimuli* and *response-produced stimuli* (stimulation resulting from a response made by the subject). The external environmental stimuli are further divided into those stimuli that are a part of the physical properties of the test and those that are a part of the surrounding context. The latter may be further divided into those associated with the room in which the test is given and those related to attributes of the test examiner. Examiner stimuli may be differentiated in terms of whether they derive from the physical properties of the examiner or from his actions or behavior. Again, his actions are divided according to whether they involve presentation of instructions, stimuli, questions, or other verbal and manipulative responses. The response-produced stimuli are divided into those initiated by stimuli involving the subject's environment and those that derive from internal stimuli. In either case they lead to responses that may be verbal, locomotor-manipulative, or visceral, and these responses in turn serve as stimuli to the subject.

Given this analysis of the stimulus conditions surrounding the administration of the projective test, Goss and Brownell suggest a number of additional concepts to be used in accounting for the associated responses. First of all, there are *receptor-orienting responses* which determine the aspects or features of the test material that will be focussed upon and experienced. Next are the concepts of primary *generalization* and primary *discrimination*. Generalization implies that when the subject has perceived a particular stimulus element in the test, this element will tend to evoke responses that have been made to similar stimuli in the past. Moreover, the more similar this stimulus element is to the stimulus that evoked this response in the past, the more strongly will the response be evoked. Likewise, when the subject has discriminated between two similar stimuli in the past (has learned to make different responses to them), he may be expected to make different responses to two test stimuli which resemble these two differentiated stimuli. Once a test stimulus has led to a particular response via the principles of primary generalization and primary discrimination, this response may facilitate further generalization or discrimination. This phenomenon of *response-mediated generalization and discrimination* may be illustrated by a situation where labelling a particular figure as "friend" would facilitate additional responses that had in the past been evoked by figures similarly labelled and differentiate these responses from those elicited by figures labelled "enemy."

The concepts we have just outlined may be considered the principal means of accounting for projective-test responses, but the response process can be further understood by means of the concepts of associative chains, habit or stimulus summation, drive and conflict. The concept of *associative chains* applies to sequences involving only words, as well as those involving both motoric and verbal elements. The authors point to the fact that once a response has been elicited, it tends, as a result of past experience, to be linked with certain further responses. It is primarily as a consequence of these links or chains that the subject emits a flow of responses following the initial identification or labelling responses. The concept of *habit or stimulus summation* accounts for the fact that two stimuli with relatively slight capacity to evoke a response may combine to provide a much stronger tendency to make the response. Furthermore, various changes in the antecedent conditions of the subject may lead to changes in *drive* which can combine in a multiplicative manner with the factors we have already discussed to elicit responses. Finally, the various tendencies to respond may exist in *conflict* or opposition to each other; Goss and Brownell believe that the unique contribution of projective techniques is to provide inferences concerning conflict.

Among the phenomena derived from conflict are inhibitory reactions, displacement, projection, and reaction formation. Following Miller (1948) the authors assume the existence of gradients of approach and avoidance to various stimulus objects and further assume that the gradient of avoidance is relatively steeper than the gradient of approach. Consistent with these assumptions, it is reasoned that when the strength of the avoidance response is stronger than the strength of the approach response, the individual will be *inhibited* or blocked in his response. Because the avoidance tendencies decrease more rapidly with distance from the original stimulus (steeper gradient of avoidance), objects which resemble the original object may elicit the inhibited response, although to a weaker degree than the original stimulus. This tendency for a somewhat weaker response to be elicited by a substitute stimulus or object is referred to as object or *stimulus displacement*. In similar manner the individual may produce a response that is related to, but not the same as, the inhibited response. This is called response or *topographic displacement*. The process of *projection* is accounted for as a simple case of stimulus displacement of a response that was originally appropriate when directed toward the self but has been inhibited because of conflicting tendencies and can only be expressed in connection with a similar but more remote object—the other person. Similarly, the process of *reaction formation* is viewed as an instance of topographic displacement in which an initial response is inhibited and replaced by a related but distinct response.

In a second paper Brownell and Goss (1957) apply stimulus-response concepts to an understanding of the antecedents of projective-test responses as well as predicting the response of subjects to new test and nontest stimuli. Initially the authors suggest that when a given *response occurs with a short latency* the examiner may assume the absence of conflict. Consequently he can predict that if the subject is shown stimulus material that is objectively more closely related than the original stimulus to the response evoked, the latency of response will become even shorter and the probability of such a response even higher. If the stimulus material is less similar, however, the investigator can expect longer latencies and lower probabilities. The situation is more complex when the examiner encounters a *long latency of response*, or even no response whatsoever, for here the slowness to respond may reflect either low associative strength between the stimulus and this response or the existence of conflict and inhibition. The authors suggest that the existence of conflict may be inferred (*a*) when there is no response even though the subject's past history suggests the likelihood of such a response; (*b*) when similar subjects provide the same response to this stimulus material with a short latency; (*c*) when there is disturbance of speech such as vacillation, changes in voice; (*d*) when the long latency is followed by a strange or bizarre response; (*e*) when there are vaso-motor changes such as blushing, sweating, and motor activity. The existence of a long latency in the absence of such signs would presumably suggest low associative strength rather than conflict. The authors consider some hypothetical means of estimating the independent strengths of the conflicting responses. They also point to the errors of measurement, as well as the shortcomings of the theoretical model in this setting, which make precise predictions from projective-test response to response in other situations impossible.

These papers serve a definite function by proposing a detailed analysis of the stimulus properties of the projective test and the testing situation. Moreover, the application of s-r concepts indicates that certain kinds of additional data would be useful in the interpretive process, for example, evidence concerning responses to nontest stimuli that bear some orderly relation to the projective-test stimuli. That there is a similarity in the behavior resulting from low associative strength (motivation) and that resulting from conflict is an interesting formulation and, if not novel, is at least presented more systematically than in the past. In addition, most of the generalizations concerning projective tests that Goss and Brownell employ in demonstrating the applicability of s-r concepts are consistent with customary clinical practice and belief.

On the other hand, as the authors make clear, this is no more than a tentative beginning in the kind of theoretical analysis needed to account, even after the fact, for the range of diverse findings and procedures that are important in customary projective testing. In particular, one may wonder how useful such an analysis can be when there is so little specification of such important properties of the model as stimulus similarity and response similarity. If the theory does not provide the investigator or clinician with a reasonable metric for assessing the degree of similarity between stimuli or responses, there is little purpose in providing carefully drawn diagrams of hypothetical relations depending upon just these dimensions. The usual qualms expressed by the unconverted over the fact that s-r theory has so little to say about the substance or content of behavior (motives, traits, the acquisitions or structures of behavior) are, of course, very relevant in the present context. The individual approaching projective techniques from the vantage of s-r analysis must rely upon some other theoretical source to suggest to him just how he should analyze or classify the response data. A final and telling criticism of this contribution concerns the relative wealth of theoretical statements and the paucity of clear translations into the language of projective testing. These papers obviously have much more to say about s-r theory than they have to say about the process of interpreting projective techniques.

Psychoanalytic Theory

The literature of projective techniques is richly endowed with casual discussions of the relationship between various projective techniques and psychoanalytic theory. As we have already seen, Rorschach was deeply influenced by psychoanalysis. His original monograph (Rorschach, 1921) makes occasional reference to psychoanalysis, but the relation between psychoanalytic theory and the Rorschach test is much more directly dealt with in his posthumous publication with Oberholzer (1923). Here the Rorschach test of a single case who had been psychoanalyzed by Oberholzer is presented and parallels between the two sources of data drawn. Unfortunately, there is virtually no attempt to draw systematic conclusions concerning the theory and the test, so the reader gains little more than an appreciation for some consistency between psychoanalytic data and Rorschach data, as well as an awareness of the extent to which Rorschach himself was influenced by this theoretical position.

There are many modern examples of the application of psychoanalytic theory to projective techniques, with the work of Rapaport (Rapaport, 1942b, 1950, 1952; Rapaport, Schafer, & Gill, 1945) and Schafer, (1954a, 1954b) providing the most skillful and influential illustrations. Holt (1954) provides an excellent general discussion of the relation of personality theory to the Rorschach test, which deals in considerable detail with psychoanalytic theory. In the same volume is a detailed discussion by Klopfer (1954) of Jungian psychoanalytic ego psychology and the Rorschach test. It is regrettable that so many of these efforts to integrate psychoanalytic theory and projective techniques have focussed exclusively upon the Rorschach test, but it is scarcely to be marveled at, in view of the test's popularity and its original close association with the psychoanalytic movement.

A masterful example of the synthesis of theory and clinical practice is provided by Schafer (1954a) in his volume on the use of psychoanalytic theory as a guide to interpetation of the Rorschach test. It is impossible to provide an adequate summary of Schafer's volume here, but fortunately some of the main points in this volume are also reported briefly in an article (Schafer, 1954b) dealing directly with the relation between psychoanalytic theory and projective testing. Let us glance quickly at the contents of this paper and then return briefly to consider the volume.

Schafer (1954b) limits his consideration of psychoanalytic theory and projective testing here to a treatment of certain points of emphasis within contemporary psychoanalysis. In particular he deals with the importance of the test situation and the relationship between tester and subject, with different levels of psychic functioning, with patterns of defense, and with the concept of ego identity. Initially he stresses *analyzing the total testing situation* and assessing its contributions to the subject's responses. He points to the parallels between transference and countertransference in the therapeutic context and the unreal although powerful expectancies, fears, and anxieties that the subject brings to the testing situation, as well as the motives, biases, and theoretical commitments that the examiner introduces into the testing situation.

A second contribution of psychoanalytic theory to the projective tester is the distinction between *different levels of psychic functioning*. Here Schafer refers to the fact that under various circumstances the individual may employ modes of thought or response typical of earlier or more primitive stages of his development. Schafer illustrates this particularly through reference to Kris's (1952) use of the concept of *regression in the service of the ego* in accounting for the creative process. He suggests that an understanding of this capacity of the individual to adaptively retreat to more primitive modes of functioning is essential to a full understanding of the process of responding to projective tests.

Schafer's third important emphasis derived from psychoanalytic theory deals with the extent to which the person's characteristic *modes of defense* determine his method of responding to projective-test stimuli. The impact of individual patterns of defense upon test performance can make the interpreter's task more difficult, but it can also provide a sensitive means of assessing this defensive structure.

A fourth derivation from psychoanalysis is the concept of *ego identity* with its emphasis upon the importance of self-conceptions and social roles internalized by the individual as a result of experience, particularly experience involving sociocultural factors and interpersonal relations. Thus, an understanding of the subject's response requires consideration of age, sex, sociocultural background and other factors which help to determine his ego identity and thus indirectly his modes of response to the projective techniques.

In his book, Schafer (1954a) begins similarly with an examination of the testing situation and the relation between examiner and subject in the light of psychoanalytic ego psychology and follows this with an examination of the contributions of unconscious, preconscious, and conscious factors in the response process, a comparison of the analysis of Rorschach responses to the analysis of dreams, and finally a consideration of the merits of content analysis and the criteria for satisfactory interpretation. The remaining and largest portion of the book is devoted to the problem of interpreting defenses from the Rorschach test. Here Schafer talks specifically about the mechanisms of repression, denial, projection, regression, isolation, reaction formation, and undoing.

In discussing the test situation, Schafer, again drawing upon the psychoanalytic concepts of transference and countertransference, asserts that complete examiner objectivity is impossible. Instead he urges the examiner to develop an awareness of his departures from impersonal objectivity and to assess their contribution to the test performance. Among the special problems contributing to the tester's lack of neutrality are confusion concerning his professional role and the tendency for clinical psychologists, in many instances, to feel inferior to other specialists. It should also be recognized that the tester enters the testing situation with a definite set of expectations or wishes. He wants an appropriate number of responses from the subject, he would like these responses to be definitely scorable, he hopes that the subject will be frank, he wants to be able to give the test in a conventional or standardized manner, and so on. Not only do these rational and relatively well-recognized personal needs affect the examiner's role in the testing situation, but certain aspects of the examiner-patient relationship play a more or less important, although largely covert, part in determining his behavior. Schafer refers to these aspects as constants because they appear to be present to some degree no matter what the personality of the individual clinician. First, there is the *voyeuristic aspect,* the role of the tester as an involved observer of the covert and overt psychic structure of the patient. Second is the *autocratic aspect,* the role of the tester in controlling and dominating the conduct of the testing session. Third is the *oracular aspect*, which pertains to the role of the clinician in drawing momentous psychological conclusions from his superior position of training and knowledge. Fourth is the *saintly aspect*, which is related to the social service, helpful, or therapeutic function of the tester.

In addition to these constants there are particular personality attributes of the tester which may contribute to or intrude upon the test relationship. Schafer characterizes these by identifying types of testers in whom particular attributes are pronounced. In this context he lists: the tester who lacks a firm sense of personal identity; the tester who is inhibited or withdrawn; the dependent or succorant tester; the intellectualizing, constricted tester; the sadistic tester; and the masochistic tester.

Just as the examiner brings certain specifiable qualities and expectations to the testing situation so too does the patient or subject. In the case of the individual being given a Rorschach test in a psychiatric setting, there are certain constants such as a sense of violated privacy, threatened loss of control in an interpersonal relationship, concern over being brought into contact with unacceptable aspects of the self, temptation to regress to passive and immature modes of response, or difficulty in coping with the broad range of freedom provided by the test situation. Patients vary in their reaction to their own responses, not only in terms of how positively or negatively they perceive them, but also in terms of the specific qualities or attributes they assign to them. In many instances these reactions are related to underlying psychosexual attitudes or points of fixation. Responses also possess a defensive aspect that shows marked variation between subjects. Among the common defensive operations encountered in response to the Rorschach test are projection, isolation, intellectualization, compulsive perfectionism, repression, denial, reaction formation, counterphobic defense, masochistic strategies, ingratiating maneuvers, and rebellious operations. Schafer points out that these qualities in the testing situation may distort responses; they may distort interpretations, by leading the examiner to arrive at faulty inferences concerning the subject; or they may, in the most favorable of cases, enrich the interpretations of the examiner.

It is evident that Schafer's analysis of the testing situation draws heavily upon psychoanalytic concepts. He emphasizes the important contributions of both conscious and unconscious motives on the part of subject and examiner alike, points to the importance of psychosexual fixation in producing attitudes that are reflected in this situation, utilizes the mechanisms of defense in describing the reaction of the patient to his own responses, and is generally guided by the concepts of transference and countertransference.

In considering the response process, the author leans heavily upon Freud's concepts of primary process and secondary process. He suggests that the test instructions encourage a mixture of free fantasy response with careful reality testing. Furthermore, it is characteristic of subjects to show fluctuation in the psychic level at which they function during the process of responding. At some points, the subject may respond consistently with the reality principle, with a full consideration of objective stimulus factors, rational and normative standards of conduct, and generally appear to be under the domination of what the psychoanalyst would call the secondary process. At other times his responses may appear to be determined by the pleasure principle, archaic inner impulse, to show little concern for the distinction between inner world and outer reality, with all sources of tension given immediate discharge—that is, the subject responds consistently with the primary process. These modes of functioning are not to be viewed as discrete and clearly differentiated but rather as continuous and blending into one another. Furthermore, the same individual at different times may respond at different levels of functioning, and of course, there are marked differences between subjects in their characteristic level of response. An important determinant of the level of psychic functioning of the individual is his capacity for regression in the service of the ego, that is, his capacity to retreat to a more primitive mode of functioning in order to serve a conscious, acceptable need or function. The operation of these shifts in level of functioning can be established through identifying variation in the accuracy, originality, and determinants of the subject's responses, as well as by changes in the attitude expressed by the subject toward his own production, toward the stimuli, and toward the examiner. Schafer points out that the range of psychic functioning in the Rorschach response provides the basis for identifying similarities and differences between this mode of response and dreaming, daydreaming, and normal perceptual processes.

Most of the remainder of the book is devoted to the interpretation of psychological defenses. This topic is introduced by a general discussion of defense that is consistent with psychoanalytic formulations; Schafer then proceeds to a careful specification of how to proceed from specific Rorschach response data to inference concerning the various mechanisms of defense.

What we have just said largely fails to convey the careful and delicate manner in which Schafer picks his way through the conceptual-empirical tangle of the Rorschach test and psychoanalytic theory. It may, however, serve to underline certain strengths and weaknesses of this approach to psychological theory and projective techniques, as well as to make clear Schafer's general reliance upon psychoanalytic concepts. The unique strengths of Schafer's contributions derive from the fact that, for once, we encounter an individual integrating theory and projective techniques who is fully informed concerning both areas involved in the synthesis. A reasonable accusation that can be leveled against most individuals who have attempted the application of s-r concepts to projective techniques is that they are considerably more at home with their theoretical conceptions than they are with the actual operations of projective testing. Schafer, however, reflects the talents of his teacher, David Rapaport, and is deeply and sensitively familiar with psychoanalytic theory and at the same time an acknowledged expert in the area of projective testing.

Schafer's analysis is, in general, highly impressive. Nevertheless, as a synthesis of theory and technique, it has a number of important shortcomings. For example, as Schafer himself notes, he has drawn upon psychoanalytic theory in a relatively casual or nonsystematic manner, taking those concepts or assumptions that seem to have particular relevance and applying them directly, with no attempt to provide a general connection between the organic theory and the operations of the test and its interpretation. Thus, although there is no question that his work contains a host of interesting and suggestive generalizations concerning the test and no doubt that his treatment is heavily influenced by psychoanalytic theory, it is by no means clear just what the systematic relation is between his view of the test and psychoanalysis. It is not even clear just what form of psychoanalytic theory is involved, since in some instances concepts not customarily considered a part of orthodox psychoanalytic theory are introduced.

If we contrast this treatment with the attempts to apply s-r concepts to projective tests, we find clear and important differences. The most important of these is that s-r theorists give explicit and systematic expositions of the theoretical concepts and make relatively few effective connections between these concepts and projective-test operations, whereas Schafer makes an ad hoc application of psychoanalytic concepts in a detailed and sophisticated manner to projective tests with the net effect of considerable illumination. There certainly can be no doubt which of these enterprises has shed most light upon projective testing, but there might be considerable doubt concerning which has supplied the clearest conceptual bridge from projective techniques to psychological theory. It is, of course, quite possible that these differences are largely determined by the current status of the two theories. Stimulus-response theory is characterized by relatively precise theoretical formulation but few statements relating the theory to complex human behavior. Psychoanalysis, on the other hand, is characterized by a marked lack of formal elegance but a relative wealth of statements linking segments of the theory to complex behavioral products.

The late David Rapaport has made distinguished contributions to both projective testing (1945, 1952) and to psychoanalytic theory (1950, 1951a, 1951b, 1953, 1958) and in several important publications he has dealt quite directly with the relation between psychoanalysis and projective testing. In his two-volume work on diagnostic testing (Rapaport, Gill, & Schafer, 1945, 1946) he provides a brief general treatment of the rationale of projective tests including an outline of the differences between the customary use of the concept of projection and the mechanisms involved in projective testing. The use of projective techniques, Rapaport suggests, rests upon the assumptions that the examiner is seeking information concerning the subject which the subject himself is unaware of or unable to communicate; and consequently these devices are closely linked to acceptance of the importance of unconscious motives. Furthermore, he reasons, some kind of underlying theory of personality is necessary, and the theory which seems most at home with unconscious motivation is psychoanalytic theory. Deciding to employ a psychoanalytic framework in the interpretation of projective-technique responses, however, is by no means the answer to all the test interpreter's problems. In fact, one of the chief dangers in such interpretation is the easy and uncritical application of psychoanalytic concepts. Rapaport suggests that the actual relation between projective-technique response and psychoanalytic theory is highly complex, if not obscure, for the test response is the outcome of involved intermediary processes and is by no means a direct manifestation of drives or motives. It is primarily an ego psychology or a theory of thinking that is needed to illuminate these responses, not a theory of drives or impulses.

Thus, Rapaport emphasizes the intimate relation between projective techniques and psychoanalytic theory, but at the same time he points to the cognitive nature of the test response and the relative weakness of traditional psychoanalytic theory in coping with this aspect of functioning. Consequently, he suggests that it is from ego psychology that the projective tester can derive the most effective assistance. Rapaport's conception of the personality structure implied by customary projective-technique procedure is summarized in the following passage:

The subject has an Ego which is the *recipient of outside stimulation,* and which may be inclined to take, to shirk, or incessantly to invoke stimulations. This Ego is also the *executor of the intentions of the unconscious strivings,* which in their particular constellation and strength are specific to the individual; as executor of these intents, the Ego may oppose them, subserve them without delay, or postpone them and by thinking prepare for their optimal realization. The Ego has a certain autonomy—autonomous energy (bound cathexes), autonomous behavior (defense mechanisms), and autonomous thought patterns—to govern perception, execution, and thought. The reception of stimulation by the Ego is not automatic but selective and to some extent distorts the stimulation to meet the needs of the subject. The execution of intentions by the Ego is likewise not an automatic discharge of internal tensions but an adaptation to the nature of the objects in reality which these intentions are aimed at or must cope with. (Rapaport, Gill, & Schafer, 1946, pp. 11-12)

Although this passage may not provide much illumination to the uninitiated, it does make clear Rapaport's commitment to an ego psychoanalytic model as a means of accounting for what is involved in projective techniques.

In his most explicit treatment of this problem, Rapaport (1952) emphasizes the need for a theory to embrace all projective techniques and furthermore, expresses his conviction that there exists already a theory of thinking (psychoanalytic) partially sufficient to this task. In a discussion of the contributions of this theory to an understanding of projective techniques, he begins by stating his belief that there are a large number of different kinds of projection. Furthermore, the type of projection, or "externalization," involved in projective techniques is by no means typical of the mechanisms of projection that the psychoanalyst has isolated and described. Thus, he indicates, an important theoretical-empirical task for the future is the further identification and study of these various externalizing processes. He states further that a general appreciation of the organizing and selective role of motivation upon perception must be coupled with an awareness that motives are by no means homogeneous and of equal status. Some forms of motivation, for example, are clearly derived from other motives, but, suggests Rapaport, the situation is even more complex than this, for under certain circumstances the derivative motives may become autonomous and operate independently of the original motive. In general, however, there is an hierarchy of motives which the investigator must keep in mind in interpreting projective tests.

Rapaport indicates that in studying cognitive processes one may focus upon the application of known concepts (fixed tools of thought), or he may examine the formation of concepts (process of thought). The more structured the test employed by the investigator, the more likely he is to be dealing with "fixed tools of thought." Actually, an adequate understanding of thought requires that both structure and process be studied.

Moreover, there is considerable variation among subjects in their "conscious experience" of the percepts that they report on projective tests. Some may feel that they are describing concrete, external reality; others present a popular response with the air of a person making a fanciful and farfetched response; still others may account for their response in terms of concurrent physiological processes, or properties of the physical stimulus. Rapaport concludes that these differences are closely related to the subject's reality-testing capacity and the degree of constriction in his inner life.

Rapaport's several treatments of projective techniques and psychological theory share many of the characteristics of Schafer's more intensive analysis. A number of interesting and suggestive connections between theory and technique are identified, but there is no systematic attempt to align the major concepts of the theory on the one hand with procedures in projective testing on the other. Thus, although what we see of the similarity between these two domains is promising, the entire venture remains highly programmatic. In this connection, it is important to note Rapaport's emphasis on the dangers of a direct and unsophisticated application of psychoanalytic concepts to projective techniques.

Nevertheless, Rapaport himself would assert that a careful examination of his major publications dealing with psychological testing (Rapaport, 1942a, 1942b, 1946, 1947, 1950, 1952; Rapaport, Gill, & Schafer, 1945, 1946; Rapaport & Schafer, 1944, 1945) will reveal implicit in them a careful, and point-by-point, linking of psycho-analytic theory and the process of interpreting projective techniques. In his words, "there is not much loud talk about psychoanalysis," but the systematic association between theory and technique is there for the discerning reader to unearth. Although this may be true, one may still object that it is the writer's responsibility to make completely explicit that which he wishes to impress upon his colleagues.

In a general exploration of the implications of personality theory for the Rorschach test, Holt (1954) limits his discussion of psycho-analysis and the Rorschach to three major topics. First, he talks at some length about David Rapaport's (Rapaport, Gill, & Schafer, 1945) linking of a psychoanalytic theory of thought to the Rorschach. Second, he considers the concept of projection and concludes, contrary to the conclusion reached in Chapter III but consistent with Rapaport's position, that no useful purpose can be served by broadening the concept of projection to include the customary processes involved in projective testing. Third, he considers the interpretation of Rorschach content and concludes that it is here that psycho-analysis has most to offer.

In his discussion of content interpretation, he points to the distinction between the *primary process* (archaic, nonlogical, image-laden mode of thought characterizing dreams and psychic world of the infant, or psychotic) and the *secondary process* (logical, reality-oriented thought process characterizing conscious activity of the normal adult). Furthermore, he suggests that the Rorschach is so designed that it is a peculiarly effective means for eliciting primitive aspects of the individual but at the same time discovers much about the manner in which the individual controls or defends against archaic impulses and images. Not only do the test responses provide general information concerning *mechanisms of defense,* but also they offer a basis for making particularly refined inferences concerning the individual's capacity for *identification* with other people. Finally, Holt considers the concept of *neutralization* (energy or behavioral trends that have been freed from their primitive sexual or aggressive origins and function with relative autonomy) and suggests that the Rorschach may also be used to measure the extent to which the individual operates under the motivation of neutralized or autonomous motives. He concludes that an adequate picture of the role of neutral energy can be achieved only if the investigator takes into consideration the possibility of ego-controlled or adaptive regression, a concept which we have already observed as a focus of Roy Schafer's attention.

Holt deals somewhat more directly with the problem of establishing points of continuity between psychoanalysis and the Rorschach test than either Rapaport or Schafer. Nevertheless, many of the same criticisms that were directed against their work can be directed against Holt's paper. Again the emphasis is only upon selected elements of the theory and technique, and again the impression is rather one of a general compatibility than a point-by-point mapping. One may reasonably assert that this detailed linking of theory and technique was not a part of the goal Holt set for himself and, indeed, that such a goal would not be practicable within the confines of a single chapter. This is undeniably the case, and yet we are not questioning here the special merit of Holt's chapter. We are asking only how well it serves to establish a bridge between psychoanalytic theory and projective testing. One may also argue that an ad hoc application of specific concepts or limited domains of the theory is the most fruitful approach to connecting theory and technique. Although it may be true that formal shortcomings of the theory or deficiencies in our knowledge of projective techniques and their operation may make a general integration of theory and test impossible, this is certainly a strong argument for the position that at present these tests lack adequate theoretical bases.

Consideration of the relation between psychoanalytic theory and projective techniques would not be compete without mention of the Blacky Test, which as we have already learned in Chapter III, was constructed by Blum (1949) to measure variables centrally involved in psychoanalytic theory. Thus, although Blum's work does little to promote any general synthesis of psychoanalytic theory and projective techniques, he has designed a projective instrument intended to provide a number of indices corresponding to psychoanalytic variables. One may argue about the success with which this instrument assesses psychoanalytic variables—clearly the evidence is as yet inadequate for an unambiguous answer to such a question—but it is evident that the tactic employed by Blum has much to offer. His approach is consistent with recent articles on the problem of construct validity (Jessor & Hammond, 1957; Loevinger, 1957), which place heavy emphasis upon the importance of taking specific theoretical matters into consideration in constructing tests rather than merely in the process of interpreting them. Of course, this admonition refers to much more than the particular variables the test is designed to assess, and in the case of the Blacky Test, many sophisticated psychoanalysts would argue that the test procedures are not, in all respects, consistent with the principles of measurement that could be derived from, or are implicit in, psychoanalytic theory. In any case, if we alter our question from which theories are at present integrated with projective techniques to which tests are specifically *dependent* upon particular psychological theories, we would have to conclude that the fate of the Blacky Test is more closely linked to the fate of a single psychological theory than is any other projective technique.

In general it appears that projective techniques and psychoanalytic theory possess many congruent elements. A considerable number of psychoanalytic concepts display real utility in accounting for, or making rational, practices common among projective-test users. This, of course, is scarcely remarkable in view of the extent to which these practices have been established by individuals influenced by psychoanalytic theory. Less convincing, however, are the steps that have been taken toward providing a careful and precise specification of the detailed relationship between psychoanalytic theory and projective techniques. Although several interesting and encouraging attempts have been made to demonstrate the utility of some portion of psychoanalytic theory in understanding or interpreting some segment of projective-technique response, a rational and carefully specified bridge from psychoanalytic theory to projective techniques remains a hope for the future—it is definitely not an accomplishment of the past.

PROJECTIVE TECHNIQUES AND PERCEPTUAL RESEARCH AND THEORY

There are a limited number of individuals interested in projective testing who have turned to particular substantive areas of psychology for guidance in how to conceive or represent the processes involved in projective testing. The most typical and influential of these approaches is exemplified by those who have looked toward motivation and perception research for illumination of projective techniques.

In the decade beginning in 1946 there was probably no area of psychological research which was so enthusiastically explored, or upon which such lavish investigative effort was expended, as the realm of motivation or personality and perception. The repeated demonstration that an identifiable role in the perceptual process could be assigned to social, personality, or organism determinants led many to feel that a new era was dawning in which even the psychophysicist could be forced to admit the essential contribution of individual differences in social and motivational variables.

Given this intense enthusiasm, in addition to the obvious fact that perceptual processes are centrally involved in every projective test, it was only natural that many would see research and theory dealing with needs and perception as promising, at last, a firm empirical and theoretical foundation upon which projective techniques could build. A number of investigators who have contributed heavily to the study of personal determinants of perception have also made serious efforts to extend their findings and generalizations to customary practices and observed findings dealing with projective techniques, and at the same time many projective testers have reached out hopefully for conceptual aid from perceptual research.

A typical example of this latter type of integration is provided in an attempt by Abt (1950) to establish the beginnings of a theoretical background for projective techniques. Although the author draws eclectically from field and organismic theory, his orientation derives its most characteristic emphasis from perception research and theory. He introduces his formulations by suggesting that instead of depending upon existing psychological theories to provide the basis for projective testing, one should instead create a "projective psychology" which employs concepts from many other theories but is primarily focussed upon a viewpoint derived from clinical use of projective techniques. He then proceeds to develop such a position, suggesting that his projective psychology is dynamic, functional, and holistic and is centered about individual or idiographic analysis. In discussing what he considers to be major conceptual trends in this area, he points to: (a) the view of personality as a process rather than a static collection of traits: (b) acceptance of this process as continuously influenced by inner states on the one hand and outer physical and social stimuli on the other; (c) utilization of field theory as the most fruitful means of ordering projective-test data; (d) acceptance of both genetic or historical and dynamic or field propositions; (e) increased interest in the "personality as a whole;" (f) intensified concern with the development of a theory adequate to describe the individual case in a clinical setting.

Turning to the topic of perception, which holds the bulk of his attention, Abt suggests that perception is centrally involved in all projective techniques and that consequently it is necessary for projective testers to agree on the nature and function of perception. He proposes that it is important to accept the selectivity of perception and, moreover, to realize that this selectivity in the stimuli to which the individual responds is determined both by *internal* and *external* factors. The external factors are equated to the autochthonous factors of Gestalt psychology and little is said about them. Of more interest to the projective tester are the internal factors which relate among other things to Roger's (1951) concept of "internal frame of reference" and involve the self-concept in a central manner. Abt suggests that projective techniques are based upon an awareness of the dual importance of internal and external factors in perception and the further knowledge that when the degree of structure in the stimulus is reduced, the operation of internal factors is facilitated. Thus projective techniques are devices intended to maximize the operation of internal factors in perception. Abt suggests that perception is ". . . an active and purposeful process which involves the whole organism in relation to its field. By its nature perceptual activity has roots that extend deeply into the whole matrix of the individual's past experiences, and the perceptual activities of the individual reach out to fashion his orientation to the future (1950, p. 52)."

Perception functions importantly to protect the individual from harmful or threatening situations and in particular to maintain his anxiety at a level he can tolerate. The perceptual process largely determines the operation of mechanisms of defense, particularly the mechanism of projection. Thus apparently Abt implies that projection is an important perceptual device employed to protect the individual against excessive quantities of anxiety. Furthermore, he suggests that since anxiety is particularly likely to be evoked in unfamiliar and ambiguous situations, it is no surprise that the unstructured stimuli of the projective test produce anxiety and in turn lead to the operation of projection.

His formulation closes with the outline of five postulates concerning the nature of personality. First, personality is a system within the individual which provides an organized relationship between stimulus and response. Second, this organization is dynamic, motivated, and has the capacity to select stimuli and control responses as an independent functioning system. Third, personality is a configuration that fits the laws of Gestalt psychology. Fourth, the development of personality involves both differentiation and integration. Fifth, the development of personality is influenced by environmental factors, including particularly cultural factors.

Abt's effort to provide a theoretical background for projective techniques may have served some useful purpose by pointing to the potential relevance of perceptual research for projective techniques, as well as by identifying elements in various psychological theories that are relevant to the activities of the projective tester. However, it is difficult to see how such an enterprise can make any important contribution either to the practicing clinician or to the individual interested in securing theoretical enlightenment concerning projective techniques. On the one hand, the theoretical statements are so general and so poorly co-ordinated that they seem unlikely to provide any new perspective concerning the psychological processes involved in projective techniques, and on the other hand, there is so little detailed consideration of the actual procedures of projective testing that even if there were theoretical illumination it would be difficult to give it empirical meaning. Abt's presentation lacks the virtues of both s-r and psychoanalytic endeavors for compared to Auld and Goss there is even less effort to provide specific linking of the theoretical ideas with actual testing procedures, and the theoretical formulations are so vague and formless as to be theoretically much less precise than the contributions of Schafer and Rapaport.

A number of investigators concerned primarily with perception have attempted to demonstrate the potential utility of perceptual theory for projective techniques and some have even carried out bridging investigations. Typical of this research is a study by Eriksen and Lazarus (1952) that attempted to demonstrate the applicability of the concept of perceptual defense to projective techniques and the actual operation of the process in responses to the Rorschach test. Using a modified version of the Rorschach which permitted the subject to accept or reject various responses to particular cards, they derived scores for three motivational areas representing the tendency of the subject to reject or refuse responses or percepts in each area. They then measured emotional disturbance in each of these areas through the use of a word-association technique and found that there was a relationship between the degree of disturbance in a particular area and the tendency to reject related Rorschach responses. This finding is viewed as evidence that perceptual defense is a determinant of Rorschach response. In a closely related study, Eriksen (1951) applied the concepts of perceptual sensitivity and perceptual defense to the Thematic Apperception Test. He demonstrated that individuals who gave evidence of perceptual sensitivity (low perceptual threshold for aggressive pictures) provided more evidence of overt or direct aggression in their TAT stories than did individuals who provided evidence of perceptual defense (high perceptual threshold for recognition of aggressive pictures). A further attempt to relate perceptual theory and projective-technique findings was carried out by Blake and Wilson (1950) who attempted to account for the relationship they observed between an independent measure of depression and the mode of responding to the Rorschach in terms of the operation of perceptual selectivity.

A more general attempt to identify areas of congruence in perceptual research and projective techniques was provided by Eriksen (1954). He suggests that most projective techniques are chiefly perceptual devices and that they share with motivation and perception research the underlying assumption that a person's motives will influence his perceptions. A large number of investigations concerned with perception have demonstrated that this assumption appears to be fully warranted; needs do, in fact, effect perception. Some of these same studies, however, have demonstrated that the operation of needs upon perception is not direct but is mediated by various defenses.

Eriksen also criticises those arguments questioning the operation of motivational factors upon perception that are based on the discovery that word frequency plays an important role in determining perceptual responses. These arguments are faulty, according to Eriksen, for the demonstration of the influence of word frequency does not rule out motivational factors. Moreover, studies controlling word frequency continue to demonstrate the operation of motivational factors. Similarly, those who have argued against the existence of perceptual defense have typically based their arguments upon inadequate data, such as that secured through the use of tabooed words in recognition studies.

Although perceptual research has supported custom among projective-technique testers by showing that needs and defenses influence perception, Eriksen suggests that this same research has also pointed to shortcomings in typical use of projective techniques. First of all, normative material is insufficient to permit one to determine just how ambiguous most projective-test material is, and consequently there is little information concerning just what constitutes reasonable or normal responses to these stimuli. Second, we know little about the adequacy of these stimuli to evoke responses relevant to the various types of motives. It seems likely that they lead to the expression of more than covert or unconscious needs. Further, since various defenses may be expected to operate, the relation between need state and projective-technique response is by no means direct. Third, the relation observed between motivational measures and perceptual measures is typically so slight that, although its mere existence may encourage the user of projective techniques, there is little basis for real optimism, in view of the very large quantity of variance in perception determined by nonmotivational variables.

Another general attempt to relate perception to projective techniques is provided by Bruner (1948). He points to the largely empirical derivation of the Rorschach test and suggests that this shortcoming be remedied by turning to perceptual research and theory. He emphasizes that what is really needed is not a theory of Rorschach perception but rather a general theory of perception which will be able to incorporate the Rorschach as a special case. In a discussion of the perceptual process he indicates that perception plays both a constructive and a defensive role. The individual constructs a world of reality to which he can adjust, and at the same time he defends himself against threatening or unpleasant parts of his world. The process of perception is intermediary between a set of stimulating conditions and a set of internal or organism states. Needs or motivational states may lead to a readiness to produce certain perceptual responses (vigilance) or to a reluctance to make or accept certain percepts (defense), although, in the normal individual, perception ordinarily is dominated by realistic or accurate percepts. Moreover, the operation of defense and vigilance has been implicitly understood and utilized by projective testers in customary Rorschach interpretation.

Investigations concerning perceptual defense suggest that there is more than one type of defense. Specifically Bruner suggests that there is sometimes an inability to develop a percept, or a "tendency to blankness," and at other times the person may develop meaningless or confused percepts, or he may develop "contravaluent" percepts that reflect a derogatory or negative set toward the stimulus object. Moreover, Bruner suggests that Rorschach administration and interpretation might be modified so as to assess these varieties of defense. Further, research has demonstrated the operation of perceptual vivification or accentuation, a process where personally relevant stimuli stand out or are emphasized. Bruner feels that if accentuation is an important part of the perceptual process, it might be worthwhile to make a more serious attempt to identify on the Rorschach those percepts that are most vivid or striking. The author closes on a hopeful note: "The future will perforce witness the coalescence of research on perception and research on diagnostics. The two belong together" (1948, p. 167).

Clearly revealed in these investigations and formulations is the conviction, shared by projective testers and perception investigators alike, that an adequate theory of perception will surely make major contributions to the understanding of projective techniques. We find instances where research has demonstrated the specific applicability of particular concepts and findings from the area of motivation and perception to customary projective-technique practice. This demonstration of logical coherence and, in some cases, specific empirical continuity between perceptual concepts and the interpretation of projective techniques is not only interesting but it provides limited support for the consistency of projective-technique practice with general psychology. All in all, however, contributions of a general theoretical nature from this quarter remain largely at the level of sentiment or intention. As yet there is certainly little in the way of a comprehensive and systematic attempt to account for the diverse procedures and phenomena that play an important part in projective testing.

One may remark upon the fact that most of these attempts at theoretical integration occurred from five to ten years ago—there is relatively little current activity of this sort. In explanation, it is easy to recall the tremendous enthusiasm that was created by the early perception and motivation research and the subsequent lessening of interest and, in some cases, reversal of personal position on major theoretical issues in this area. At the peak of interest in these phenomena, it was natural that the role of perceptual processes in projective techniques should be emphasized and efforts made to bring these techniques and perception research into association. With a general slackening of interest in the impact of motivation upon perception and a tendency to reaffirm the importance of structural factors in perception, it is understandable that the integration of perception and projective techniques seems currently less significant.

MINIATURE THEORIES CONCERNED WITH PROJECTIVE TECHNIQUES

On occasion attempts have been made to provide a specific theoretical analysis of particular types of response to projective techniques or particular empirical findings involving projective techniques. These are endeavors that, at least for the moment, shrug off the responsibility of providing a general theory applicable to all aspects of all projective techniques and turn instead to some more limited goal. Implicit in such a strategy is the assumption that with the construction of a sufficient number of efficient theories of this sort the task of constructing a general theory of projective techniques may become surmountable. As illustrative of such approaches let us take a quick look at efforts to account for the relation between fantasy aggression and overt or behavioral aggression as well as attempts to provide a theoretical rationale for the Movement response on the Rorschach test.

Fantasy and Overt Aggression

One of the central problems facing the individual using projective techniques concerns the association between overt or manifest evidence of a motive and its covert or fantasy expression. Furthermore, among the wide variety of psychological dimensions studied by psychologists, none is of wider interest than aggression. Consequently it is easy to understand why a number of investigators and theorists have concerned themselves with exploring and formulating the relation between overt and covert aggression.

The first explicit treatment of this problem was provided by Murray (1943) in the *Manual* for the TAT. He cautions users of the TAT against assuming that behavioral tendencies strongly manifested in TAT stories will be strongly present in overt behavior. It is true that there generally is a slight positive relationship between fantasy and overt indices of motives, but there are many particular exceptions to this weak over-all relation. Experience has shown that stories told to the first ten cards are likely to be more closely related to overt behavior than stories told to the second ten cards. This implies that the nature of the stimulus material will play a role in determining the relative overtness or covertness of the responses evoked, and the second ten TAT cards, because of their bizarre nature, are more likely to evoke responses that deviate from typical overt responses. A further clarifying principle is provided by his suggestion that where a given dimension of behavior is not negatively sanctioned or restricted by the surrounding culture, there is likely to be a strong relation between the fantasy response and the behavioral response. He then cites findings indicating a correlation of +.40 or more between fantasy measures and overt measures for such variables as abasement, dominance, nurturance, passivity and dejection. There is, however, a negative correlation for sex, and no evidence for any association between overt and fantasy aggression and achievement. That there is substantially no correlation between aggression and fantasy behavior, Murray suggests, may be due, at least in part, to the negative sanction of this motive in our society. However, one must admit that Murray's parallel observation under comparable circumstances of no correlation for achievement and a negative correlation for sex suggests that the conditions must be more complex than his interpretation implies.

At almost the same time Sanford, one of Murray's students, advanced a similar, although considerably more involved, formulation concerning the relation between fantasy needs and overt behavior. He also reported a new set of relevant empirical findings (Sanford, et al., 1943), including a low, nonsignificant correlation (+.15) between aggression as measured by a projective technique and aggression as measured in overt behavior, and for other needs a measure of association ranging from +.41 to —.44. He attempts to account for these findings through considering five factors: the strength of the motive, the existence of cultural restriction, conflict between needs, opportunity for overt gratification of the need, and the ego strength or self-control of the subject. Thus, in accounting for negative association or contrast between fantasy manifestation and overt manifestation, he suggests: ". . . some needs are frequently inhibited, owing chiefly to cultural prohibitions or to conflicts with other needs, and operate the more forcibly in fantasy the less the gratification which can be attained through overt behavior; and conversely, the more successful the overt activity of the need the less the residual tension which gives rise to fantasy." (p. 282) When there is positive association or congruence between the overt and fantasy measures, he reasons:

... a need will be manifested, according to the degree of its strength, both in fantasy and in behavior if that need does not conflict with the mores—or their internal representative—and it is to some extent frustrated by a lack of ability or of opportunity. Second, that a need which is in conflict with moral prohibitions or with self-respect will nevertheless be expressed in behavior as well as in fantasy if the need is strong and the subject's capacity for self-control is relatively weak. Third, needs which are both encouraged and frowned upon in our culture according to what modes or objects they employ will sometimes be manifested both in fantasy and in behavior, their modes and objects being relatively primitive or infantile in the first instance, relatively acceptable socially in the second. (p. 282-284)

A subsequent study by Mussen and Naylor (1954) built upon and extended somewhat Sanford's reasoning in an investigation of aggressive behavior in a group of lower-class subjects. The investigators reasoned that both Murray and Sanford had drawn their subjects from middle-class backgrounds where aggressive behavior was punished and inhibited and that consequently there was little relation between fantasy and overt aggression. However, in lower-class subjects with whom there had been less attempt to suppress aggressive behavior, those subjects who show a large amount of fantasy aggression should also show a large amount of overt aggression. Employing a group of lower-class boys who had been sent to a juvenile home and using the TAT and ratings of overt aggression, Mussen and Naylor found evidence that confirmed their prediction. The authors then reasoned that even within the same social class there must be differences in the extent to which individuals have been punished following aggression and, consequently, differences in the relation between overt and fantasy expression of aggression. Specifically, they predicted that individuals who showed a high ratio of anticipation of punishment following acts of aggression in their TAT stories would demonstrate less overt aggression than individuals who showed little anticipation of punishment following aggression. Again, their findings confirmed the prediction.

Kagan (1956) suggested that an adequate understanding of the relation between fantasy and overt aggression necessitated consideration of the nature of the stimulus material evoking the fantasy aggression, as well as the factors we have already considered. He also believed that in order to predict overt behavior one needed to know not only the strength of the relevant motive but also the degree of anxiety surrounding it. Further, he reasoned that the fantasy measure of aggression should correspond directly to the type of aggressive behavior to be predicted rather than be a mixture of all types of aggressive responses.

In order to test the cogency of his reasoning, he administered a set of modified TAT pictures to a group of young boys and secured teacher's ratings that permitted him to divide the subjects into five groups in terms of tendency to start fights and freely express anger. The TAT pictures he used varied in the extent to which they were directly linked to aggression. Kagan predicted that those pictures that were most manifestly related to aggressiveness were most likely to arouse anxiety and that, consequently, aggression expressed to these pictures would be most closely associated with the overt measure of aggression. His findings were generally supportive of his prediction, with those pictures judged to be most closely related to aggression proving most predictive of overt aggression. In similar fashion, when the TAT stories were scored for aggression in terms of fighting alone, the relation to the criterion proved to be much higher than it was when a similar measure derived from all types of aggression was employed. One should note the relationship between his reasoning concerning the importance of the stimulus material and Murray's generalization concerning the tendency of the first ten cards to be more predictive of overt behavior than the second ten cards.

In a recent study Lesser (1957) attempted a careful investigation of the role of punishment of aggression in the past history of the individual as a determinant of the relation between overt and fantasy aggression. He argued that fantasy and overt aggression should be positively related when the mother was relatively accepting of aggression in her child, and negatively related when the mother was unable to accept aggression in her child. Utilizing a modified set of TAT pictures, a set of peer ratings of overt aggression, and a questionnaire-interview with mothers of the subjects, Lesser attempted to examine the role of maternal acceptance or rejection of aggression in her children, in this fantasy-overt behavior relationship. Among the 23 children whose mothers were relatively accepting of aggression there was a significant positive correlation (+.43) between fantasy aggression and overt aggression, whereas among the 21 children whose mothers discouraged aggression there was a significant negative correlation (−.41). Combining the two sets of subjects provided an over-all correlation between fantasy and overt aggression that was slight and nonsignificant (+.07). Thus, the over-all correlation is virtually the same as that reported by Murray and Sanford, and yet when the group is appropriately subdivided, substantial correlations are observed.

A number of other formulations and investigations have been advanced to account for the relation between overt and fantasy aggression, but even the preceding handful of studies is sufficient to reveal many of the strengths and weaknesses of this approach to the general problem of the projective instrument and its theory. The obvious advantages of such an approach are the relatively close relation between theoretical formulation and empirical research and, consistently, the relatively clear implications of such studies for the individual interested in the practical application of the instrument. Although the problem these investigators have set themselves is carefully circumscribed, a satisfactory solution will clearly provide evidence and formulation of general significance for the user of projective tests. The principal shortcoming of this tactic is the absence of any general framework for either technique or theory. That is, only a small aspect of the test is related to psychological theory, and the theory it is related to is often ad hoc and unsystematic. Thus, the number of such individual bridges that might have to be constructed before we would have an adequate connection between general theory and technique could prove to be very great.

There is, nonetheless, something appealing about an approach so modest and direct as this. It seems likely to produce a real minimum of pretentious theoretical speculation and a maximum of relevant investigation to link with the theoretical statements advanced. Thus, although such an approach to the creation of a general theory of the instrument may seem long and forbidding, the path is much more clearly marked and perhaps more likely to lead to fruitful consequences than most, if not all, of the paths we have mapped thus far.

The Movement Response

There have been various attempts to isolate special types of response to projective tests and to subject them to a concerted theoretical-empirical analysis, and perhaps the best example of this approach is provided by studies of the Movement response (M) on the Rorschach test. Commencing with Rorschach (1921) himself, observers have consistently given this response a central role in the interpretation of the test. Some have even concluded with Piotrowski (1957) that the M response is the most important of all aspects of Rorschach response. Kinesthetic or Movement responses are defined by Rorschach (1921) as those where ". . . visual memories of movements observed, imagined or executed previously . . . have had a determining influence in addition to the consciousness of the form of the blot" (p. 22).

Most of Rorschach's own efforts were devoted to reporting empirical correlates of the M response and the ratio of Movement responses to Color responses, but he provided virtually no rationale for the empirical observations he reported. The most important of his generalizations concerns the relation between M responses and "inner life" and the particular type of M response and general personality characteristics. He suggests that a high incidence of M responses is indicative of a tendency toward productive intelligence and active associative processes and a high ratio of M responses to Color responses is indicative of a tendency to turn in upon one's self, or choose an inner life rather than a mode of adjustment emphasizing relations to the outer world. Furthermore, M responses may be seen as involving either flexion or extension, and Rorschach indicates that "Subjects who usually see extension movements are fundamentally different from those who see only bent, burdened, or twisted figures. . . . Subjects who see extension movements are active individuals with strong drive toward self-assertion, though they often show neurotic inhibitions. Those who see flexion movements are passive, resigned, neurasthenic individuals" (p. 29).

These important empirical generalizations by Rorschach have guided users of his test for almost four decades, but until quite recently there have been very few attempts to provide a theoretical account of this relationship. The two exceptions are papers by Furrer

(1925) and Binder (1932), the contents of which have been briefly summarized by Schachtel (1950). Furrer proposes that the *M* responses are derivatives of actual or symbolic movements that represent indirect satisfactions of unexpressed drives, particularly sexual drives. He suggests that the sexual drives are denied overt expression and are consequently given substitute expression in the form of overt acts such as play and that finally this process leads to fantasy expression of these actions. The Movement response on the Rorschach represents one instance of such fantasy expression of denied motor actions. Schachtel suggests that although the emphasis in this analysis is upon sexual drives, Furrer is willing to accept the Movement response as indicative generally of drives or "attitudes toward the world." Binder accepts Furrer's account and goes on to propose that presentation of the blot activates motor tendencies linked with drive states and that the individual then perceives the blot in such a manner that his motor tendencies are projected upon the blot.

Rapaport (1945) has adopted the view that Movement responses occur in connection with the perception of "unbalanced material." That is, when the subject arrives at a percept which is assymetrical, unbalanced, or of poor proportion, there is a general tendency to reorganize the perceptual field to achieve better balance or a "good Gestalt." This tendency toward reorganization is experienced as the Movement response. Because the subject reports the response to be partially determined by movement does not mean he actually experienced a kinesthetic sensation at the time of the percept. For Rapaport, response to a projective technique involves both a perceptual process and an associative process and the existence of *M* responses suggests the richness and flexibility of both of these processes. The *M* response is also indicative of the capacity of the person to delay direct expression of impulses and thus provides an index of ego strength and the capacity for thought.

Heinz Werner (1945), who is well known for his sensory-tonic theory of perception (Wapner & Werner, 1957; Werner, 1948), has presented an analysis of the Movement response in which he cites considerable empirical evidence suggesting an opposition between the perception of movement and physical motility. He also has attempted to show the consistency of this finding with Rorschach's empirical generalizations as well as with important assumptions in sensory-tonic theory. Werner suggests a distinction between various types of perceived motion: *real motion* (perception of an object continuously changing its position); *stroboscopic motion* (motion perceived from discontinuous movement of an object in space, as in the case of two lines alternately exposed which are in different spatial positions); *illusory motion* (apparent movement of stationary objects as in the autokinetic effect); and *empathic movement* (impression of movement in stationary object but with no sense of object being displaced, as in the Rorschach Movement response). Studies that Werner and others have carried out indicate an opposition or contrast between motility or hyperactivity and the capacity for stroboscopic, illusory, and emphatic motion perception.

Werner suggests that it has been typical for psychologists to treat sensory functions as independent of motor processes but that in actuality they are heavily interdependent. In his words, "A common dynamic property binds both sensory and motor processes. This common factor is, most probably, tonicity" (1945, p. 325). Further, he reasons that "Available tonic energy may either be released through body movement, or may increase tonicity in a sensory area, bringing about spatial displacement and illustory motion." (1945, p. 325) It is worth noting that this assumption of a shared energic basis of motor and perceptual activity has been central to a theoretical position that has led Werner and his associates to a rich variety of investigations, most of which have produced confirmatory findings.

Generally considered the most important contribution to a theoretical understanding of the *M* response is a paper by Schachtel (1950) which is one of a series of papers (1941, 1943, 1945, 1950) providing a detailed examination of elements of Rorschach response. In this essay he links the Movement response to the process of projection and attempts to show why such responses should have the diverse psychological significance that most Rorschach investigators attribute to them. Schachtel emphasizes that all of the determinants of the Rorschach scoring system (Form, Color, Movement) involve ways of relating to objects in the outer world. Thus, to understand the *M* response one must understand the type of object relationship which leads to, or is reflected in, this type of perception. This object relationship may be understood only after an examination of the perceptual experience involved in seeing this particular determinant in the Rorschach. The key to understanding this perceptual process is the mechanism of projection which, for Schachtel, is an unconscious process, although its results (the qualities attributed to the outer world) may or may not be conscious.

In the case of the Movement response, inhibited movements or kinesthetic sensations are projected upon the blot. This response is "purely projected," since the blot is, of course, completely stationary and any tendency toward movement must be provided by the perceiver. According to Schachtel (1950), the projection of kinesthetic sensations is particularly important:

Since kinesthetic sensations are the only way in which man has direct, inner, physical experience of himself and his characteristic movements, postures, and tensions, they are deeply and intimately connected with the central layers of the personality. In kinesthetic perception the subject, stimulated by the perception of the object, projects *his* sensation of movement or posture onto the object, thereby establishing a type of relatedness in which he may feel inside of himself the movement or posture seen in the object. (p. 99).

In view of the crucial nature of these kinesthetic sensations and the tendency to project them into external objects, it is not surprising that kinesthetic or Movement responses often reveal the basic attitudes of the perceiver. Not only his tendency toward activity and passivity, which, as we have seen, Rorschach considered related to extensor and flexor movements, but any important attitude or quality may be reflected in the particular type of movement perceived. In other words, Schachtel suggests that the Movement response is important because it represents a projection of kinesthetic sensations which, in turn, are involved in the person's most intimate and characteristic self-perceptions.

A recent volume by Piotrowski (1957) elaborates earlier assertions by the author (Piotrowski, 1937) emphasizing, contrary to Rorschach's views, the *consistency* between overt response and the *M* response. Where Rorschach saw *M* responses as indicative of inner life and inhibited movements or overt responses, Piotrowski considers the *M* response indicative of the individual's major overt patterns of adjustment. He considers the *M* response sensitive to ". . . a real tendency which exercises a direct although not an exclusive control over overt behavior . . . a steering mechanism which directs the individual to play certain definite roles in those interhuman relationships that are vital to him; the *M* (responses) determine external conduct directly or indirectly but always materially and, therefore, are accessible to direct observation in the external motor behavior of the subject . . ." (1957, p. 141).

Piotrowski also suggests that the appearance of M is dependent upon an understanding of human relationships, and consequently, it is not present in the earliest years of childhood. Furthermore, the existence of a large number of M responses indicates a very keen awareness of the nature of interpersonal relations, and related to this is Piotrowski's generalization: "An intimate, intense, and lasting harmonious relationship between persons differing markedly in the numbers of their M seems impossible." (p. 181) He feels that the development of M responses takes place only when the person has discovered that satisfactory interpersonal relations do not follow automatically from spontaneous or direct expression of motives and impulses. Thus, the development of this capacity is dependent upon some interference or frustration in important interpersonal relations, particularly those involving the mother and father. Piotrowski suggests that the child's effort to arrive at a stable and satisfactory relationship with his mother and father develops consistent and stable views of the world and means of relating to these figures, which Piotrowski refers to as prototypal roles because of their pervasive impact and significance. The M response is a particularly sensitive indicator of these maternal and paternal roles, particularly when they are characterized by self-assertion, compliance, and indecisiveness.

A series of investigations by Singer and his associates (Meltzoff, Singer, & Korchin, 1953; Singer, Meltzoff, & Goldman, 1952; Singer & Spohn, 1954) have provided empirical evidence supporting some of the theoretical contentions we have just examined. Their research has centered about the behavioral correlates of the Movement response, and in addition to their empirical work, they have attempted to show the consistency of Rorschach's ideas and their findings with Werner's sensory-tonic theory. Their studies revealed that various states of motor inhibition (writing a short phrase as slowly as possible or remaining motionless in an awkward position) in normal subjects tended to produce an increase in M responses on the Rorschach. In a group of schizophrenics those subjects with a high ratio of M responses to Color responses consistently showed a longer inhibition time in a writing task and less activity in a free response situation. Thus, these findings tend to support Rorschach's statements concerning the negative association between Movement responses and overt action as well as to confirm derivations from Werner's theory.

These attempts to provide a theoretical foundation for the M response have the advantage of sharply reducing the amount of empirical data with which the theorist must cope, but thus far they have produced little in the way of a simplification of theoretical statements. The theoretical formulations still seem to be ad hoc rather than systematic, and they are by no means consistent. On the other hand, some of the formulations do suggest clear empirical consequences and in certain cases these consequences have been tested. There seems little doubt that further development of theory and research in connection with this single dimension of response would have important implications for a general theory of projective techniques. Moreover, the achievement of such a limited goal seems well within our present resources.

ASSUMPTIONS IMPLIED BY CUSTOMARY INTERPRETATION OF PROJECTIVE TECHNIQUES

Here we are concerned with an attempt to provide a theoretical statement that is adequate to encompass all of the major findings and practices in projective testing and is focussed primarily upon the projective techniques rather than upon a general theory of behavior or upon some special theory developed in another realm of psychology. We might consider it an effort to develop a minimum or *status quo* theory of projective techniques.

It is evident that the current state of projective testing militates against any completely satisfactory presentation of a set of underlying assumptions from which can be deduced all the procedural steps employed routinely in the use of these techniques. However, there is certainly no harm, and there might be some benefit, in attempting this feat. Such an enterprise is interesting not only because it provides one measure of how rational and consistent current practice is, but also because it might eventually provide a means of embracing and unifying a number of devices that hitherto have been treated as relatively independent. Furthermore, the outcome of such an approach should certainly emphasize the continuity between general psychological theory and investigation and projective testing.

It might even provide eventually the basis for a more effective link between projective techniques and existing psychological theory than do current attempts to bring about such a union by direct methods.

Although the following statements are generally treated as assumptions or "givens," in the process of interpreting projective techniques, there is considerable empirical evidence that can be used to support some of these assumptions. Space limitations make it impossible for us to examine such evidence here, although the interested reader will find an array of relevant evidence for a similar set of assumptions specific to the TAT in a paper by Lindzey (1952). It will be clear to the reader that each assumption could be greatly amplified (with exceptions, special considerations, definition of terms, and so on) but here we shall limit ourself to brief over-all statements.

The most general assumption underlying projective testing is:

If an individual is presented with a stimulus situation permitting variable responses, the particular responses he emits will reflect his characteristic response patterns and tendencies to response.

It is further assumed that:

If the response alternatives are relatively unlimited, a wider range of response tendencies will be revealed than would be possible if the alternatives were narrowly restricted.

Beyond this:

If the response setting is divorced from the customary constraints of reality, it may be possible to assess not only those response tendencies which are known to the subject and that he is willing to admit but also those he is unwilling to admit and those of which he is not even aware.

At this point we have simply a small set of assumptions implying that what an individual will do in a free response setting largely divorced from reality is partly determined by his characteristic response tendencies—both those of which he is aware and those of which he is unaware. Not all of the subject's behavior in the test situation is determined by these response tendencies, however, and we customarily encounter at this point a set of assumptions concerned with the various other conditions or factors that determine the subject's test response. These may be referred to as variance-contributing factors, and the task of the interpreter is, of course, to correctly link the responses to their underlying classes of factors or conditions.

The particular response alternatives emitted are determined not only by enduring dispositions or motives but also by intervening processes such as the individual's defenses and his cognitive style.
Although the test interpreter is ordinarily interested almost exclusively in the class of events or variables we have just described (motives and controlling processes), he usually is willing to admit that the test response is also influenced by some or all of the following factors.

The response alternatives produced or selected are determined in part by: (a) temporary affective and dispositional states (for example, annoyance, frustration, elation, sadness); (b) ability and performance factors (for example, general intelligence, verbal facility); (c) stimulus factors (for example, color, size, content, shading); and (d) response sets (for example, speed, accuracy, conformity).

All of these factors operate directly to determine the nature of the subject's responses, but there is a further class of determinants that operates indirectly or through the mediation of one or more of these processes.

The definition that the subject assigns to the testing situation (its meaning for him) serves to influence the operation of response sets as well as temporary affective and dispositional states.

This is an assumption that admits the psychological variability of objectively standard stimulus conditions. This variability in the perception of the testing situation is, in part, attributable to known determinants.

The definition of the test situation is influenced by such factors as: (a) the relation between the examiner and the subject which in turn is influenced by the personality of the examiner; (b) the physical setting in which the test is administered; (c) the immediate past life experience of the subject; (d) the test-relevant past experience of the subject; (e) various procedural factors such as the instructions accompanying the administration of the test.

A further closely related assumption is that:

The significant groups to which an individual has belonged (social class, ethnic group, culture) will influence the interpretation he will make of the testing situation and will also have something to do with the particular achievement or performance factors that characterize the subject.

We now see that the responses produced by the subject in the test situation are, in part, determined by factors of considerable interest to the psychological investigator. Unfortunately we see with equal clarity that these responses are heavily overdetermined and that many factors of little interest to the typical interpreter play a role in response determination. Thus, there is still an ominous gap between the subject's test responses and a set of specific statements concerning his characteristic response tendencies or personality, and there is plentiful opportunity for error on the part of the unwary in the inference process. In the effort to provide some means of going from the subject's often voluminous responses to specified inferences concerning his motives or response tendencies, it is typically assumed that:

There is a direct or isomorphic relation between the subject's responses in the test situation and his characteristic behavior, that is, those responses or motives directly acted out or clearly implied in the test situation also exist as behavior tendencies in the subject's ordinary life.

The situation is more complicated than this, however, as:

Certain formal, noncontent, or stylistic regularities in test response are related to the subject's characteristic behavior tendencies, in spite of a lack of isomorphy or evident meaningful relation between the test response and the predicted behavior; for example, movement responses may indicate a rich inner life or the ratio of verbs to adjectives may be related to obsessional tendencies.

The complications are only beginning to appear, for:

The subject's characteristic response tendencies are sometimes reflected indirectly or symbolically in the response alternatives selected or created in the test situation.

To add still another complication:

An absence of responses that seem appropriate to, or are characteristically emitted in, a particular stimulus situation may indicate the importance or existence of these omitted response tendencies in the subject's everyday life.

At last we find a few simplifying assumptions:

Those responses elicited or produced under a variety of different stimulus conditions are particularly likely to mirror important aspects of the subject.

A further clue as to the most significant areas of response is provided by the assumption that:

Test responses that do not seem particularly called for by the stimulus situation are more likely to reflect important characteristics of the subject than those responses that are clearly appropriate to the stimulus material.

In very much the same vein, it is customary to assume that:

Responses that deviate from those typically made by other subjects in this situation are more likely to reveal important characteristics of the subject than responses much like those made by most other subjects.

Not only is it important to compare the subject's responses with the responses of others but also with other responses he himself has displayed, for:

Responses that differ markedly from the responses that the same subject has made to similar situations are likely to be more significant than responses which closely resemble those that he has made to other situations.

It may appear that there is a logical conflict between this assumption and the earlier assumption of the importance of consistent responses to different stimuli. Actually this assumption is intended to identify areas of disturbance or affective arousal and generally is applied only under circumstances where there has been some degree of stability of response across stimuli to provide a basis for identifying a deviant response.

A further technique for isolating the most important response elements is the assumption:

Responses that seem to imply primitive, nonlogical, or bizarre approaches to the stimulus situation are more likely to reflect important or significant characteristics than those that clearly comply to logical or rational principles of thought or association.

This is about as far as convention will take us, and it is clear that we are still a long way short of our goal of being able to derive specific interpretive rules. It is true that most such rules are more or less clearly related to one of the above assumptions, but this is a weak and unsatisfactory type of contiguity. Let us then ask the significant question, what further assumptions would be necessary in order for us to descend from our still rather abstract level to the specific level of concrete test interpretation?

First of all, we need an assumption concerning:

When are responses to be interpreted directly and when are they to be interpreted symbolically or indirectly? We have already seen that there is commonly assumed to be an isomorphic relationship between the acts or impulses expressed in the projective-technique responses and the subject's own tendencies or motives. However, we have also learned that there is sometimes an indirect or symbolic relation between the content of the projective-technique response and the underlying tendency of the subject. Clearly, we need a set of principles to guide us as to when we are to make a literal or direct translation and when we are to search for a latent or hidden significance. There are, of course, a number of contributions that provide some insight into this dilemma, with Freud's (1911) distinction between the primary process and the secondary process representing an important beginning on the road to formulating these principles.

This assumption by itself, is not enough, for we must also have an assumption (or set of assumptions) concerning:

How are symbolic transformations to be performed so as to recover the latent or hidden significance of the response? A great deal of psychoanalysis, of course, has been concerned with just this issue, and Freud's (1900) treatment of the dream work and the process of reconstructing the latent content from the manifest content provides an excellent beginning to the solution of this problem. However, there are few who would contend that we are even close to a clear specification of a set of assumptions designed to take us from symbol to referent.

Further, it is necessary to provide an assumption indicating:

When are behavioral tendencies (motives) to be linked to public, private, or unconscious areas of response? We have seen that there is virtually complete agreement among projective testers that responses elicited by these devices reflect not only covert or private tendencies, but also conscious and public aspects of behavior. Given this state of multidetermination, the interpreter must have some set of principles to guide him in linking his inferences to the appropriate level of behavior. This problem is obviously related to the matter of when symbolic transformations are needed, but it is considerably more general, for it is not only in the case of symbolic interpretations that the material revealed is unconscious or private.

A fourth missing assumption would tell us:

How to distinguish between responses that reflect temporary instigations as opposed to those that reflect enduring dispositions. Although the user of projective techniques is typically interested primarily or solely in dispositions, or enduring personality qualities, we have seen that most would agree that these devices also reflect situational tendencies and fleeting states. Thus, in order to arrive at appropriate interpretations, the test interpreter should have some set of rules for choosing between those tendencies that are of only passing or temporary significance and those that are a continuing part of the subject's psychological make-up.

Finally, we need one or more assumptions to guide us in:

Assessing the defensive or controlling mechanisms that operate to influence the expression of drive states or enduring dispositions. If we accept the common assumption that defenses or other mechanisms operate to control the expression of drives or motives, we clearly need some means of assessing or interpreting the role of these factors. As we have seen, there has been considerable attention directed upon this problem, the most impressive instance of which is Schafer's (1954a) discussion of the Rorschach test and the mechanisms of defense. However, again we must conclude that there is no agreed-upon set of principles that can be applied to projective techniques generally.

It is clear that even with these additional assumptions there is still an important gap in the interpretive process which can be filled only when we have provided: a set of specific *empirical definitions* (to show what is meant, for instance, when a response is said to be "bizarre" or "intimately tied to the stimulus material."); *appropriate norms* to permit a reasonable answer to questions concerning how most subjects do, in fact, respond to a given stimulus; and a more or less general *set of specified relationships between formal test characteristics and psychological qualities of the storyteller.*

As the reader will have noted, it would be wrong to suggest that we have no information concerning what we should assume in regard to each of these issues. Actually, there is much relevant information, some of it based upon considerable evidence and fortified by theoretical considerations. Nevertheless, in none of these cases does there seem to be a sufficiently clear basis for agreement among persons working with various projective techniques to permit even a tentative assumptive solution to the problem.

The preceding statement of normative assumptions which underly customary projective-technique interpretation leaves us with several clear impressions. First, it is evident that projective techniques are not completely rationalized and that a considerable gap remains between the act of interpretation and a single coherent set of assumptions or underlying principles. Second, the numerous assumptions that can be made explicit share important features with a good many psychological theories. It would be an easy task, for example, to demonstrate that many of the assumptions we have stated are similar to, or identical with, elements of psychoanalytic theory. Third, there are substantial areas of assumptive similarity or agreement shared by virtually all projective techniques. This agreement suggests that there are indeed important underlying similarities in these instruments and that, consequently, the goal of an integrative theory may not be unattainable.

A GENERAL APPRAISAL OF THE
RELATION BETWEEN PSYCHOLOGICAL THEORY
AND PROJECTIVE TECHNIQUES

What is the significance of all this for the general relation between projective techniques and psychological theory? Can we provide a summary statement indicating just how successfully these two domains have been integrated? Can we say anything about the relative merit or promise of the various approaches we have examined?

The over-all relation between psychological theory and projective techniques is easy to describe. These realms are neither alien nor are they on intimate terms. There is no doubt that a great deal of customary projective-technique interpretation is highly congruent with the major assumptions of important psychological theories. For example, the principle concepts of systems such as psychoanalysis and stimulus-response theory can be brought readily into some kind of relationship with important elements of projective-technique response and interpretation. Moreover, special theories such as those developed in conjunction with perceptual data also appear to be generally congruent with conceptions and procedures of the projective tester. Even our statement of the assumptions underlying projective tests makes clear that these derived assumptions share much with various currently popular psychological theories, and there is little in these statements to conflict with most such theories.

So much for the positive evidence; what of the negative? At no place have we found a coherent, explicit, and illuminating statement bringing together any acceptable psychological theory and practice and findings in projective testing. Even the attempts to relate psychoanalytic theory, the intellectual father of most projective techniques, have been relatively fragmentary and more stimulating than systematic. In part this is a matter of intention. None of the major figures in this area has set himself the task of providing such a systematic integration. Clearly, Rapaport and Schafer are responsible for the best examples of such synthesis, and they have either not considered a detailed and comprehensive approach worthwhile or have felt that the present state of psychoanalytic theory and projective testing militates against the success of such an effort. In general, those expositions that have been theoretically most explicit, for example those of Goss and Brownell, have been most precariously related to projective techniques and have provided the least illumination of interpretive practices. Even the array of underlying assumptions in projective techniques leaves us considerably short of a theoretical foundation giving reasonably explicit principles for interpreting projective techniques.

It seems clear, then, that we cannot at present imply that projective techniques may be justified because of their close association with powerful psychological theories. Although they are generally congruent with one or more of the most influential of such theories, this relationship is too weak and nonspecific to permit one to use it as a compelling reason for why these devices work or are to be preferred over alternative measures. Having pointed this out, we must hasten to add that this less than exact meeting of the two areas is by no means solely attributable to shortcomings in projective testing or even in the competence or interest of individuals who have carried out such analyses. The simple truth of the matter is that both stimulus-response theory and psychoanalytic theory themselves possess flaws that make any exact linking of the substantive area and the theory extremely difficult. One could even go a step further and question whether the demonstrated utility of these psychological theories is sufficient to make a careful linking of procedure with theory much of an advantage in any case. Although the query is a reasonable one, this is scarcely the place to pursue such a question, and it may suffice simply to assert that whatever the flaws of these theories, they are commonly accepted by psychologists as possessing some capacity to provide license or indicate merit among empirical devices or domains of inquiry. Therefore, a mapping of technique into psychological theory must be considered by customary standards a worthwhile goal.

We may generalize, then, that there is considerable congruence between common interpretive practice and various theoretical vantages. Whether we attempt to provide a set of normative assumptions, turn to related areas of investigation and formulation, or examine systematic theoretical positions, it appears that much of what the projective tester does is rational and consistent with explicit theoretical formulations. However, equally clear is the definite gap between many of the specific interpretive acts that form a part of the projective tester's repertoire and the comforting background of theory. It would be unfair to conclude from our discussion that the interpretation of projective tests is contradictory to psychological theory —the fact is, let us repeat, that it is generally congruent! On the other hand, it would be equally unfair to conclude that any theory provides a clear and definite rationale for these tests and their application.

What of the promise of the various avenues of integration we have discussed? Although no definitive conclusions can be reached, it does seem that some of these approaches are more appealing than others. As we have already indicated, the building of *miniature theories* concerned with particular types of response or particular empirical relations seems in many ways a more attainable and less grandiose approach than most of the other avenues. Certainly this type of enterprise deserves to be continued. The contributions of *perceptual theory* to an understanding of projective techniques appear at this point to have been limited, and interest in this form of integration has diminished. Consequently, it is probably reasonable to view this approach as less promising than the other alternatives. The attempt to ferret out the *assumptions* implicit in the present use of projective techniques is an interesting exercise in soul searching and should have the healthy effect of leading to a more earnest attempt to make explicit that which is now implicit. Furthermore, it has the modest merit of identifying areas in which necessary assumptions are not agreed upon and, thus, point to important problems for investigation and formulation. In regard to *systematic theory* and projective techniques, it seems clear that developments on both sides are necessary before a smooth fit can be reasonably expected. Nonetheless, something more can be done in this area than has thus far been attempted. The stimulating work of Schafer and Rapaport could certainly be extended by someone who set himself the self-conscious task of exploring carefully, *systematically, and explicitly* the relations between psychoanalytic theory and projective tests. Both historically and substantively, psychoanalysis has had such an intimate association with projective techniques that further exploration of this sort seems likely to prove rewarding. At present there is less basis for optimism about the probable outcome of efforts to link stimulus-response theory and projective techniques.

In conclusion, projective techniques are congruent with much of psychological theory, but they are not carefully mapped into any existing theory. Utilization of such techniques cannot be justified by means of the theoretical cogency or warrant of these instruments. The process of carefully linking technique with theory remains a task for the future.

REFERENCES

ABT, L. E. A theory of projective psychology. In L. E. Abt & L. Bellak (Eds.), *Projective psychology: clinical approaches to the total personality.* New York: Knopf, 1950. Pp. 33-66.

ATKINSON, J. W. Exploration using imaginative thought to assess the strength of human motives. In M. R. Jones (Ed.), *Nebraska symposium on motivation, 1954.* Lincoln: Univer. of Nebraska Press, 1954. Pp. 56-112.

ATKINSON, J. W., (Ed.) *Motives in fantasy, action, and society.* Princeton: Van Nostrand, 1958a.

ATKINSON, J. W. Thematic apperceptive measurement of motives within the context of a theory of motivation. In J. W. Atkinson (Ed.), *Motives in fantasy, action, and society.* Princeton: Van Nostrand, 1958b. Pp. 596-616.

AULD, F. Contributions of behavior theory to projective techniques. *J. proj. Tech.,* 1954, 18, 421-426.

BINDER, H. *Die Helldunkel deutungen im psychodiagnostichen Experiment von Rorschach.* Zurich: Art Inst. Orell Fuessli, 1932.

BLAKE, R. R., & WILSON, G. P., Jr. Perceptual selectivity in Rorschach determinants as a function of depressive tendencies. *J. abn, soc. Psychol.,* 1950, 45, 459-472.

BLUM, G. S. A study of the psychoanalytic theory of psychosexual development. *Genet. Psychol. Monogr.,* 1949, 39, 3-99.

BROWNELL, Marjorie H., & Goss, A. E. Stimulus-response analysis of inferences from projective test behavior. *J. Pers.*, 1957, 25, 525-538.

BRUNER, J. S. IV. Perceptual theory and the Rorschach Test. *J. Pers.*, 1948, 17, 157-168.

DEUTSCH, M. Field theory and projective techniques. *J. proj. Tech.*, 1954, 18, 427-434.

ERIKSEN, C. W. Some implications for TAT interpretation arising from need and perception experiments. *J. Pers.*, 1951, 19, 282-288.

ERIKSEN, C. W. Needs in perception and projective techniques. *J. proj. Tech.*, 1954, 18, 435-440.

ERIKSEN, C. W., & LAZARUS, R. S. Perceptual defense and projective tests. *J. abn. soc. Psychol.*, 1952, 47, 302-308.

FREUD, S. The interpretation of dreams. In J. Strachey (Ed.), *The complete psychological works of Sigmund Freud.* Vols. 4 & 5. London: Hogarth, 1953. (Originally published in 1900.)

FREUD, S. Formulations on the two principles of mental functioning. In J. Strachey (Ed.), *The complete psychological works of Sigmund Freud.* Vol. 12. London: Hogarth, 1958. Pp. 218-226. (Originally published in 1911.) Pp. 13-21.

FURRER, A. Über die Bedeutung der 'B' im Rorschachschen Versuch. *Imago*, 1925, 11, 58-83.

GEORGE, C. E., & BONNEY, W. C. Rorschach's affect-color hypothesis and adaptation-level theory. *Psychol. Rev.*, 1956, 63, 294-298.

GOSS, A. E., & BROWNELL, Marjorie H. Stimulus-response concepts and principles applied to projective test behavior. *J. Pers.*, 1957, 25, 505-523.

HANFMANN, Eugenia. William Stern on "Projective Techniques." *J. Pers.*, 1952, 21, 1-21.

HOLT, R. R. Implications of some contemporary personality theories for Rorschach rationale. In B. Klopfer, Mary D. Ainsworth, W. G. Klopfer, & R. R. Holt, *Developments in the Rorschach Technique.* Vol. 1. *Technique and theory.* New York: Harcourt, Brace & World, 1954. Pp. 501-560.

HOLZBERG, J. The relevance of personality theory for projective methods. *J. proj. Tech.*, 1954, 18, 418-420.

JESSOR, R., & HAMMOND, K. R. Construct validity and the Taylor Anxiety Scale. *Psychol. Bull.*, 1957, 54, 161-170.

KAGAN, J. The measurement of overt aggression from fantasy. *J. abn. soc. Psychol.*, 1956, 52, 390-393.

KLOPFER, B. Rorschach hypotheses and ego psychology. In B. Klopfer, Mary D. Ainsworth, W. G. Klopfer, & R. R. Holt, *Developments in the Rorschach Technique.* Vol. 1. *Technique and theory.* New York: Harcourt, Brace & World, 1954. Pp. 561-598.

Kris, E. *Psychoanalytic explorations in art.* New York: International Universities Press, 1952.

Lesser, G. S. The relationship between overt and fantasy aggression as a function of maternal response to aggression. *J. abn. soc. Psychol.*, 1957, 55, 218-221.

Lindzey, G. Thematic Apperception Test: interpretive assumptions and related empirical evidence. *Psychol. Bull.*, 1952, 49, 1-25.

Loevinger, Jane. Objective tests as instruments of psychological theory. *Psychol. Reports*, 1957, 3, 635-694.

McClelland, D. C. Some social consequences of achievement motivation. In M. R. Jones (Ed.), *Nebraska symposium on motivation, 1955.* Lincoln: Univer. of Nebraska Press, 1955. Pp. 41-65.

McClelland, D. C., Atkinson, J. W., Clark, R. A., & Lowell, E. L. *The achievement motive.* New York: Appleton-Century-Crofts, 1953.

Meltzoff, J., Singer, J. L., & Korchin, S. J. Motor inhibition and Rorschach movement responses: a test of the sensory-tonic theory. *J. Pers.*, 1953, 21, 400-410.

Miller, N. E. Comments on theoretical models: illustrated by the development of a theory of conflict behavior. *J. Pers.*, 1951, 20, 82-100.

Murray, H. A. *Thematic Apperception Test Manual.* Cambridge: Harvard Univer. Press, 1943.

Murstein, B. I. A conceptual model of projective techniques applied to stimulus variations with thematic techniques. *J. consult. Psychol.*, 1959, 23, 3-14.

Mussen, P. H., & Naylor, H. K. The relationships between overt and fantasy aggression. *J. abn. soc. Psychol.*, 1954, 49, 235-240.

Piotrowski, Z. A. The M, FM, and m responses as indicators of changes in personality. *Rorschach Res. Exch.*, 1937, 1, 148-156.

Piotrowski, Z. A. *Perceptanalysis: a fundamentally reworked, expanded, and systematized Rorschach Method.* New York: Macmillan, 1957.

Rapaport, D. *Emotions and memory.* New York: International Universities Press, 1950.

Rapaport, D. Principles underlying projective techniques. *Character & Pers.*, 1942, 10, 213-219.

Rapaport, D. (with Roy Schafer) The Rorschach Test: a clinical evaluation. *Bull. Menninger Clin.*, 1945, 9, 73-77.

Rapaport, D. Principles underlying non-projective tests of personality. *Ann. N.Y. Acad. Sci.*, 1946, 46, 643-652.

Rapaport, D. Psychological testing: its practical and its heuristic significance. *Samiksa J. Indian Psycho-Analyt. Soc.*, 1947, 1, 245-262.

Rapaport, D. On the psychoanalytic theory of thinking. *Int. J. Psychoanal.*, 1950, 31, 161-170.

RAPAPORT, D. The theoretical implications of diagnostic testing procedures. *Int. Cong. Psychiat. Reports*, 1950, 2, 241-271.

RAPAPORT, D. The autonomy of the ego. *Bull. Menninger Clinic*, 1951*a*, 15, 113-123.

RAPAPORT, D., (Ed.) *Organization and pathology of thought*. New York: Columbia Univer. Press, 1951*b*.

RAPAPORT, D. Projective techniques and the theory of thinking. *J. proj. Tech.*, 1952, 16, 269-275.

RAPAPORT, D. On the psychoanalytic theory of affects. *Int. J. Psychoanal.*, 1953, 34, 177-198.

RAPAPORT, D. The theory of ego autonomy: a generalization. *Bull. Menninger Clinic*, 1958, 22, 13-35.

RAPAPORT, D., GILL, M., & SCHAFER, R. *Diagnostic psychological testing: the theory, statistical evaluation and diagnostic application of a battery of tests*. Vol. 1. Chicago: Year Book Publishers, 1945.

RAPAPORT, D., GILL, M., & SCHAFER, R. *Diagnostic psychological testing: the theory, statistical evaluation and diagnostic application of a battery of tests*. Vol. 2. Chicago: Year Book Publishers, 1946.

ROGERS, C. R. *Client-centered therapy: its current practice, implications, and theory*. Boston: Houghton-Mifflin, 1951.

RORSCHACH, H. *Psychodiagnostics: a diagnostic test based on perception*. (4th ed.) New York: Grune & Stratton, 1942. (Originally published in 1921.)

RORSCHACH, H., & OBERHOLZER, E. The application of the form interpretation test. In H. Rorschach, *Psychodiagnostics: a diagnostic test based on perception*. (4th ed.) New York: Grune & Stratton, 1942. (Originally published in 1921.) Pp. 184-216.

SANFORD, R. N., ADKINS, Margaret M., MILLER, R. B., & COBB, Elizabeth A. Physique, personality and scholarship. *Monogr. Soc. Res. Child Develop.*, 1943, 8, No. 34.

SCHACHTEL, E. G. On color and affect: Contributions to an understanding of Rorschach's test, II. *Psychiat.*, 1943, 6, 393-409.

SCHACHTEL, E. G. The dynamic perception and the symbolism of form with special reference to the Rorschach test. *Psychiat.*, 1941, 4, 79-96.

SCHACHTEL, E. G. Subjective definitions of the Rorschach test situation and their effect on test performance: Contributions to an understanding of Rorschach's test, III. *Psychiat.*, 1945, 8, 419-448.

SCHACHTEL, E. G. Projection and its relation to character attitudes and creativity in the kinesthetic responses: Contributions to an understanding of Rorschach's test, IV. *Psychiat.*, 1950, 13, 69-100.

SCHAFER, R., & RAPAPORT, D. The scatter in diagnostic intelligence testing. *Character & Pers.*, 1944, 12, 275-284.

SCHAFER, R. *Psychoanalytic interpretation in Rorschach testing: theory and application.* New York: Grune & Stratton, 1954a.

SCHAFER, R. Some applications of contemporary psychoanalytic theory to projective testing. *J. proj. Tech.*, 1954b, 18, 441-448.

SINGER, J. L., MELTZOFF, J., & GOLDMAN, G. D. Rorschach movement responses following motor inhibition and hyperactivity. *J. consult. Psychol.*, 1952, 16, 359-364.

SINGER, J. L., & SPOHN, H. E. Some behavioral correlates of Rorschach's experience-type. *J. consult. Psychol.*, 1954, 18, 1-9.

WAPNER, S., & WERNER, H. *Perceptual development.* Worcester, Mass.: Clark Univer. Press, 1957.

WERNER, H. Motion and motion perception: a study on vicarious functioning. *J. Psychol.*, 1945, 19, 317-327.

WERNER, H. *Comparative psychology of mental development.* (Rev. ed.) New York: Follett, 1948.

5. The Interpretive Process: Some Hazards and General Issues

We have now defined in general terms the nature of projective techniques, we have examined their theoretical underpinnings, and we have surveyed extensively, even if briefly, a wide array of these devices. Included in our discussion of the individual tests has been some consideration of the process whereby each is interpreted. It seems appropriate now to turn to whatever general remarks can be made regarding the interpretative process.

It will be obvious to the reader that this discussion must leave many questions unanswered. In fact, the most we can hope to accomplish in the space of the present chapter is to provide a viewpoint that, however helpful, will need to be supplemented and elaborated before it can be applied successfully to any specific technique. Our major intent is to caution the reader against certain shortcomings or flaws in interpretation often associated with these tests and to introduce briefly certain general issues. These few remarks can be effectively enriched by examining them against the background provided by one or more of the many treatises, identified in Chapter III, that deal with the specific details of analyzing projective test responses.

Although there are many ways in which the process of interpreting projective techniques can be represented, *our choice is to view it as an attempt to link variation in test performance to appropriate determinants or antecedent conditions.* Sensitive interpretation is a matter of correctly sorting out the considerable number of variance-contributing factors that underlie performance on a projective test. In other words, the responses to a projective test derive from a variety of different sources, and the analyst's task is to attach a specified response, or cluster of responses, to its underlying source. Obviously, for any particular analyst concerned with a particular problem, certain of these sources will represent only error variance, or variability that is of no significance or interest. The identification of such sources remains important if one is to be certain that the responses they determine are not used as the basis for unwarranted personality inferences.

In a highly general sense the process of mapping projective-technique responses into appropriate personality generalizations is no different than any other process of making inferences. In this case, the interpreter has, on the one hand, an array of qualitative data and, on the other hand, a set of dimensions or terms that may be used in describing personality. To bridge the gap between these two domains, he has at his disposal whatever power may be generated by the assumptions outlined in our earlier discussion of psychological theory and projective techniques, and he also has a number of highly specific interpretive rules (for example, Beck, 1944, 1945; Klopfer, Ainsworth, Klopfer, & Holt, 1954; Lindzey, Bradford, Tejessey, & Davids, 1959).

The simplest initial approach is to assume that the content revealed in the various protocols directly reflects personality attributes of the storyteller. If, for example, the responses reveal aggressive impulses, the storyteller is aggressive; if the responses are constrained and restricted, the storyteller is constrained and restricted. The task of the analyst then becomes little more than summarizing economically the variety of different reflections of motives or personality attributes provided by the test responses. If we accept such a tactic, we may treat any individual pattern of response as indicative of some isomorphic or corresponding personality syndrome and, similarly, any set of differences in response between two or more groups as deriving from differences in underlying personality attributes. Such an approach is typical of many, if not most, cross-cultural studies employing projective techniques.

Recollection of our earlier discussion of the general assumptions underlying interpretation of these tests makes clear that any such direct transformation of projective-technique response into personality attribute is not only hazardous, but inconsistent with most of what is known and believed concerning these devices. More specifically, it is generally agreed that responses to projective techniques are controlled by a variety of determinants, only a small number of which are likely to be of strategic interest to any single investigator. Thus, in part, projective-technique responses are determined by: temporary affective states, stimulus factors, response sets, ability and performance factors, definition of the testing situation, situational factors, and the relation between examiner and subject. At least as important as all of these specific determinants is the contribution of random or chance factors. Let us briefly discuss each of these determinants, beginning with the role of chance.

Whether we are considering the individual performance of a single subject on a particular projective test or examining group differences in response to one or more tests, it is obvious that some response elements must be related only to random or *chance factors*. Given the requirement that the respondent provide a set of responses to a particular stimulus, we can confidently expect that some proportion of the resultant responses will show no variation with any of the factors of interest to the psychological tester or personality analyst. That is, some of the responses will not be correlated with, or reflect, enduring motives, areas of conflict, characteristic defenses, modes of cognitive control, or similar attributes. In similar vein, one would not expect any two groups of subjects, no matter how psychologically similar they were, to provide *exactly* the same pattern of responses to projective tests.

One of the essential features of human performance is its variability, variability between individuals and variability within the same individual on successive occasions, and by no means all of this variability is to be assigned to real and important psychological differences or changes in the individual. In areas of behavior that have been carefully studied, findings clearly indicate an appreciable amount of response variation that is not linked to any significant determinant and is best understood as chance fluctuation. Consequently, before placing any heavy interpretive load upon a particular response, it is essential that the investigator consider seriously the possibility that what he has observed is no more than random or noninterpretable oscillation.

How is the analyst to winnow the meaningful and stable grain of his response data from the random chaff? In the case of group comparisons, most common in cross-cultural applications of projective tests, the typical method will necessitate transformation of the response data into some numerical form and the application of more or less conventional statistical techniques for testing distribution differences. Actually, as we shall see, most analysts have used some type of quantification in analyzing their projective-test protocols, so that the application of some variety of statistical reasoning is within the realm of possibility.

Where the analyst is concerned with the individual case, the application of statistical analysis is much more difficult, although under special circumstances and with a high degree of motivation and skill, it is possible. Ordinarily, however, the analyst can best protect himself against the sin of interpreting random phenomena by being consistently conservative in his inferences and using internal checks, or evidence of consistency from various response areas, before accepting a particular response element as indicative of a particular motive or personality attribute. Thus, if the investigator resists the temptation to base interpretations upon isolated response elements and seeks multiple supporting indices for his generalizations, he is not likely to end up with his case resting on random responses or chance fluctuations.

Let us assume the analyst has satisfied himself and the competent critic that the response phenomena on which he wishes to build a personality interpretation are not mere outgrowths of some random process. Even then he can be sure of his personality inference only after a number of further alternatives have been pursued.

First of all, there is the possibility that the response in which he is interested is no more than a product of a *temporary affective state* or a fleeting deprivation. In our discussion of interpretive assumptions we suggested that it is conventionally agreed that projective tests often mirror temporary or adventitious psychological states that may have little to do with the enduring motives or characteristic conflicts of the respondent. This is not solely a matter of belief; there is excellent empirical evidence demonstrating the co-variation of projective-technique responses with a variety of special states (Clark, 1952; Crandall, 1951; Lindzey & Herman, 1955; Lord, 1950; Pattie, 1954; Sanford, 1937; Shipley & Veroff, 1952; Singer, Meltzoff, & Goldman, 1952). Clearly the sophisticated investigator must consider carefully the possibility of unusual factors in the immediate past of his subjects that might generate emotions or motives not ordinarily characteristic of these persons but which would influence test response. Subjects tested in the midst of a famine might be expected to give evidence of oral needs that would not usually be present; those tested following some dire threat to their existence or some emotion-arousing ritual might be expected to respond to projective techniques in a manner suggesting affects or motives not representative of their usual state. Thus, before the investigator can make dependable infer-ences concerning the motivational structure of conflicts of his sub-jects, he must assure himself that at the time of testing they were not experiencing special or adventitious emotions and motives. We shall return in a moment to discuss certain classes of events that are par-ticularly significant or important in the production of temporary affective states.

Having disposed of random factors and temporary affective states as determiners of the response events to be interpreted, atten-tion might well be directed toward the role of *stimulus factors*. There is ample evidence from a variety of convincing sources (Kenny, 1954; Kenny & Bijou, 1953; Lindzey & Goldberg, 1953; Siipola, 1950) on the salient role played by stimulus factors in controlling and de-termining responses to projective techniques. This observation has a dual implication. First, we cannot safely assume that responses with a particular motivational content or stylistic quality are necessarily indicative of some personality attribute, for it may be that the par-ticular stimulus material elicits such responses regularly from most or all subjects. Second, if we wish to compare the performance of two groups, we must have stimulus constancy in order for the comparison to offer much promise of valid findings. Thus, the introduction of special sets of stimulus material for use in a particular culture cre-ates almost insurmountable problems for meaningful cross-cultural comparisons. Moreover, the use of such novel stimulus material creates problems for interpretation even within the target society. The specific interpretive rules associated with each test are often closely linked with the traditional stimulus material, and changes in the stimuli may at least impair, if not destroy, their validity.

Although stimulus constancy represents an important goal of the cross-cultural investigator, one must remember that the same ob-jective stimulus may not necessarily have the same value or meaning in different cultural settings. For example, employing TAT pictures that depict scenes involving clothing, housing, and equipment char-acteristic of Western European culture in a comparative study involving subjects from a Western European society and a nonliterate African society is not likely to provide for constancy across the two cultures in terms of the effective or perceived stimulus. Thus, in comparisons involving cultures that are dramatically different it may be necessary to avoid the use of stimulus material that has any specific cultural content in order for there to be any possibility of stimulus equivalence.

The wise investigator is therefore certain to assure himself of stimulus constancy when comparisons between groups are envisaged, and moreover, he is cautious about interpreting responses to projective-test stimuli when there is not a great deal of available information concerning the typical responses elicited by these stimuli. Finally, he is aware that maintaining constancy of the objective stimulus in different cultural settings does not guarantee constancy of the effective or perceived stimulus.

A further consideration of importance for the interpreter is the type of *response sets* with which his subjects have operated. Beginning with the work of Cronbach (1946), there have been many investigations demonstrating that performance on psychological tests, even highly structured instruments that permit little variation in response, is systematically influenced by the guiding set or intention of the subject. That is, some subjects may be oriented toward responding quickly, above all else, whereas others may be set toward accuracy or precision as their primary guiding principle. Still others may strive to attain originality, or quantity, or normality. This is not to imply that such sets are necessarily unrelated to underlying personality variables, although little is known concerning those personality links. Even granting such an association, however, the operation of these sets serves to influence and distort material used to provide inferences concerning quite distinct or unrelated psychological variables. For example, the subject who interprets his instructions as suggesting the essential importance of originality in TAT stories may, in the process of striving for originality, create stories that give unusual evidence of conflict, bizarreness, and primitive affect. A subject equally disturbed but not set so strongly toward originality would ordinarily produce stories that appeared much closer to the norm.

Consequently, the competent investigator is obliged to learn something about the set or sets with which his subjects approach the test. Particularly where cross-cultural comparisons are attempted, and where we might expect that different cultural patterns would lead to an emphasis upon quite different aspects of performance, this should be a matter of deep concern. It is altogether possible that marked cultural differences in the type of response elicited by projective techniques may be attributed not to personality differences between subjects but rather to differences in response set generated by distinct cultures.

Even if the analyst has disposed of all the factors we have considered thus far, he is still not faced with a clear interpretive path. There remain a number of further determinants to be considered, including *individual differences in ability or performance factors.* Again we have firm belief, as well as clear empirical findings (Altus & Thompson, 1949; Horrall, 1957; Ruess, 1958; Vernon, 1935; Webb & Hilden, 1953), to indicate that projective-technique response is heavily influenced by intelligence and such related factors as verbal skill. Not only does the more intelligent and more verbally facile subject give more, or longer, responses, but also it has been shown that a variety of measures representing motivational variables are related to verbal productivity (Lindzey & Goldberg, 1953; Lindzey & Silverman, 1959; Magnusson, 1959). Thus, if we are to compare the performance of two or more subjects or groups of subjects, it is important to know something about the extent to which they are comparable in intelligence, literacy, education, verbal facility, and so forth, before we can safely assume that observed response differences reflect the existence of differences in personality structure. The cross-cultural investigator will obviously find it essential to consider the contribution of such factors, particularly when subjects are asked to perform in something other than their native language.

All of the factors we have just discussed may be considered to influence projective-technique response directly. A further cluster of determinants of equal significance derives its importance from the extent to which they influence or determine one or more of the factors already outlined.

Perhaps the most important of these mediating factors is the *definition of the testing situation* that is constructed by the respondent. It is obvious that there is almost endless variation in the respondent's interpretation of the testing situation and its significance for him. An individual subject may look upon the testing situation as a playful setting in which he is able to relax and respond without concern for everyday reality and constraint; he may look upon it as a threatening assessment in which his every thought and response is potentially capable of leading to dire and unpleasant circumstances and where he must exercise a maximum of alertness and caution to protect himself against harm; he may view the entire production as foolishness which he is willing to indulge for whatever material or indirect benefit he receives; or he may view the testing situation as closely related to known and significant activities and consequently he may be set to respond in an earnest and highly motivated fashion.

There seems little doubt that the particular affective states that are temporarily active, as well as the response sets that may be expected to operate, are intimately linked to the meaning of the test situation for the respondent. Clearly the person who sees the examiner as a magical and potentially harmful observer of the subject's inner world will experience different emotions and motives than the subject who views the entire procedure as a rather amusing and frivolous game.

These observations imply that, so far as possible, the sophisticated analyst should secure from his subjects as much information as he can concerning their understanding of the function of the testing situation and its implications for their lives. Where the testing situation has been defined in such a manner as to make anxiety, rage, sexuality, or other motives or emotions appropriate, it is obviously hazardous to interpret test evidence of such motives as indicative of the importance of these factors in the characteristic behavior of the subjects. Similarly, when different cultural groups are being compared, the interpreter should be very much aware of the possibility that differences in cultural patterns may lead to different definitions of the testing situation and thus produce evidence for personality differences that do not, in fact, exist.

Still another dimension that may influence some of the determinants already discussed is the *situational factor.* Here we refer to such considerations as the physical and social setting in which the test is administered, the detailed instructions presented to the subject, or any other external influence immediately acting upon the subject. Clearly the meaning assigned to the testing procedure will vary depending upon whether the test is administered in the home, a hospital, a school, or a church. Further, each of these settings may have associated with it appropriate response sets and temporary affects. In support of this view, we know on the basis of controlled studies (Masling, 1960) that administration of projective tests in a solitary or in a group setting (Kimble, 1945), with or without an examiner present (Bernstein, 1956), with varying levels of illumination

(Weisskopf, 1950), with or without time pressure (Siipola & Taylor, 1952), or with varying instructions (Calden & Cohen, 1953; Henry & Rotter, 1956; Weisskopf & Dieppa, 1951) has significant effects upon the test responses elicited.

Consequently, the sophisticated interpreter is again faced with the necessity of making certain that those test responses he wishes to compare have been collected under circumstances where there was sufficient homogeneity in the testing situation to ensure that the response elements to be interpreted can be assumed confidently to be linked with variation in personality attribute rather than with variation in the situational factor. This does not, of course, imply that in order to be compared two sets of test results must have been collected under identical circumstances. It does suggest that reasonable caution dictates a careful examination of whatever differences in situational events existed, with particular reference to the possibility that this variation may have produced the response differences of interpretive interest.

A peculiarly important component of the situational factor is the nature of the *relation between subject and examiner,* which clearly is an essential determinant of variation in the definition of the testing situation. There are many dimensions along which this relationship can vary. The respondent may view the examiner as a superior, a peer, or an inferior; he may consider him to be benevolent and supportive, or threatening and malignant; he may look upon him as a mysterious seeker of the hidden, or simply as one who wishes to know more about the people with whom he is talking; he may be seen as an informed member of the same culture or as an uninformed stranger who knows little or nothing of the local culture.

It is well known within our culture that the identity of the examiner (Baughman, 1951; Kenny & Bijou, 1953; Lord, 1950), whether he is of the same sex or of different sex than the respondent (Clark, 1952; Curtis & Wolf, 1951), and likewise whether he is supportive, hostile, or neutral to the respondent (Bellak, 1944; Lord, 1950), influences obtained results. In view of these and similar findings it seems very likely that variations in the respondent's view of the examiner will have profound effects upon test responses.

This changeable relation between examiner and subject may be expected to control or mediate the nature of test responses primarily because of its capacity to influence the meaning of the testing situation and thus, in turn, to control response sets and temporary affective states within the subject. Depending upon whether the relation between the subject and examiner is warm and supportive or cool and impersonal, the subject may be disposed to provide material that is intimate and revealing or conventional and remote. The subject may feel on trial and attempt to produce lengthy or numerous responses, or he may feel quite relaxed and be motivated to give only those responses that occur to him easily and without strain. Depending upon the conduct and personality of the examiner and the history of his relationship with the subject, he may evoke anxiety, hostility, sexuality, rivalry, or many other affective or motivational responses. These states, consistently with what has already been said, may be expected to determine, in part, the nature of the resultant protocols, regardless of the enduring personality of the subject.

It is an evident conclusion that before a particular response element can be used interpretively with confidence, the potential role of the examiner-respondent relation must be examined carefully. Particularly where comparisons are made between test responses collected in different cultures, one should be quite concerned over differences between the various examiners in age, sex, testing experience, contact with the culture, prestige, personality, clinical skill, and professional role. Where there is variation between examiners in these qualities, substantive differences between test responses secured in the different cultures must be viewed suspiciously and interpreted in the light of the expected influence of such differences upon test response.

This general discussion of the process of interpretation of projective techniques leads to two important conclusions. First, it is *impossible to interpret projective-technique data meaningfully without a considerable amount of detailed information concerning the circumstances under which these data were collected.* An adequate understanding of the psychological meaning of the test responses is dependent upon a full awareness of just how the responses were elicited and by whom. Second, valid interpretation of projective techniques demands that the *analyst carefully examine the potential contribution of nonpersonality factors to the test responses he wishes to employ in his personality interpretations.* Only if the role of nonpersonality factors as determinants of test response is considered exhaustively can the analyst place much confidence in his generalizations concerning personality.

There can be no doubt that if the typical culture-and-personality investigator collected this important information concerning the circumstances of testing and carefully appraised the role of non-personality factors as determinants of test performance, he would be far advanced over his typical clinical colleague. In other words, the cautions advanced in this chapter do not represent a simple extension of general psychological practice in the interpretation of these tests. Quite the contrary, customary clinical practice largely overlooks the importance of many of these considerations in spite of the fact that few, if any, well-trained psychologists would disagree with them on principle.

TO QUANTIFY OR NOT?

There are few areas of psychology where sentiments concerning the inherent dangers and shortcomings of quantification are stronger than in the domain of projective testing. Users of these tests are typically imbued with a primary concern for the individual case, and they manifest the suspicion of statistics that is so often a corollary of clinical practice. Efforts to map methods of analysis and interpretation into the number system have often been greeted with disdain or open hostility by persons working in this area.

In spite of this resistance to quantification, there seems little doubt that if we define this term broadly enough, we can argue strongly that all serious investigators must resort to some type of quantification. By defining this term broadly, I mean simply that "yes-no" or "presence-absence" applied to a particular attribute or configuration shall be considered a form of quantification.

In many cases, the interpreter will wish to discuss the relative incidence of particular kinds of responses, such as Movement responses, Whole responses, sexual words, aggressive acts, and under these circumstances a direct counting operation with the eventual aim of statistical analysis seems both logical, desirable, and directly feasible. There are, of course, a variety of technical problems involved in the statistical analysis of this kind of data (Cronbach, 1949) but to avoid these problems by shunning quantification and statistical analysis is scarcely a rational alternative. The dangers of this tactic far outweigh any risks involved in a reasonably cautious application of statistical technique.

In other cases, the analyst may be unable or unwilling to signify just what response elements have led him to the interpretations he proposes. In this situation, it is often possible to treat the interpretation as the object of analysis and to observe the incidence of certain kinds of interpretative responses to protocols derived from various groups or collected in different settings. Thus, even though the investigator is not able or willing to specify elements of response for analysis, it is possible to treat the interpreter and the test together and to derive units for analysis from their joint product.

Finally, the interpretations may be presented as a set of organic entities, no one of which is meaningful if subjected to analysis or separation into individual interpretive statements. Even here it is possible to use matching techniques (Vernon, 1935) which will permit the investigator to test the association between these interpretations and various other measures; for example, blind matches might be made between the interpretations and personality descriptions derived from other observational sources including ethnological data, or sets of interpretations based upon projective techniques representing various cultures might be sorted or matched with other interpretations drawn from the same sources (for example, Kaplan, 1955).

It should be understood clearly that one of the essential contributions of quantification is to permit simple and meaningful estimates of the role of chance; and we have already agreed that such estimates play an essential role in the proper use of these instruments. An additional important function is to permit the identification of relationships that could not be established through a casual, or even a careful, examination of the data by the unaided observer.

The aim of this discussion is not to imply that all worthwhile investigation must involve the elaborate use of numbers and statistical analysis, but, rather, to defend the simple assertion that more often than not it is possible to use numbers at some stage in the interpretive process in such a manner as to facilitate, not conflict with, the goals of the investigator.

OVERT VERSUS COVERT

As we agreed in our discussion earlier, it is customary to assume that personality inferences derived from projective techniques refer to covert or unconscious aspects of behavior. However, available evidence indicates overwhelmingly that these devices reflect conscious as well as unconscious, overt as well as covert, public as well as private. Because these test responses are overdetermined, it is clear that the interpreter of projective tests cannot assume safely that his interpretations automatically refer to some single level of behavior.

There are a variety of crude generalizations concerning the conditions under which response elements refer to particular levels of behavior (for example, motives expressed under circumstances remote from everyday life are likely to be covert or unconscious; the avoidance of appropriate percepts related to particular motives suggests the unconscious operation of these motives; motives accomplished by frustration, guilt, or punishment are likely to be unconscious; motives expressed in a context of rational and realistic achievement are likely to be overt or conscious), but unfortunately there is little or no evidence to demonstrate the empirical warrant of such statement. There are, in fact, some tentative findings suggesting that those elements of projective-test response most readily objectified or subject to specific and operational analysis are also most closely related to the overt or public aspects of behavior (Lindzey & Tejessy, 1956).

In any event, unless the investigator has available a good deal of information from sources other than projective techniques which makes clear whether or not a given motive or disposition is expressed overtly, he is poorly advised to assume that the motives expressed in projective-test response are necessarily linked to any single domain or level of behavior. This indicates once again the strategic superiority of the investigator who is able to interpret his projective-technique responses against a rich background of supplementary information.

GROUP FINDINGS AND INTERPRETATIONS VS. INDIVIDUAL FINDINGS AND INTERPRETATIONS

As we shall discover, a very large proportion of the anthropological studies employing projective techniques have utilized these instruments in order to permit group comparisons. Such a procedure is in marked contrast to the typical clinical use of these instruments, where the modal approach involves a careful examination of individual results with an attempt to arrive at generalizations applicable only to the unique case.

Although there are a variety of means of deriving group results from projective techniques, ranging from the simple averaging of individual scores or indices to relatively complex configural approaches, they all require the collapse of a set of widely different protocols into a small number of categories, interpretive statements, or index numbers. This attempt to capture the nature of the group through combining the results of many individual tests seems anathema to most persons accustomed to employing these tests in a clinical setting. There is no doubt that the procedure does pose problems that are not present when generalizations are restricted to the individual case. In the individual approach there is available typically a wide variety of information from other observational sources that can be combined with the projective-technique results and utilized to reject or provide support for particular inferences. Furthermore, the generalizations refer to a single, relatively homogeneous person rather than to a group of diverse persons. Finally, the clinician presumably arrives at his final inferences through a delicate process of sifting very carefully a variety of response data in terms of general principles of interpretation in search of those few formulations that fit best the complex observations. It would be very unusual for the investigator utilizing a large group of protocols to be able to analyze his response data in comparable detail.

In spite of these difficulties, there are compensating advantages that adhere to the group results and interpretations. One of the chief difficulties of the clinician in the empirical court of science is that he finds it difficult or impossible to provide the kind of quantitative analysis that often seems necessary to convince others of the chastity of the observer's inferences. In contrast, the group analysis usually makes it relatively simple to provide a sample of observations that can be tested statistically for similarity or difference in comparison to some other set of observations. In the individual clinical case an enormous weight must rest upon the adequacy of a single observational sample, and consequently it is essential that the measuring instruments meet the highest standards of precision. In the group comparison, on the other hand, the investigator can often afford a good deal of error or wobble in his measuring instrument and still expect to arrive at sound generalizations because of the large number of observations. Even when it comes to the matter of additional information available to the clinician concerning the behavior of his patient, the group investigator may also utilize such additional sources; indeed as we have already suggested, it is an unwise investigator who fails to employ them.

All in all, the investigator must be exceedingly careful in making group comparisons to be sure that he does not produce a quantitative or qualitative artifact that bears little or no resemblance to any individual member of the group being studied. However, if he takes suitable precautions to be sure that his group results are, in fact, related to individual patterns of response and if he then couples his results with suitable quantitative analysis, there seems no reason to expect this product to be necessarily inferior to the individual case report of the clinician. Indeed, there are many who would argue that the group investigator occupies a strategic position generally superior to that of the clinician.

We have now completed our general discussion of projective techniques, and it remains for us to examine in some detail their application in cross-cultural studies. It will be a matter of considerable interest to observe the extent to which the cautions and hazards discussed in this chapter have played a role in actual investigations in this area.

REFERENCES

Altus, W. D., & Thompson, G. M. The Rorschach as a measure of intelligence. *J. consult. Psychol.*, 1949, 13, 341-347.

Baughman, E. E. Rorschach scores as a function of examiner differences. *J. proj. Tech.*, 1951, 15, 243-249.

Baughman, E. E. The role of the stimulus in Rorschach responses. *Psychol. Bull.*, 1958, 55, 121-147.

Beck, S. J. *Rorschach's Test.* Vol. I. *Basic processes.* New York: Grune Stratton, 1944.

Beck, S. J. *Rorschach's Test.* Vol. II. *A variety of personality pictures.* New York: Grune & Stratton, 1945.

Bellak, L. The concept of projection: an experimental investigation and study of the concept. *Psychiatry*, 1944, 7, 353-370.

Bernstein, L. The examiner as inhibiting factor in clinical testing. *J. consult. Psychol.*, 1956, 20, 287-290.

CALDEN, G., & COHEN, L. B. The relationship of ego-involvement and test definition to Rorschach test performance. *J. proj. Tech.*, 1953, 17, 300-311.

CLARK, R. A. The projective measurement of experimentally induced levels of sexual motivation. *J. exp. Psychol.*, 1952, 391-399.

CRANDALL, V. J. Induced frustration and punishment reward expectancy in thematic apperception stories. *J. consult. Psychol.*, 1951, 15, 400-404.

CRONBACH, L. J. Response sets and test validity. *Educ. Psychol. Measmt.*, 1946, 6, 475-494.

CRONBACH, L. J. Statistical methods applied to Rorschach scores: a review. *Psychol. Bull.*, 1949, 46, 393-429.

CURTIS, H. S., & WOLF, Elizabeth B. The influence of the sex of the examiner on the prediction of sex responses on the Rorschach. *Amer. Psychologist*, 1951, 6, 345-346. (Abstract)

HENRY, Edith, & ROTTER, J. B. Situational influence on Rorschach responses. *J. consult. Psychol.*, 1956, 20, 457-462.

HORRALL, Bernice M. Academic performance and personality adjustments of highly intelligent college students. *Genet. Psychol. Monogr.*, 1957, 55, 3-83.

KAPLAN, B. A study of Rorschach responses in four cultures. *Peabody Museum of Harvard University Papers*, 1954, 42, No. 2.

KENNY, D. T. Transcendence indices, extent of personality factors in fantasy responses, and the ambiguity of TAT cards. *J. consult. Psychol.*, 1954, 18, 345-348.

KENNY, D. T., & BIJOU, S. W. Ambiguity of pictures and extent of personality factors in fantasy responses. *J. consult. Psychol.*, 1953, 17, 283-288.

KIMBLE, G. A. Social influence on Rorschach records. *J. abnorm. soc. Psychol.*, 1945, 40, 89-93.

KLOPFER, B., AINSWORTH, Mary D., KLOPFER, W. G., & HOLT, R. R. *Developments in the Rorschach technique*. Vol. I. *Technique and theory*. New York: Harcourt, Brace & World, 1954.

LINDZEY, G., BRADFORD, Jean, TEJESSY, Charlotte, & DAVIDS, A. Thematic Apperception Test: An interpretive lexicon for clinician and investigator. *J. clin. Psychol. Monogr. Suppl.*, 1959, No. 12.

LINDZEY, G., & GOLDBERG, M. Motivational differences between male and female as measured by the Thematic Apperception Test. *J. Pers.*, 1953, 22, 101-117.

LINDZEY, G., & HERMAN, P. S. Thematic Apperception Test: A note on reliability and situational validity. *J. proj. Tech.*, 1955, 19, 36-42.

LINDZEY, G., & SILVERMAN, M. Thematic Apperception Test: Techniques of group administration, sex differences, and the role of verbal productivity. *J. Pers.*, 1959, 27, 311-323.

LINDZEY, G., & TEJESSY, Charlotte. Thematic Apperception Test: Indices of aggression in relation to measures of overt and covert behavior. *Am. J. Orthopsychiat.*, 1956, 26, 567-576.

LORD, Edith. Experimentally induced variations in Rorschach performance. *Psychol. Monogr.*, 1950, 64, No. 10.

MAGNUSSON, D. *A study of ratings based on TAT.* Stockholm: Swedish Council for Personnel Administration, 1959.

MASLING, J. The influence of situational and interpersonal variables in projective testing. *Psychol. Bull.*, 1960, 57, 65-85.

PATTIE, F. A. The effect of hypnotically induced hostility on Rorschach responses. *J. clin. Psychol.*, 1954, 10, 161-164.

RUESS, A. L. Some cultural and personality aspects of mental retardation. *Am. J. ment. Def.*, 1958, 63, 50-59.

SANFORD, R. N. The effects of abstinence from food upon imaginal processes: a further experiment. *J. Psychol.*, 1937, 3, 145-159.

SHIPLEY, T. E., & VEROFF, J. A. A projective measure of need for affiliation. *J. exp. Psychol.*, 1952, 43, 349-356.

SHPOLA, Elsa M. The influence of color on reactions to ink blots. *J. Pers.*, 1950, 18, 358-382.

SHPOLA, Elsa M., & TAYLOR, Vivian. Reactions to ink blots under free and pressure conditions. *J. Pers.*, 1952, 21 22-47.

SINGER, J. L., MELTZOFF, J., & GOLDMAN, G. D. Rorschach movement responses following motor inhibition and hyperactivity. *J. consult. Psychol.*, 1952, 16, 359-364.

VERNON, P. E. The significance of the Rorschach Test. *Brit. J. Med. Psychol.*, 1935, 15, 199-217.

WEBB, W. B., & HILDEN, A. H. Verbal and intellectual ability as factors in projective-test results. *J. proj. Tech.*, 1953, 17, 102-103.

WEISSKOPF, Edith A. An experimental study of the effect of brightness and ambiguity on projection in the Thematic Apperception Test. *J. Psychol.*, 1950, 29, 407-416.

WEISSKOPF, Edith A., & DIEPPA, J. J. Experimentally induced faking of TAT responses. *J. consult. Psychol.*, 1951, 15, 469-474.

6. The Case Against Projective Techniques in Cross-Cultural Investigation

IN THE FIRST CHAPTER of this volume we noted an increase in the application of projective techniques by anthropologists. We also examined some of the pioneer investigations in this area and discussed indications from various quarters suggesting that these techniques are not accepted with equal enthusiasm by all. The present chapter is intended to examine more carefully some of these same issues as a preliminary to a general discussion of the studies that have been carried out in cross-cultural settings. Specifically, I will attempt here to appraise the major criticisms that have been made of this type of application of projective techniques, and in the following chapter I shall present a detailed summary and evaluation of the principal studies that have been carried out in nonliterate settings. Once we have examined the imputed and existing flaws of these instruments in the hands of the cross-cultural worker, we can turn to the problem of assessing the likely contribution of projective techniques to the anthropologist or kindred investigator.

We have already encountered some evidence of doubt concerning the potential merit of projective techniques in anthropological research, but we have seen thus far only a small fragment of the negative sentiments uttered. The bulk of the criticism, however, has originated with a small number of critics, the most vigorous of whom have generally adopted the view that contemporary anthropology would be well rid of projective techniques and their dubious contributions. Our enumeration of published criticisms will result in a list of more than a dozen specific accusations. This indeed appears to be a serious indictment, particularly when we examine the criticisms and find that some of them are uncomfortably accurate.

In considering these issues let us divide them into three clusters according to the cogency of the criticism: First are the objections that seem demonstrably invalid, nonrelevant, or insupportable. Second are the reservations that are essentially accurate but overlook the generality of the issue and the extent to which it can be applied to alternative approaches as well as to projective techniques. Third, we find those sound objections that should be seriously considered by every cross-cultural investigator who weighs the possibility of employing projective techniques in his research.

UNWARRANTED CRITICISMS

We are concerned here with a small group of objections that seem to have no firm basis in fact but rather to reflect a lack of sophistication concerning projective techniques or general methods of data collection. If there is a single underlying error in these criticisms, it is that the writer has failed to fight the battle of abstraction successfully. That is, in a number of instances the critic seems to be saying that projective techniques force an abstract, limited, or segmental view of human behavior upon the investigator; whereas if he would simply remain a naturalistic observer he could avoid the restrictive clutch of instruments and see the society or culture as a whole. This is sheer nonsense! No one sees a culture or an individual whole, with or without projective techniques. Furthermore, these devices certainly do not force upon the anthropologist a segmental view of the individual or society. In fact, we have already seen that one of the attributes of these measures that seems to attract many users is the somewhat dubious virtue of ordinarily *not* committing the investigator to any particular set of dimensions or variables.

No matter what approach the ethnologist employs in securing his data, he must select and choose what he observes and reports. His choice lies between making this determination implicitly or explicitly, and whichever basis he elects, there seems no reason to expect that *in principle* projective techniques will fail to mesh with his plans. The likelihood of projective tests contributing worthwhile data derives not from their segmental or holistic qualities but rather from their special sensitivity to certain areas of behavior that may or may not be of interest to a particular anthropologist. In a moment we shall return to this point for further discussion.

1. *The projective technique comes between the observer and his basic data—human behavior.* In contrast to the interview, where personality can be observed directly, the projective technique places a screen between the anthropologist and his informant and thus limits or restricts what can be observed (Henry, 1955).

This argument asserts two patently false propositions. First, it suggests that responses to projective techniques are not "behavior." In actuality these products are response data, just as much as any other form of behavior, and they have secured the special attention given them solely because many have believed that they provide a good inferential base for the observer concerned with assessing personality. Second, the suggestion that personality may be observed directly in the interview is a literal example of the lack of sophistication concerning abstraction that we have just discussed. Personality is not about to be observed "directly" in the interview, or any other place. The statement, often attributed to L. J. Henderson, that "A fact is a receptor experience in terms of a conceptual scheme" may somewhat overstate the case, but certainly it is clear that any personality inference depends upon a set of prior assumptions and empirical rules—assumptions and rules which operate fully as directly with the projective technique as with the interview. Thus, if the individual is interested in personality variables, the projective test should by no means be considered a "screen" blocking off the investigator from his basic data. Quite the reverse, it is intended to facilitate behavioral observations of a relevant sort.

2. *The use of projective techniques is narrowing* and leads the anthropologist to give up his opportunity to ". . . observe *real* (not laboratory models), relatively small, complete human societies as wholes." (Henry, 1955, p. 267)

This objection rests upon much the same premises as those we have just discussed, and it seems fully as vulnerable to counterargument as the first criticism. Neither the anthropologist, the sociologist, nor any other social scientist observes society as a whole, although it is true that he may attend to many or to only a few aspects of the society, and he may study these aspects independently or, within limits posed by technical problems, in interaction. If we assume that the anthropologist is, in fact, interested in studying as many aspects of the functioning society as he can, it seems perfectly consistent for him to decide to employ, among other techniques, the projective technique. Use of this device will certainly broaden his observational base somewhat, and if he is not giving up some other set of observations for the sake of projective-technique data, it is obvious that he is closer to the elusive "whole" than he was without the projective technique. No one, to my knowledge, argues that the projective technique should be employed in isolation, and it is only under such circumstances that one might reasonably conclude that this device is narrowing. There is a legitimate area of concern surrounding the possibility (or indeed probability) that in the process of collecting projective-technique data, the investigator is not simply adding to his data but rather is making a substitution for some other alternative, and we shall return to this question.

3. When tests of any sort (including projective techniques) are used, *the investigator* must not only worry about the possibility of his own personal factors and past history influencing the inferences he arrives at, but also he *must worry about the past history of the instrument and its effect upon his inferences.* (Mensh & Henry, 1953).

This objection seems to overlook completely the fact that one of the major factors in the development of all instruments is the effort to reduce the extent to which the investigator must take into account his own past history and its influential role in data collection and analysis. A private, individual, largely unspecified, process of observation and inference-making is given up in favor of a more general and intersubjective set of considerations. Moreover, as this implies, an instrument has a very different past history from that of an individual; it is a public and recoverable past, and the interested investigator can, depending somewhat upon the instrument, learn a great deal about this past. Most important, he can learn a good deal about the present operating characteristics of the instrument, which, after all, is the really important question, for it would be ludicrous to suggest that the doctor or patient who wishes to use a thermometer, or the butcher or scientist who wishes to use a scale, must understand the history of their instrument in order to use it successfully.

In other words, projective techniques, as well as other instruments, are intended to reduce the importance of personal qualities of the observer (including his past history), and it is the present functioning of the projective technique that is of primary interest to the investigator, not its past. Even so, the past of the technique is much more objective and communicable than the individual observer's past.

4. Projective techniques measure the end product of a process of development; they do not provide information concerning the events or determinants that have played an important role in the process of growth and development. If behavior is conceived of as involving antecedent and consequent events, then it may be argued that *projective techniques tell us little or nothing about the antecedent events and instead measure consequent behavior or outcomes.* (Mensh & Henry, 1953)

This argument rests upon the assumption that the primary task of the student of behavior is to establish antecedent-consequent relations rather than to establish correlations between co-existing events or to identify structural or enduring attributes of the person. Suffice it to say that among psychologists and other social scientists there is by no means firm agreement concerning the relative merit or importance of these two approaches and that, consequently, even if they believe projective techniques are insensitive to antecedent events, this conclusion will have little or no negative implication for many investigators.

More compelling is the observation that projective techniques are not limited to providing information concerning end processes any more than are other techniques. For example, if the investigator employs projective techniques at one point in time (or with one particular age group) and then relates measures derived from this administration to measures based upon subsequent performance (or performance of an older age group), he may be using the projective technique as an antecedent measure in a perfectly legitimate sense. Or the investigator may use projective techniques administered in adulthood to form the basis for inferences concerning past experiences. Although this is hazardous procedure, there is no guarantee that it is more hazardous than relying solely upon a contemporary interview for retrospective report concerning past events or experiences. In other words, depending upon the circumstances under which the projective technique is employed, it may provide perfectly legitimate inferences concerning antecedent events, and in any case, the relative importance of measures of antecedent events is by no means agreed upon by social scientists.

5. *Projective techniques involve fixed categories* so that the investigator who uses them must resign himself to slicing the world of reality in a manner consistent with these particular variables or categories. By dictating the categories or variables that may be used, the instrument is implicitly dictating the theory of behavior or personality that will be employed, and in many cases this is not the theory of choice for the anthropologist (Henry, 1955).

In our discussion of the nature of projective techniques, as well as in our consideration of problems of interpretation, it was made clear that "fixed categories" are, generally speaking, about as much of a problem with projective techniques as overemphasis upon operationism is with psychoanalysis, or idolatry of holism is with students of operant conditioning. For the most part, projective techniques do not come equipped with fixed categories (or indeed any categories), and where fixed categories are recommended, it is typically very easy to find another authority who will recommend a different set of categories, or, for that matter, no categories at all. In fact, one of the principal reasons for the wide popularity of projective techniques is precisely the absence of specific and delimited scoring schemes that commit the user to a particular set of variables. As for the statement that the use of projective techniques implies commitment to a particular theory of behavior, our long discussion of the relation between psychological theory and projective techniques has certainly emphasized the fragile and fleeting ties between most projective tests and any form of psychological theory. In general, it seems an obvious conclusion that among the many difficulties associated with projective techniques, neither fixed categories nor tight theoretical linkage are cause for much concern.

OVERGENERALIZED CRITICISMS

Here our attention is directed to a set of critical evaluations concerning the contribution of projective techniques to anthropology that are appropriate in that they point to real and identifiable shortcomings in the use of these devices. They are deficient, however, in their failure to place projective techniques in an appropriate context of comparison with other data-collecting devices or in their willingness to consider the steps that can be taken to minimize these problems. In other words, these criticisms are leveled against projective techniques without any serious consideration of their appropriateness when directed against those instruments that the critic himself has used, or would use, in the anthropological setting, and typically there is little recognition of the existence of available resources for minimizing such problems.

1. The use of *projective techniques* tends to *impose* upon the anthropologist the *language of pathology* so that entire groups of apparently well-functioning persons may be described in the language of the closed ward. Terms and concepts that have particular pertinence to psychiatric diagnosis or the therapeutic situation are not necessarily appropriate for describing the individual who is functioning effectively in his natural social setting. (Abel, 1948; Henry, 1955; Lantz, 1948)

There seems little doubt that the majority of applications of projective techniques have led to interpretive statements heavily flavored with terms or concepts that originated in the world of abnormal behavior or clinical psychiatry. An ingenious study by Little and Shneidman (1959) provides dramatic evidence of the tendency for even very sophisticated users of projective techniques to see pathology where normalcy should be. This state of affairs, however, is less a commentary upon projective techniques than upon the entire field of personality assessment. In fact, some of the leading exponents of projective tests, for example, Henry A. Murray, have valiantly labored to develop conceptions that owe more to the normal personality than to the neurotic or psychotic. Moreover, the extensive use of the instruments in studies of normal (Atkinson, 1958; McClelland, *et al.*, 1953; Murray, 1938) and supranormal (Roe, 1951*a*, 1951*b*) functioning in our own society makes clear the absence of any exclusive tie to psychopathology. In any case, the use of the interview to assess personality factors, particularly the psychiatric interview which appeals to Jules Henry as providing invaluable experience for the anthropologist, is at least as steeped in the language of pathology. It should also be pointed out that there is some supporting evidence and widespread belief concerning the assumption that an understanding of normal behavior can be advanced by means of insights, concepts, and instruments developed with the psychologically ill. The danger here lies not in the use of such concepts but in their blind use, not in their extrapolation to normal behavior but in the rigid and unwavering determination of the clinician to see pathology in every subject.

It is reasonable to suggest that projective techniques in use are often linked with concepts and terms derived from the study of abnormal behavior, but one should remember that this link is not inevitable and is probably no more pronounced than it is for most other devices used to assess personality. Finally, there is considerable reason to consider normal and abnormal behavior as continuous rather than discontinuous, so that concepts originating in the study of deviant behavior may well prove illuminating in regard to the normal range of behavior. In spite of these justifications for the current use of projective techniques, it remains clear that the investigator who employs these techniques in a stereotyped manner completely consistent with that used in psychiatric diagnosis is not likely to secure information of maximum utility to the person concerned with personality in a cultural setting.

2. The *interview provides ethnographic and personality data* simultaneously, whereas the *projective technique can provide*, at best, *only information concerning personality.* Consequently, the interview technique is a superior instrument and to be preferred. (Henry, 1955)

There seems little doubt that the interview is a superior means of collecting ethnographic data, although there is no reason why projective techniques could not be employed within a limited context for procuring such information. Indeed, on rare occasions, projective-technique responses have been used to provide inferences concerning aspects of culture (Hobson, 1954; Honigmann, 1949; Leighton & Kluckhohn, 1947). The question of whether in the hands of the ordinary ethnologist the interview provides personality information comparable to that provided by the projective technique remains an unanswered empirical question.

The most important consideration in connection with Henry's point, however, is that the projective technique is not ordinarily used to supplant the interview or field observation, and consequently its adequacy as a cultural measure is not at issue, but only its contribution to an understanding of motivational or personality dimensions. Kaplan (1957), for example, concludes that the Rorschach is not a legitimate instrument to employ in the study of culture but goes on to suggest that ". . . if one of Henry's purposes in going into the field was to study personality he would be very foolish not to consider seriously, at least, whether projective techniques could not help him in his task" (p. 108). It seems reasonable to conclude that although on occasion projective techniques might be used to assess cultural dimensions, this attribute of the test is not an important consideration in evaluating its potential merit for the anthropologist. Consequently, the superiority of the interview as an ethnographic tool seems only vaguely relevant to any decision concerning the use of projective tests in cross-cultural settings.

3. There are *special* quantitative or *statistical problems* involved *in the analysis of projective-technique data* which make it difficult or impossible to apply conventional statistical analysis and thus raise serious doubts concerning the dependability of findings based on projective tests. (Mensh & Henry, 1953)

There is little doubt that a number of special problems beset the investigator who wishes to transform the typically qualitative data of the projective test into some set of numbers that can be treated statistically. In spite of these difficulties, numerous investigators have succeeded in making these transformations in such a manner as to result in meaningful quantitative results. The greater the familiarity of the projective-technique user with specific cautions, such as those presented by Cronbach (1949), the more likely he is to analyze his data in an elegant and revealing manner. Moreover, the more sophisticated the analyst is in measurement theory and statistical analysis, the greater the likelihood of a fruitful outcome. But then, in what area of social science would the same statements not apply?

The most important question here is not whether the data of the projective technique pose difficult problems for quantitative analysis, but rather whether these problems are more severe or incapacitating than the difficulties posed by alternative techniques. If we look upon the unstructured interview as the most likely alternative, the answer must surely be negative. Whatever difficulties there are in mapping Rorschach or TAT responses into sets of numbers, these seem slight in comparison to the task of quantifying the results of the clinical interview. Much the same could be said for direct observation, analysis of life-history material, or other potential approaches. Consequently, on a comparative basis, the quantitative ailments of projective techniques do not seem to be unduly severe.

4. Even among projective-technique experts there is *no agreement on how these techniques should be analyzed and interpreted*, and consequently it seems unlikely that the anthropologist, much less experienced in this area, can pick his way without serious difficulty. (Henry, 1955)

In previous chapters we have seen something of the extent of agreement on principles of interpretation for projective techniques; and no one could assert safely that there is anything approaching consensus. If we compare the plight of the person who wishes to administer and interpret the Wechsler-Bellevue or Stanford-Binet tests of intelligence with the person who wishes to administer the TAT or Rorschach, there can be little doubt who has the firmest guidelines or who will have to make the largest number of arbitrary decisions. This does indeed suggest that the anthropologist with little or no training in psychology, and only a passing contact with projective techniques, is not likely to secure much benefit from their use.

Again, however, we must raise the question of how firm the procedural rules and interpretive assumptions are for the investigator who chooses an alternative technique for appraising personality. The answer seems obvious—rules for making inferences from data generally considered to reveal personality (dreams, interview, observation) are sparse and inadequate. Whether the anthropologist uses projective techniques or direct observation or clinical interviews, he is likely to find little in the way of well-worn paths of demonstrated utility to guide him to the inferences he wishes to attain. In fact, for all of the ambiguity in regard to interpreting projective techniques, these devices are better structured than some of their likely alternatives.

5. It is almost certain that within a given culture there will be different degrees of compliance with the request to respond to projective techniques. Presumably variation in personality factors as well as status, sex, and role would contribute to this uneven willingness to participate in projective-test procedures. Consequently, these techniques *elicit data* from a group of subjects *that is* not only *nonrepresentative,* but nonrepresentative to an unknown degree. (Nadel, 1955)

There is no doubt that Nadel has identified a consideration that could lead to considerable error in inferences concerning a group or society if the investigator did not take careful steps to compensate for it. The existence of various factors associated with willingness to subject oneself to projective tests makes it evident that the field worker must operate with independent definitions of the nature of the group he wishes to assess—independent, that is, of the whim or willingness of the informant—and must be prepared either to secure respondents fitting these characteristics or else to accept the potential vulnerability of his data to sampling error. The main point to be made here is that a sampling problem exists, but there are various procedures that can be followed in the effort to solve such problems.

It should also be pointed out that these sampling problems are with the field worker constantly. Not only is there a differential willingness to participate in projective testing, there is also a differential willingness to be interviewed, to permit the anthropologist to enter the home or village, to provide a life history, or indeed to interact with the investigator under any circumstance. The field worker must be alert constantly to the extent to which his own personal characteristics, his sponsors, his techniques, his mastery of the language, and other inescapable attributes limit and select who responds and how they respond. Presumably all well-trained ethnologists are aware of these problems and are prepared to take whatever technical and strategic steps are necessary to minimize their effects upon data. Thus, with projective tests, as well as with all other data-collecting devices, the field worker must be prepared to defend his study against the threat of selective and nonrepresentative response data.

6. Implicit in the use of projective techniques is the *assumption that the* "deepest" *or most covert aspects of personality are the most interesting* and valuable. Furthermore, the use of these devices in other cultures implies that there is a consistent tendency in these alien cultural settings for the development of unconscious motives and conflicts, and yet there is little or no evidence to support such a point of view (Henry, 1955).

It is clear that projective techniques have traditionally been linked with the pursuit of covert motives, and we have seen this clearly demonstrated in earlier chapters. Furthermore, many investigators, including such well-known psychologists as Allport (1953), and Murray (1958), have raised serious questions concerning the extent to which current human research may be slighting the accessible or overt side of personality in favor of the unconscious or latent. Thus, Henry's caution carries considerable general sanction. It seems thoroughly desirable that the anthropologist give serious consideration to alternative techniques that may be less closely linked to pursuit of the covert side of personality. He should also be aware, however, that projective techniques do not reflect merely, or perhaps mostly, covert aspects of personality. Thus, even if he is interested in surface manifestations, it is quite likely that he will secure some evidence of these manifestations from the projective techniques. The real problem, as we have already seen, is to determine how to link inferences derived from projective tests to their appropriate level of overtness.

The question of whether there is evidence for the operation of unconscious motives or processes in nonliterate cultures is far too complex for us to dispose of satisfactorily here. Suffice it to say that in many nonliterate cultures procedures that have convinced observers in our own culture of the operation or reality of unconscious processes (for example, hypnosis, free association) have been applied with apparently parallel results. Personally, I would consider the assumption that the mental apparatus of the nonliterate and the Western European possess certain basic similarities, such as those involved in the repression process, so minimal and so much less demanding than other assumptions made by most or all personality and culture investigators as to be most unobjectionable.

7. It is *not possible to use projective techniques to compare with interview material or field observation without serious contamination* as a result of the knowledge that the interpreter of the projective technique protocols has concerning the culture. Thus, the results of projective techniques cannot be used as a check upon the accuracy of personality inferences based upon observation. (Mensh & Henry, 1953)

It should be clear that only under special circumstances is it essential for the investigator to protect himself against the possibility of contamination of projective-technique interpretations by other sources of information. This will be important in inquiries to appraise the importance of various sources of data, investigations that attempt to demonstrate the independent contribution of these sources of information, or studies that relate personality findings to other sets of data, such as ethnographic description or child-rearing practices. In many cases the investigator is primarily concerned with maximizing the likelihood of valid personality estimates, and then it may be advisable to introduce a maximum of "contamination," that is, to provide the projective-test interpreter with as much information concerning the culture and its individual members as he can successfully absorb.

Even in those cases where the question of contamination is crucial, it is perfectly possible to have projective techniques interpreted with no contamination of the interpretation through prior knowledge of the culture or the individuals who have been tested. One need merely distinguish sharply between the process of data collection and the process of data analysis or interpretation. Studies making this distinction have been conducted, as we shall see, and more and better investigations of this variety could be carried out in the future.

Thus, there is nothing intrinsic in the test that leads to the flaw the critics have cited. The difficulty becomes manifest only with faulty design. Furthermore, in some studies contamination of projective-technique interpretations is not even an appropriate or important issue.

ON-TARGET CRITICISMS

The objections to follow are those that seem closest to the heart of the matter. Here we find a group of comments that deal with genuine shortcomings of projective techniques or considerations in regard to their use that in many circumstances may dissuade the sophisticated investigator from employing them.

1. The anthropologist *must never be content to collect projective data alone.* His basic data must come from other observational sources, since the possibility of a meaningful interpretation of the projective techniques rests upon a full array of ethnographic data. (Honigmann, 1955; Nadel, 1955)

This point is obviously more caveat than criticism. However, there is an element of criticism, for the statement implies that by itself the projective technique does not provide data that may be interpreted without ambiguity. As the reader will recall from previous chapters, this implication is completely supported by existing opinion and evidence. It would indeed be injudicious to attempt to understand the significance of projective-technique responses of nonliterate subjects without considerable information from other sources concerning the overt behavior, the culture, and other dimensions important to the subjects of the study.

This point does not simply imply that the field worker must aspire to more than projective-technique data, for what sophisticated field worker is likely to remain content with this type of data alone? More important is the implication that the person seriously interested in the analysis of projective-technique responses must attempt to secure a maximum context of relevant and overlapping data to aid him in accounting for observed projective-technique findings in a psychologically supportable manner.

2. *Projective techniques rest upon subtle language differences,* and yet they are often given with the aid of interpreters or through the medium of a language with which the subject is only dimly familiar, so that it is virtually impossible to provide basic data of any precision. (Nadel, 1955)

There is little question that variation in language resulting from the use of interpreters or of an unfamiliar tongue, introduces serious problems for many kinds of analyses of projective technique data. More serious is the fact that linguistic differences between cultures, even if the other problems do not exist, may introduce variation in projective-technique response that may not be attributed to personality variation.

This difficulty is not always an important one; depending somewhat upon the particular technique or method of analysis, the structure of the relevant language may play a central or only a peripheral role. Clearly, if one is analyzing TAT protocols in terms of word counts or parts of speech, a precise control over the conditions under which the verbal responses are elicited is necessary. On the other hand, if one is engaged in thematic analysis or story rating, the same degree of precision may not be necessary. Likewise, the importance of variation in the details of verbal behavior will be much more important in the TAT or Rorschach than in the Draw-A-Person test.

There is no way of eliminating the problems posed by language differences between informant and investigator, but it is certainly possible to decrease the role of this factor as a source of contamination by making sure that the person who administers and interprets the test is familiar with the language, by employing techniques that place less reliance upon verbal response, or by utilizing methods of analysis not intimately linked to the details of language usage. Most important of all, the test interpreter must be alert to the possibility that response variation in alien cultural settings may be, in part, or whole, attributed to linguistic differences or artificial constraints upon verbal productions rather than to personality differences.

3. The anthropologist is always under heavy time pressure in collecting the full range of data he considers necessary or important. Consequently, *by including projective techniques* in his array of data-collecting procedures, he *ordinarily omits some procedure he might*

otherwise have employed. This comment suggests that the projective technique must always compete with other potentially valuable sources of data. (Nadel, 1955)

It is undeniable that the decision to include one or more projective techniques in a particular study is by implication to limit the range of other instruments or the amount of time and energy invested in them. Whether this proves to be a decisive negative consideration will depend upon the goals of the investigator and the demonstrated utility of the alternative devices. Thus, if the investigator is little interested in personality devices, he will not wish to give up other instruments or their intensive use for projective-techniques. Of course, if he considers himself a skilled appraiser of personality through the unstructured interview, he will be unwilling to shorten interview time for the sake of the projective technique. Unfortunately, the relative effectiveness of the various instruments that might be used for securing personality data in the cross-cultural setting is by no means evident. It is clear, however, that the field worker should not ordinarily look upon the decision to use projective techniques in this setting as a decision to be made without consideration of alternative devices for collecting data. It is virtually always a paired-comparison decision rather than a judgment of absolute merit.

4. However valid projective techniques may be within our own society, it remains *a task for the future to demonstrate* that they possess *cross-cultural validity.* The principles of interpretation and rules for diagnosis that work within Western European culture may or may not be relevant for interpreting the responses of individuals from societies in other parts of the world. Until some demonstration of this general validity of the instruments has been made, it seems unwise to employ projective tests in nonliterate societies as the basis for providing personality inferences. (Adcock & Ritchie, 1958; Gladwin & Sarason, 1953; Nadel, 1955)

As we have already implied, evaluation of the validity of projective techniques is an enormously complex matter. Much of the next chapter will be devoted to an examination of some of the evidence that might be used to provide a tentative and incomplete answer to the question of whether projective tests have any demonstrable utility in anthropological research. What we have already said concerning the general validity of these tests in our own culture must make clear, however, that the investigator cannot utilize these instruments with a sense of conviction or certainty in alien cultural settings. This does not mean that they cannot or will not have any utility but merely that the degree of sensitivity and reliability remains to a considerable extent unknown. The use of unvalidated or partially validated tests creates problems that are well known, and it is more justifiable under some circumstances than under certain others. We will consider some of these circumstances later.

These are the broad criticisms that have been raised against the use of projective techniques in anthropological research. Let us now see how well they apply to a wide array of such investigation. When we have examined these studies in some detail, we may then ask what appear, in fact, to have been the typical flaws or shortcomings of these studies; what the general contributions of projective techniques seem to have consisted of; and what promise these instruments hold for the future in this area of research.

REFERENCES

ABEL, Theodora M. The Rorschach test in the study of culture. *Rorschach Res. Exch.*, 1948, 12, 79-93.

ADCOCK, C. J., & RITCHIE, J. E. Intercultural use of Rorschach. *Amer. Anthrop.*, 1958, 60, 881-892.

ALLPORT, G. W. The trend in motivational theory. *Amer. J. Orthopsychiat.*, 1953, 23, 107-119.

ATKINSON, J. W., (Ed.) *Motives in fantasy, action and society.* Princeton, N.J.: Van Nostrand, 1958.

CRONBACH, L. Statistical methods applied to Rorschach scores: a review. *Psychol. Bull.*, 1949, 46, 393-429.

GLADWIN, T., & SARASON, S. B. *Truk: man in paradise.* New York: Wenner-Gren Foundation, 1953.

HENRY, J. Symposium: Projective testing in ethnography. *Amer. Anthrop.*, 1955, 57, 245-247, 264-269.

HOBSON, R. Navaho acquisitive values. *Peabody Museum of Harvard University Papers*, 1954, 42, No. 3.

HONIGMANN, J. J. Culture and ethos of Kaska society. *Yale University Publications in Anthropology*, 1949, No. 40.

HONIGMANN, J. J. Symposium: Projective testing in ethnography. *Amer. Anthrop.*, 1955, 57, 253-256.

KAPLAN, B. Personality and social structure. In J. B. Gittler (Ed.), *Review of sociology*. New York: Wiley, 1957. Pp. 87-126.

LANTZ, H. Rorschach testing in pre-literate cultures. *Amer. J. Orthopsychiat.*, 1948, 18, 287-291.

LEIGHTON, Dorothea, & KLUCKHOHN, C. *Children of the people.* Cambridge, Mass.: Harvard Univer. Press, 1947.

LITTLE, K. B., & SHNEIDMAN, E. S. Congruencies among interpretations of psychological test and anamnestic data. *Psychol. Monogr.*, 1959, 73, No. 6.

McCLELLAND, D. C., ATKINSON, J. W., CLARK, R. A., & LOWELL, E. L. *The achievement motive.* New York: Appleton-Century-Crofts, 1953.

MENSH, I., & HENRY, J. Direct observation and psychological tests in anthropological field work. *Amer. Anthrop.*, 1953, 55, 461-480.

MURRAY, H. A. *Explorations in personality.* New York: Oxford, 1938.

MURRAY, H. A. Drive, time, strategy, measurement and our way of life. In G. Lindzey (Ed.), *Assessment of human motives*. New York: Rinehart, 1958. Pp. 183-196.

NADEL, S. F. Symposium: Projective testing in ethnography. *Amer. Anthrop.*, 1955, 57, 247-250.

ROE, Anne. A psychological study of physical scientists. *Genet. Psychol. Monogr.*, 1951a, 43, 121-235.

ROE, Anne. A psychological study of eminent biologists. *Psychol. Monogr.*, 1951b, 65, No. 14.

7. Cross-Cultural Applications of Projective Techniques

THE ARRAY OF CRITICISMS we have just discussed represents the indictment of projective techniques in cross-cultural research. It is our present task to turn to the relevant evidence and judge the merit of the indictment.

The evidence we shall turn to lies embedded in an unwieldy mass of complex investigations, and our efforts to assess it will involve a relatively extensive survey of actual anthropological investigations employing projective techniques. Although the survey will undoubtedly fail to attain total inclusiveness, it will almost surely encompass examples of all the major types of investigation in this domain. The review will not only assist in evaluating the contribution of projective techniques in this setting, but it will also serve as a detailed summary of an important domain of contemporary research. In a final section of this chapter, we will attempt to provide some generalizations concerning the characteristic shortcomings or weaknesses of these studies.

In outlining these investigations, we shall deal extensively with matters of procedure and method because our interest is in arriving at a general conclusion concerning the contribution of these studies and because knowledge of the empirical procedures is essential if we are to form any judgment of the over-all merit of these studies. No attempt has been made here to distinguish between anthropological studies carried out by psychologists and psychological studies carried out by anthropologists. Any study was eligible for inclusion that utilized projective techniques in a nonliterate or a cross-cultural setting, provided the study did not deal exclusively with European or modern American societies.

We have not hesitated to criticize these studies where it seems appropriate, but it should be clear that the amount of criticism directed at a given study is in no sense a measure of its general merit. Many highly significant investigations are fraught with empirical flaws, and there are some studies that involve a high degree of procedural sophistication and yet offer little in the way of enduring interest and value.

In examining these inquiries, what evaluative considerations should be foremost in our thinking? Although there is no finite limit to the relevant considerations, the following questions represent issues likely to be of particular importance in judging the merit of a study and the potential contribution of projective techniques to its findings. It will become obvious that we have not approached every study with an explicit query on each of these points, but these questions have served as a general guide in our attempt to appraise these investigations.

1. Is there a full *description of the circumstances surrounding the administration of the projective technique?* How are subjects selected and what are they told about the examiner and the test?

2. Is a language *interpreter* employed in the administration of the projective technique?

3. Is the *relation between the testing situation and the cultural context* of the study *explored?* Is the significance of the test-taking activities within the framework of the local culture considered?

4. Is the *process of making personality inferences* from the projective technique *specified?* Is the report of *results derived from field observation and projective techniques sufficiently delineated* that it is clear when the investigator is talking about statements based upon one source of data and when he is referring to the other?

5. Is the projective technique *scored according to a scheme* that has some *demonstrated sensitivity and stability?*

6. Is the *presentation* of the projective-technique *findings quantitative or qualitative?*

7. Does the investigator make a serious attempt to assess the role of *chance factors* in determining his findings? How many comparisons or relationships have been examined in the process of identifying significant or dramatic findings to report?

8. Are projective-technique *findings explored from the point of*

view of alternative hypotheses that would account for the results without involving personality factors?

9. Is the *analyst* of the projective techniques *familiar with the culture* and the individuals whose protocols he is interpreting?

10. Is the person who interprets the projective techniques *aware of the prior hypotheses or expectations of the investigator?*

11. Are the personality inferences derived from the projective techniques *integrated with the other data and findings?*

We have elected to divide these studies into several groups according to the major intention of the investigator. This analysis was begun with the plan of classifying studies according to the degree of empirical control imposed in the study. However, this basis for distinction proved tedious and relatively unrevealing, with the result that a more substantive set of categories was devised and studies were classified in terms of whether they seemed to have dealt primarily with national character, acculturation, personality development, or procedural issues.

NATIONAL CHARACTER—MODAL PERSONALITY

It seems safe to say that if social scientists had not been intrigued with the concept of national character (modal personality, basic personality type, ethos, and such) from almost the time they were weaned from the concept of the group mind, there never would have been any fever over the use of projective techniques in anthropological research. It was largely the powerful attraction exerted by the notion of typical group or cultural personality attributes which lead the anthropologist and psychologist to devise or adapt personality instruments for cross-cultural application. A companion interest was the association between particular institutions or cultural patterns and personality constellations. Consistently, we find a large portion of the anthropological research utilizing projective techniques has been executed by investigators whose primary intent was to study national character or modal personality patterns.

By now a classic in the culture and personality area is Cora Du Bois' *People of Alor* (1944). As part of this comprehensive study, the investigator administered the Rorschach test to 37 informants, 17 males and 20 females, and these protocols were interpreted by Emil

Oberholzer, well-known psychoanalyst and early collaborator with Hermann Rorschach. In her volume, Du Bois presents initially what she refers to as a psychocultural synthesis, which consists of a description of the developmental process among the Alorese and an outline of the major institutions of the society. This includes both cultural material and psychological or personality generalizations. There is also a general discussion by Abraham Kardiner of personality determinants in the Alorese culture and following this a series of nine autobiographies accompanied by Kardiner's interpretive remarks.

The Rorschach scoring and analysis by Oberholzer were carried out with presumably little or no knowledge of either the Alorese culture or of the individual subjects. We are told that the ethnologist and psychologist compared rankings on a number of personality variables for a small number of subjects. They found that ranks derived from the Rorschach showed so much correspondence with ranks derived from the anthropologist's field observations that Oberholzer felt principles of interpretation used customarily with European and American subjects could be generalized fruitfully to the Alorese. The report of the Rorschach data includes a description of average scores, for the most part limited to the male subjects, coupled with a number of specific interpretations of these findings. There is also some comparative data derived from Swiss subjects. In addition, there is a comparison of the average male and average female scores and an extended discussion of individual variation from the modal pattern. The latter discussion includes detailed summaries of several individual protocols and personality descriptions of some of the same subjects whose life histories and interpretive analyses were presented earlier.

The general portrait of the Alorese that Oberholzer infers emphasizes the fearfulness, suspicion, and distrust of these people; their apathy, indifference, and lack of vigor; their egocentricity and greed; the shallowness of their interpersonal relations; their lack of emotional responsiveness; and the absence of neurotic conflict or repression in their personalities. It is difficult to depict here the correspondence between these generalizations and the psychocultural descriptions provided by Du Bois, as well as the life histories and their psychological interpretations by Du Bois and Kardiner, but it seems reasonable to say that almost any reader must be impressed with their congruity. No formal analysis is attempted by the author, and consequently the reader himself is responsible for making the comparison. There is little doubt, however, that whatever the underlying basis for the similarity, there is a striking resemblance between the portraits of the Alorese provided by the anthropologist and by the Rorschach analyst.

The ethnologist also administered a word association test and a drawing test to some of her informants and this material was subjected to a more limited analysis. The word association measure consisted of 100 words chosen from the language of the Alorese on the basis of emotional significance and frequency. It was administered to 17 men and 19 women with slightly modified instructions. There was no measure of latency of response. Du Bois presents a summary of modal responses to certain words and also reports sex differences for some words but engages in little interpretation, aside from some rather speculative suggestions in regard to sex differences in sexual adjustment and uncertainty concerning sexual role. Although admitting that her use of the instrument is fragmentary and inadequate, the author suggests that ". . . the use of a word association test phrased in the terms of the local culture and in connection with psychocultural investigations seems promising . . ." (p. 563).

Drawings were collected from 33 boys and 22 girls who were given pencil and paper and asked to draw something. They were permitted 30 minutes in which to execute their drawings. The investigator presents a content analysis of the drawings for boys and girls as well as a number of illustrative pictures. Application of the Goodenough scale of intelligence demonstrates for the boys a mental age only half of their chronological age while the female subjects are even lower. The drawings were also given to a person experienced in the psychological analysis of drawings who provided a number of interpretive statements which the anthropologist considered consistent with her own inferences based on direct observation.

The most important portion of the study of Alorese for our purposes is the Rorschach analysis and here we find several strongly positive features. First of all, the analysis of the protocols was carried out with little or no knowledge of the individual subjects and their culture. Second, the Rorschach analyst is a person of considerable stature in the field so that whatever advantage may accrue to the test as a consequence of experience and talent should presumably be fully represented in this study. Third, there is a clear delineation between inferences based upon Rorschach data and those derived from other sources of observation. Fourth, there is a wealth of direct observation, life-history data, and interpretive material to be used in providing standards for comparison with the Rorschach interpretations. Fifth, the personality inferences extracted from the Rorschach are carefully linked to specified response characteristics.

Surprisingly enough, in view of the many excellent features we have just identified, we find almost no report of the conditions under which the Rorschach was given. Thus, although we are apprised of the identity of the interpreter of the test, we are told little or nothing about the process of administration, either in regard to the Rorschach experience of Dr. Du Bois or the circumstances under which the data were collected. Furthermore, in spite of the extensive consideration of the psychology and culture of these people, there is no serious effort to examine the impact of the culture upon the test-taking process. Another regrettable feature of the study lies in the failure to attempt any formal or controlled comparison between the interpretive statements of Oberholzer and the statements provided by Du Bois and Kardiner based upon observational data. We have already agreed that the similarity between these two sets of formulations is impressive, but the case would be greatly strengthened if a controlled demonstration of this association had been made. The reader would also benefit from a more detailed account of just what information was given to Dr. Oberholzer prior to his Rorschach analyses. We are told that the interpretation was made without knowledge of the culture, but the analyst must have been told something about the nature of the study and the purpose of his participation. Moreover, we find in the section written by Oberholzer that the individual subjects are identified by name, and the name includes reference to their social role (interpreter, genealogist, seer, and so on). Even this limited information would be a powerful source of bias if it was available prior to the interpretation. If Oberholzer knew that one subject was an interpreter and that another was a seer, it would not be surprising if the psychological portraits he constructed resembled those constructed by Kardiner. Whatever differences there might be in the data each had, they shared determining information concerning a distinctive social role.

In the comparison of Swiss and Alorese protocols, one might wish that the findings had been strengthened by means of statistical analysis and that somewhat more attention had been paid to background differences between the two samples, aside from culture, that might contribute to response variation. Finally, Oberholzer indicates that preliminary analysis of the Rorschach protocols and a comparison on specific dimensions with the rankings of the anthropologist revealed a high degree of concordance. If this is so, it is certainly unfortunate that a systematic record of these rankings was not preserved and reported, for this finding would be at least as interesting as anything else included in the report. It also seems possible that this session with Dr. Du Bois must have violated somewhat the "blindness" of Oberholzer's subsequent analysis. At the very least, a comparison of rankings would lead to the ethnologist confirming or rejecting, on the basis of her data, Rorschach generalizations concerning particular subjects on particular personality dimensions.

In Ruth Benedict's (1946) well-known *The chrysanthemum and the sword,* there is a passing reference to a set of Rorschach tests collected by Dorothea Leighton from Japanese subjects in a wartime relocation camp. This source of data is often referred to in discussions of projective techniques in anthropological research, but in actual fact there is so little information in Benedict's volume concerning either how these data have contributed to her generalizations about Japanese character or the actual data and their collection, that it is impossible to describe or evaluate this study.

Honigmann's (1949) monograph dealing with the culture and ethos (group personality) of the Kaska Indians includes a rather extensive treatment of the personality of these people as viewed from the perspective of life-history material and Rorschach findings. The author's generalizations about the character or ethos of the Kaska were based upon a variety of information secured from rather close observation of a small number of informants, as well as general observation of a larger number of subjects. For those subjects who were studied intensively, there was available some or all of the following sources of data: the Rorschach test (19 adults and 9 children); a "personality data sheet" which consisted of a log of specific behavior or events that might be considered indicative of personality attributes; and for nine of the subjects, two or more relatively unstructured life-history interviews. Where dreams or folk tales were available, they too were included in the record.

The author implies that his description of the Kaska personality was derived first from participant-observation data and second from the life-history and test data: "Two principal steps may be distinguished in the analytical process: first, the inference of socially patterned dominant motivations from ethnographic data and, second, the inference of this system from the personality data, including interviews, Rorschach records, dreams, folk tales, and the casual bits of conversation and items of behavior noted on the P-data sheets" (p. 25).

The Rorschach tests were administered in English without the use of an interpreter, and typically the adult informants were given cigarettes freely during the testing period as a form of reward. Although the administration began with a standard inquiry period, it soon developed that the subjects, particularly children, became so impatient with the second round of exposure to the same cards that it was necessary to conduct the inquiry directly after the initial responses had been elicited. Consequently, for 13 of the subjects a standard inquiry was conducted, whereas for the remaining 15 it was not. For most of the female subjects, the test was administered by the wife of the anthropologist. The total group consisted of 14 adult males, five adult females, five boys, and four girls.

In referring to his method of scoring Rorschach protocols, the author cites a number of well-known contributors to the Rorschach literature and indicates that their writings were consulted. Most of the results of the psychological testing are presented in connection with a description of the ideational culture of the Kaska, and there is tabular material summarizing the average results for the adult and child groups on the dimensions of location, determinants, content, popularity, and number of responses. The ethos of the Kaska is described in a separate chapter organized about a series of "dominant motivations" including egocentricity, utilitarianism, deference, flexibility, dependence, emotional isolation. Under each of these headings there is a detailed discussion of the findings supporting the importance of this variable as a determinant of Kaska behavior, including a consideration of the appropriate Rorschach results as well as individual behavior and ethnographic data. After presenting these findings, the author attempts to synthesize them and to provide some explanation for their salience in this group by means of developmental considerations and theoretical speculation. These latter sections are not specifically linked to Rorschach findings. An appendix presents personality portraits of five individuals who were studied intensively and includes, for four of the subjects, Rorschach psychograms together with their interpretations.

There are a number of positive features to Honigmann's analysis and presentation. First, he presents a good deal of summary data concerning the scored Rorschach responses, both for individual cases and for specified groups. His interpretive statements, consequently, can be assessed against the background of reported response elements. Moreover, he frequently anchors his use of a particular pattern of response as indicative of a certain motivational tendency to specific references in the literature. Second, there is a wealth of observational material dealing with related dimensions of behavior that can be used to support or refute any particular Rorschach interpretation. Third, the administration and interpretation of the Rorschach were carried out by individuals familiar with the culture of the Kaska who might be expected to secure better response data to begin with, as well as to make better use of this material in subsequent interpretation, than persons lacking such familiarity.

On the negative side, the monograph supplies rather scant information concerning the factors which determined the selection of Rorschach subjects, in addition to a limited report concerning details of test administration and the relation of test-taking to the cultural context. Although the interpretative process is adequately described and accompanied by a good deal of response data, there appears to be no serious attempt to assess the influence of cultural variation or the particular testing situation upon the pattern of test results. It is also true that the discussion of "dominant motivations" suggests to the reader that the author had arrived at a conception of these dimensions on the basis of general observation of the Kaska and had then proceeded to examine the Rorschach for evidence that fitted directly with these conceptions. This impression is strengthened by the rather precarious connection between some of the personality variables discussed and their Rorschach indices. For example, $F+/F-$ was treated as a measure of egocentricity, and per cent of $M, FM, m,$ as indicative of utilitarianism. There is no statistical analysis of the Rorschach findings, although quantitative data is presented. In general, one may question whether the substance of this investigator's report would have differed appreciably if he had conducted the same field work but had not administered the Rorschach.

One of the most highly regarded of modern anthropological monographs is the community study of the Tepoztlan conducted by Lewis (1951). This inquiry represents the second time in two decades that this Mexican community has been studied, for some seventeen years earlier Redfield had conducted a study that resulted in his influential *Tepoztlan—a Mexican Village* (1930). Included in the more recent study was an extensive program of Rorschach testing, and the results of this effort are summarized in a chapter entitled "The People as Seen from Their Rorschach Tests" written by Theodora Abel and Renata Calabresi.

The Rorschach protocols were collected by Ruth Lewis, wife of the principal investigator, with the intent of securing tests from individuals of both sexes and of different age groups. The testing was initiated in families where assistants had been living and where good rapport had already been established. Furthermore, the practice was followed of beginning with the adults in the family and then extending the testing to include the younger members of the family. Some of the testing was carried out in school surroundings, although there were two conspicuous difficulties here: the relatively low status of schools in this culture and the fact that the administration, which required the tester and the subject to be alone together, was suspect. This problem was made more acute by a local healer who felt threatened by the project doctor and responded by circulating pornographic pictures, which, he asserted, were the pictures being used in the Rorschach testing sessions. Although the testing assistants worked through the families and used various gifts to motivate the subjects, the children had considerable difficulty with the test, and this problem was exaggerated by the local conviction that it was not good to study or think too much. In the end the investigators were able to secure 106 usable protocols, almost evenly divided between the two sexes and including representatives of the following age groups: older adults, younger adults, adolescents, children just before puberty, and young children.

In presenting the results of their analysis, Abel and Calabresi (1951) first consider the group as a whole, then compare their findings in this group with the findings of other investigators, and finally focus their attention upon comparisons within the Tepoztlan group itself. The authors had only limited exposure to the culture of their subjects, for prior to writing this chapter ". . . they had seen three short published articles of mine [Lewis] one of which dealt with inter-personal relations. In addition, they had read an early version of one of my family studies" (p. 306). In describing the group as a whole, Abel and Calabresi point to the subjects' concrete rather than abstract approach to the blots ($D>W$) and the relative balance between inner and outer life, as reflected in the roughly equal frequency of Movement and Color responses. Their responses show more interest in animals than in people or human relations and little evidence of overt aggression or hostility. Their contact with the external world is realistic as reflected in F per cent and $F+$ per cent, and yet they are not so dominated by reality perception as to be incapable of impulse (FC) or fantasy (M).

The authors compare the frequency of response (R) of the Tepoztecans to that of white and Negro subjects in our own culture, Guatemalan subjects (Billig, Gillin, & Davidson, 1947, 1948), and American Indian subjects (Hallowell, 1942), noting that only in comparison to the Guatemalan subjects do the Tepoztecans appear more productive. The Guatemalan subjects were divided into an Indian group and a Ladinos group (higher-status group of Spanish descent), and the authors suggest that the quality of response of the Tepoztecans resembles the Ladinos in the incidence of Human Movement and Color responses. This result may be partially a consequence of the fact that unlike the Guatemalan Indians, the Tepoztecans do not live adjacent to a higher-status group from whom they must withdraw or submit. When compared to Hallowell's Ojibwa Indians, the Mexican subjects showed a much lower incidence of Human Movement responses which suggested to the authors a more constricted inner life.

The remaining portion of the chapter is devoted to a discussion of age and sex differences in Rorschach performance in Tepoztlan. The authors present in tabular form high and low trends for males and females in each of the five age groups. A high trend indicates that 60 per cent of the particular subgroup scored above the median for the group as a whole, whereas a low trend indicates that 60 per cent of the group scored below the median for the group as a whole. There is a detailed discussion of these results which focuses on sex differences at the various ages, and the chief conclusion of the authors concerns:

... the opposite course taken by the life cycle of the men and women. Women appear to be initiated early in their role of life, and are consistently expected to avoid sex as a source of pleasure. They follow a well-defined line of development, with conscious control over their feelings and impulses, but in later years they assume the dominant role in society. Men experience more discontinuity and inconsistency in behavior; they are

likely to be more exuberant than women but also more anxious and insecure. As they grow older, they lose their dominant position, and the older
adults appear disturbed, impulsive, and anxious. They seem to be losing
the grip on society that the older women are taking over. (Abel & Calabresi, 1951, p. 318)

In discussing the group as a whole, the authors emphasize the lack
of friendliness and co-operativeness of the people, their rigidity, and
yet their realistic perception of the outer world. The Tepoztecans
apparently have neither an active fantasy life nor warm and enduring
interpersonal relations.

Perhaps the most impressive aspect of this analysis is the extent
to which the authors have carefully linked their personality inferences to identified elements of test performance. As a result of their
table indicating age and sex trends, as well as numerous statements
interspersed through the text, the reader is given an excellent idea
of what types of response led the authors to particular conclusions
concerning the personality of their informants. Another outstanding
feature of this study is the careful description of the circumstances
under which the tests were administered. As we have seen, the ethnologist not only indicates the approach to the subjects he used, but
also he comments freely upon the obstacles and difficulties he encountered in the process of administering the Rorschach. This section is of value in assessing the present findings, and it contains material of potential interest for those who might consider the use of
projective techniques in similar cultural settings. In this same context, some attention is paid to the influence of the local culture upon
response to the tests. A final commendable feature of this report is
the extensive use of comparative data, both within the culture under
study and in relation to the findings of other investigators working
in different societies.

Perhaps the most serious flaw of this study has to do with the
relation between the ethnological data and the projective-test data.
First of all, it should be noted that the personality inferences derived
from the Rorschach are presented in a separate chapter and no formal attempt is made to examine their continuity or discontinuity
with findings derived from other sources. Thus, even though many
of the statements by Abel and Calabresi refer specifically to the local
culture (as in the previous quotation), no attempt is made to appraise the accuracy of these by so much as a footnote. The entire

responsibility for examining these findings against the background of ethnological data rests with the reader. The second flaw is the puzzling report that the interpreters of the test were given access to some, but not much, information concerning the Tepoztlan culture. Such an approach loses the advantages of either extreme. The data are contaminated by some knowledge, so that we can no longer consider the Rorschach findings to be independent of the ethnology, and yet the Rorschach is interpreted without a full knowledge of the local norms and conventions. It would have been much better either to have kept the interpreters completely ignorant of the surrounding culture or else to have urged them to saturate themselves with this material.

One may also regret that with such extensive quantitative results the authors made no attempt to employ simple statistical analysis to permit a rough estimation of the role of chance factors. Further, the use of differences between the findings in this study and the findings of other investigators seems somewhat questionable. Although these differences are discussd at some length, there is little or no attempt to exploit or develop their psychological significance. A final criticism of the study is that the analysts failed at any point to consider seriously the possible role of nonpersonality factors in producing the findings under discussion. This is true in spite of the fact that the discussion of the conditions under which the test was administered provides at least some data that could be employed fruitfully in such an analysis. Several of these same criticisms were pointed out by Dr. Abel herself in a paper delivered at the First Inter-American Congress of Psychology (1953).

Included among the studies comprising the Coordinated Investigation of Micronesian Anthropology is an investigation by Joseph and Murray (1951) of the Chamorro and Carolinian groups on the island of Saipan. The intent of this study was not only to provide a general personality description of individuals in these two cultural groups but also to deal with problems posed by the interaction between the American culture and the culture of Saipan.

The subjects of this investigation were principally a group of 200 children and 30 adults, and the relevant findings, in the present context, are those derived from the Rorschach. The children included 100 boys and 100 girls between the ages of five and seventeen and there were an even number of Chamorros and Carolinians. Through a public-address system the subjects were informed of the plans for testing, and they were asked by name to report to the local school at an assigned time for the purpose of test administration. Most of the children appeared submissive and co-operative, and they were tested with the aid of interpreters whom they knew. The actual choice of subjects was from a census list and was carried out in a roughly random manner so that there is little doubt that this sample is more representative of the community from which they were chosen than is typically true in anthropological investigations. The adult sample consisted of 15 men and 15 women all of whom were Chamorros and who represented a high level of success within their own community and in dealing with Western culture. That the adult sample was relatively small and nonrepresentative was a consequence of pressure of time, and the decision to focus upon the Chamorros derived from the fact that they were the majority group on Saipan.

The authors discuss some of the difficulties encountered in the cross-cultural application of the Rorschach test but conclude that in spite of these, the instrument has much to offer in this setting. In support of the test, they point to the fact that in their testing of frankly psychotic Saipanese they found the protocols of these subjects to ". . . show the same disintegrated patterns and serious decrease or loss of reality testing as the records of psychotic members of our own culture" (p. 144). They point to the unfortunate fact that time limits placed upon the worker in the field have usually made it impossible to deal adequately with Rorschach responses both quantitatively and qualitatively. Although they recognize the importance of both approaches, for a variety of reasons the authors elected the quantitative approach as representing an important first step in the development of the tool for cross-cultural purposes. Thus, their report focuses upon ranges, frequencies, and averages of the various scorable elements of the Rorschach for the special groups we have just described. The authors label their result the "Rorschach group personality" and recommend it as a convenient abstraction useful in determining individuals who depart from the group, as well as in comparing the group with other groups.

The results of the children's Rorschach test are summarized in the form of actual distributions of responses of boys and girls within each of the cultural groups for a large number of scoring categories.

Given these relatively objective findings, the authors discuss their psychological significance, proceeding on the assumption that ". . . most of the psychological equivalents of the test have universal value . . ." (p. 191). The over-all impression that the investigators arrive at concerning the personality of both cultural groups is relatively negative: "According to the Rorschach findings, the Saipanese children were functioning on a precarious level of adjustment. Their anxiety tolerance was low. They showed remarkable similarities with the 'institution children' in our society . . ." (p. 193). This evidence of malfunctioning was not ascribed to biological factors or generally inferior perceptual capacities by the authors, because there were some records that displayed a high form level and considerable originality, and some of the children who did poorly on the Rorschach test performed very well on other psychological tests. In view of this, the authors conclude that the inferior Rorschach performance was a consequence of "psychogenic disturbance." The most deviant aspects of the children's response have to do not with bizarre percepts but rather with a great deal of vagueness and a tendency to repeat the same percept to various stimuli. The protocols, as a group, suggest little abstract capacity and limited imaginative ability, with relatively good capacity for practical thinking. From the content of the Rorschach responses, the investigators conclude that the most salient problem of the children, which accounts for their low tolerance for anxiety, is a loss of self-esteem.

A comparison of the two groups of children revealed that the "Chamorro children were less reckless in their mental approach, more 'objective' and more differentiating in their thinking. . . . The Carolinians seemed even more subjective in their thinking, but, at the same time, more shrewdly practical" (pp. 195-196). The Chamorro children appeared more emotionally mature, whereas the Carolinians appeared more spontaneous emotionally and more at ease in social interaction.

The Rorschach results for the Chamorro adults are again reported by first summarizing the distribution of responses for a number of scoring categories and then proceeding to interpretation of the group pattern. In comparison to the children the investigators conclude: ". . . the adults were on the average better endowed than the children, that they functioned on a much higher level of adjustment, but that they showed symptoms of the same types of emotional disturbance, although their defenses were better developed" (p.

223). Anxiety was less pervasive than in the children, and there was evidence of better developed mechanisms of defense.

It is interesting to note that although performance on the intelligence tests and the Bender Gestalt test did not differentiate the Chamorros and Carolinian children effectively, performance on the Rorschach did.

While the children of both groups showed a general pattern of anxiety and submissiveness, and most of them obviously functioned on a lower level than their capacities warranted, anxiety in the Chamorros seemed to be a more chronic condition and to have given rise to certain specific defense mechanisms, while the Carolinians appeared more exposed to panic-like states but also showed surprising recoverability. Affectively, the Carolinians were distinguished from the more inhibited Chamorros by their comparatively high spontaneity and markedly uncontrolled emotionality. (p. 292)

This monograph compares favorably with comparable investigations on a number of counts. One of the most valuable features of the study is the extensive experience that Alice Joseph has had with projective techniques in alien cultures. Furthermore, the large sample and the relatively random manner in which the children were selected suggest that the Rorschach responses are far more representative of the target population than is true of many other studies. We find a pleasing degree of explicitness in describing the Rorschach responses of the various groups of subjects, and the personality inferences derived from these data are carefully linked to specific data. Although the test findings are presented separately from ethnographic and interview data, the authors have not hesitated to draw upon multiple sources in accounting for the behavior of their informants. The investigators report in some detail the specific conditions surrounding administration of the tests and in so doing describe a number of factors that seem likely to have influenced their findings. To be applauded also is the fact that both administration and interpretation of the Rorschach test was carried out by individuals thoroughly familiar with the test and with the local culture.

On the negative side, we may note that the possible contribution to Rorschach responses of nonpersonality differences between Chamorro and Carolinian subjects is not explored. Furthermore, the entire interpretation rests upon assumptions in regard to the continuity of test response between our own culture and this alien culture, that can scarcely be supported by evidence and that might be strongly opposed on rational grounds. Thus, the negative psychological portrait of the children of Saipan which emerges from the Rorschach interpretation may well reflect cultural and situational factors rather than genuine personality dispositions. The marked differences in the techniques used to select and test children and adult subjects make the few generalizations concerning differences between these two groups hazardous. Again there is no attempt to apply any type of statistical analysis, and consequently we have little basis for deciding when obtained differences in average score are due to anything more than random variation.

An unusually interesting and sophisticated application of projective techniques in anthropological research is Wallace's (1952a) use of the Rorschach to assess the modal personality of the Tuscarora Indians. Although the primary goal of this study was the description of the modal personality structure of a heavily acculturated Iroquois tribe, the author also examined the relation between personality attributes and the local culture and attempted a comparison of the modal personalities of the Tuscarora and Ojibwa Indians.

The principal findings of the study are based upon 70 Rorschach protocols, all but one of which were collected by the investigator or his wife. This sample was selected after the investigator had conducted a census of the Tuscarora and was intended to reflect the age and sex characteristics of the adult groups as a whole. The majority of the subjects were selected by one of the members of the family with which the ethnologist was living, following age and sex specifications provided by Wallace. Later in the study, the investigator became concerned about the possible bias this procedure might create and began to select subjects independently of his informant. He suggests, "It cannot be asserted that the sample is proportionally representative insofar as socioeconomic status, chieftainship, matronhood, lacrosse-playing, alcoholism, and a variety of other important factors are concerned; but most of the many possible categories have at least one representative. On the whole, the writer is satisfied that the present sample is really a fair representation of Tuscarora society" (p. 42). The test was administered under standard conditions except that the testing was done at the convenience of the informant, with a good deal of consequent variation in physical location, social setting, illumination, and such.

The analysis was carried out following Klopfer's scoring procedures. Having completed the scoring of the 70 records, Wallace identified the modal score for each of the 21 scores or dimensions that were of principle interest to him. Given the mode, he computed confidence limits for each modal score so that any score falling outside of this range could be said to deviate significantly ($p < .03$) from the mode. Thus, for each of the 21 scores he had a definition of what constituted a modal range of response, and he proceeded to identify all of those individual records that fell within this range on all scores. There were 26 cases in this modal class and an additional 16 cases that were considered submodal, that is, their psychograms showed substantial resemblance to the modal profile. This left 28 deviant cases that could not be considered to reflect the modal type. Having identified the 26 modal records, Wallace averaged the scores for each of the dimensions, thus arriving at a single psychogram that represented the average of the modal records. This psychogram was then interpreted by the author and Dr. and Mrs. Hallowell, utilizing Klopfer's principles of interpretation and with full awareness of Wallace's direct observation of the subjects.

Initially the author was impressed with the relative similarity between the modal profile of his subjects and that which might be expected for typical American subjects. Following a detailed interpretation of the profile, however, Wallace suggests:

. . . The Tuscarora modal personality type . . . (displays) (1) on a basic but presumably largely unconscious level, a strong urge to be allowed to become passive and dependent; (2) a fear of rejection and punishment by the environment and by the self for these demands; (3) a compensatory drive to be hyperindependent, aggressive, self-sufficient; (4) an ultimate incapacity to feel, to adapt, to evaluate the environment realistically, and a concomitant dependence upon categories, stereotypes, and deductive logic. (p. 75)

Following this general description, there is some discussion of deviant cases and a brief consideration of the relation between these personality findings and the Tuscarora culture.

A final section of the monograph is devoted to a comparison of the modal personality of the Tuscarora and Ojibwa. This rests upon the data we have described and on a set of 102 Ojibwa Rorschach protocols obtained from Hallowell and subjected to the method of analysis we have just discussed. Basing his comparison completely upon these modal profiles, Wallace arrives at the conclusion that the Ojibwa and Tuscarora modal personalities are markedly different although they show some points of similarity. These differences and similarities are then discussed in the light of discrepancies between the two cultures.

In a separate publication, Wallace (1952b) emphasizes the extreme diversity in personality structure displayed by his Tuscarora subjects. On this basis he reasons that the concept of a national character or a common personality type might better be replaced by a modal personality which is ". . . a type of personality more closely approximated by more individuals than any other type . . ." (p. 750).

In many important respects this study serves as a model investigation. Probably nowhere in the literature is there a more detailed and revealing account of the circumstances under which projective-technique data were collected. Moreover, the test-taking behavior of the informants is examined against the background of cultural convention. The scoring of the Rorschach protocols is conventional but carefully described, and the steps that the author has taken in identifying his modal type represent a skillful and interesting approach to the problem of arriving at group representativeness. Most impressive is not the superiority of his method over other approaches that might have been used but rather the thoughtfulness with which this approach was elected and the consistency with which it was carried out. The need to recognize the difference between a series of similar individual profiles and an average profile, arrived at by combining many different profiles, seems obvious when it has been pointed out, but very few workers in this area have recognized the problem, let alone attempted to cope with it. Moreover, Wallace shows considerable skill, both conceptually and to some extent empirically, in maintaining a clear distinction between personality inferences and cultural inferences. The sample of subjects appears to be relatively representative, and even more impressive is Wallace's capacity to examine the various sources of bias or contamination that might have operated and his frank and revealing description of how the sample was collected. A final noteworthy quality in this research is the author's broad awareness of relevant technical issues spanning several disciplines.

There are a number of minor criticisms that can be raised against Wallace's findings (sampling bias, effects of conditions under which test is administered, and so on), but the author is so clearly aware of these problems and so disarming in the tentativeness with which he presents his findings that it would be graceless to dwell upon these matters. There are also a host of empirical problems involved in the comparison of the Ojibwa and the Tuscarora, such matters as differences in examiners, scoring and use of interpreter, that undoubtedly make any comparison between the modal profiles of these two samples little more than suggestive. The most surprising shortcoming of the study is the failure of the author, in spite of his conceptual clarity and his clear awareness of the problem, to protect his inferences concerning the modal personality from information concerning the Tuscarora culture. As we have said earlier, under some circumstances an investigator may not be concerned with separating cultural and personality data, but in studies such as Wallace's, where the investigator wishes to relate his personality data to patterns of culture, it is important to preserve the independence of the two bodies of data. In view of this, it is surprising to find that the author interpreted the modal Rorschach results, checking "Rorschach conclusions for congruence with his impressions of people and behavior patterns which he remembered." (1952a, p. 70) Even more surprising is the investigator's report that a "blind" interpretation of the same Rorschach data was carried out by a psychologist and is contained in the author's files, followed by no further mention of this very interesting source of data.

A recent study by Straus and Straus (1957) utilizes the Rorschach test to study children on the island of Ceylon. The investigators set out to investigate the modal personality of the Sinhalese, to compare the Rorschach performance of this group with a comparable American group, and to test the hypothesis that Sinhalese children are insecure. The projective test was administered to a total of 73 children, including all 34 children attending school in a small highland village, and 39 children (every third child) attending school in a larger city. The children averaged a little less than 10 years in age and, with only four exceptions, the test was administered in the school setting in the native language by three senior students from the University of Ceylon. These collaborators were given special instructions prior to the beginning of data collection and worked under the direct supervision of the investigators. Almost all of the children appeared co-operative and eager to do well.

The authors report the median and quartile deviation for each of the conventional Rorschach scores and compare many of these scores with the medians reported by Ames, Learned, Metraux, and Walker (1952) in a study of American children's Rorschach responses. The statistical significance of the difference between the Sinhalese scores and the scores for the American children is tested individually in all cases where the data permit. The authors, on examination of the reported quartile deviations for the various scores, conclude that a sufficient number of the subjects fall within a narrow range on these scores that ". . . the results of this study give some support to the validity and utility of the concepts of national character and modal personality" (Straus & Straus, 1957, p. 110). They also conclude that, although the Rorschach protocols of the Sinhalese children are markedly different from typical American Rorschach protocols, they nevertheless show considerable resemblance to protocols obtained from American subjects of comparable age. The hypothesis that the Sinhalese children are characterized by a high degree of insecurity appears to be confirmed in the judgment of the investigators. In describing the Sinhalese subjects, the authors place particular emphasis upon their restriction of emotional response, absence of rich inner life and creativity, high incidence of anxiety and insecurity, and their cautious practicality.

A number of positive features of this study are readily apparent. The sample is certainly more representative of the populations from which it was drawn than is often the case in such studies. We are told something about how the testing was conducted and the attitude of the respondents toward the test. Furthermore, this test-taking attitude is taken into account in discussing the basis for some of the findings. In particular, the high R and low rate of card rejection by the Sinhalese subjects are viewed against the background of local culture and the test-taking attitude of respondents. Furthermore, to compare the newly collected Rorschach protocols carefully with normative data from an American group of similar age is a much more reasonable procedure than to rely upon impressions of general European-American norms as have other investigators. Further confidence in the findings derives from the investigators' willingness to test the statistical significance of observed differences and the objective reporting of medians and deviation measures for the Sinhalese.

The major shortcoming of this study is the lack of satisfactory comparability between the American and Sinhalese children, since this comparison plays a central role in almost all of the authors' inferences. The fact that the American Rorschachs were collected by examiners who must have had a very different amount of Rorschach training and type of professional background from the examiners in the present study; the likelihood of enormous variation between the comparison groups in socioeconomic, demographic, and other characteristics not an integral part of the dominant culture to which they belong; and, finally, the probability that the subjects vary a great deal in their attitudes toward the test and the testing process—all this impairs confidence in the reported findings. Actually, the authors note the existence of such differences but do not fully exploit their potential impact upon the obtained results. In brief, these investigators, along with most other authors, have failed to make a sufficiently diligent examination of the nonpersonality factors that may have contributed to the aspects of test performance upon which their interpretations are based. One final objection concerns the admittedly qualitative judgment the authors make in concluding that the variation about the reported medians is not sufficient to discourage the application of general descriptive terms to this group. Although there are no firm standards here, I can only report, from another vantage, that examination of the quartile deviations for the various Rorschach scores suggests to me that there is a great deal of variation and consequently that interpretations which rest solely upon measures of central tendency are restricted in their usefulness. Thus, there seems no firm empirical basis either for supporting or for infirming the utility of the concept of national character.

In a further study involving the same Sinhalese subjects, Straus (1957) attempted to relate toilet-training and feeding practices in childhood to personality as measured by the Rorschach test. Information concerning feeding (oral frustration) was secured through interviews and was summarized by means of six specific items (for example, fed on schedule, bottle fed, sudden weaning) that were assigned weighed scores. These weighted scores were then summated leading to a single index that could range theoretically from 0 to 9. Toilet training was similarly represented by a total of seven weighted items, which led to an anal-frustration index that could range from 0 to 11.

Each of these sets of scores was then related to a number of specific dimensions drawn from the Rorschach on the basis of a prior expectation that such psychological variables would be associated with toilet training or feeding experience. Prior expectation was determined chiefly by a summary prepared by Honigmann (1949) of the personality attributes that have been reported to be associated with severity of weaning and toilet training. The scoring of the Rorschach protocols is not reported in detail in this article (Straus, 1957), but it was derived from Klopfer (Klopfer, Ainsworth, Klopfer, & Holt, 1954) and included ratings for the following general variables: maladjustment, emotional disturbance, need for affection, anxiety, insecurity, aggression, passivity, inadequacy, constriction. In addition, four specific Rorschach scores (for example, F per cent over 50; D per cent over 70) were related to the measure of anal frustration. In all, there were 22 tests of association between the various personality measures and the indices of early experience, and five of these proved to be significant at or below the 10 per cent level. In view of the fact that so few of the relationships achieved this rather permissive standard of significance, and the further fact that all of those associations that proved significant were in a direction opposite to that predicted, the investigator concluded that there was no evidence for any association between early feeding experience or toilet training and personality.

The advantages and disadvantages we have just discussed in connection with the previous study (Straus & Straus, 1957) are, for the most part, equally applicable here (Straus, 1957). The chief superiority of this study derives from its skirting the necessity of comparing two cultural groups that are as poorly matched as those employed in the first study. In general, the present study involves relatively full specification of objective techniques of analysis and a more sophisticated statistical analysis of the resultant data than is characteristic of studies in this area. On the negative side, one may question, of course, whether the Rorschach variables represent the underlying variables they were intended to assess with sufficient fidelity to constitute a fair test of the relationships at issue. The sophisticated student of psychoanalytic theory would almost surely object to the suggestion that the empirical relationships under test represent derivations from psychoanalytic theory. He would undoubtedly feel that a very general summary such as Honigmann's does not constitute an acceptable basis for generating predictions from this theory.

Richards (1954) reports a further Rorschach study that focuses upon acculturated Chinese. The findings in this case are derived from 35 Rorschach records collected by Francis Hsu from a group of Chinese subjects living in Hawaii. The subjects included 27 males and 8 females and ranged in age from 16 to 60. The average age for the female subjects was 25 and for the male subjects, 41. They were drawn from the upper socioeconomic class, and most had completed high school or had some college education. The psychologist scored and interpreted the protocols without any background information other than that the subjects were Chinese and lived in Hawaii.

Averages for a number of conventional Rorschach dimensions are reported and compared with Klopfer's characterization of an ideal healthy American, with the average Rorschach profile for a group of American soldiers, and with Beck's (Beck, Rabin, Thiesen, Molish, and Thetford, 1950) normal sample. In addition, Richards compares the Rorschach performance of male and female subjects and introduces a number of concrete illustrations from the protocols in the process of interpreting the findings reported.

The author concludes that there is no single personality quality that is characteristic of these Chinese subjects. Although they show considerable variability, their average performance differs relatively little from the performance of the American subjects in the various comparison groups. When female Chinese subjects are compared with males, they appear to show more anxiety and depression in response to the "father figure," to be more oriented toward inner life, and to display more evidence of masculine protest. The male subjects, on the other hand, show more evidence of disturbance in sexual and interpersonal relations, seem less spontaneous, and are more concerned with prestige and social conformity. Richards also points out that the absence of comparable Rorschach data for non-Chinese Hawaiians is an important deficiency in this study.

Perhaps the most positive aspect of this study is the author's caution in generalizing from his data and his thoroughly justified concern over the absence of a suitable control group of non-Chinese Hawaiians. Also, there appears to be a higher degree of "blindness" in this study than in most such studies. The interpreter seems to have known very little about either the culture, the intent of the investigator, or the special characteristics of the subjects whose protocols he interpreted.

The fact that this study is reported as a "progress report" tends to disarm the critic. However, if we take the study as it is reported, it seems vulnerable to many criticisms, including the author's failure to make clear the precise purpose of the study. If we assume that a characterization of the modal personality of this subgroup is an important aim, a number of flaws become immediately apparent. First, the various American groups with which the Chinese subjects are compared are far from being comparable on many dimensions other than nationality or cultural background, and consequently it is impossible to interpret meaningfully the observed differences. Second, even the comparison of the male and female Chinese subjects appears relatively fruitless in view of age differences and the very small number of female subjects. There is, of course, virtually no information concerning the selection of subjects or the circumstances surrounding the administration of the test, and no effort is made to estimate the role of chance factors in producing the observed differences between sexes and comparison groups. There is little or no attempt to relate the personality observations to other types of information such as ethnological data. All in all, one may seriously question whether such a study leads to any useful outcome.

One of the many outgrowths of the Harvard Values Project is an interesting application of the Rorschach test in the study of modal personality in four distinct cultural groups sharing a common geographic location. With the intent of testing "the prevailing idea that there are wide personality differences between cultures," Kaplan (1954, p. vii) administered the Rorschach to a total of 170 subjects, half of whom were veterans and half nonveterans. Included in the sample were 53 Zuni subjects, 27 Navaho subjects, 20 Mormon subjects, and 23 Spanish-American subjects, ranging in age from 17 to 47.

Kaplan provides a careful account of the circumstances under which the testing was carried out, describing the most important details separately for each of the four groups. In general, the administration was informal and dictated by convenience of the subject and by the attempt to maximize rapport with him. Between the groups there was a good deal of variation in the circumstances surrounding selection of subjects and administration of the test, for example, about two thirds of the Navaho were tested with the aid of an interpreter, but the other groups were tested in English; Navaho and Spanish-American subjects were paid one dollar for their cooperation, but the other subjects were given no payment. With the Zuni, the investigator encountered considerable resistance and suspicion, culminating in the rumor that he was a German spy, apparently because of the German words on the Rorschach folder. The investigator is frank to admit that this circumstance not only influenced the attitudes and behavior of the subjects, but also led to detectable changes in the investigator, who was thereafter inclined to attribute hostility to all Zunis with whom he interacted. Of the other groups, the Mormon subjects seemed to respond to the test much as white American subjects whom the investigator had tested elsewhere; the Navaho subjects seemed unaware of the personal nature of the test responses and were unusually free and spontaneous in their behavior in the test situation; whereas the Spanish-American subjects tended to give brief responses and seemed to the investigator to make little effort to perform well.

The Rorschach protocols were scored following the recommendations of Klopfer and Kelley (1942), although only 14 of the 27 variables analyzed were used in the study proper. This reduction in the number of variables was an effort to reduce the likelihood of capitalizing on chance factors in the statistical analysis. Variables were eliminated that had a very low incidence or were heavily dependent upon other variables. In an appendix the investigator reports individual scores for each subject on 25 Rorschach variables.

By means of analysis of variance and chi-square, the four groups were compared for the 14 Rorschach variables. The findings indicated that on five of the variables ($FC, CF, T/R, FC', m$) there were differences between the four cultures that were significant at the 5 per cent level. An additional three variables ($R, M, FC:CF$) approached this level of significance. When the four groups were compared individually by means of a t test on eight Rorschach variables, 13 of the 48 comparisons revealed significance at the 5 per cent level. A comparison, for these same variables, of the variance between the four cultures and the variance within the individual cultures, revealed that the within-group variance was much greater than the between-group variance. This finding suggests that, at least for these dimensions, the four groups are characterized more by overlap than distinctiveness. A further comparison of the four cultures in terms of variability of these scores revealed that there were significant differences in 22 of 48 comparisons. This suggests that the cultures are more readily distinguished by variability than by average performance, as only 13 of the comparisons concerned with mean differences were significant. Kaplan concludes:

The significant differences between means, while not very great in number, are nevertheless very definite, and they indicate the presence of real differences, however small, between cultures . . . the variability of the scores was found to be exceptionally high. A very high degree of overlap among the groups is present, and this, coupled with the small size of the differences that do appear, indicates that the variability of individuals in any one culture is greater than the variability between cultures. (Kaplan, 1954, p. 18)

Inspection of the group averages on the Rorschach indices provided strong evidence suggesting that the Spanish-American group was more constricted than the other groups. Kaplan discusses this in the light of lack of involvement and effort on the part of these subjects and suggests that it is impossible to know whether this behavior reflects underlying personality attributes that might legitimately be considered related to the concept of modal personality or whether it derives from "superficial cultural injunctions or situational factors."

The four groups were also compared in terms of Popular responses, and the frequencies for each culture of a large number of specific responses are reported in tabular form. Examination of these data leads to the conclusion that "there is substantial similarity among the four cultures as to the frequency of the most popular responses" (p. 22). A simple comparison of the four groups in terms of two aspects of Rorschach content (Animal responses and kinds of action) revealed no marked differences between the groups.

Taking all of his findings into consideration, the investigator concludes ". . . concepts such as modal personality are appropriate to personality material such as we have collected, but . . . their applicability is limited and will vary from culture to culture and from one kind of personality material to another" (p. 31). Perhaps the major emphasis of these concluding remarks is upon the great variability in personality within the individual cultures studied. Kaplan suggests, "Anthropologists have in general tended to underestimate individual variability within cultures" (p. 32).

In a variety of respects this investigation attains unusually high standards. We find, to begin with, that Kaplan has provided a careful description of the circumstances under which the Rorschach data were collected from each of the four groups. Furthermore, he has not hesitated to report information concerning difficulties encountered in the field situation that many investigators would have been tempted to conceal, or at least to discuss only in informal conversation. The positive impact of this candor is strengthened by Kluckhohn's report,

in the foreword, that his observation of Kaplan in the field setting indicated that the psychologist had unusual skill in securing effective
co-operation from his subjects. Almost unique among investigations
in this area is the author's attempt to utilize information concerning
subjects' reaction to the test situation in his consideration of some of
the observed findings (constriction of the Spanish-American group).
The efforts of the investigator to determine whether the Rorschach
protocols of the four groups are largely similar, or clearly distinctive,
are most impressive both because of the relatively high degree of
rigor in the analysis and because of the variety of different ways in
which the investigator approaches the question. Kaplan's efforts to
control for chance factors are as careful and meaningful as those of
any worker in this area. His findings on the variability of personality
within a single culture represent an important substantive contribution.

Perhaps the major flaw of this study lies in the questionable
comparability of the four cultural groups. Aside from cultural differences, it seems likely that these groups varied considerably on a
variety of attributes that, as our earlier discussion has implied, could
be expected to influence test performance, for example, education,
age, facility with English, experience with tests. It is unfortunate that
we are not given more information concerning such characteristics.
Perhaps the most dramatic differences between the groups have to do
with the fact that the circumstances of test administration were
materially different in the four cultures. As we have seen, interpreters were necessary for half of the Navaho but not for the other
groups; the Navaho and Spanish-American subjects were paid to
participate and the Zuni and Mormon subjects were not; the
Spanish-American subjects were largely recruited in a bar, whereas
the other subjects were contacted in very different social settings,
with the examiner cast in different social roles. We have already commented upon the investigator's serious concern with the test setting
in attempting to understand the constriction of the Spanish-American
subjects. It is regrettable that this same concern was not extended to
other differences revealed in the comparison of the four groups on the
various Rorschach variables.

One further quality of this study to which some readers might
object is the extremely limited attempt on the part of the investigator
to give his findings psychological flesh. That is, almost all of the dis-

cussion revolves around the existence of group differences on Rorschach dimensions, and virtually no attempt is made to discuss the substantive nature or meaning of these differences.

A recent study that has attracted considerable favorable attention is the investigation of Indian national character by Carstairs (1957). The investigator, a British psychiatrist trained in anthropology, set out to do his own field work in the tradition of McDougall and Rivers. The study began as an attempt to examine the effectiveness of Adolph Meyer's psychobiology in accounting for the process of personality formation in an Eastern society, but in process, it was converted to an examination of the "essential differences between Indian and Western personality structure." It also attempted to identify "the means whereby group personality characteristics are transmitted."

The investigation was conducted in a Hindu village that had not been heavily influenced by Western culture and that included members of the three highest Hindu castes. The principal data collected by the investigator during his ten months of observation were derived from intensive, nondirective interviews. Carstairs encouraged his informants to tell him in detail about how they had grown up in their family and community but permitted them to range widely in terms of the topics they discussed. He also inquired about dreams and asked for associations to these. Finally, most informants took the Raven Progressive Matrices test of intelligence, the Rorschach test, and a specially devised word association test. The interviews were for the most part conducted in Hindustani and spanned between ten and twenty hours for each subject. Forty-five male life histories divided among the three highest Hindu castes (Rajputs, 13; Brahmins, 11; Banias, 12) and Moslems (9) were collected. Local convention made it impossible for the investigator to conduct such prolonged interviews with female informants, and consequently all of the informants were male. Eight other case histories were attempted but had to be abandoned for reasons that the author specifies.

The findings are reported in terms of a description of the village in which the study took place, a very brief description of each informant who participated in the study, followed by consideration successively of interpersonal relations, family relationships, Hindu body image, religion, fantasy, those traits common to the three castes, and those that differentiate them. The author then presents a brief but very interesting discussion of the problem of subjective influences upon data collection, his own concern over this problem midway through the study, and his resultant effort to cope with the problem by observing a group of Bhil tribesmen who were considered to be sharply differentiated from the Hindu villagers. The development of the Hindu personality is considered extensively in connection with conscious processes and unconscious processes. In a separate section of the book, detailed life histories are presented for three informants who represent each of the three castes.

Virtually all of this is presented without reference to projective techniques, and there is good reason to believe that the author was directly influenced very little by responses to these tests. The one exception to this generalization is the fact that each of the three life histories contains a complete summary of the Rorschach test and an individual interpretation. For the two subjects who took the word association test, there is also brief mention of some of the important features of their responses to this test. An appendix includes a summary of the number of delayed word association responses to each of the 60 stimulus words for the Rajput, Brahmin, Bania, and Moslem subjects as well as a qualitative discussion of the relation between certain response tendencies and characteristics of the group and the relation between individual response tendencies and characteristics of the individual informants. The author says, "In practice, this test proved most useful in indicating areas of emotional involvement of individual subjects, hence suggesting topics for further talk" (p. 321). The same appendix also includes a summary statement by Dr. Rosemary Gordon, who performed the interpretations of the three Rorschach tests included in the individual case histories, in which she indicates that her interpretive approach to the protocols was much the same as would have been employed if the subjects had been European. She also identifies some of the problems involved in such a procedure. The author indicates that a separate publication is planned to report in detail the results of the Rorschach test. The overall impression one secures from the author is that the Rorschach findings are consistent with the interpretations derived from the clinical interviews and direct observation.

Easily the most attractive feature of this study derives from the clinical sophistication of the investigator and the fact that he successfully employed an interview technique that might be expected to utilize to the maximum his clinical skills. In addition, his familiarity with the language and, at least broadly, the culture of his subjects as well as his professional training in anthropology, provide an appealing link between the ethnological and the psychological. In view of this, it is not surprising that his psychocultural interpretations make much more successful use of covert dimensions of personality than is usual.

It is difficult to evaluate the study as an application of projective techniques because so little of the monograph deals with the tests or their results. Clearly the interpretation of the Rorschach and word association test responses could be carried out within a context of relevant information concerning each subject that should maximize the sensitivity of the tests. Furthermore, the familiarity of the author with psychoanalytic concepts and his concern with the covert side of personality should make it possible for him to integrate effectively projective-technique findings and the remainder of his data. However, the present report of Rorschach and word association test findings is so brief and unrevealing that thus far these advantages have not been utilized. Moreover, if the projective findings are eventually reported in reasonable detail, the investigators will surely encounter many of the typical problems we have discussed previously having to do with sampling procedure and the contribution of nonpersonality factors to test performance.

Included among the applications of projective techniques in nonliterate settings are a small number of studies that explore personality differences associated with various subcultural groupings. The distinction here is typically at the level of role or status, and sex differences have proved to be the most popular analytic target—perhaps because of the relative ease and objectivity with which this group designation can be made.

One such study (Spindler & Spindler, 1958) we shall discuss in the following section. However, a recent investigation by Abel and Metraux (1959), dealing with sex differences in the natives of Montserrat, an island in the British West Indies, seems best discussed here. In this study a battery of projective techniques, including the Szondi and Rorschach, was administered to a group of 34 male and 33 female subjects ranging in age from fourteen to seventy. These subjects were selected from the residents of a small mountain community of about 500 persons. Although other tests were administered (Pfister Pyramid Test, Lowenfeld Mosaic Test), only the Rorschach and Szondi revealed clear sex differences, and it is upon these test findings that the investigators rest their discussion.

In general, Abel and Metraux report their results in a series of empirical generalizations followed by citation of the test data that provided the basis for the interpretation and, in some cases, the results of tests of significance for the frequency differences between sexes. The natives of Montserrat as a whole are characterized by strong unconscious dependency needs, a lack of repression, free expression of affect, a practical, nonabstract orientation toward the outer world, and little understanding of inner psychological processes. When the females are compared with males, they share unconscious dependency needs but show more of a tendency to "accept and cling to objects" and are more imaginative and creative in their inner life. Adolescents seem generally to have more anxiety than adults, but the female adolescent seems better able to cope with this anxiety than the male. The investigators also suggest that there are more deviant male subjects than female subjects, although they caution that this may possibly be an artifact produced by selection of subjects. In conclusion, the authors discuss some of the aspects of Montserrat and its culture that might contribute to the development of psychological sex differences.

Positive qualities of this report include the explicitness with which interpretations concerning modal characteristics and personality differences between sexes are linked to clearly identified aspects of test response. Moreover, in a number of instances these reported differences are tested for their statistical significance. Furthermore, the attempt to work with specified groups within a single culture is an empirical approach that avoids many of the dangers or difficulties involved in cross-cultural comparisons.

On the negative side, one may remark upon the failure to integrate adequately the psychological findings and the cultural discussion, the complete absence of any presentation of the details of testing and sampling, and the report of a few isolated statistics with no indication of how many other statistics may have been computed or rejected on the basis of an inspection of the results for the two sexes. Most disappointing of all is the failure to describe the male and female samples adequately, with the result that it is impossible to know whether to attribute the observed findings to sex differences, age differences, educational differences, socioeconomic differences, or other factors. Actually, some of this missing information can be obtained from other publications by Dr. Abel not cited in the present article. In part, then, our criticism may be seen as directed against incomplete and fragmented research reports.

ACCULTURATION

One of the traditional meeting grounds for psychologist and anthropologist is the area of culture change and acculturation. It is precisely where cultural modes are displaced or altered that the role of individual psychological factors is likely to be most apparent and to seem most important. An adequate account of these cultural processes, their determinants and their concomitants, demands an understanding of associated psychological processes. In view of this, it seems quite natural that a considerable quantity of the applications of projective techniques in anthropological research should have taken place in the hands of investigators concerned with acculturation.

There are few anthropologists who have been more seriously and wisely concerned with the process of acculturation than Irving Hallowell, and there is none who has applied projective techniques in this setting so extensively. In the opening chapter of this volume, we identified Hallowell as one of the early and important investigators interested in the use of projective techniques in cross-cultural settings. We also examined briefly some of the findings reported in one of his early studies of the Ojibwa (Salteaux) concerned with the psychological aspects of acculturation. His years of devoted investigation of this American Indian group are further revealed in a more recent publication (Hallowell, 1955), outlining the results of extensive Rorschach investigation of three Ojibwa settlements. He reports findings based upon 217 subjects divided among two Berens River groups (Inland and Lakeside) and the Lac du Flambeau group. All three groups share original Algonkian culture, but they show marked differences in the extent to which they have become acculturated to the white culture, with the Flambeau the most heavily acculturated and the Inland Ojibwa the least acculturated.

Given extensive Rorschach data for three differentiated groups, it remained for Hallowell to score the Rorschach protocols according to conventional procedures (Klopfer) and then to compare the three groups in terms of their performance on these Rorschach scores. In addition to this usual Rorschach analysis, the investigator scored all protocols according to a set of signs of adjustment developed by Davidson (1943) in a personality study of children. The distributions of conventional Rorschach scores and adjustment scores are reported for each of the three groups, and the average differences between the groups are tested for statistical significance using simple techniques.

The author begins his analysis with a general description of the Ojibwa modal personality, which he sees as congruent with the aboriginal Algonkian culture and thus as a kind of generic personality type for these people. In this description he emphasizes surface friendliness, latent aggression and anxiety, shallow human relations, introversion, and frequent use of the mechanism of projection. A qualitative examination of the Rorschach protocols of the least acculturated group (Inland) provides a concordant impression, and Hallowell cites a number of group averages on Rorschach indices to support this generalization. A comparison of this personality portrait with the findings for the Lakeside and Lac du Flambeau groups reveals "the continuity of the same basic psychological pattern through these stages of acculturation. There is a persistent core of generic traits which can be identified as Ojibwa" (Hallowell, 1955, p. 351).

In spite of these important similarities, Hallowell feels there are significant differences among the settlements, the most striking of which have to do with the Lac du Flambeau, where the author feels there are definite signs of psychological malfunction. "It is at Flambeau where we can see reflected in the Rorschach data an introversive personality structure being pushed to the limits of its functional adequacy" (pp. 351-352). These impressions are strengthened by comparison of the three groups in incidence of signs of adjustment. There is no difference between the two Berens River groups, but significant differences appear between both of these groups and the Flambeau group, with the latter group displaying inferior adjustment. Hallowell feels that the absence of any appreciable difference in adjustment between the Inland and Lakeside group, in spite of their difference in acculturation, implies that in assessing the relationship between adjustment and acculturation one must take into consideration such factors as the speed with which the acculturation is carried out and the extent to which the equivalents of aboriginal institutions can be found in the newly acquired culture. The hypothesized association between personality and acculturation is, thus, highly complex.

There are few if any anthropological studies using projective techniques where the investigator is more thoroughly familiar with the culture, the overt behavior, and the test response of his subjects than in this one. Hallowell has collected an impressive array of historical, cultural, and personality data concerning the Ojibwa, and consequently his generalizations from the Rorschach are much more effectively embedded in contextual information than is true of most such studies. Not only do we find an impressively large sample of subjects in this study, but also we find that the protocols are subjected to an analysis resulting in quantitative scores and that a serious attempt is made to subject these scores to simple statistical treatment.

Perhaps the major criticism of Hallowell's study is that he fails to examine the possible impact of varying degrees of acculturation upon test-taking behavior, aside from its influence through personality variation. It is clear that the Flambeau, by virtue of being more heavily acculturated, may also have a different set of attitudes toward the anthropologist, a different set of linguistic skills, a different set of hypotheses concerning just what the examiner is attempting to accomplish, different degrees of education, and so forth. These qualities could well produce variation in Rorschach performance not directly attributable to personality changes accompanying acculturation. Also, one cannot help wishing that the author had been more specific about the circumstances under which the data were collected in the three different groups. If, as seems likely, different examiners were used in collecting the data in some of the groups, we might expect this to play an important role in producing performance differences, particularly if the examiners varied in their experience with the test and in the field.

Although we have agreed that one should not quibble at length over method of statistical analysis, when such an approach is itself still a novelty, it does seem regrettable that the author failed to utilize the results of his statistical analysis of Rorschach scores in his general discussion of group differences. There appears to be no attempt whatsoever to single out and emphasize those findings that the quantitative analysis suggest to be most clear-cut or striking. There is no attempt to protect the Rorschach scoring against contamination by a knowledge of the culture and its representatives. Further, on the basis of earlier studies, Hallowell must undoubtedly have expected certain general personality patterns and group differences to emerge, and yet he reports no steps that were taken to prevent the operation of such a bias. One may also question the applicability of an adjustment scale developed upon American children to a group of adult, partially acculturated Ojibwa. It is true that Hallowell is aware of this danger and that his pattern of results provides partial (although contaminated) evidence in support of his choice of measure.

Not only has Hallowell studied the Ojibwa extensively using the Rorschach and customary methods of anthropology, but also Caudill (1949) has applied the TAT in this setting. His chief purpose was to compare the existing personality of the Flambeau Reservation Ojibwa with the much less acculturated Berens River Ojibwa and thus to secure some insight into the association between cultural change and personality change.

Caudill administered ten TAT cards selected from the standard set to a total of 88 subjects consisting of school children ranging in age from seven to sixteen and including approximately 40 per cent of all the children enrolled in the local school. The subjects were evenly divided in terms of sex and were selected so as to show a rough correspondence to the number of children in each age group in the school. The TAT protocols were analyzed in terms of formal and content variables developed by William Henry (1947) in his comparative study of American Indian tribes. They included such dimensions as length of story, number of intraceptive remarks, number of interpretive remarks, intraceptive remarks referring to hostile interpersonal relations or to warm interpersonal relations, intraceptive remarks suggesting anxiety or deprivation, denial and hostility from the environment. The average scores for these variables and others are presented separately for both male and female subjects, and the results are discussed with additional interpretive material. Caudill also presents a summary picture of the personality of the Flambeau children that appears to be derived from knowledge of the culture as well as general interpretation of the TAT protocols. His general conclusion is that these subjects constitute a "psychologically badly damaged group" (1949, p. 423), and he cites illustrative protocols that suggest to him primitive and diffuse aggression as well as infantile dependency needs, anxiety, and a lack of inner strength.

Caudill's most general conclusion is, "It does not seem likely that the impact of Western civilization alone on the Flambeau Ojibwa could give rise to the psychological pattern reflected in the data . . ." (p. 423). Thus, he concludes that there is considerable continuity between the personality manifestations presently displayed by the acculturated subjects of his study and the Berens River subjects studied by Hallowell. Specifically, he cites Hallowell's report, based upon Rorschach analysis, that his subjects displayed ". . . a general feeling of apprehensiveness, a suspiciousness, a lack of development of close emotional ties, an individualism, and a great deal of carefully concealed interpersonal aggression . . ." and suggests that much of this is congruent with the outcome of the analysis of his TAT protocols. Caudill goes on to reason that although there is much evidence for "persistence of Ojibwa personality over a long span of time . . ." (p. 425), there is also evidence for change and that all of those personality changes with acculturation have been negative.

Caudill's study involves a relatively large sample of the group under study; the investigator has employed a set of variables previously used in a cross-cultural setting; an attempt is made to present quantitative findings; and the interpreter of the protocols appears to have a general familiarity with the Ojibwa culture. All this is to the good.

On the other side of the ledger, we may remark upon the lack of information concerning the circumstances under which the test was administered, the inadequate specification of the details of analysis of the TAT protocols, the failure to attempt any estimate of the role of chance factors in producing the differences reported, the lack of clear differentiation between statements based upon projective-technique response and those based upon a general knowledge of the culture, and the high incidence of interpretive statements concerning TAT performance not tied to any particular element of response or else linked only to an illustrative passage from a TAT story. Perhaps most serious of all the objections that can be raised to this study is the difficulty of arriving at a conclusion concerning similarities and differences between the Berens River and Flambeau Ojibwa on the basis of general interpretive statements derived from two different projective techniques, administered under different conditions, by different examiners at different times. All in all, it seems clear that the complexity of the relation between the TAT and Rorschach alone is sufficient to make any such interpretive exercise excessively hazardous.

A frequently cited investigation, making use of Rorschach data to assist in understanding the acculturation process, is Barnouw's (1950) study of the Wisconsin Chippewa (Ojibwa). This research grew out of the Columbia seminar conducted by Linton and Kardiner and involved the collection of both TAT and Rorschach data. Although the investigator made some use of projective-technique data, the emphasis of the study is upon personality inferences based upon ethnographic data. The author attempts to relate the personality of the Chippewa to their culture and culture change over a span of centuries.

We are told that Barnouw had available 107 Rorschach protocols collected by the author and two other investigators (one male and one female), but there appears to be no report of the number of TAT protocols available. The results reported take the form chiefly of interpretations by Klopfer and appear in connection with a discussion of "The Individual in Chippewa Society" and several extensive case histories.

In a discussion of fear and isolation among the Chippewa, the author indicates that Rorschach findings generally suggest greater insecurity on the part of male subjects than female subjects. In support of this interpretation, the author cites longer response time, higher rate of card rejection, and lower incidence of Human Movement responses by the male subjects. Consistent findings of this sort are reported for a number of groups varying in age and acculturation. Also singled out for emphasis is the very low incidence of Color responses. Out of 107 records there were 53 that gave no evidence of any Color response whatsoever. This is interpreted as indicative of the emotional isolation of the subjects. The investigator reports: "Dr. Klopfer believes that the rarity of Color responses among the Chippewa implies that the individual is under pressure to become as emotionally independent of his environment as possible, and to expect very little from others. This assessment, of course, is essentially in agreement with the personality picture which has been described in the preceding pages" (p. 27). The author notes some inconsistency between his findings in regard to Color responses, and those reported by Hallowell for subjects from the same and culturally similar tribes.

Interpretations based upon the Rorschach are included in two of the three life histories, and material from the TAT is reported in one of these same life histories. In the case including both the TAT and Rorschach, the author finds congruence between the findings suggested by these two sources, and he also considers them consistent with the evidence secured from autobiographical report and observation. He suggests that "If it were not for their value as a check and corroboration, I might have spared John the uneasiness aroused by the Thematic Apperception Test for there is little in the projective-test material which does not also appear in the biographical data" (p. 111). The analysis by Bruno Klopfer of the Rorschach in the other case is also viewed as fitting closely with the material in the biography.

The outstanding features of this study are the rather large number of projective-technique protocols available for analysis and the sophistication, indeed the distinction, of the analyst of most of the Rorschach protocols. There are a vast number of shortcomings to the study, most serious of which are the failure to specify adequately the sample, the method of administration, or the method of analysis of the projective-technique data. However, the very slight weight that Barnouw places upon these data makes it appear injudicious to take a sharply critical view of his study. It is clear, of course, because of the lack of important empirical controls, that Dr. Barnouw's conclusions concerning the overlap between the inferences derived from the projective techniques and those based upon autobiographical report cannot be given very heavy weight.

A stimulating and sophisticated study utilizing the Rorschach to investigate psychological aspects of acculturation is the investigation of the Wisconsin Menomini by Spindler. This inquiry, in both conception and method, builds upon the earlier work by Hallowell but possesses certain important, novel features. An unusual aspect in the reporting of this investigation is one article solely devoted to a detailed discussion of the design of the study (Spindler and Goldschmidt, 1952). The bulk of the substantive findings, however, are reported in a monograph (Spindler, 1955) and two articles (Spindler, 1952; Spindler and Spindler, 1958).

Interested in the association between personality characteristics and degree of acculturation, Spindler attempted to define a sociocultural variable and a personality variable and then correlate the two measures. The personality variable was equated to performance on the Rorschach test, whereas the sociocultural variable was assessed chiefly on the basis of religious activities. Sixty-eight male subjects were studied in all, and they were restricted to members of the society who, in biological descent, were at least one-half Menomini and were more than 21 years of age. The subjects represented a 20 per cent sample of all members of the society of these specifications. Spindler describes the selection of subjects as follows:

The persons studied were selected to represent all degrees of observable socioeconomic status from the richest to the poorest; and all degrees of cultural participation from Medicine Lodge to bridge club. . . . At each sociocultural level, a few known individuals, friendly to me, were treated with first, then a minimum of three other names of other persons was obtained from them and at least one of these persons was obtained as a case, using his acquaintance with the first subject as a means of introduction. These cases in turn designated other possibilities. A number of other cases were "picked up" as contacts were made in many casual conversations. (Spindler, 1955, p. 11)

The eventual grouping of the subjects was largely dependent upon the religious affiliation of the subjects and the extent of their participation in their religion or religions. On this basis four groups were identified: (*a*) the Native-Oriented group (Medicine Lodge-Dream Dance group), which was least acculturated and most resembled the aboriginal culture; (*b*) the Peyote Cult group, which was transitional in terms of acculturation and characterized by use of peyote and active participation in the associated religious sect; (*c*) a further Transitional group that was characterized by minimal participation in both Catholic and native religions; (*d*) a group consisting of those born into the Catholic Church who had maintained their association with the church. The last group was ultimately divided into two groups largely on the basis of socioeconomic differences (Elite Acculturated Group and Lower-Status Acculturated group), thus making a total of five groups. The meaningfulness of these distinctions, established on the basis of religious affiliation and a gross measure of socioeconomic status, was tested by comparing the groups on a large number of items (24) taken from an interview schedule (including items concerned with income, knowledge of Menomini language and lore, group affiliations, and so forth) and demonstrating that the groups were appropriately differentiated. Finally, a group of 12 white subjects who were living on the reservation were included as a control group.

The Rorschach test was administered in a standard manner, except that for all subjects a trial blot was used, and in four cases it was necessary to use the services of an interpreter. The investigator reports he encountered no particular difficulty in administering the test, and the protocols secured with the assistance of interpreters appeared "comparable in length and detail" to the other protocols.

The Rorschach analysis was limited to formal indices rather than content scores, and in all Spindler utilized 21 scores and combinations of scores. The individual scores for each subject are reported in an appendix. The association between the Rorschach indices and the five differentiated sociocultural groups and control group was determined by means of chi-square and Fisher's exact test. The basic procedure was to dichotomize each Rorschach variable and then to compare the distribution of subjects in the resultant two categories for all combinations of the six groups under study. Thus the distribution of scores for each of the 21 Rorschach variables was compared for each of the 15 pairs of groups, for example, Peyote group versus Transitional group, Medicine Lodge group versus Elite Acculturated group, and so forth.

The extreme groups (Native-Oriented and Elite Acculturated) showed differences in the distribution of scores that were significant at the 5 per cent level or below in eight of the 21 Rorschach indices. Similar comparisons for other pairs suggested that the Peyote group was psychologically the most distinct (13 of the Rorschach variables are significantly different from the Native-Oriented group, 5 for the Transitional group, 6 for the Lower-Status Acculturated and 6 for the Elite Acculturated). In a separate paper, Spindler (1952) uses these findings to support the hypothesis that the Peyote group members, as a consequence of their social deviance and disorganization, display a "systematic deviation in personality type" regardless of variation in early childhood experience.

The Transitional group, although psychologically differentiated from other groups, was not so distinctive as the Peyote group. The Elite Acculturated and Lower-Status Acculturated groups were relatively similar to each other, differing significantly on only two of the 21 variables. The white control group appeared to be psychologically distinct from the Native-Oriented group (Medicine Lodge) and from the Peyote group, but they showed little evidence of difference from the Transitional group (1 Rorschach variable), the Lower-Status Acculturated group (3 Rorschach variables), or the Elite Acculturated group (0 Rorschach variables). The findings from this analysis lead the investigator to conclude:

The extremes of the established continuum exhibit psychological as well as sociocultural differentiation. The differentiating psychological adaptations away from the native-oriented base are in large degree shared by both acculturated categories, but these two groups bear a different relationship to the transitional category, with which the lower-status group exhibits no clear-cut distinction. The position of the transitional group in relation to both extremes of the continuum denotes psychological as well as sociocultural transition. The Peyote Cult group deviates systematically from all other Menomini categories. Disregarding this deviation, there is evidence of a general continuum of psychological adaptations that parallels the sociocultural continuum. (Spindler, 1955, p. 206)

Having carried out the quantitative comparison of the groups and demonstrated to his satisfaction the existence of important psychological differences differentiating the groups and associated with the differences in acculturation, Spindler proceeded to examine the nature of the psychological attributes that typify the different groups. First he turned to the Medicine Lodge-Dream Dance or Native-Oriented group for what he refers to as a base line against which other personality patterns can be viewed as deviations. Using the same dichotomous treatment of variables employed in the previous analysis, he constructed a group psychogram that represented the modal or most frequent of each of the 21 variables. Spindler was aware that this procedure involves some distortion, but he points out that the lowest incidence of members of the group sharing any score represented in the psychogram is 58 per cent and the most important interpretations that he makes are based upon characteristics displayed by 70 per cent or more of the members of the group. Thus, the elements in the psychogram are displayed by many individual members of the group. Analysis of the group psychogram suggests that:

The typical native-oriented Menomini personality is highly intratensive, sensitive to the environment but able to maintain equilibrium despite its variations, lacking generally in overt emotional responsiveness and exhibiting a high degree of rational control over it when it does appear, motivated more by biologically oriented survival drives than by self-projective imaginatively creative ones, intellectually uncomplicated but adequate in terms of its setting, lacking in rigidity or constriction, without evidence of the usual forms of anxiety, tension, or internal conflict and, in general, psychologically adequate to the demands placed upon it within its own sociocultural setting. (Spindler, 1955, p. 206)

This group psychogram is then compared to a comparable summary graph based upon the Rorschach responses of 44 Inland Ojibwa studied by Hallowell. The reader will recall that the Inland group was the least acculturated of the three Ojibwa groups studied and therefore occupied a position roughly equivalent to the Native-Oriented group in the present study. The two psychograms suggest considerable personality similarity ". . . especially in the areas of overt emotional responsiveness and control, and in the high degree of intratensivity. Differences were noted in the greater tendency toward rigidity and the greater emphasis on self-projective imaginative creativity displayed by the Ojibwa" (p. 207). The personality resemblance between these two groups is attributed by the author to their common cultural heritage, whereas the differences appear accountable in terms either of subcultural variation or differences in degree of acculturation.

Having completed a psychological description of the Native-Oriented, Spindler proceeds to examine each of the other groups and to provide general personality descriptions with particular emphasis upon the indices that differentiate these groups from other groups. Thus, a portrait of each of the groups is presented which emphasizes the psychological differences between that group and every other group, and these psychological differences are considered in relation to the sociocultural context in which they occur. A final chapter provides group or average psychograms for each of the Menomini groups and a frankly subjective discussion of the personality pattern of these groups in relation to the problems of adjustment faced by the members of the group, with particular emphasis upon acculturation demands. In general, Spindler appears to find evidence for better personality organization and emotional control in the two extreme groups (Native-Oriented and Elite Acculturated) with the Peyote group and the Transitional group displaying disturbances that are believed to be a function of the "social and cultural dislocation" to which they have been exposed.

A continuation of this investigation (Spindler & Spindler, 1958) involved a comparison of the Rorschach performance of the subjects we have just discussed with a group of 61 female subjects selected in comparable manner so as to be distributed along the acculturation continuum. The investigators were interested in comparing the psychological adaptations of male and female subjects to the same acculturation demands. Before attempting any direct comparison of the two sexes, the differences between the female acculturation groups in Rorschach performance was examined using the method we have just discussed. To the investigators' surprise, there was no evidence for any appreciable personality differences between the five groups, thus suggesting that the females were responding to the acculturation process quite differently from the males.

A direct comparison of all female and all male subjects, regardless of acculturation group, revealed marked Rorschach differences and, encouraged by these findings, the Spindlers attempted to devise a means of comparing male and female subjects within each of the acculturation groups. To achieve this end, they adopted Wallace's (1952) device for determining the modal personality, which we have already discussed. Using this method, they eventually obtained a modal profile representative of the male subjects and a modal profile representative of the female subjects. A comparison of the two profiles displayed a number of differences and supported the conclusion that there is ". . . a picture of disturbance, tension, and diffuse anxiety, and decrease in emotional controls among the modal males that is not represented among the females" (Spindler & Spindler, 1958, pp. 223-224). Having identified the modal personality for both sexes, it remained to examine for each sex the relationship between this modal personality and the acculturation groups. Three different methods of making this comparison were utilized, the simplest of which was simply to compute the per cent of the modal personality cases that belong to each of the acculturation groups. The different methods agreed in suggesting that the modal personality of the female subject occurs most often in the Native-Oriented group, but is present in large numbers in all groups except for the Elite Acculturated. Among the male subjects the modal personality typically occurs much higher (more acculturated) on the acculturation scale, and there is generally a lower incidence of the modal personality among the male subjects. The authors suggest that "the picture of disjunctive psychological adaptation for the males and continuous adaptation for the females is strengthened by the fact that only 12 per cent of the males in the whole sample are in the modal class, and 25 per cent of the females" (p. 228).

In discussing this lower incidence of modal personality among the male subjects, as well as the tendency for the highest incidence of modal personalities to occur among subjects who are at least transitional in their acculturation status, the authors draw upon the social and cultural conditions within which these individuals have developed. The somewhat less healthy, and certainly less modal, picture of the male subjects is believed to reflect associated difficulties these persons have encountered in their social context. "Menomini women do not encounter the sharply disjunctive role expectations in acculturation that the men do . . . for the males, the new roles that they must necessarily appropriate in acculturation and that dominate their lives, are in sharp conflict with what they have had 'built into' their personality systems by their usually less acculturated parents . . ." (pp. 230-231).

These investigations and their outcomes reveal a healthy focus and problem orientation. Unlike many culture and personality investigators, the Spindlers have approached the field armed with a coherent and reasonably simple question; specifically, they wished to measure two variables and assess the relation between them. Furthermore, their attempts to measure the acculturation variable are much more systematic and objective than those of other investigators concerned with similar problems. Their analysis of the projective-technique protocols is explicit, direct, and leads to quantitative results, and the outcomes of this analysis are reported in detail. Furthermore, they make a serious and reasonable effort to control for the contribution of chance factors. The discussion of psychological characteristics derived from projective techniques is clearly differentiated from inferences based upon other sources of data but is evaluated directly in the light of the social or cultural setting. In many respects, then, this is a model study: the purpose is explicit, the major variables are measured objectively, the results are quantified and subjected to statistical evaluation, and the findings are placed in a cultural context.

Even a model study, however, may be expected to display some shortcomings. Perhaps the most important of these, in the present case, is the failure to examine the possible role of nonpersonality factors in producing the differences observed between groups. It is true that the groups differ demonstrably in acculturation, but it is also true that they differ in age, education, and other factors that might influence projective-technique response. It is further true that the cultural beliefs and customs of these groups show some variation, and it might be that these factors would influence the subjects' attitude or set toward the test situation, and consequently their responses, without the mediation of any personality differences. Along this line, it seems unfortunate that the investigator does not identify the four subjects who were given the Rorschach with the aid of an interpreter. If, as seems likely, these were all members of the Native-Oriented group, it certainly would have been desirable to remove these four subjects from the group comparison to see if this had any appreciable effect upon the analysis.

Although Spindler displays both ingenuity and sophistication in his treatment of data, there is little question but that his dichotomizing of Rorschach variables reduces the sensitivity of these measures greatly. Moreover, as he points out, there are serious problems associated with the use of the reconstructed group profiles as representative of the individual members of the group. The joint paper by the Spindlers tacitly accepts these criticisms and employs the device used previously by Wallace. The investigator also points out that the group which is labelled a white control group does not actually serve this purpose, for the whites who have married Menomini women and live on the reservation are undoubtedly atypical of most members of white society. Finally, it may be pointed out that Spindler makes no attempt to qualify, or appraise the usefulness of, conventional Klopfer scoring of the Rorschach protocols. Information concerning the culture of the Menomini is used to examine and discuss the personality findings, but the process whereby these findings are attained (Rorschach testing) is not examined against the background of the local culture. In general, the results of this study are completely dependent upon the cross-cultural applicability not only of the Rorschach but also of the specific interpretive rules of Bruno Klopfer.

A study by Abel and Hsu (1949) provides information relevant to the modal personality of the Chinese as well as personality correlates of acculturation and sex variation in this group. The investigators secured Rorschach protocols from 15 males who had been born and largely educated in China, 10 males who were born and educated in America, 12 females who were born and largely educated in China, and 19 females who were born and educated in America. Some of the tests were administered in 1945 and others in 1948, with three different female examiners collecting the data. The protocols were analyzed in a manner consistent with Klopfer's scoring system, and the average results for the four groups are presented for a number of specific scores under the conventional headings of *approach, determinants,* and *content.* The differences in average scores are discussed in terms of their probable significance for personality differences between the three groups, and particularly in connection with variation in the content of responses, an attempt is made to relate these response differences and associated personality inferences with aspects of the Chinese culture and the problems encountered in moving from the Chinese culture to the American culture.

The authors conclude that the traditional emphasis of the Chinese culture upon control of impulse, balance between inner self and outer world, and preservation of psychological distance between self and others is reflected in the personality patterns revealed by the subjects born in China. As a group, they display strong tendencies toward conformity, restraint of affect, and remote interpersonal relations, with free and spontaneous expression evidenced only in special areas such as those having to do with nature and oral activities. When the male and female subjects born in China are compared, the females display greater flexibility, somewhat more freedom in expression of affect, and superior imaginative powers. The American-born Chinese display evidence of a higher incidence of adjustment problems and greater anxiety, as well as more spontaneity and expression of affect, when compared to the subjects born in China. Of the American-born subjects, the females appear to deal with their adjustment problems more directly and to make less use of repressive mechanisms than the males.

To the credit of Abel and Hsu is their relatively explicit linking of personality statements to specific differences in Rorschach scores, their reporting of average scores on a large number of Rorschach variables for the groups being studied, and the thorough knowledge of the Chinese culture possessed by one of the authors. It is regrettable that so little information is provided concerning the circumstances under which the Rorschach was administered and the subjects selected. We are told enough to make clear that the tests were administered by three different examiners at widely separated periods of time. If these different examiners and times were not evenly balanced in the four groups studied, it is obvious that some or most of the differences reported could have resulted from this shortcoming in design. The authors wisely comment upon the fact that the sex of the examiners may have had a differential effect upon the male and female subjects and thus contributed to the observed sex differences. Further, one cannot help but wonder whether the Chinese- and American-born subjects may have varied in command of the English language, age, level of education, and other factors that would have influenced test response, quite aside from the acculturation process. Finally, there is no attempt to test the statistical significance of the differences between the four groups in Rorschach scores which are used interpretively.

A study of value change and its determinants among Navaho veterans is reported by Vogt (1951) as part of the Harvard Comparative Study of Values in Five Societies. The investigation dealt with a group of 15 young Navaho males, 12 of whom were returned veterans of World War II, and three of whom were nonveterans of comparable age. Vogt was concerned with the three broad problems: factors influencing value change under conditions of culture contact; the role of culture contact during armed forces service in producing value change; and the discovery of which aspects of Navaho culture are relatively changeable and which are resistant to change. Of primary interest here is the first problem, for it was in this connection that the projective-technique data was used as evidence. The author, in defining his problem somewhat more specifically, predicted that personal and social factors would play a role in determining who would accept elements from the foreign value system and made the specific prediction that ". . . a greater degree of value change can be anticipated in cases marked by *personal* conflict and insecurity, and by *social* deviation from the traditional patterns of Navaho society" (p. 4).

The principal data of this investigation consisted of life histories collected by the author through the use of a nondirective approach followed by a structured inquiry designed to cover areas omitted during the spontaneous narration. Approximately half of the informants were able to provide this material in English, and in the remaining cases an interpreter who was a relative or close friend of the informant was used. These life histories were supplemented by observation and informal discussions with the subjects and their families and local leaders over a 10-month period as well as interview and observational data collected over a 12-year period on the same persons by various ethnologists. Finally, formal interviews intended to measure present values were conducted with each of the informants.

The projective techniques included the standard TAT and Rorschach test and a newly designed "veterans' form" of the TAT and Sentence Completion Test. The revised TAT consisted of pictures of Navaho veterans in situations typical of the white and of the Navaho culture. The Rorschach and some of the other tests were administered by a collaborating psychologist (Bert Kaplan), but the remainder of the tests were administered by Vogt. The interpretation of all the projective-technique data was carried out by Dr. Kaplan.

The data of the study are presented in the form of a series of life histories systematically organized about a number of focal points. Each individual account includes a section presenting the background of the person (chiefly family), preservice experience, service experience, postwar experience, personality data, current value system, and an interpretation. The last section attempts to integrate the previous information in such a manner as to account for whatever changes in values have been observed. The report of personality data typically begins with a brief description of the informant from the view of the ethnologist and follows with a personality description derived from the psychologist's interpretation of the individual tests. These interpretations consist of personality inferences with no attempt at justification in terms of raw data or method of analysis. Finally, the actual responses of the informants to the projective tests are presented for 10 of the 15 cases, with an indication that the remaining 5 cases will be presented fully in a forthcoming publication.

On the basis of the personality data, in conjunction with the ethnographic findings, the following conclusions are suggested. First, there seems to have been more variation and less uniformity in personality structure than seems consistent with a conception of modal personality or basic personality type. Second, the greater the acculturation the less evidence of satisfying emotional relations with others and the greater the evidence for personal conflict and insecurity. Third, the existence of personal insecurity and conflict does not necessarily lead to acculturation, for the individual may choose instead to turn toward alcohol addiction, he may withdraw, or he may intensify his commitment to traditional Navaho values.

There are many things about this interesting study of Vogt's that are noteworthy. We encounter a rather complete description of the local culture and the relation between the anthropologist and his informants as well as a specification of certain special qualities (custom of storytelling) that have obvious implications for the response of the Navaho to particular projective techniques. Further, we find that the raw material from the personality instruments is presented fully for most of the subjects. There is no attempt to rely solely upon projective techniques in making personality appraisals, but rather this data is combined with life history and observational data. Finally, in the presentation of the case histories, personality inferences are carefully linked to the particular projective technique upon which they were based.

It is not surprising, in view of the breadth of Vogt's problem and human limitations of time and energy, that there are also certain flaws in this study. Perhaps the most serious shortcoming is the fact that we are provided with scarcely any information concerning how the personality inferences were derived from the raw protocols. Thus, we encounter such statements as: "In the Murray Thematic Apperception Test we discover that Jo is too much concerned with achievement, rebellion, ambition, competition, and economic success to be a particularly happy or stable personality" (Vogt, 1951, p. 43). Such a statement concerning someone in our own society made by an individual who has tested hundreds of persons in this society, and, furthermore, has the advantage of reported experiences of dozens of other investigators who have worked with the same group, would be suspect. When it is made with no indication of the data base, other than a reference to the TAT, in connection with a subject who is one of 15 subjects within this particular culture who have taken the TAT, the statement has little meaning.

Related to the lack of any indication of how one gets from the raw protocols to the personality inferences is the absence of any form of quantification, and this, in turn, is related to the absence of any attempt to assess the role of chance factors. If Vogt were employing his protective-technique data to provide the basis for suggestive or descriptive findings, there would be little reason to object to his preference for qualitative analysis. However, when he suggests that his findings test or confirm hypotheses, however tentatively, he has some obligation to make at least a crude estimate of whether these findings represent anything other than the operation of random processes.

Through most of the discussion of findings and conclusions, Vogt considers the relation between personality factors and culture change as though the former were determining the latter, in spite of the fact that he has no control over the temporal dimension. In other words, he is at best reporting association, and this association can have no implication of cause, or antecedent-consequent, without the collection of data of a sort that is totally absent from this study. It is true that there is a brief section (p. 108) concerning the interdependency of values and personality, but this isolated paragraph is scarcely sufficient to offset the fact that the statement of problem, report of findings, and conclusions, all tend to be stated in a form that implies unidirectional causation.

Finally, there is a disappointing lack of information concerning the details of administration of the projective techniques. Although there is a rather full discussion of the general data-collection procedures, there is much less information concerning the personality instruments. For example, we are told that two examiners gave the various instruments, but aside from the Rorschach we are not told which examiner gave the tests to which individuals, nor are we told anything about the other examiner. For example, how familiar was he with the purpose of the present study? How much contact did he have with the Navaho culture? What we have just said implies not only that we cannot tell whether the findings reported are a product of situational factors, but also we are unable to estimate the extent to which the data is contaminated by knowledge on the part of the test interpreter (sometimes administrator) of the hypotheses to be tested and degree of acculturation of the subjects.

Several interesting reports have resulted from an interdisciplinary study of Japanese Americans in Chicago. Utilizing representatives of anthropology, sociology, psychology, and psychoanalysis, an attempt was made to examine intensively the psychological characteristics of groups of Japanese who had undergone varying degrees of acculturation. The results of the study were intended to illuminate the psychological correlates of acculturation and also to provide some basis for understanding the relative ease and success with which the Japanese have solved the problems of American acculturation.

One aspect of this study dealt with the Thematic Apperception Test as a means of arriving at information concerning the personality and values of the subjects under study (Caudill, 1952). A selected group of 14 cards from the standard TAT was administered to 30 Issei (first generation, born in Japan) and 40 Nisei (second generation, born in America) subjects. TAT protocols were obtained also from a group of 40 white lower-middle-class subjects and 20 white upper-lower-class subjects. Japanese subjects were selected from a large available sample ". . . to include individuals representative of all types of adjustment so that the widest possible range would be obtained" (p. 19). The white subjects were obtained from other research projects and were matched with the Nisei subjects in age and, for some subjects, in socioeconomic status. The TAT protocols for the white and Japanese subjects overlapped for only five cards.

The TAT analysis centered about the stories told to nine TAT cards and was concerned with three broad variables: parental and familial adjustment; goals, life tasks, and self-attitudes; and interpersonal adjustment including social, marital, and sexual relationships. The TAT stories to be scored were selected so that each of the broad dimensions could be related to stories told to three cards. For each card specific categories for analysis were established, and all stories were classified in terms of these categories. The results of this analysis are presented in the form of a series of tables that summarize the incidence of the various types of response to each card, for each of the groups being studied. These results are presented separately for the various TAT cards and are clustered in terms of the broad variables, for example, for Card 6BM we find that the total incidence of "mother rejects son" is 3 for 15 male Issei, 1 for 15 female Issei, 3 for 20 male Nisei, and so on. For many of the categories, there is no data for the white, female lower-middle-class subjects and the male and female white upper-lower-class subjects. These tabulations are then given a general psychological interpretation, with frequent citing of specific TAT stories to illustrate the process under discussion. In addition, Caudill presents a general summary of modes of personality adjustment of the Japanese subjects as inferred from the TAT protocols and several illustrative cases in which no attempt is made to summarize objective results of analysis. Here, he simply presents clinical interpretations and illustrative material from the raw protocols.

The author concludes that the Issei men and women are characterized by two conforming modes of adjustment, one consisting of "successful self-assertion and labile emotional control" and the second involving "passive self-submergence." In addition, a third mode, typical of the Issei women, but not men, involves a rebellious rejection of the norms of the dominant society. Among the Nisei three similar modes are identified: one involves "positive self-assertion with good reality ties and emotional freedom," whereas a second mode, typical only of men, is "a conforming and often defeated adjustment." The third and rather unusual mode, that is also typical of the men, is a "rebellious, aggressive adjustment." On the basis of the objective analysis and clinical interpretation, Caudill arrives at the conclusion that there exists ". . . a direct continuity between the values and adaptive mechanisms of the Issei and the Nisei. Also, in many areas, the values and adaptive mechanisms of the Nisei and the lower-middle-class are highly compatible, while the upper-lower-class diverges from both these groups and presents a different psychological adjustment" (p. 65). He also suggests that although the Japanese and white middle-class share similar goals or values, the Japanese are much more restricted or limited in terms of the instrumental means that can be used in arriving at these goals. Although personality similarities of the Nisei and Issei are emphasized, the author does identify a number of specific deviations and also points to differences between the male and female Japanese subjects.

This study displays a number of attractive qualities, including a relatively large sample of subjects, some attempt at objective analysis of TAT protocols, and the existence of multiple comparison groups. Further, the analysis and much of the data collection were carried out by an individual trained in anthropology and experienced in the interpretation of this type of projective technique. A further advantage to this investigation was the collection of a considerable amount of additional personal, demographic, and cultural information concerning the subjects which could be used as a background against which to interpret the significance of the TAT findings.

In contrast to these important assets, one may comment upon the relative scarcity of information concerning the circumstances under which the data were collected, the absence of detailed information concerning much of the interpretive process, and the lack of comparability of the various groups included in the study. We are told virtually nothing about the identity and background of the person or persons administering the test, the selection of subjects, the site of the testing, the influence of language skill upon test performance or, indeed, in what language the test was administered. Although Caudill does provide a general statement of the categories in terms of which the stories were analyzed, this description is highly general and provides no information concerning such obvious problems as rater reliability and internal consistency. More important, most of the interpretive statements in the monograph are generalizations specifically linked only to illustrative material, and thus, they remain at the level of clinical impression rather than objective demonstration. It is also true that although the investigator collected data from various comparison groups and engaged in a partial categorical analysis, there is no attempt to test the statistical significance of variation between the different groups on these objective indices. In any case, a large number of important differences between these groups (nature of test administration, age of subject, language facility of subject, educational background, and so on) make it unreasonable to assume that observed differences reflect personality variation.

In general, it should be clear that findings of the sort reported in this study should not be considered controlled empirical demonstrations of group similarities and differences. The projective-technique data and the circumstances under which they were collected are sufficiently uncontrolled so that these results exist as the generalizations of a sensitive observer with little in the way of control over ordinary sources of bias or chance factors.

A second paper (DeVos, 1954) from the same study of Japanese-Americans describes the results of a comparison of Rorschach protocols secured from Issei, Nisei, and Kibei (American-born Japanese who were sent back to Japan for at least part of their education) and from American normals, neurotics, and schizophrenics. The comparison of these groups is limited to quantified variables, and no attempt is made to provide general clinical interpretations of the protocols. The author describes the study as "an attempt to demonstrate some of the prevalent elements of personality structure underlying manifest behavior as they change . . . with acculturation" (p. 154).

Rorschach protocols were obtained from a sample of subjects selected from the larger population of Chicago Japanese-Americans included in the parent study by means of an approximately random procedure. The normal, neurotic, and schizophrenic protocols came from another research project. In all there were 280 protocols included in the analysis, divided into 50 Issei, 30 Kibei, 60 Nisei, 60 normal Americans, 50 neurotic Americans, and 30 schizophrenic Americans. There are differences in age, education, socioeconomic status, and language facility between a number of these comparison groups. In an effort to examine the role of age as a determinant of Rorschach response, DeVos compared groups of American subjects averaging 26 years of age and 46 years of age in their test performance and, finding no difference, concluded that the age factor does not account for the differences observed at other points in the study, when groups that differed in age as well as in acculturation or race were compared. The investigator reports in some detail the kinds of problems encountered in the testing situation, particularly the effect of individual differences in English language facility. The fact that the examiner could speak some Japanese and had an effective understanding of the language helped to minimize the influence of these language differences.

The major results of the study are presented in several chapters dealing with intellectual organization and ego controls, control of emotional response, and affective symbolism. Within each chapter the results for conventional Rorschach indices related to these broad dimensions are presented for each of the comparison groups, and the distributions of these scores are tested statistically for significant differences. The findings provide the basis for a number of generalizations concerning differences between the Japanese-American and the American subjects. However, they also suggest important differences between the Issei, Kibei, and Nisei, at least some of which can be interpreted as suggesting that the more acculturated group (Nisei) has moved toward the American norm. In most respects the Kibei tend to fall midway between the Issei and Nisei. Thus the personality patterns appear to reflect the position of these groups in regard to the Japanese-American cultures.

Illustrative of the type of generalizations provided by the author are the following. The Japanese-Americans, in contrast to the normal Americans, are characterized by a high degree of intellectual and personal rigidity, they display marked ambition or striving in the intellectual sphere which often outstrips their actual capacity, they display body pre-occupation and sado-masochistic tendencies in the content of their responses, and they provide evidence of greater maladjustment. When the Nisei and Issei are compared, we find that the Nisei are characterized by less rigidity, less maladjustment, similar intellectual striving, and similar, although less severe, inhibitions in the expression of affect.

In a separate monograph DeVos (1955) reports a set of findings based upon the same subjects but centered about an analysis of the Rorschach protocols in terms of measures of maladjustment and rigidity developed by Fisher (1950) in a study of American subjects. On both the rigidity and maladjustment scales, the Issei and Kibei had significantly higher scores than the Nisei, who tended to be more like the normal American subjects. On the maladjustment scale the Issei and Kibei average scores were similar to the average for the neurotic American subjects and lower than the schizophrenic average. Again we find the most acculturated group showing the closest personality resemblance to the normal Americans.

A fourth report, written jointly by Caudill and DeVos (1956), utilizes both the Rorschach and TAT data we have just described to provide the basis for a discussion of achievement goals and their relation to culture and to personality factors in these Japanese-American subjects.

Most of the positive features commented upon in connection with Caudill's study are equally applicable here, such as, size of sample, multiple comparison groups and existence of a wide variety of additional information concerning the subjects. In addition, one may remark upon the investigator's detailed reporting of aspects of the testing situation and the culture of the subjects. Further, DeVos provides us with considerable information concerning the objective analysis to which his response data was subjected and the outcomes of this analysis are presented in careful detail. We find considerable awareness of the major statistical problems confronting the user of the Rorschach and the statistical analysis employed appears relatively defensible. Further, the interpretation is largely limited to findings that seem unlikely to have been produced solely by chance factors. The author also shows awareness of the serious problems posed by the age differences between his comparison groups, and he takes at least minimal steps to appraise the importance of this lack of control.

On the critical side, we are again faced with important differences, other than those of primary interest (acculturation), between the groups being compared. Most important are the differences in age and language facility between the various groups of Japanese-Americans. As we have commented, the investigator is aware of this problem and has provided limited data concerning Rorschach variation with age differences. These data, however, are not sufficiently general or directly applicable to the area of concern to eliminate the problem. There is also the difference in availability of information concerning the circumstances of testing for Japanese-American subjects and for American subjects, as well as differences in identity of examiner, purpose of study, test situation, and so forth. All in all, it seems relatively safe to conclude that DeVos' comparisons among the various Japanese-American groups are more meaningful than the comparisons between these groups and the American subjects.

Utilizing the Rorschach data secured from 116 Zuni, Navaho, Mormons, and Spanish-American subjects, Kaplan (1954) compared the performance of those subjects who had been veterans with the performance of nonveteran subjects, in search of personality differences associated with this differential exposure to the dominant white culture. His expectation was that the greater differences between Zuni and Navaho culture and the dominant culture would lead to clear personality differences between veterans and nonveterans that would not be present in the Mormon and Spanish-American subjects.

The details of the collection and analysis of this data have already been considered in our discussion of Kaplan's inquiry into the modal personality of these groups. In the phase of investigation we are concerned with here, the investigator subjected each of eight Rorschach variables (W, F per cent, A per cent, M, R, FC, CF, T/R) to individual analysis of variance with the emphasis upon the difference between veteran and nonveteran performance. Veterans and nonveterans showed significant differences on two of the eight scores and several others approached significance. Kaplan concludes that ". . . both Movement and Color responses are increased to a significant degree in the veteran groups. As may be seen . . . this difference occurred in each of the four cultures" (p. 33).

Thus, the Rorschach reflected changes with armed-service experience, but the changes did not agree with the investigator's prior expectations. Kaplan suggests three factors that might have accounted for the different Rorschach performance of the veterans —changes in the cognitive view of the testing situation, changes in the attitudes of the veterans toward this setting, and changes in personality structure. As the following statement suggests, Kaplan is inclined to emphasize the probable role of attitudinal changes: "We must therefore reject the conclusion that our results reflect personality differences between veteran and nonveteran, even though we admit this is a possibility. It seems to the writer that the most likely explanation lies at the attitudinal level" (p. 35).

The positive features of Kaplan's research, which we commented upon earlier, are equally applicable here, as are the negative. Perhaps the only additional point that should be made is that the investigator does not appear to have convincing evidence for the consistency of Rorschach change across all four groups. Actual examination of the tabled results suggests to this observer that the two groups closest to the dominant culture (Mormon and Spanish-American) appear to show smaller differences between veterans and nonveterans. In any case, having decided to employ analysis of variance for his problem, the investigator should clearly have approached this particular question through an examination of the evidence for interaction between veteran status and group membership. In addition, it seems that the findings are quite ambiguous in regard to what may have produced the changes in Rorschach scores and there is no basis other than speculation for suggesting that this difference derived from attitude changes.

A study of individuals developing in a "society under stress" is reported by Alexander and Anderson (1957). Using a modified TAT they studied a group of Northern Cheyenne children to secure information concerning their perceptions. The general expectation of the investigators was that social isolation, deprived socioeconomic conditions, and the conflict between aboriginal culture and contemporary forces within their society would have detectable effects upon the perceptions of these children.

A newly developed TAT, consisting of five cards, was administered to the Cheyenne children by the field worker, with the request that the stories be written. The stories were analyzed in terms of three attributes: stimuli (stimuli presented in picture *versus* stimuli introduced by subject); emotional expressions (positive *versus* negative); meaning of external forces (beneficent *versus* hostile). Examination of the results of this classification revealed that the interests of the subjects, as suggested by the stimuli they introduced, are in "human beings, simple things that individual human beings make, and the rocks, hills, and rivers of their world" (p. 54). The findings for the emotional attribute suggest that the subjects express little emotion and what they do express is negative. Similarly the meaning assigned to external forces is largely hostile. The authors conclude:

As we stated at the beginning, we cannot establish a direct cause and effect relationship between the forces of the culture and individual perceptual experience. However, we can say there is a coexistence between the conditions of deprivation and disintegration in the security systems of a culture and the perceptions of the individual. (pp. 54-55)

The positive features of this study are chiefly the explicitness with which the TAT analysis is reported, the extensive prior experience of the psychologist with this instrument, and the thorough knowledge of the culture possessed by the ethnographer. On the negative side, we find distressingly little information concerning the circumstances surrounding the collection of data, including a failure even to report how many subjects were included in the study. Perhaps the most serious difficulty with the study, however, is that the investigators have employed a new set of stimulus materials and have attempted to make generalizations based upon responses to them in the absence of either normative data or a suitable control group. In addition, the test was administered in written form to children who might be expected to have difficulty with the English language. The essential importance of stimulus factors as determinants of TAT response, in addition to the probable negative influence of written administration of the test to subjects of this age, implies that the results of this TAT analysis can only be considered completely ambiguous at present. Whether the negative emotions and negative environmental forces perceived by these children are more or less than might be expected of normal, happy children is impossible to say. All in all, one may reasonably question whether even tentative conclusions can be derived from such data.

An unusual approach to the study of acculturation and its psychological correlates is reported by the psychologist Leonard Doob (1957). This investigator describes a preliminary study of three African societies (Ganda, Luo, and Zulus) that utilized a battery of direct and indirect psychological measures. On the basis of prior theory and empirical findings as well as current observation, Doob arrived at nine hypotheses concerning correlates of acculturation (contact with dominant white society). Illustrative of these hypotheses and the measures to be used in testing the predictions are the following:

> More of those with relatively greater contact feel generally frustrated and hence are generally aggressive . . . *Measures*: expressed feelings about the present and future . . . a projective situation (What do you see here? Would you say that he is happy or unhappy?); Expressed hostility . . . More of those with relatively greater contact are sensitive to other human beings . . . *Measures*: "human" responses to the Rorschach plates and TAT-type drawings; and the tendency to accept the suggestion during the "testing-the-limits" procedure on the Rorschach. (pp. 150-151)

Acculturation was equated to education and leadership. That is, Doob assumes that those who receive more education and occupy positions of leadership are exposed to more contacts with whites and thus are more acculturated. Within each of the three societies, groups of subjects were tested who were considered high and low in education and high and low in leadership. All subjects were males, and an effort was made to achieve randomness, although practical difficulties made it impossible to come close to this goal. In all, a total of 139 Ganda, 47 Luo, and 106 Zulus were studied, and each subject completed approximately two hours of testing which Doob describes in the following manner: "A schedule was devised which included census-type questions; direct and projective questions concerning attitudes and values; three formal tests seeking to ascertain modes of perception or ability to solve problems; four Rorschach plates . . . two experiments, one to study the influence of, and the ability to recall a communication and the other to study suggestibility" (p. 148). The testing took place in a variety of physical and social settings but always with the aid of an interpreter. Some of the subjects were given a small payment for their participation but most were not.

The results of the study are reported in the form of a series of proportions for each of the hypotheses. The proportions report, for the high and low education and high and low leadership groups within each of the three cultures, the number of test items that discriminated in the predicted direction, as compared to those that discriminated in the direction opposite to that predicted. Thus, under the column heading *Luo-Education,* we find the proportion 9/1 opposite the row heading *Antagonism toward Authorities.* This implies that there were 10 test items or scores presumed to be related to this variable and for 9 of these the difference between those high and low in education among the Luo was in a direction congruent with Doob's hypothesis. In addition to reporting this table of results, the investigator subjects each proportion to the simple sign test and identifies those proportions that deviate from chance at the 10 per cent, 5 per cent, and 1 per cent levels. It is somewhat difficult to derive general implications from these findings, but Doob appears to feel that the general trend is favorable to the hypothesis ("Eight of the nine hypotheses tend to be verified in one or more of the societies.") (p. 159) and, further, that the variable of education appears to be more revealing than the variable of leadership.

This study is of particular interest since it involves a well-known social psychologist operating in what has traditionally been the domain of the social anthropologist. In view of this, it is not surprising to find the study featuring the rather unusual distinction of a set of hypotheses. Thus, whatever may be good or bad about Doob's hypotheses, he has attempted to generalize past experience and current knowledge of the phenomena under study, and consequently, he has generated a core of empirical problems about which to center his investigation. The psychological measures he employed are varied and numerous, and they suggest somewhat greater psychological sophistication and skill than the typical one-instrument study. Moreover, there is a reasonable amount of detail concerning the circumstances under which the tests were administered, and the investigator used simple quantitative and statistical techniques in analyzing and reporting his findings.

One serious shortcoming of this study is the somewhat questionable empirical hold that the investigator has upon the concept of acculturation. By equating variation in acculturation only to amount of education or leadership status, one is unlikely to reveal much concerning psychological processes underlying acculturation. Not only is there the serious question of just how close the association may be between these indices and the underlying variable of acculturation, but there is the more important fact that many kinds of test performance (including projective-test response) vary directly with education and that there are likely to be personality differences between leader and nonleader. Thus, positive findings may have little to do with personality variables associated with contact with white society, and may have much more to do with aspects of education and leadership independent of acculturation. In general, it may be said that although this is a cross-cultural study, there is very little culture in it. Doob makes little or no attempt either to describe the three cultures studied or to relate specific test differences to particular aspects of these cultures. There is also relatively little detail in the description of the testing instruments and virtually no mention of the manner in which the data were analyzed in order to provide support or refutation for the specific hypotheses. It is true that Doob describes the study as a pilot investigation, but one might still hope for a more adequate account of his procedures of data collection and analysis.

An interesting and ingenious attempt to relate personality to culture change was carried out by DeVos and Miner (1958) in a study comparing a group of Algerians who inhabited an oasis with another group who had been born in the same site but had moved to the urban setting of Algiers. The subjects consisted of 64 male Arabs who for the most part were between twenty and fifty years of age. Twenty of the subjects had never lived away from the oasis for more than four months, 28 had lived in Algiers for more than a quarter of their lives, and the remaining 16 fell between the two extremes in their past residence. The mixed group was not used in the comparison of Oasis and Urban subjects but only to contribute to findings concerning the Arab group as a whole. The subjects in the different groups were not selected for comparability on demographic variables, nor were they randomly chosen. However, the investigators report that they were roughly comparable in terms of the most obvious demographic characteristics.

The personality data were derived from Rorschach tests administered by the anthropologist (Miner) with the assistance of a tape recorder that permitted verbatim transcription of responses. The test protocols were scored independently by two assistants according to a scheme developed by DeVos (1955) for such variables as rigidity, maladjustment, anxiety, hostility, and positive and negative affect. Discrepancies in the scoring were resolved by DeVos.

When the Arab responses were examined as a group and compared descriptively with groups of normal, neurotic, and schizophrenic American subjects (the same samples employed by DeVos in his study of Japanese acculturation), there were certain distinguishing features. Interestingly enough, among these group characteristics were a number that paralleled those reported by Bleuler and Bleuler (1935) in their early and rather poorly controlled study. A formal comparison involving simple statistics revealed a number of significant differences between the Algerian sample and American samples in terms of rigidity, maladjustment, anxiety, and so forth. There were also some statistically significant differences between the Oasis and Urban Arab groups. For example, the Urban group showed greater variability in scores on rigidity, more unpleasant content in their responses, and greater hostility.

The investigators also tested the association between certain specific Rorschach dimensions and specific "cultural beliefs." Certain culturally determined practices were assessed by means of an interview, and subjects were classified in terms of their attitudes toward cleanliness, seclusion of women, punishment of children, and belief in the supernatural. There were a total of 13 classificatory categories under these headings which the investigators tried to associate with Rorschach indices of rigidity, maladjustment, positive Rorschach content, body preoccupation, and hostility. A number of significant associations were found (for example, individuals high in rigidity tended to believe that female seclusion should last to 56 years of age or older, and they tended to beat children rather than deprive them of food for punishment). These associations are discussed in the context of traditional Arab culture as well as the culture change caused by the shift from oasis to urban life. The investigators conclude:

. . . The evidence from Rorschach protocols, when viewed in relation to seclusion practices, discipline of children, and religious beliefs, shows a consistent pattern, namely, that attenuation of traditional beliefs in the urbanized Arabs is related to increasing intrapsychic tensions that are expressed in symbolic form in Rorschach content in a number of individuals. (DeVos & Miner, 1958, p. 267)

One of the attractive features of this study is the use of comparison groups within the same culture as well as from a distinct culture. In addition, we find the investigators making use of suitable techniques to objectify their projective-technique protocols and employing simple statistics to examine differences between the various groups. The investigators show a healthy interest in reliability of projective-technique scoring and have analyzed the tests under circumstances where it would be easy to protect fully against contamination of data through knowledge of the acculturation status of the subjects. The report of the study does not indicate, however, whether or not the test scorers were given information about which subjects belonged to the Oasis and which to the Urban groups. The investigators also make an explicit attempt to relate personality findings to cultural practice and indicate that in a further publication, this topic will be dealt with even more extensively.

There is the usual difficulty in equivalence of groups being compared which is particularly important in the case of the comparison of the Algerian groups with the American groups. There is so much diversity between these groups in terms of demographic variables, the testing situation, and test analysis that it is difficult to have much confidence in any of the obtained results. The comparison of the Oasis and Urban groups appears considerably safer, although even here there are important shortcomings in the method of selecting subjects. The relationship between cultural practice and personality seems to be on the firmest ground, but even here one has reservations concerning the large number of relationships tested (42) and the limited number that attain statistical significance (11). Again we are told less about the circumstances under which the test was administered than we would like to know. For example, the relation between acculturation and Rorschach performance or between cultural practice and the Rorschach could readily reflect differences in the ease with which the examiner was able to establish rapport, differences in language fluency, or differences in familiarity with comparable settings or procedures; without there necessarily being personality differences between groups or associated with cultural practice. A more detailed report of this study is contained in a recent monograph by Miner & DeVos (1960).

PERSONALITY DEVELOPMENT IN NONLITERATE CULTURAL SETTINGS

Most anthropological studies employing projective techniques show at least some concern with personality development. Consequently, it may seem that the above heading is broad enough to include all of the studies appropriate to this chapter. However, there are some studies that focus on the description and understanding of personality in a particular culture, whereas other investigations are primarily concerned with identification of a modal personality or the process of acculturation, even though they make considerable reference to personality development. It is with the studies aimed directly at the process of personality development that we are concerned here.

Perhaps the most extensive application of projective techniques in a cross-cultural setting yet reported was the Indian Education Research Project, conducted jointly by the United States Bureau of Indian Affairs and the Committee on Human Development of the University of Chicago. This program of research centered about the personality development of children aged six to eighteen in five American Indian tribes: Hopi, Navaho, Papago, Sioux, and Zuni. The stated goals of this research were to ". . . investigate, analyze, and compare the development of personality in five American Indian tribes in the context of the total environment setting—social, cultural, geographical, and historical—for implications in regard to Indian administration" (Joseph, Spicer, & Chesky, 1949, p. vii). The study utilized existing ethnological data, conducted new ethnographic inquiries, and carried out extensive programs of psychological testing and interviewing in order to describe the personality and the developmental process within each of the five tribes. Among the psychological tests employed were: the Arthur Point Performance Scale, Stewart's Emotional Response Test, Goodenough's Draw-a-Man Test, Bavelas' Moral Ideology Test, the TAT, the Rorschach, and free drawings. Some indication of the extensiveness of this study may be secured by simply examining the number of projective tests administered to four of the tribes:

	Rorschach	TAT	Free Drawing
Navaho	110	109	148
Papago	117	63	130
Sioux	154	130	—
Hopi	185	105	141

The first volume to appear in this series was a charming little book by Thompson and Joseph (1944) entitled *The Hopi Way*. In the process of presenting a broad outline of personality development among the Hopi and its relation to the forbidding physical setting and culture of these people, the authors include a good deal of personality description derived from projective techniques. The book is written in a relatively nontechnical manner, with little attempt to document statements and an obvious interest in presenting the material so that it will be understood readily, even by the general reader. Consequently, it is not easy to identify those personality inferences derived from projective tests rather than from other sources. The reader should note that in some instances portions of the data have been reported in greater detail elsewhere. For example, Henry (1947) presents both details of analysis and further comparisons involving the TAT data.

The section of the Thompson and Joseph volume that clearly owes most to the projective tests is entitled "What lies below the surface?" These passages show that the authors utilized both quantitative and qualitative analysis in interpreting the Rorschach and Thematic Apperception Tests. The results of the Rorschach test suggets that these children display a great deal of individual variation, but at the same time, they share a kind of controlled complexity. That is, their personality is highly differentiated and yet subjected to a careful and efficient over-all control. Consistent with this is the fact that it is unusual to find a subject characterized by emotional impulsiveness. The subjects display more investment in their inner, subjective world than in the outer world of reality, and yet they are not free and uninhibited in their fantasy life. Their relation to the surrounding world is careful or cautious and involves close attention to details. There is also evidence of a capacity for resistance or stubbornness.

In comparison to other Indian children, the Hopi show more evidence of free-floating or diffuse anxiety, and the test interpreters suggest that the careful control or rigidity of these children may be a device whereby this anxiety can be controlled or lessened. The authors consider these personality attributes to be understandable in view of the developmental context of the Hopi: "The price the average Hopi child has to pay for his survival in such an environment of actual and potential dangers seems to be the limitation and frequent frustration of his own desires, emotions and ambitions. Apparently not too seldom deriving from it is the generation of inside pressure which, without adequate outlet, accumulates and arouses a feeling of discomfort or fear" (Thompson & Joseph, 1944, p. 110). This personality pattern is considered by Thompson and Joseph as functional and adaptive given the culture and physical surroundings of these children.

The responses of the children to the TAT were quite congruent with what has already been reported. Again there was consistent evidence of balance and careful control and little evidence of strong emotional impulsiveness. Furthermore, the hero, or self, seemed less important than the group in these stories, and there was little evidence of direct aggression. The authors suggest that the responses to the TAT are not only consistent with the Rorschach inferences but also with the results concerning the Hopi culture obtained with other instruments and through observation and interviewing. Findings derived from the TAT are also utilized extensively in a chapter concerned with Hopi hostility, which is devoted to accounting for the high incidence of malicious gossip and accusations of witchcraft in this society. The authors suggest that such evidence might be used to support the interpretation of a paranoid trend among these people, but they go on to suggest that this interpretation is not supported by their data. Rather, it appears that this behavior can be understood as a natural reaction to a cultural system that provides heavy restriction against expression of overt aggression and exerts a high degree of control over interpersonal relations. The TAT protocols confirm the existence of covert aggressive tendencies which seem centered about the techniques of control used on the children, especially by the mother. Thompson and Joseph point to the image of the Spider Woman, who is one of the most important of the mythological personages of this culture and is both powerful and malignant, as reflecting these same impulses.

Next in this series was *Warriors Without Weapons,* the well-known analysis of the Pine Ridge Sioux by MacGregor (1946). Here the results of the projective tests are presented in a chapter devoted to a general description of covert aspects of behavior and in a further section of the book that presents ten case histories. The interpretation of these tests is presented in terms of a detailed "Outline for Individual Case Analysis," prepared by William Henry. Results of the individual tests were matched with information provided by the other sources of information (tests, observation) concerning the individual children with the result that "A high correlation among the findings appeared" (p. 218).

The Rorschach and TAT results are organized under the topics: insecurity, anxiety and its effects, and age and sex differences. The general personality picture presented emphasizes powerful repressive forces, lack of spontaneity, and weak drives. The author concludes that the adjustment of the Sioux places heavy stress upon defensive fantasy. The children are more restrained than either white or Navaho children, and their inner life seems as inhibited as their outer expression. The outer world is conceived as hostile and threatening, and the children tend to be insecure, without purpose and passive. The pervasive and powerful anxiety leads to inhibition, shallow relations with other people, and a tendency to respond with images or stories of escape on the projective tests. In general, the younger children display better organized personalities than the adolescents and are likewise less withdrawn.

When compared to the other studies in this series, there is considerably more attempt to anchor personality inferences in the actual response data provided by the projective tests. There are numerous instances, particularly with the TAT, where generalizations concerning personality are followed by concrete indications of the types of projective-technique data which have led to these statements. Further, there appears to be less casual interweaving of observational or behavioral evidence with the data of the projective techniques. We are also told more about the form that the modification of the TAT has taken, and the modified instructions which accompanied the test are present for the first time.

The portion of this program of research dealing with personality development among the Navaho is summarized in a volume by Leighton and Kluckhohn (1947). The subjects in this study are divided into three subgroups (Shiprock, Ramah, and Navaho Mountain), and the actual testing procedures in each of these settings is described in considerable detail with, in some instances, illustrative material in the form of rather complete field notes.

Description of the process whereby these tests were interpreted is again rather scanty. The Rorschach protocols and their interpretations are included in an appendix which summarizes, for boys and girls in each of four age groups and the three communities, the distribution of the following Rorschach scores: number of responses, per cent of subjects rejecting one or more blots, manner of approach (Whole, Detail, etc.), per cent of subjects with $M>FM$, per cent of subjects with $FC>CF$, and per cent of Popular and Original responses. In presenting the results of this testing process, the authors first provide a general description of the test responses, indicating that both Rorschach and TAT responses ". . . tend to be short, literal, commonplace descriptions with little elaboration or imaginative detail" (p. 176). The remainder of a brief chapter dealing with results of the projective testing is devoted to an examination of age, sex, and regional differences in personality. Most of the statements are quite general and not only give little hint of what inference process has lead to them but, in many cases, do not even indicate the instrument from which they were derived. There is again evidence of a mixture of data from observation with data from the projective techniques. Typical of the descriptive statements provided is the following generalization concerning children in the five-to seven-year group:

At this age the children are rather shy and unable to express themselves easily, even in their own language. Their concepts are often rather vague, and it is impossible to get them to specify what they mean. They are, on the whole, quite restrained, and they control their reactions consciously. They are less controlled in their relations to the outer world than in giving expression to their inner urges. They are a little anxious in a general way and feel subject to their parents' authority. (p. 178)

A series of 16 brief case histories is presented which includes personality statements inferred from the projective techniques but again with little specification of the process leading to the generalization.

The fourth volume in the series deals with personality development among the Papago Indians (Joseph, Spicer, & Chesky, 1949). We are told little about the interpretation of the projective tests other than that comparable test results for four other Indian tribes and a group of white children facilitated interpretation of the tests in relation to tribal characteristics, whereas individual interpretations leaned heavily upon averages for various subgroups as well as findings for the group as a whole. Not only were averages computed for the group as a whole but also for the two tribal communities separately (Eastern Papago and Western Papago), for the two sexes, and for four age groups (six to seven, eight to ten, eleven to thirteen, fourteen to eighteen). In presenting the test interpretations the authors indicate that no documentation for the interpretations is provided because of the technical nature of the basic data and, further, because a separate volume concerned with the Rorschach findings for all five tribes included in the study is to be published.

The main Rorschach findings are summarized as follows:

1. Papago children's average personality structure reveals no elaborate complexity of traits or subtle differentiation of existing traits.
2. Papago children show spontaneity, limited range but intensity of emotions, a relatively precarious control and discipline, and a peculiar swing between realistic participation in the life about them and extreme withdrawal.
3. Against outer and inner conflicts they seem to defend themselves essentially by evasion and by subjective interpretation of facts and feelings.
4. Though they are able to form clear concepts and to categorize them, the children reveal a tendency to disregard this capacity, enforcing their associative thoughts upon objects of reality. Thus their intellectual approach seems to be largely subjective interpretation instead of objective and analytical. (pp. 215-216)

Most of the remainder of the section devoted to the covert aspects of personality examines the cultural and situational factors that appear related to these personality attributes. In general, these passive, subjective, and somewhat withdrawn personalities are viewed as consistent with the history and culture of their tribe. This group has regularly emphasized withdrawal rather than overt resistance and has placed heavy emphasis upon the supernatural.

The results for the Thematic Apperception Test are given little attention other than some remarks upon their consistency with the findings derived from the Rorschach. Brief mention of results from this instrument is included in a series of case histories presented at the end of the volume, but again there is no indication, for either the Rorschach or TAT, of how these personality inferences were achieved.

Although the various studies we have just described are reported separately and possess distinctive features, they are sufficiently alike so that, particularly since they are part of an over-all program of research, it seems legitimate to evaluate them together. They have many ideal qualities: As we have noted, the number of subjects tested exceeds that of any comparable investigation, and, in general, the subjects tend to be more representative of the group being investigated than in most similar studies. There are a variety of comparative groups, including differentiated groups within most of the tribes studied, which can be used in interpreting test findings. There is also a large bulk of ethnological data available to be used in conjunction with the inferences concerning personality derived from the projective tests. In some cases we are given at least illustrative raw data from the projective tests and in several instances there are relatively comprehensive discussions of the circumstances under which the tests were administered.

These research reports are made singularly difficult to criticize by the authors' decision to place most of the technical details concerning their use of projective techniques in separate publications. Thus, the reader will note that many objections to these reports might have been answered if material comparable to that included in William Henry's monograph, which we have already mentioned, had been included in the present volumes. This decision to exclude the details of projective testing may, of course, be fully justifiable in terms of the goals of the investigators and the audience with which they wished to communicate. However, it has deprived these studies of much of their potential technical merit. Furthermore, the promised technical monograph reporting Rorschach findings has never even been published.

Logically enough, in view of what has just been said, the major criticism of these studies is that they tell the reader altogether too little about the interpretive process. In most instances we are told virtually nothing concerning what it was in the projective-technique protocols that led the writers to the personality inferences they report. Furthermore, in many instances the personality generalizations are presented in such a manner that it is not clear whether they are based upon observational data, nonprojective tests, or projective techniques. The volumes vary somewhat, with *Warriors Without Weapons* providing the clearest link between data and inference, but in all cases there is far too little description of how the projective techniques were analyzed and what kinds of comparisons permitted the particular inferences reported. There is, of course, no indication of any effort to rule out the role of chance factors; in fact, it is only through an occasional reference that we know that the projective-technique protocols were subjected to objective analysis.

In some of the studies there is also a tendency to place the material derived from the projective techniques in a separate chapter with little effort to integrate it with the remainder of the volume. Although the volumes vary in this respect, there is generally a less systematic description of the circumstances under which the tests were administered and the extent to which the testing procedures meshed with the existing culture than one would hope to find. Furthermore, there is relatively little attempt to explore the contribution of nonpersonality factors to performance on the projective tests.

An extensive investigation of a Guatemalan community by Billig, Gillin, and Davidson (1947, 1948) utilized the Rorschach test in an effort to unearth differences between the Indians and Ladinos of the village of San Luis. The Indians maintained a predominantly Mayan culture, whereas the Ladino culture was largely European. The authors describe the Indian culture as more "folklore" and more localized, whereas the Ladinos are described as oriented toward the outside world and as having a somewhat less stable culture. The two groups existed in an ordered relationship, with the Ladinos looked upon as superior and the Indians as inferior.

The investigators set out to answer three questions. First, they were interested in whether there were distinct personality differences between the Indians and Ladinos. Second, they were concerned with whether there was any evidence for the influence of the local social system upon the formation of adult personality. Third, they inquired into whether there were any personality factors associated with the role of curer or witch doctor. In addition to a relatively complete ethnology, a series of personality sketches and life histories were collected, and the Rorschach test was administered to all of the subjects. The ethnologist made brief summary descriptions of these individuals prior to the administration of the Rorschach, and the authors report that "It was surprising that a 'blind' interpretation of the Rorschach records agreed in almost all cases with the ethnologist's opinions" (Billig, Gillin, & Davidson, 1947, p. 166).

The Rorschachs were administered in a rented house with only the subject and the tester present, and Spanish was used to communicate with the subjects. Local custom made it impossible for the examiner, a man, to be alone with female subjects, so the group studied consisted solely of male subjects, except for one female healer who was tested in her own home. The major part of the sample consisted of 60 men, divided equally among Ladinos and Indians and distributed evenly among six age groups. Within each of these categories an effort was made to select representative subjects. Additional Rorschach records were secured from six Indian witch doctors, one Ladino healer, and one Indian who had undergone a magical cure and was studied intensively. The Rorschach tests were analyzed following the recommendations of Klopfer and Kelley (1942) and the results are presented in separate sections dealing with the Ladino personality, the Indian personality, Indian and Ladino adolescents, the acculturation process, and the personality of the witch doctor.

In reporting these findings the authors present a wealth of detail, including psychograms for all of the subjects as well as distributions of a variety of important scores and ratios for the various special groups. An examination of the records of the Ladinos suggests that according to the ratio of Movement to Color responses, these subjects are more introtensive than extratensive, but that most typically they are constricted, showing a low incidence of both types of response. Consistently, the investigators conclude that their intellectual processes are inhibited and lacking in free expression. Out of 25 adult Ladinos the authors report finding only one who showed a rich and uninhibited capacity to use his creative powers. There is little evidence of anxiety in the protocols, presumably because these subjects withdraw from situations that are potentially anxiety-arousing. Most of the evidence concerning drives or motives suggests that these are crude and unsocialized and that the subjects maintain them in check by direct inhibition, which in turn leads to a shallow emotional life with only occasional impulsive expression of these emotions. Not only are the Ladinos lacking in any rich inner resources, they also appear to be poorly oriented toward the everyday world and its demands. The general personality portrait presented by the authors is that of a group incapable of deep and rewarding relations with self or others.

The Indian subjects resemble the Ladinos in Movement-Color ratio, where there is a high incidence of constricted records, but they are differentiated in that those who show a tendency for predominance of one type of response are most frequently extraversive, that is, show a relatively high proportion of Color responses. Among the Ladinos the incidence of intraversive tendencies was higher than the incidence of extraversive. Examination of the VIII + IX + X per cent in addition to the ratio of $FM + m$ to $Fc + c + C'$ leads the authors to conclude ". . . that we are not dealing with well-adjusted individuals, but rather with somewhat rigid persons finding it essential to restrict their natural inclinations and inhibiting their reactions to both inner and outer stimulation" (p. 328). The low incidence of Detail responses suggests an inability to deal with ordinary realistic problems, whereas the high incidence of Whole responses is coupled with a low incidence of $W+$ or well-formed Whole responses, suggesting intellectual impoverishment or serious emotional problems. The authors feel that the relatively low incidence of Color responses among these subjects may reflect a high degree of inhibition and restriction imposed by the local culture upon these people. There is an almost total lack of Human Movement responses, and the authors infer from this an inadequate inner life and little or no creative ability. In summarizing their inferences concerning the psychic life of the Indians, the authors suggest:

. . . The life of the adult Indian is dominated by his primitive drives and early fixations. He does not respond readily to outside stimulation. His emotional life is shallow; his intellectual accomplishments and his creative abilities are very limited. . . . Because of his tendencies to brush aside outside occurrences, he is unaware of difficulties evolving from community life. He approaches his world by means of all-inclusive generalities and rationalizations. When he attempts to face objective reality, he gets lost in the problems of his everyday life, which becomes so overwhelming to him that he is incapable of solving them. (p. 345)

In a section concerned with acculturation, the authors compare the performance of the Ladinos and Indians and suggest that the personality differences observed are a product of the different degrees of acculturation of the two groups. They conclude that both groups manifest an intense concern with primitive, unacculturated drives as manifested by a very high incidence of Form-Movement responses. They are also similar in their tendency toward a balance between Movement and Color but with a tendency toward constriction. The Ladinos are somewhat more extratensive and the Indians somewhat intraversive. Stereotyped responses are more frequent among the Indians than among the Ladinos, and the Indians generally seem somewhat less well-prepared to meet the demands of daily living. There is somewhat more rigidity (per cent of Form responses) and a higher incidence of oppositional tendencies (Space responses) among the Ladinos than among the Indians. An examination of Rorschachs of the adolescents in the two groups reveals a high degree of similarity and suggests to the authors that the effect of the process of socialization is to produce selective differences in these groups as adults. The Ladino adolescents appear to be more emotionally responsive, more closely related to external reality, and better able to think in conventional terms. Both groups seem to be intellectually rigid, as suggested by their high F per cent, and both groups seem superior to the adults in creative capacity, as suggested by the incidence of Movement responses.

In presenting the Rorschach results for the witch doctors, the authors first consider the case of a patient and then present in detail the cases of the female Ladinos and one Indian healer, following this with a joint consideration of the six witch doctors. The group, in general, appears less rigid (lower F per cent) than the other members of their society, and their higher incidence of Movement responses suggests greater potentiality for creativity. Moreover, the Indian healers seem to be predominantly introversive, whereas the other Indians studied tended to be balanced between introversion and extroversion. Consistently, four of the curers show strong evidence of schizoid tendencies, and, the authors report, a fifth would probably be judged schizophrenic in our society. On the basis of their analysis of these Rorschachs, the authors accept the hypothesis that there is a distinctive personality type accompanying the role of witch doctor.

The report of this study is particularly commendable because of the care with which the investigators have described the circumstances under which the personality data were collected and the detail with which the raw material upon which personality inferences are based is presented. The authors also provide a relatively clear indication of the interpretive process and, in comparison to other studies of this era, display a relatively explicit awareness of the extent to which the local culture influences the testing process.

On the negative side, we find little consideration of the various factors, other than personality differences, that could have produced the observed differences in Rorschach performance. For example, all of the protocols were collected in Spanish, and it is unlikely that both Ladinos and Indians were equally fluent in this language. In spite of this, the authors show no inclination to consider language difference an important potential contributor to the differences in Rorschach performance. Furthermore, the general status difference between the two cultural groups, remarked upon by the authors, clearly might be expected to influence response to the test administrator and his Rorschach cards. The report of a "blind analysis" of the Rorschach and correlation of the results of this analysis with inferences based upon the ethnologist's observations is much too cryptic to carry conviction. Nothing is said concerning the form of the personality inferences made by the ethnologist or the manner in which the comparison was made with the Rorschach findings, and this, after all, is the crux of the matter. The authors also use percentages throughout their report, even when such figures may be quite misleading, as in the case of results based upon a total of five subjects. Furthermore, there is no attempt to assess the role of chance factors in producing the differences observed. The interpretation of the Rorschach appears somewhat pedantic, as it is based upon a literal transposition of specific interpretive generalizations (derived from Klopfer and Kelley, 1942), many of which seem questionable and all of which were based upon a sample that does not even remotely resemble the present samples. One might argue that it is this interpretive procedure which led to personality descriptions that are singularly devoid of positive elements and generally paint a picture of bleak pathology. Findings based upon the Rorschach and results derived from field observation are sometimes presented in such a manner that it is difficult to know whether inferences are based upon one source, the other, or both.

An unusually original and provocative inquiry is reported by Gladwin and Sarason (1953) in a volume entitled *Truk: Man in Paradise.* This research, part of the Coordinated Investigation of Micronesian Anthropology, centered about the study of personality development among the Trukese. The investigators offer a detailed description of the various stages of development among the Trukese and illustrate these with an unusually full life history of a female informant. The results of the personality tests are summarized by Sarason, and subsequently Gladwin attempts to synthesize the psychological and cultural findings in a chapter concerned with personality development in this particular cultural setting.

Although the ethnological data were derived from a variety of different sources, including the notes and manuscripts of colleagues participating in the same study, the data of principal interest to us were obtained from Gladwin's administration of the Rorschach and a modified TAT to 12 men ranging in age from 13 to 56 and 13 women ranging from 14 to 50. The field worker wished to include within his sample some subjects who were unusual or atypical, and he began by securing from 10 informants judgments as to which males and females were particularly liked and particularly disliked. On this basis the six males and six females who were most popular and the six of each sex who were least popular were identified, and three of each were selected at random for inclusion in the study. From those subjects not at the extremes in popularity, an additional five of each sex were selected at random, and one additional male subject was included because of his active role in assisting the anthropologist. Each of these subjects provided a life history and took the Kohs Block Test, the Rorschach test, and the Thematic Apperception Test.

Before going into the field the psychologist and anthropologist discussed test administration, and the anthropologist was given experience in administering the tests to American subjects. More important, it was agreed that Gladwin would attempt, whatever the exigencies of the field situation, to maintain the treatment of the different subjects as nearly constant as possible. Further, it was decided that he would attempt to have the subjects indicate the location of their Rorschach responses on tracing paper. The actual administration of the Rorschach followed conventional procedure except that the inquiry was conducted following the responses to each card, rather than at the end of the series, and for some subjects, a trial blot was shown to the subjects before the regular series. The tracing paper was used to locate responses where it seemed desirable and feasible. The TAT cards employed were a modified set developed by William A. Lessa for use in Micronesia and included 18 pictures and one blank card. It was early decided that the test was too long and difficult for the subjects and five pictures and the blank card were eliminated. A good deal of prompting was necessary in administering the TAT in order to get satisfactory stories from the subjects, particularly on the first few cards.

The interpretation of the Rorschach and TAT protocols was carried out by Sarason, and in the case of the Rorschach, this process is specified in more detail than in any other cultural study with which I am familiar. Thus, the investigator deliberately attempted to make as public as possible not only the interpretations and the raw data upon which they were based but also the process of inference that permitted him to go from one to the other. After reading all of the Rorschach protocols several times:

I then interpreted each record, response by response, in the presence of Gladwin who wrote down what I said. His presence was necessary for several reasons: (a) when one is interpreting a record he has not administered, it is unusual not to have questions arise which only the administrator can answer—in the case of non-Western records more than the usual quota of questions should be expected; (b) since the Trukese referred to animals, plants, etc., with which I was not familiar, Gladwin was the logical person to judge whether a response to a given blot area was a "good fit"; (c) I wanted to state the interpretations so that they conveyed to another person, with knowledge of the Rorschach, what aspects of the responses I was using, Gladwin's function being to ask questions ("that's not clear," "it's vague," etc.) which would force me to be specific about the referents of my own statements. (p. 219)

After the individual records had been interpreted, Sarason developed a general description of the group based upon the entire 23 protocols. It was only when all of this had been completed that he moved on to the interpretation of the TAT. Here the pressure of time forced him to interpret the test according to "the usual clinical manner" with no attempt to make explicit the inference process. Again a general personality description of the subjects was prepared.

Case histories for the 23 subjects studied intensively are presented individually, and the authors include in the appendices individual test protocols for each of the subjects and, in the case of the Rorschach, a complete running account of Sarason's interpretive speculations as he derived personality inferences from the protocols.

Sarason shows explicit and serious concern over the possibility that his interaction with Gladwin may have served to bias or contaminate his interpretations. However, as the following quotation indicates, he concludes that such an effect was not likely:

The only information I ever requested of Gladwin was (*a*) whether an individual was unduly upset by the testing or appeared markedly evasive —*I never asked for or received information about an individual's behavior outside the testing situation*, and questions concerning test behavior were asked in only a few cases; (*b*) whether ghosts, as I had already concluded, were malevolent spirits; and (*c*) whether the Trukese habit (in the tests) of responding in the form of a question was a form of "talking aloud" or was directed to the examiner in a dependent way—the answer received was that it was not directed to the examiner. I would like to emphasize that Gladwin's function was not to discuss my statements but to insure that the relation between my conclusions and the data were clear. (p. 220)

The results of Dr. Sarason's interpretations of the Rorschach protocols led him to describe the Trukese as concrete and rigid in their thought, inhibited in response to novel situations, unable to respond freely in affective areas, superficial in their interpersonal relations, and characterized by severe sexual conflicts. In spite of these generally shared characteristics, the investigator was impressed with the diversity and variation within these protocols. On the basis of the TAT protocols, Sarason suggests that the Trukese men and women live in serious conflict with each other and that much of this opposition is related to sexual activity. Further, interpersonal relations are typically shallow, parents tend to be inconsistent in their treatment of children, and the Trukese have severe anxieties centering about food and separation. Sarason also suggests that the members of this culture tend toward a passive existence rather than an active, industrious life, and that these subjects as a group have difficulty in expressing hostility overtly.

Once these generalizations and a host of related interpretations were presented, the anthropologist confronted them with ethnographic data. In doing this, he found evidence for both contradiction and continuity. The general impression is one of surprising concordance, with those instances of discrepancy usually being accountable on the basis of the psychologist's having had insufficient information concerning the culture while making his interpretations.

Gladwin used the projective-technique findings to shape and guide his analysis and interpretation of the cultural data in his psychocultural outline of the process of personality development in Truk. Sarason also considered the consistency of the projective-test results and the ethnographic findings, arriving at the conclusion that "Psychological tests can be interpreted in a manner so as to give conclusions which correspond rather well with ethnographic data" (p. 455). In emphasizing the importance of the potential error contributed by the psychologist to studies such as the present one, Sarason provides a number of interesting strictures against the Rorschach test in anthropological research, particularly when the investigator depends upon conventional scoring categories. His general position is that the utility of these scores is by no means clearly demonstrated in our own society, and in view of the additional problems involved in their application in an alien culture, their use hardly seems warranted. His own preference is to examine the Rorschach protocols not as the basis for a set of formal scores but rather as a relatively standardized sample of behavior that may provide inferences concerning how the subject will behave in other settings. Given this conviction it is understandable that he would state:

One does not have to read far in the Rorschach literature in order to conclude that some workers view the scoring categories as the chief if not sole basis for interpretation. . . . (or) The most flagrant examples of the use, or abuse, of the "counting" method are those studies in which a more or less homogeneous group of subjects is given the Rorschach, the frequencies computed, and the interpretation written in such a manner as to suggest that the constellation of frequencies is somehow unique for this group and that the behavioral characteristics described in the interpretation are valid. (p. 435)

Sarason points to the potential contribution of psychological tests in directing the attention of the anthropologist toward generalizations or problems that he might otherwise have overlooked. He also suggests that the information secured from the Rorschach and TAT is sufficiently different so that both instruments should be used where possible. In a final summing up, Gladwin again states that the psychological results influenced the treatment of the field data. "The test results provided a number of hypotheses and made evident several relationships within ethnographic data which were not apparent during the initial 'anthropological' analysis" (p. 460).

This point is elaborated in a separate paper (Gladwin, 1953) discussing sex differences among the Trukese. Gladwin makes clear that after four years of contact with these people he returned home convinced that men were dominant and generally more secure than the women who appeared ". . . subservient, insecure, and afraid to express themselves in the presence of their lords and masters" (p. 306). Much to his surprise the analysis of the projective-technique protocols suggested to Sarason that men were more anxious than women and less competent to deal with ambiguous or conflict situations. Prodded by this finding, Gladwin took a second look at the ethnographic data and found, again to his surprise, a considerable amount of information (incidence of suicide attempts, successful resistance to parental pressure in regard to marriage, male and female role in adulterous relations, treatment of brother and sister at puberty when they must be separated by cultural decree, and so on) which supported Sarason's interpretation and forced the anthropologist to a new formulation which seemed considerably more "economical and inclusive" than his earlier position. In conclusion he suggests:

The use of independently and adequately interpreted projective tests in the study of personality and culture can serve others, as it served me, in forcing a re-examination of data with which it is easy to become all too familiar and in exposing previously unsuspected relationships within the data which can then be further explored. On the other hand, by no means all of Dr. Sarason's conclusions stood up unmodified under examination. . . . While we can strongly urge, therefore, the more extensive use of projective tests in conjunction with the collection of as many other sorts of information as possible in the study of personality in other societies, equally we should warn against the unreserved acceptance of test interpretations alone as a means of arriving at a description of the psychological attributes of the people under study. (p. 309)

This is clearly one of the most important anthropological studies employing projective techniques yet to be conducted. Its importance stems initially from the novelty of its approach and is sustained by the interest of the findings and the excellence of the reporting. It is perhaps the only study in this domain where the results of the psychological tests clearly have had a heavy influence upon the analysis of ethnographic data. Furthermore, we find a refreshingly effective collaboration between psychologist and anthropologist so that, although some important controls against contamination of data are fully maintained, the psychologist is able to secure certain essential information from the ethnologist as he proceeds with his interpretive task. Moreover, we find happily that the two investigators actually began their collaboration prior to field work and reached some important agreements in regard to aspects of the data collection. As part of this picture, Sarason shows much more interest in the immediate context of the psychological examination than is typical of projective-test interpreters. The avoidance of conventional scoring categories represents a further interesting and unusual aspect of the study. The selection of the sample and the process of administering the test are adequately reported, and most unusual is the fullness with which Sarason has reported the process whereby he interpreted the Rorschach protocols. Clearly the detail and explicitness with which the Rorschach interpretation is discussed is not only unusual in anthropological research but would be distinctive in projective-technique research in any setting. It is also heartening to find both investigators convinced of the existence of substantial congruence between projective-technique findings and ethnographic report and able to cite numerous instances of parallel passages derived from these two data sources.

This matter of the association between ethnographic data and projective-technique findings leads directly to the major flaw of the study. The measure of association between these two sets of inferences, or two sources of data, is nothing more than the judgment or verbal report of the two investigators. This is indeed a dubious means of determining such an essential relation. Sarason specifically identifies this flaw in the study and suggests four considerations that might be used to object to the judgment of congruence by Gladwin and Sarason (possible bias in favor of congruence, test interpretations so general as to fit with many different independent generalizations, so many generalizations from projective techniques that some are certain to be congruent, investigators so familiar with each other's ideas that they impute more than is literally present in statements by the other). He reasons that "Ideally the evaluation of congruence should be done by several independent judges with appropriate backgrounds," and suggests that "this was obviously not feasible for the present study" (p. 445). This statement makes sense only as a description of the personal impossibility of such a step, since on technical grounds such an operation would be completely feasible although not easy to execute. When we remember that these investigators skillfully, and at cost of considerable time, carried out the psychological interpretations under carefully controlled conditions, one may regret that they did not extend their controls somewhat.

Of what merit is it to protect so carefully against contamination of data at the level of analysis when the eventual comparison of the two sets of data is to be so hopelessly contaminated? Athough multiple trained judges would be desirable, there are many ways in which the problem of comparing inferences from ethnographic and projective-technique data can be approached, including various matching devices. In any case, it would be important not only to rule out observer bias of various kinds, but also it would obviously be necessary, if we are to have full confidence in the outcome, to provide some basis for testing the role of chance factors in producing whatever degree of congruity is observed. Chance is a potent factor, particularly when the study includes only 23 subjects.

One may also take issue with the authors' stringency in rejecting conventional scoring approaches to projective tests. It is true that there is no magic assurance these will function satisfactorily in this setting, neither is there any assurance that alternative approaches will function effectively.

PROCEDURAL STUDIES

We are concerned here with studies primarily intended to explore matters of method or procedure rather than to unearth substantive findings. The investigation that attempts to demonstrate the cross-cultural applicability of projective techniques, that tries to devise some means of compensating for a known difficulty in using these techniques in this setting, or that centers upon the comparison of ethnographic data and projective-technique data would fall under this heading.

One of the most extensive considerations of the usefulness of projective techniques in the hands of the anthropologist is provided by Hallowell (1955) in a general discussion of the use of the Rorschach in studies of culture and personality. He suggests that a satisfactory psychological test for use in anthropological field work should possess the following qualities: (1) it should be neither theoretically nor practically culture bound; (2) it should be adaptable so that it can be administered without undue difficulty to nonliterate subjects; (3) it should be usable with children as well as adults; (4) it should permit inferences concerning the group as a whole as well as individual members of the group. A general discussion of his own and others' experience with projective techniques in alien cultures leads him to the conclusion that the Rorschach can be utilized cross culturally. He suggests that ". . . the raw data necessary for interpretation can be elicited because a universal function of human perception is exploited" (p. 45).

In support of this important conclusion he considers several streams of evidence, beginning with productivity or number of responses to the Rorschach. He finds that when he compares several American samples with a wide variety of samples from other cultures, there is considerable similarity at least in terms of average productivity. Furthermore, he suggests that even in groups where the productivity is low, as in the case of the Flambeau Ojibwa, the records shed psychological light upon the subjects. He also examines the content of Rorschach responses in a number of different cultures and again reports that the proportion of Human and Animal responses shows considerable constancy, even in subjects drawn from diverse cultural settings. Consideration of his own findings, as well as the research of others, in connection with Movement responses and Popular responses leads him to conclude that although there are problems involved in the cross-cultural application of the Rorschach, used properly it can provide the analyst with important information.

Hallowell's observations are of importance not only because of his detailed familiarity with the use of the Rorschach in anthropological field work, but also because he attempts to draw upon the extensive experience and findings of other ethnologists. Thus, his comparison of the number of responses and the incidence of Human and Animal responses in a wide variety of different cultures represents one of the few attempts to examine Rorschach performance in a genuinely broad cultural context. The primary difficulty with this type of analysis is that once the author leaves the level of assertion or generalization based upon his own experience, with no empirical control of quantitative evidence, his position becomes infirm. In the case of productivity, for example, if Hallowell finds a high degree of constancy across diverse cultures, one may argue that this shows the practical usefulness of the test in different cultural settings, or one may argue with equal cogency that this displays the insensitivity of the test to cultural variation and concomitant personality differences. Equally ambiguous is his report that in his studies of the Ojibwa and in Spindler's studies of the Menomini, productivity appears to vary with acculturation, but in the one case the association is positive and in the other, negative. Even when the reader gives serious attention to Hallowell's suggestion that the important underlying variable may be personal adjustment, these findings seem to give a very weak basis for his conclusion that ". . . we now have unequivocal evidence that lack of productivity is no bar to the cross-cultural use of the Rorschach test" (p. 48).

We have already referred to William Henry's (1947) pioneer application of the Thematic Apperception Test as part of the Indian Education Research Project, and it seems appropriate to outline the study in more detail here because of its focus upon the usefulness or validity of the TAT in a cross-cultural setting. Henry used a modification of the TAT, consisting of 11 pictures redrawn so as to be appropriate for his Indian subjects, which was administered individually to Hopi and Navaho children ranging in age from two to eighteen and evenly divided in sex. The tests were administered by different examiners to the Hopi and the Navaho children, and in cases where there was difficulty with the English language an interpreter was employed. For each subject there was available also life-history material, Rorschach test results, results of a free-drawing test, and results of a battery of tests including a measure of emotional response, moral ideology, rules of games, and moral judgment. All of this material was collected and analyzed independently of the TAT data.

After completing some preliminary studies which suggested the TAT was providing useful information concerning these subjects, Henry established a scheme for analyzing the TAT protocols in terms of seven major areas of functioning: mental approach, creativity and imagination, behavioral approach, family dynamics, inner adjustment and defense mechanisms, emotional reactivity, and sexual adjustment. He then attempted to assess the validity of his TAT analysis by two studies, the first inquired into the extent to which the individual analyses applied accurately only to the child whose TAT was being interpreted and not to other children. Here, he was attempting to demonstrate that the descriptions were not couched in general enough terms to be applicable to almost any individual. Personality descriptions based upon the TAT, upon the Rorschach, upon the life history, and upon the test battery were prepared independently for each of eight Navaho girls and given to three judges. Thus, each judge had in his possession 32 separate personality descriptions, some of which belonged together (were for the same person), whereas others were unrelated. There were 24 matches, in all, involving the TAT and some other instrument, and the chance expectancy was that three of these matches would be performed correctly. The first judge had 18 correct matchings, the second judge matched correctly all 24 pairs, and the third judge had 15 correct matches. Thus, the findings provide positive evidence for the validity of the TAT inferences. It is worth noting that the second judge was most familiar with the culture of the children and the first judge next most familiar, so that there is some slight evidence that familiarity with the social and cultural setting of the individuals was an important aid in the interpretive process.

In the second validity study the scheme of analysis was applied to 16 Navaho children ranging in age from 6 to 17 and including eight boys and eight girls. In addition, the independent analyses of the Rorschach, life history, test battery, and free drawing were examined in terms of each of the areas included in the TAT analysis. Whenever there was a statement in one of the other analyses that bore upon an area included in the TAT analysis, this statement was rated on a three-point scale in terms of its agreement or disagreement with the TAT interpretive statement. For the 16 subjects there were a total of 451 instances where the TAT analysis showed overlap with the interpretations based on other evidence, and 375 of these were judged to be in essential agreement, 66 were judged to be in partial agreement, and 10 were judged to be in disagreement. Thus, the findings present a rather strong case for the similarity of the interpretations inferred from the TAT protocols and those inferred independently from quite different data sources. The reliability of the ratings was examined for three cases with three judges repeating independently the judgments of the experimental judge and the results showed moderate reliability. The results of these studies led Henry to the following sanguine conclusion:

As can be seen in the foregoing quantitative analysis and as was clear from the qualitative analysis in the clinical conference, the TAT had cut across and integrated all the other techniques used in this research . . . the TAT gave personality descriptions that were consistent with other known data on the case and which also contributed new and helpful information on the personality of the subject. The analyses gave a general picture of the personality structure and the emotional development of the individual and, in addition, provided this description in a behavioral and social context that made possible demonstration of personality variables in overt behavior and of the motivational background of behavior. (p. 82)

The remainder of Henry's study was devoted to examining the validity of psychological generalizations concerning the Hopi and Navaho as a group. For these purposes 102 TAT protocols were used from the Hopi and 104 from the Navaho. For each culture a composite picture of the psychological makeup of the group was derived from the analysis of the TAT protocols, and this was then compared at specific points with evidence provided by field work with these people. In addition, the personality descriptions were read and judged for essential accuracy by experienced anthropologists familiar with the society. Finally, in the case of the Navaho, it was possible to compare the results of the TAT analysis with the results of a similar analysis based upon Rorschach protocols for the same group. In every case the general findings supported the effectiveness of the TAT as a tool for description of the personality characteristics of a group. Henry concludes:

With regard to the use of the TAT for studies of society, it is indicated both by the approval of the anthropologists who reviewed the reports and by the degree to which the details of the reports check with the anthropological field data, that the TAT data was of sufficiently high validity and make sufficient contribution to the study of the society to justify its conclusion in the total Research on Indian Education and to have a strong claim on inclusion in future studies of personality and culture. (p. 126)

Henry's study is early, extensive, and ingenious. The number of subjects included in the various phases of the study is impressively large, the independent information available for validation purposes is remarkably full, and the author's analysis of the TAT procotols is original, sensitive, and very detailed. Moreover, there is an unusually careful outline of the procedure followed in analyzing the projective-test data. Finally, we find that the TAT interpretation is transformed into a quantitative outcome in a number of instances, and in some cases findings are subjected to simple statistical analysis.

It is difficult to find fault with this study, particularly in view of its inventive quality; however, it has some observable shortcomings. We are given relatively little information concerning the testing context, and the author displays no concern over the fact that the TAT was administered to Hopi and Navaho subjects by different examiners and that an interpreter was used for some subjects and not for others. All in all, these differences would make the attempt to compare or differentiate these two groups on the basis of test performance quite hazardous. Of course, Henry's primary emphasis upon the relation between the TAT and independent measures of the same subjects negates this criticism to some extent. It is also true that comparison of the general characterizations of the Hopi and Navaho subjects with ethnographic data and Rorschach data is relatively impressionistic and uncontrolled so that prior belief or expectation might influence the outcome considerably. In the end, however, perhaps the only important objection is the plaintive remark that the association reported by Henry between TAT and Rorschach ratings in this alien culture setting is so much closer than that observed in the society in which these devices originated that one cannot help being somewhat puzzled.

Margaret Mead's technical monograph on the Mountain Arapesh (1949) includes a life history of one of her informants, Unabelin, as well as his complete Rorschach protocol and four different interpretations of these responses provided by various analysts. The circumstances surrounding the administration of this Rorschach test are particularly interesting, for it was in 1931 that the author set out for New Guinea—long before there was much general interest on the part of anthropologists, or even psychologists, in projective techniques. A suggestion by David Levy, who introduced the Rorschach in this country, led Dr. Mead to include this device among her data-collecting procedures.

Upon returning from her field work, some of her protocols were submitted to Rorschach authorities who pronounced them unscorable, presumably because of the absence of any location chart. More than a decade later when the case of Unabelin was being prepared for publication, Dr. Mead examined the Rorschach protocol and concluded, on the basis of published reports of the use of the Rorschach in nonliterate societies, that this record would lend itself to interpretation. Consequently, with the aid of Jane Belo, she translated her verbal notes concerning location of the percepts on the blots onto a conventional location chart and submitted the record to Bruno Klopfer, Molly Harrower (and Florence Miale), Martha Wolfenstein, and Theodora Abel. Slightly different material was used in interpreting the test since two different sets of scores were employed by the analysts (Belo's & Abel's); one analysis (by Harrower & Miale) was performed without recourse to formal scores; and at least one of the interpreters (Klopfer) was able to ask Dr. Mead questions about the culture as he proceeded with his interpretation. Furthermore, the interpreters approached their task with somewhat different orientations, and in at least the case of Abel's interpretation, there was an effort to emphasize the "cultural relevance of the material" (p. 371).

So far as the details of the administration of the test are concerned, we are told that it was given in the fourth interview session, and the detailed contents of the preceding three sessions are reproduced so that it is easily possible to estimate the adequacy of the rapport between examiner and informant. Moreover, the test was administered in pidgin English except where ambiguity seemed particularly likely, in which case the native word was employed.

It would be unreasonable for us to attempt to summarize the four interpretations here, but certain general remarks can be made. First, the analyses are highly diversified, not only in the variables that are focused upon, but also in length and detail. Klopfer's analysis is immediate and associative; he responds with initial impressions and interpretations to the individual responses in sequence, and there is no attempt at an over-all synthesis or summary personality portrait. The interpretation was made in conversation with Dr. Mead, was stenographically recorded, and is reported verbatim. In similar fashion, Harrower and Miale discussed the interpretation of the protocols and then summarized their interpretive conclusions by means of dictation. Wolfenstein's very brief and somewhat general interpretation was based solely upon Jane Belo's scoring of the protocols. Theodora Abel, employing her own scoring of the protocols, prepared a fairly detailed portrait of Unabelin with some attempt to refer interpretations to their cultural context, although it is not clear how much, if any, information she had concerning the Arapesh culture.

In her discussion of these interpretations, Mead emphasizes her belief that the various personality portraits show a "high degree of agreement" (p. 358) and that they fit rather well with inferences provided by the ethnologist. She suggests that the Rorschach test serves to increase communication between anthropologist and psychologist and for this reason alone is worth inclusion among the field techniques of the anthropologist. She questions whether the Rorschach records told her anything about the Arapesh culture that she did not already know, although she concludes from her discussion with Dr. Klopfer that the technique might be used to identify elements within the culture that are of particular emotional salience.

This study is of interest mainly because of the very early period at which it was carried out, the detailed reporting of some of the interpretive acts, and the prestige of the investigators and interpreters. As Mead makes clear, the study was carried out under adverse conditions. It is primarily the subjective impressions of the merit of the test reported by Mead and the detailed recording of the process whereby Klopfer arrived at inferences concerning the respondent that endow this report with contemporary significance. It is also true that we have here a much more complete ethnography than is customary in personality and culture studies and a wealth of interview data relevant to an understanding of Unabelin and his culture. The author also provides a detailed report of the Rorschach responses as well as the results of a formal scoring of the protocols.

The frankly exploratory nature of the study and the report make it understandable that the administration of the instrument would depart from customary technique and that the scoring would be carried out with difficulty. Somewhat more difficult to justify is the procedure followed in the interpretation and the process whereby Mead reached conclusions concerning the results of these interpretations. Here the root difficulty is that the investigator appears to have had no particular question in mind that she hoped to answer with these data. The fact that the psychologists possessed different data, different information concerning the culture, and set themselves different goals in their interpretive activities makes it clearly impossible for the study to provide much enlightenment on any question of the use of projective techniques. Equally difficult to defend is the fact that there is no attempt at careful comparison of the various interpretations with each other or with the ethnographic findings. In other words, Mead's conclusions on the agreement between interpreters and between Rorschach interpretation and ethnographer are apparently based simply upon inspection of the relevant material. Furthermore, these conclusions seem clearly contradicted by manifest disagreements between the various interpretations as well as by their obvious failure to deal with the same personality areas. In other words, it is not clear that her conclusions are warranted by the data, and it is certain that without some objective comparison of the various sets of data, it would be hard to convince the neutral observer of the legitimacy of these inferences.

A further study, involving the same Rorschach protocols collected from the Navaho, Zuni, Mormon, and Spanish-American subjects already mentioned, was conducted by Kaplan, Rickers-Ovsiankina, and Joseph (1956). This study was intended to answer the question of whether the Rorschach protocols from four distinct cultural groups could be accurately grouped or sorted by individuals who were unaware of the origin of the protocols.

In the first part of the study an experienced Rorschach analyst with no knowledge of the cultures involved was given a set of 24 protocols and asked to sort them into the four cultural groups that they represented. The protocols were then divided in half, and the first 12 protocols were grouped into the four cultural groups. The interpreter was then asked to take the second 12 protocols and match each with one of the four established groups. The results of these analyses revealed that the interpreter was unable to sort or match the protocols with sufficient success to indicate anything more than a chance performance. In the second part of the study an equally experienced Rorschach interpreter who also had considerable experience in cross-cultural study of personality and some contact with the four cultures under investigation was given the same two tasks. In this case the accuracy of her sorts and matches was significantly better than could have been expected on the basis of chance alone. The difference in performance is interpreted as deriving from the greater cultural contact of the second interpreter and her consequent ability to form psychological hypotheses concerning the kinds of differences that might be expected between the cultural groups.

The third part of the study involved the application of discriminant function, a statistical method for differentiation of groups on the basis of multiple scores or dimensions, to the entire group of 116 protocols from the four cultures. Each pair of cultures was compared in terms of eight Rorschach variables, and the three most discriminating variables were chosen for use in the further analysis. In addition, the protocols were divided into half with the first half being used to determine, by means of the discriminant function, the most efficient means of classifying the groups in terms of the three variables and the second half being used to test the generality or validity of this classification. The results of the analysis indicated that the method, derived from the discriminant function approach and utilizing the eight Rorschach variables, performed somewhat better than would be expected by chance but that it was not a powerful tool for classifying the Rorschach protocols according to culture.

The authors conclude: "These results suggest that Rorschachs from the four cultures are different enough to be sorted with considerable success. This differentiation is more possible with some cultures than with others. It is facilitated by a knowledge of the cultures" (p. 178). In addition, they suggest that the Rorschach differences between cultures provide "a strong presumption that certain personality characteristics of the individuals in these cultures are also different" (p. 178), although they are aware that certain cultural differences might lead to performance differences on the Rorschach that could be mistaken for personality differences. In support of the fact that the differences in Rorschach results between cultures cannot be accounted for solely in terms of differences in cultural content, they point to the fact that Kaplan's (1955) investigation with protocols from these same cultures revealed no "substantial differences among the cultures" in several content areas. They also discuss the possible impact of cultural differences upon interpretation of the test situation and the consequent danger that these differences might lead to response differences that, again, would reflect the culture and not the individual personality.

We have already considered the relative strengths and deficits of this inquiry in our discussion of Kaplan's study of the modal personality, and it will suffice here to suggest that, although there are certain technical problems with the study, it is a singularly objective and interesting demonstration of a type of investigation needed in much larger quantity.

An unusual study that involved repeated psychological testing of two Navaho children over a period of five years and the independent interpretation of some of the projective techniques by different persons is reported by Kluckhohn and Rosenzweig (1949). In this investigation life-history information as well as responses to the Rorschach and other psychological tests were collected initially in 1942, at which time the subjects were six and seven years of age. They were then retested in 1946 with a different set of measures, and in 1947 the Rorschach was administered again.

Of primary interest here are the results for the two administrations of the Rorschach. Following the first administration this test was interpreted by the examiner, a psychiatrist, and then independently by an anthropologist, a psychologist, and a second psychiatrist. Only the first two interpreters were familiar with Navaho cultures, and only the first knew the particular subjects. The interpretive statements of these four investigators were then compared in terms of eight major categories (degree and mode of control, responsiveness of emotional energies, mental approach, creative capacities, intellectual level, security, maturity, prognosis) with a number of alternative descriptive phrases included under each of these headings. The authors report, for each of the four interpreters, the presence or absence of statements fitting all of the subcategories, thus permitting a judgment of the consistency of the clinicians' personality inferences. The authors suggest: "It is clear that there is a remarkable degree of agreement among the four interpretations, three of them done 'blind' " (p. 269).

The 1947 Rorschach was administered and interpreted by a psychologist who had seen the interpretations of the 1942 Rorschachs. His interpretations are reported qualitatively and in reasonable detail so as to permit a comparison with the earlier Rorschach findings, as well as the life-history information, and the qualitative interpretations from the other tests. The authors feel that the basic personality pattern revealed in the second set of interpretations is the same and that the changes reported are accountable in terms of normal maturational changes and special situational factors. Taking all of the test results into consideration, Kluckhohn and Rosenzweig conclude that

The picture obtained of these two personalities by different testers and interpreters using a variety of projective techniques is, on the whole, remarkably consistent. . . . The personality diagnoses made on the basis of projective tests also check well with the impressions of another set of field workers who used ordinary interview and observation methods. In short, the present paper constitutes a partial validation of projective tests in another culture, with the caution that significant results are peculiarly dependent upon the relationship between tester and subject. (pp. 277-278)

Several of the tests administered in 1942 were re-administered some ten months later by a different field worker, and the results of these administrations lead the authors to emphasize the importance of the language in which the test is administered, as well as the degree of rapport that the examiner has established with the subject. When the TAT was administered to one of the subjects in Navaho rather than English, the protocol was more than five times as long; and variation of the same magnitude was revealed when the examiner had been living with the family for a week prior to administering the test.

The attempt to measure consistency of interpretation of Rorschach protocols by independent investigators with various degrees of familiarity with the relevant culture represents an extremely important and novel feature of this study. Furthermore, the repeated testing of the same subjects over a period of years, and under different conditions, points to essential problems that are, as yet, virtually unapproached. The analysis of the four interpretations in terms of specific categories of interpretations reveals a healthy interest in moving beyond general impression to controlled inference. Furthermore, the intensive study of a small number of subjects provides an interesting and useful supplement to the usual study involving the analysis of limited amounts of information for large numbers of subjects.

Virtually all of the criticisms that can be made of this study have to do with additional empirical controls that might ideally have been included in order to provide a firmer empirical base for the conclusions of the writers. For example, there is no objective or formal comparison of the interpretations based upon the projective techniques and those based upon direct observation and life-history material. Conclusions concerning the congruence of projective techniques with other data sources remain impressions rather than demonstrations. Furthermore, even in the admirable analysis and comparison of the interpretations of the four investigators, there is an uncomfortable degree of ambiguity in regard to just how much consistency is revealed. Certain descriptive categories are so regularly found in almost all interpretations of projective-technique protocols (for example, presence of anxiety, or difficulty in controlling emotional response) that agreement on these items may say little about the extent to which interpreters agree in statements that differentiate one subject from another. Further, even if one accepts all subcategories as meaningfully differentiating subjects, there is still no indication of which specific categories are considered consistent and which inconsistent or mutually exclusive. Thus, for one of the subjects there are only two statements for which all four judges make the same interpretation, and there are 19 subcategories into which the interpretation of only one judge falls. The point is not that the judges appear to be inconsisent but, rather, that without a more meaningful analysis of their interpretations there are many readers who would not concur with the authors' statement that there is a "remarkable degree of agreement" among the various interpreters. There are a number of additional procedural objections that could be cited, such as the exposure of the second Rorschach examiner to the interpretations of the first Rorschach, thus making impossible any statements concerning consistency over time, or in the instrument, without concern over contamination of the second interpretation by knowledge of the first. All of these points do not detract from the important merits we have already cited or from the role of this study in pointing to significant areas of investigation that have been largely neglected.

An unconventional cross-cultural study employing the Rorschach test is reported by Adcock (1951), who subjected Rorschach scores, derived from a group of New Zealand and a group of Cook Island subjects, to factor analysis. The broad intent of the investigator was to identify personality factors that could be attributed to constitutional factors and other personality dimensions that could be attributed to cultural factors.

The Rorschach data utilized in the study were derived from 88 protocols secured from Cook Island children by an anthropologist and scored by a third person who administered the same test to 30 New Zealand children and scored these protocols. A total of 15 conventional Rorschach scores were subjected to factor analysis, according to Thurstone's multiple-group method, for each of the two groups of subjects. The results suggested the existence of four factors for each group. Although the investigator does not label the factors, they might be referred to crudely as fluency, autism, constriction, and concrete or nonabstract thinking. The items and item loadings in the two groups are very similar for three of the factors but show considerable variation for the constriction factor. The author reasons that the three common factors may be basic personality dimensions which appear in similar form in all cultures, whereas the form of the remaining factor depends upon the particular cultural context.

The most important feature of this study is the willingness of the investigator to submit personality data secured from culturally diverse subjects to a relatively explicit and rational analytic treatment, which permits the investigator to find evidence on an objective basis for either cultural diversity or continuity. The communality of the Rorschach for the two cultures provides at least some basis for defending the cross-cultural sensitivity of the instrument. That is, if the same factors can be extracted from sets of scores secured under these diverse circumstances, there is at least some support for the inference that similar kinds of psychological processes are operating in the functioning of the test in the two different cultures.

There are two major flaws in the study. The first has to do with the relatively slight concern that Adcock has shown for the basic data used in his analysis. He was not involved in the collection of any of the data, and he reports little or nothing concerning the subjects or the circumstances under which the tests were administered. Furthermore, we discover nothing about the details of scoring, or the cautions taken to protect against the various kinds of bias that might have operated in the scoring. The second criticism has to do with the technical problems involved in a factor analysis of these data. Obviously the scores utilized in this study are far from meeting the customary assumptions of factor analysis, and some or all of the factors extracted may be considered artifacts, rather than underlying psychological reality. For example, the first factor, as Adcock correctly points out, is largely derived from the lack of independence among the various Rorschach scores. Furthermore, the consistency of factor pattern from one culture to the other may as easily reflect the scoring practices of the same Rorschach interpreter as the tendency of the subjects in different cultures to respond in parallel fashion.

Adcock's conviction that factor analysis is the instrument whereby the cross-cultural effectiveness of the Rorschach can be gauged is further revealed in a second paper concerned with the

Rorschach performance of white and Maori subjects (Adcock & Ritchie, 1958). The subjects were divided into three Maori groups (Adults, Upper-Class High School and Training College) and one white group (Upper-Class High School). The Rorschach tests were scored in terms of an unspecified number of variables of which 21 scores "gave meaningful results" and were included in the factor analyses which were conducted individually for each of the four groups. This procedure led to five factors: Imaginative Thinking (present in all four groups); Mature Spontaneity (present in all four groups); Introversion (present in the adult and Training College samples but not in the High School groups); Insecurity (which appeared only in the Maori High School group); Affective Extraversion (which appeared only in the white High School group).

Having extracted these five factors, the investigators proceeded to compare matched samples of Maori and white subjects on the individual Rorschach scores. A comparison of the Maori and white High School subjects revealed a number of significant differences concerning which the investigators report, "We were startled to find that they were substantially the same variables as appeared in our first Rorschach factor. . . . The ethnic differences can be explained almost wholly in terms of differences with regard to this one factor, imaginative thinking" (p. 887). A similar comparison of matched white subjects and the more select Training College Maoris reveals little difference between the two groups, thus suggesting the tendency of acculturation to eliminate the major group differences. The authors indicate their conviction that these findings recommend extreme caution in applying the Rorschach in different cultural settings, for the importance of the Imaginative Thinking factor is so great that "If the culture is one where imaginative activity is not encouraged, then the Rorschach tester has difficulty in collecting an adequate sample of verbal behavior from each subject for the usual interpretations to be applied" (p. 889). The authors also point to the two factors that appeared in only one of the groups under study (Insecurity and Affective Extraversion) as probably representing the outcome of cultural influences.

The firm and somewhat patronizing conclusions of the investigators merit report:

The facts noted above . . . suggest . . . that the problems involved in interpreting the data from one culture by reference to the norms of another culture are of such magnitude that the game may not be worth the candle. Few anthropologists would be equipped, or prepared, to conduct a validating factor analysis of their Rorschach data. When they are able to do so, the results of this attempted validation may be of such a nature as to suggest, as do our own results, that the Rorschach is of so little value for testing purposes in a "nonliterary" or "imagination-deficient" non-Western culture that anthropologists should only use the test with extreme caution, fully cognizant of its many hidden weaknesses, or that better still, they should look around for another and better personality-testing instrument to pack into their field kit. (p. 891)

The comments concerning Adcock's earlier study are fully applicable here. Again there is the advantage of an objective analytic tool, but again there is an absolute minimum of information concerning the administration of the test, the nature of the subjects and their selection, the cultural context, and the process of analyzing the Rorschach protocols. Virtually all of the detailed discussion is reserved for consideration of the statistical analysis. With so little concern over, or respect for, the basic data, it is hard to take seriously the authors' strictures concerning the limited utility of the Rorschach in cross-cultural research, even if we grant the applicability of factor analysis in this setting.

An exceptionally neat and well-presented investigation, intended to explore the extent to which projective-technique data validly reflect the culture and modal personality of a nonliterate culture, is reported by Lessa and Spiegelman (1954). These investigators studied a group of subjects from the Ulithi Atoll, one of the Caroline Islands of Micronesia, using a modified TAT.

The form of the TAT is the same as that employed in the study by Gladwin and Sarason (1953) and was devised specifically for use with natives of Micronesia. The test included a total of 14 pictures. The ethnographer administered the test with the aid of four native assistants who were trained in the administration of the test and "knew how to write fairly well" (p. 264). The authors report that the "longest and most imaginative" stories were those elicited by the trained anthropologist. In all, a group of 99 subjects were tested and they were divided approximately evenly in terms of sex and four age groups (5-11, 12-21, 22-40, 41 and over). The protocols were analyzed by means of a slightly modified version of a scheme developed by Fine (1955). The reliability of scoring of the categories was examined for 30 randomly selected cases with two judges scoring the stories independently. Reliability proved to be generally high with only one of 44 categories failing to show respectable agreement between judges. This category was slightly modified and subsequently an acceptable degree of reliability was demonstrated.

The interpretations of the test results were made by a psychologist, who read 20 protocols in order to decide upon the actual grouping to be employed, who knew that the material came from a non-Western culture, presumably "primitive," and who had seen the test pictures with their Micronesian figures; but otherwise knew nothing of the culture or identity of the subjects. He clustered the 44 categories under seven broad headings (story characteristics, catastrophes, goals, means to goals, feelings, interpersonal relationships —formal, interpersonal relationships—informal), and the numerical averages for each of the categories for each of the sex and age groups are reported in tabular form. The psychologist then proceeded to develop descriptions of these people, both generally and in terms of subgroup differences, basing his inferences so far as possible solely upon the quantitative results before him. In other words, his description of Ulithian behavior and personality was based not upon the raw protocols but upon the results of the quantitative analyses of these protocols.

The authors present verbatim, under each of the major headings, the description the psychologist inferred from the projective-technique data and follow this with the ethnologist's careful examination of this description for its fit with ethnographic observation and inference. At the end of this chapter, the psychologist arrives at an over-all personality portrait of the Ulithian subjects and the ethnologist attempts to generalize concerning his impressions of the closeness of fit of the two sets of data: "After many accurate interpretations of Ulithian personality and culture, many of them happily arrived at by reversing previous tentative interpretations, the foregoing summary draws a picture in high accord with the observations made in the field by the ethnographer. . . . There are minor discrepancies of trivial nature . . . but these alter nothing in the essential outlines of the basic personality type here offered to us" (Lessa & Spiegelman, 1954, p. 299). The authors suggest that the degree of congruence between the psychologist's interpretations and the ethnologist's data exceeded by a good deal the expectations of either investigator. They also remark upon the fact that the projective-technique protocols reveal not only personality attributes but also aspects of the ongoing activities and culture of these people. In spite of their warm enthusiasm for the future of this technique in cross-cultural research, they point out that the projective technique did not add information to what the ethnologist already knew but rather ". . . seemed to provide an independent verification of what was observed in the field" (p. 300).

Not only is the reporting of this study a model of clarity, but the same coherence is reflected in its design and execution. The purpose is clearly stated, the analysis of the projective technique is explicit and objective (including a reliability analysis—a real rarity in anthropological use of these instruments), the psychologist's interpretations were made with very good controls against the possibility of contamination by ethnographic data, and the comparison of the two domains of data is carried out in an orderly and explicit manner. The study obviously offers important information concerning the potential utility of this variety of projective technique in a cross-cultural setting.

Inevitably, there are objections that can be raised to this investigation: the contaminating effect upon the psychologist of viewing the stimulus material with its explicit message concerning the cultural identity of the subjects, the limitations upon the sensitivity of the psychologist's interpretations imposed by working primarily with scores rather than scores and protocols, the questionable practice of having many of the protocols collected by native assistants and with no indication that the different examiners were evenly spread across the various groups, and the failure to examine the test performance in the light of the cultural context. Almost all of these factors, however, would be expected to work against congruence of the two sets of data, and thus they are at least partially countered by the positive findings reported. Thus, the major flaw is the procedure used in testing the congruence of projective-technique findings and ethnographic findings. In comparison to most other studies, the procedure is highly defensible for it is explicit, detailed, and arranged about specified areas of behavior. Nevertheless, the masses of data to be compared are so great and include so many statements of varying degrees of similarity that it is obviously possible for the ethnologist's preconceptions to have a determining effect. The argument here is not that Lessa has necessarily distorted his recall or judgment but rather that when such complex decisions must be made without objective procedures, we can almost guarantee that there will be different results if the data is examined by judges of widely different commitment or prior belief. Thus, we cannot be certain that the encouraging results of this study are not in part or whole a reflection of the positive set of the investigators toward projective techniques.

A Rorschach study of the Ute was carried out by Hauck (1955) as part of a co-ordinated program of investigation under the direction of E. A. Hoebel. The investigator was primarily concerned with identifying personality characteristics of the Ute and personality variation associated with age. A total of 107 full-blood Utes, who lived in roughly the same area, were tested and their performance on the Rorschach was compared with data collected by Beck on normal American subjects. The subjects were divided into four age groups ranging from childhood to old age.

The results of the Rorschach interpretation are presented in the form of a free discussion of personality attributes typical of the Utes, or particular age groups, with no reference to the underlying test data or the kind of test analysis that led to these inferences. Somewhat more interesting, from the point of view of our present discussion, is a section concerned with "field methods and procedures" in which Hauck discusses casually, and somewhat unsystematically, various problems he encountered in his field work and the way in which he attempted to cope with them. The investigator reports that he considered using the Rorschach test, Draw-A-Person Test, Moral Ideology Test, Body Word-Association Test, Emotional Response Test, Goodenough Intelligence Test, and Rosenzweig's Picture Frustration Study but found that only the Rorschach and Draw-A-Person tests were "good testing tools among the Utes." He eventually decided to introduce the study to the subjects as a study of the "art of the Ute Indians." There were a number of revisions of customary Rorschach administration, many of them corresponding to the practice of other cross-cultural investigators, for example, conducting the inquiry after each card and testing the subjects in their native environment rather than in a standard testing situation. There is also a discussion of the devices that the investigator used in establishing and maintaining rapport with his subjects.

We are given so little information concerning the actual projective-technique findings and the procedures utilized in analyzing the projective-technique protocols that it is impossible to evaluate the significance or legitimacy of the findings reported. Consequently, the most interesting portion of this study has to do with the report of procedural problems and tactics. Although this section is worth examination by any person contemplating the use of the Rorschach in cross-cultural research, there are portions of the report to which many would object. For example, the decision to introduce the study as something that it clearly isn't (a study of art) seems questionable, particularly since many other cross-cultural investigators have found it possible to provide a reason for administering projective techniques without deceiving the subject about the investigator's interests.

An interesting paper by Honigmann and Carrera (1957) reports an attempt to evaluate the cross-cultural usefulness of Machover's Draw-A-Person Test. Drawings were obtained from a small (9) group of Eskimo children and a small (14) group of Cree Indian children. The Eskimo drawings were secured by the anthropologist, but the data from the Cree subjects were collected in a school setting. In both cases an attempt was made to follow Machover's recommendations for administration, although it was not possible to get male and female drawings from all subjects and notes on the subjects' performance were not obtained in every case.

The psychologist who conducted the analysis of the pictures knew only that the drawings came from Cree Indian and Eskimo children (but not which pictures came from which culture) and the age and sex of the individual subjects. He attempted four different kinds of analysis. First, he derived a qualitative interpretation of the individual protocols according to Machover's general principles and then, grouping the interpretations for the Eskimo and Cree subjects, prepared general personality descriptions for each group. Second, again drawing upon Machover's interpretive principles, he developed three rating scales that were intended to measure aggression-submission, dependence-independence, and intrapersonal sexual conflicts. Comparison of the groups on these three scales revealed no significant differences, although there was a trend in the direction of inferior sexual adjustment on the part of the Cree Indian subjects. Scoring the drawings in terms of Goodenough's scale of intelligence revealed an average IQ of 86 for the Indians and 64 for the Eskimos, a difference that attained conventional statistical significance. The fourth analysis utilized a scale developed by Machover to measure the extent to which the individual is influenced by his immediate perceptual environment. The investigators found no evidence for any difference between the two groups on this measure.

The authors conclude:

According to procedures 1, 2, and 4, presently available criteria for interpreting the Machover test do not show the nine Eskimo and fourteen Indian subjects to reflect the differences that a field worker observes between the overt behavior of Eskimo and Indian adults and children. Relatively intensive field work . . . also suggests some profound covert personality differences in the individuals of each group that are not brought out by test as applied to the particular subjects. In general, personality data revealed by the test are meager. (pp. 652-653)

The investigators also object to the measured IQ of the Eskimo children, suggesting that the field experience of the anthropologist makes it clear that these individuals are not subnormal in intelligence. All in all ". . . it would appear that the Machover technique offers little promise for anthropological field study" (p. 654).

Among the commendable features to this study are the relatively objective analysis to which the projective-technique data were subjected, the protection of the psychological interpreter from contamination by ethnological data, and the serious attempt to examine projective-technique findings in the light of detailed results of field work. Unfortunately, the shortcomings in the study are drastic. The sample size, the departures from conventional test administration, and the irregular sampling procedure make clear that only a rash optimist would attempt to generalize the results of this study. The comparison of projective-technique findings with ethnographic data is frankly subjective and, with the exception of the matter of intelligence, is sufficiently complex and ambiguous to leave the neutral observer anything but convinced of the incompatibility of projective-technique interpretation and field-work data. This is particularly so when the complexities of the covert side of personality are introduced. One might well question what would have happened if Honigmann had undertaken a similar study of the Rorschach test with the same lack of commitment to that instrument that he here displays to the drawing technique. It seems very likely that a similar "no confidence" vote might have been registered although, as the reader will recall, Honigmann employed the Rorschach extensively, and with some enthusiasm, in a study we discussed previously.

WHAT WERE THE MODAL FLAWS IN THESE STUDIES?

Our extensive discussion of research has been accompanied by a variety of critical remarks concerning difficulties or infirmities in these studies. A reasonable question derived from this survey concerns the degree to which these flaws are typical or normative. To what extent has investigation in this area suffered from identifiable weaknesses that could have been avoided and which undoubtedly have interferred with the empirical harvest of these investigations? It will also be of interest to note the congruence or disparity between these existing flaws and the imputed shortcomings that we examined in the previous chapter.

Let us begin with the question of the *independence* or "blindness" of the *personality inferences derived from the projective-technique protocols*. In our initial discussion of this issue we suggested that, contrary to the view of some critics, there is nothing intrinsic in projective techniques to prevent the investigator from deriving independent or uncontaminated inferences from the projective technique. Furthermore, we suggested that it would not be necessary or desirable in all studies to maintain complete independence between the projective-technique data and other sources of data.

Our survey of research suggests several further conclusions concerning this problem. First, there are few studies in which any serious attempt has been made to protect the interpreter of the psychological test from knowledge concerning the culture of the individuals being appraised. Second, of those studies that have attempted to provide some degree of protection against contamination, only a small number were successful. Even worse, many studies appear to combine the unattractive features of both approaches to this problem. That is, a number of studies deprive the interpreter of a maximum of contextual information, which might be expected to improve the accuracy of his interpretations, and yet they permit him sufficient knowledge so that his interpretations are not free from suspicion of contamination, or influence, by other sources of data. Thus, his interpretations are neither maximally valid nor are they really independent or "blind." Third, of those studies that have attempted to protect against bias from cultural or other observational data, there are none that provide a clear demonstration of the fit between the independent inferences derived from the projective-technique data and those derived from other data sources. In other words, there is no single study that provides a compelling demonstration of the independent merit of the inferences derived from projective-technique protocols when compared to inferences secured from other vantages.

The importance of "blind" analysis of projective techniques is easily overestimated. What we have already said concerning the interpretation of these instruments makes clear that one cannot expect such instruments to function even close to their normal level of effectiveness when the interpretations are made with little or no contextual information concerning the subject, the testing situation, and the culture. In spite of this, it is somewhat surprising, when one considers the number of studies that have been conducted in this area, that not one has combined independence of analysis of projective techniques with suitable checks against random factors and bias in the comparison of the projective-technique inferences with inferences derived from traditional data sources. The *tendency* of almost all investigators *to rely upon subjective impression when relating projective-technique data and inferences derived from traditional ethnological sources* is, to say the least, unfortunate. The complexity and extensity of the data involved in such comparisons make it essential that an objective basis of comparison be employed if we are to place much reliance upon the conclusions. Future studies aimed at overcoming these deficiencies would be most welcome to the person interested in applying projective techniques in this setting.

A striking and very surprising shortcoming that characterizes most of the studies we have discussed is a *failure to provide a full description of the circumstances under which the test is administered.* One might expect that the anthropologist, with his traditional focus upon external constraint and social determinism, would show an unusual sensitivity to the role of situational and cultural influences on response to projective techniques. Not only do the anthropologists fail to give full consideration to these factors, but most of those studies where the testing situation is described relatively satisfactory have actually been conducted by psychologists, or else they have involved a psychologist as a collaborator. Presumably the resolution to this paradox lies not in the psychologist's appreciation for the general importance of cultural-situational factors, but rather in the anthropologist's lack of appreciation for the extreme importance of immediate or situational factors in determining projective-technique response. The anthropologist often appears to have accepted the projective technique as a relatively immutable device that can be administered in a standard manner and scored in an objective fashion, with the consequence of specifiable results quite independent of variation in the surrounding world. As our discussion has already made clear, this is by no means the case; a sensitive and dependable outcome from projective-technique data depends upon a full understanding of the context within which the test was administered.

Related to the previous point is a *general failure* on the part of many, if not most, investigators *to explore the possible contribution of nonpersonality factors* to the observed projective-technique findings. This lack of sensitive concern includes a failure to consider fully the role of situational factors, and it also extends to a tendency to overlook the role of chance factors, as well as a host of other parameters such as age, rapport, education, or sex, which are known to influence performance on projective techniques. In other words, given a particular group difference in projective-technique performance, it is the task of the investigator to explore a variety of possible determinants of this difference, and only one class of these determinants is concerned with personality differences. The importance of this caution has been thoroughly documented in our discussion of the interpretive process. In general, most investigators appear to have assumed that when significant test differences have been observed, the interpretive task is complete and one may safely invoke personality differences. This is clearly not the case!

The significance or probable meaning of the test-taking activity when viewed through the lenses of the local culture would appear to be a natural concern for the ethnographer. Strangely enough, few investigators have shown much detailed interest in this problem and those that have, consistently fail to extend this analysis into the interpretation of projective-test performance or findings. That is, they may discuss the relation between test-taking activity and cultural prescription and yet show no interest in the extent to which such prescription may have influenced the particular response dimensions used as a base for generalizations concerning personality.

Related to the previous point is an apparent unawareness of the importance of the *examiner's influence upon test performance*. Many of the studies we have reported tell us little or nothing concerning the skill, training, or even identity of the person administering the projective technique, in spite of the impressive array of evidence considered earlier which makes clear the importance of this factor as a determinant of projective-test response. This casual attitude toward the role of the examiner has led in a number of studies to comparing test results for culturally differentiated groups where the instruments have been administered by examiners who vary in age, sex, training, or cultural background and attributing all variation in test performance to personality differences between the groups. There is every reason to look with suspicion upon findings generated by such a procedure.

The comparison of differentiated groups has played an essential role in many or most of the studies we have examined. Unfortunately, we have observed a general *failure to select for comparison, groups sufficiently well matched* on parameters of known relevance to make group differences in projective-test performance meaningful or significant. In most cases, comparison groups that are culturally diverse prove upon close examination to be diverse also in age, education, language facility, socioeconomic status, and similar dimensions. Thus, differences between these groups cannot be attributed confidently to the role of cultural difference or variation in acculturation for they may equally well be due to the contribution of one or more of the uncontrolled parameters. This problem is particularly pronounced in the case of the studies of acculturation and national character where the group comparisons typically lie at the core of the study.

A defect of many of these studies that must come as a painful surprise to most champions of the projective technique is the tendency toward *mechanical application of scoring systems and interpretive generalizations* developed in connection with the study of educated European and American subjects. To most observers, it has appeared that the users of projective techniques have been the strongest resisters to actuarial methods and psychometric procedures. If such were the case, one would expect the interpretation of projective-technique protocols in anthropological research to rely upon various complex and elusive cues, or clinical judgments, entailing the testing context, the individual subject, and a variety of other information. The typical report gives quite the contrary impression, for we find a willingness to equate a particular type of projective-technique response regularly to a particular personality attribute. Actually, if we removed from this literature all interpretive statements dependent upon Klopfer's specific generalizations, we would probably eliminate three quarters of the results we have examined. The point that is being made here is that most users of projective techniques have appeared too ready to adopt slavishly those conventional scoring practices current in the clinical use of these instruments in our own society.

One of the difficulties with many of these studies is a tendency to present the *findings derived from projective techniques* as a little island of results completely *isolated from the data derived from traditional anthropological techniques.* Thus, we may find a relatively complete ethnography and included within the same book covers, but totally unintegrated with this ethnography, a report of the results of a program of projective testing. Such a procedure loses the potential contribution of the cultural context to the understanding of the test results and at the same time makes it impossible for test findings to contribute to the analysis of the ethnographic data. An obverse of this difficulty is the tendency to report personality findings in such a manner that it is impossible to tell what data the statements are based on. The results of direct observation, interviewing, analysis of myths and art products, and analysis of projective-test results may all have contributed to the personality picture, but there is no indication of the specific role of any one of these data sources. Such a procedure is particularly undesirable for the reader who would like to make some estimate of the contribution of the various techniques, but it is also generally somewhat unhealthy because of the rather different status of these various kinds of data and the consequent confusion as to how much confidence can be invested in the various findings reported.

A recurrent difficulty in the studies we have surveyed is the *tendency to take group averages and treat them as descriptive of the group as a whole.* This procedure is particularly prevalent in studies employing the Rorschach test, where many investigators have secured averages for the various Rorschach scores or ratios and then have proceeded to develop a psychogram from these group averages and to interpret this average psychogram as representative of the personality of the group. In actual fact the group may include no single member whose psychogram closely resembles the average profile. The essential error in this procedure is its failure to take into consideration the likelihood of wide differences in test performance among the members of a single culture.

Perhaps the most discouraging reflection that can be made on these studies is that there is relatively *little evidence of cumulation of sophistication* and wisdom. The studies carried out in the past five years, as a group, seem to be little superior to those reported a decade or more ago. Explicit consideration of particular problems such as sampling, statistical treatment, or difficulties involved in using average scores, and suggested solutions of the problems do not appear to have led to any increase in the awareness of these problems and their potential solutions. There are some exceptions to this generalization, perhaps the most notable being the tendency in recent investigations to provide much more explicit inference links between personality interpretation and projective-technique response and the parallel readiness to transform projective-technique data into some type of quantitative product.

How do the flaws we have identified compare with the published objections that we outlined earlier? It seems clear that many, although by no means all, of the objections raised by interested authorities are reflected in actual practice. It is also evident that the cautions emphasized in our discussion of the interpretive process have not often been heeded by these investigators. Perhaps the most revealing general comment that can be made is that more of the observed or actual shortcomings have to do with features of the particular investigation rather than shortcomings of the projective test itself, whereas more of the published objections have to do with intrinsic features of the test rather than with its application.

So much for the substance and shortcomings of studies involving projective techniques in cross-cultural settings. Let us now concern ourselves with the actual or potential contribution of these investigations.

REFERENCES

ABEL, Theodora M., & CALABRESI, Renata A. The people (Tepoztecans) from their Rorschach tests. In O. Lewis, *Life in a Mexican village: Tepoztlan restudied.* Urbana: Univer. of Illinois Press, 1951. Pp. 306-318; 463-490.

ABEL, Theodora M., & HSU, F. L. K. Some aspects of personality of Chinese as revealed by the Rorschach test. *Rorschach Res. Exch.*, 1949, 13, 285-301.

ABEL, Theodora M., & METRAUX, Rhoda. Sex differences in a Negro peasant community, Montserrat, B. W. I., *J. proj. Tech.*, 1959, 23, 127-133.

ADCOCK, C. J. A factorial approach to Rorschach interpretation. *J. gen. Psychol.*, 1951, 44, 261-272.

ADCOCK, C. J., & RITCHIE, J. E. Intercultural use of Rorschach. *Amer. Anthrop.*, 1958, 60, 881-892.

ALEXANDER, T., & ANDERSON, R. Children in a society under stress. *Behav. Sci.*, 1957, 2, 46-55.

AMES, Louise B., LEARNED, J., METRAUX, Rhoda, & WALKER, R. *Child Rorschach responses: developmental trends from 2 to 10 years.* New York: Hoeber, 1952.

BARNOUW, V. Acculturation and personality among the Wisconsin Chippewa. *Amer. Anthrop. Assoc. Memoir*, 1950, No. 72.

BECK, S. J., RABIN, A. I., THIESEN, W. C., MOLISH, H., & THETFORD, W. N. The normal personality as projected in the Rorschach test. *J. Psychol.*, 1950, 30, 241-298.

BENEDICT, Ruth. *The chrysanthemum and the sword: patterns of Japanese culture.* Boston: Houghton Mifflin, 1946.

BILLIG, O., GILLIN, J., & DAVIDSON, W. Aspects of personality and culture in a Guatemalan community: ethnological and Rorschach approaches. Part I. *J. Personality*, 1947, 16, 153-187.

BILLIG, O., GILLIN, J., & DAVIDSON, W. Aspects of personality and culture in a Guatemalan community: ethnological and Rorschach approaches. Part II. *J. Personality*, 1948, 16, 326-368.

BLEULER, M. & BLEULER, R. Rorschach's ink-blot test and racial psychology. *Character & Pers.*, 1935, 4, 97-114.

CARSTAIRS, G. M. *The twice-born: a study of a community of high-caste Hindus.* London: Hogarth, 1957.

CAUDILL, W. Psychological characteristics of acculturated Wisconsin Ojibwa children. *Amer. Anthrop.*, 1949, 51, 409-427.

CAUDILL, W. Japanese-American personality and acculturation. *Genet. Psychol. Monogr.*, 1952, 45, 3-102.

CAUDILL, W., & DEVOS, G. Achievement culture and personality: the case of the Japanese Americans. *Amer. Anthrop.*, 1956, 58, 1102-1126.

DAVIDSON, Helen H. *Personality and economic background: a study of highly intelligent children.* New York: King Crown's Press, 1943.

DEVOS, G. A comparison of the personality differences in two generations of Japanese Americans by means of the Rorschach Test. *Nagoya J. Med. Sci.*, 1954, 17, 153-265.

DeVos, G. A quantitative Rorschach assessment of maladjustment and rigidity in acculturating Japanese Americans. *Genet. Psychol. Monogr.*, 1955, 52, 51-87.

DeVos, G., & Miner, H. Algerian culture and personality in change. *Sociometry*, 1958, 21, 255-268.

Doob, L. W. An introduction to the psychology of acculturation. *J. soc. Psychol.*, 1957, 45, 143-160.

Du Bois, Cora. *The people of Alor.* Minneapolis: Univer. Minnesota Press, 1944.

Fine, R. A scoring scheme and manual for the TAT and other verbal projective techniques. *J. proj. Tech.*, 1955, 19, 306-309.

Fisher, S. Patterns of personality rigidity and some of their determinants. *Psychol. Monogr.*, 1950, 64, No. 1.

Gladwin, T. The role of man and woman on Truk: a problem in personality and culture. *Transactions of the New York Acad. Sci.*, Ser. II, 1953, 15, 305-309.

Gladwin, T., & Sarason, S. B. *Truk: man in paradise.* New York: Wenner-Gren Foundation, 1953.

Hallowell, A. I. Acculturation processes and personality changes as indicated by the Rorschach technique. *Rorschach Res. Exch.*, 1942, 6, 42-50.

Hallowell, A. I. *Culture and experience.* Philadelphia: Univer. Pennsylvania Press, 1955.

Hauck, P. A. Ute Rorschach performances and some notes on field problems and methods. *Univer. Utah Anthropological Papers*, 1955, No. 23.

Henry, J., & Spiro, M. E. Psychological techniques. Projective tests in field work. In A. I. Kroeber (Ed.), *Anthropology today.* Chicago: Univer. Chicago Press, 1953. Pp. 417-429.

Henry, W. E. The Thematic Apperception Technique in the study of culture-personality relations. *Genet Psychol. Monogr.*, 1947, 35, 3-135.

Honigmann, J. J. Culture and ethos of Kaska society. *Yale University Publications in Anthropology*, 1949, No. 40.

Honigmann, J. J., & Carrera, R. N. Cross-cultural use of Machover's figure drawing test. *Amer. Anthrop.*, 1957, 59, 650-654.

Joseph, Alice, & Murray, Veronica F. *Chamorros and Carolinians of Saipan: personality studies.* Cambridge, Mass.: Harvard Univer. Press, 1951.

Joseph, Alice, Spicer, Rosamund B., & Chesky, Jane. *The desert people: A study of the Papago Indians.* Chicago: Univer. Chicago Press, 1949.

Kaplan, B. A study of Rorschach responses in four cultures. *Peabody Museum of Harvard University Papers*, 1955, 42, No. 2.

Kaplan, B., Rickers-Ovsiankina, Maria A., & Joseph, Alice. An attempt to sort Rorschach records from four cultures. *J. proj. Tech.*, 1956, 20, 172-180.

KLOPFER, B., & KELLEY, D. M. *The Rorschach Technique.* New York: Harcourt, Brace & World, 1942.

KLOPFER, B., AINSWORTH, Mary D., KLOPFER, W. G., & HOLT, R. R. *Developments in the Rorschach technique.* Vol. 1. *Technique and theory.* New York: Harcourt, Brace & World, 1954.

KLUCKHOHN, C. The personal document in anthropological science. In L. Gottschalk, C. Kluckhohn, & R. Angell, The use of personal documents in history, anthropology and sociology. *Soc. Sci. Res. Council. Bull.*, 1945, No. 53, 79-173.

KLUCKHOHN, C., & ROSENZWEIG, Janine C. Two Navaho children over a five-year period. *Amer. J. Orthopsychiatry*, 1949, 19, 266-278.

LEIGHTON, Dorothea, & KLUCKHOHN, C. *Children of the people.* Cambridge, Mass.: Harvard Univer. Press, 1947.

LESSA, W. A., & SPIEGELMAN, M. Ulithian personality as seen through ethnological materials and thematic test analysis. *University of California Publications in Culture and Society*, 1954, 2, 243-301.

LEWIS, O. *Life in a Mexican village: Tepoztlan restudied.* Urbana: Univer. Illinois Press, 1951.

MACGREGOR, G. *Warriors without weapons*: A study of the society and personality development of the Pine Ridge Sioux. Chicago: Univer. Chicago Press, 1946.

MEAD, Margaret. The Mountain Arapesh V: The record of Unabelin with Rorschach analysis. *Anthrop. Papers Am. Museum Nat. Hist.*, 1949.

MINER, H. M., & DEVOS, G. *Oasis and casbah: Algerian culture and personality in change.* Univer. Michigan, *Museum of Anthropology Papers*, 1960, No. 15.

REDFIELD, R. *Tepoztlan—a Mexican village.* Chicago: Univer. Chicago Press, 1930.

RICHARDS, T. W. The Chinese in Hawaii: a Rorschach report. In F. L. K. Hsu (Ed.), *Culture and personality.* New York: Abelard-Schuman, 1954. Pp. 67-89.

SPINDLER, G. D. Personality and Peyotism in Menomini Indian acculturation. *Psychiatry*, 1952, 15, 151-159.

SPINDLER, G. D. Sociocultural and psychological processes in Menomini acculturation. *University of California Publications in Cultural Sociology*, 1955, 5.

SPINDLER, G. D., & GOLDSCHMIDT, W. Experimental design in the study of culture change. *Southwest J. Anthrop.*, 1952, 8, 68-83.

SPINDLER, Louise, & SPINDLER, G. D. Male and female adaptations in culture change. *Amer. Anthrop.*, 1958, 60, 217-233.

STRAUS, M. A. Anal and oral frustration in relation to Sinhalese personality. *Sociometry*, 1957, 20, 21-31.

STRAUS, M. A., & STRAUS, Jacqueline H. Personal insecurity and Sinhalese social structure. Rorschach evidence for primary school children. *East. Anthrop.*, 1957, 10, 97-111.

THOMPSON, Laura, & JOSEPH, Alice. *The Hopi way*. Chicago: Univer. Chicago Press, 1944.

VOGT, E. Z. Navaho veterans: a study of changing values. *Peabody Museum of Harvard University Papers*, 1951, Vol. 41.

WALLACE, A. F. C. The modal personality structure of the Tuscarora Indians as revealed by the Rorschach Test. *Bull. Bur. Amer. Ethnol.*, 1952a, No. 150.

WALLACE, A. F. C. Individual differences and cultural uniformities. *Amer. soc. Rev.*, 1952b, 17, 747-750.

8. The Contribution of Projective Techniques to Anthropological Research

WE HAVE NOW EXAMINED an indictment of projective techniques in cultural research and, more painfully, we have surveyed the relevant evidence. Our present task is to agree upon a verdict. Regrettably we find ourselves faced with the very dilemma that confronted so many of the investigators whose work we have just discussed. On the one hand, there is an apparently simple question; on the other hand, an enormous amount of data, almost none of it in a form that lends itself to quantification or easy comparability. Small wonder if those whose work we have seemed so ready to criticize should choose to scoff at the inference process to follow.

Let us first consider the major purposes for which projective techniques can be employed in anthropological investigation and follow this with a discussion of the empirical findings in this area to which projective techniques have contributed materially. We can then consider the evidence for selective preference of one type of projective test over other types and finally turn to the task of providing a general appraisal of the past and probable future contribution of these techniques in cross-cultural research.

WHAT ARE THE PURPOSES?

There are several ways in which an answer to this question can be approached. We might attempt to identify the problem areas where projective techniques have been employed. Or, we could consider the kinds of functional or tactical roles that have been assigned to projective tests in anthropological research. In either case we are considering the relation between projective tests and varying investigative intents.

Our survey of the relevant research literature makes it easy to answer the question of which problem areas typically have appeared to be fruitful sites for the application of projective techniques. We have already remarked that the bulk of cross-cultural application of these devices has been carried out by investigators interested in either national character or in the acculturation process. Although we have observed a handful of studies concerned with personality development in a particular cultural setting, group differences at a subcultural level, or even in the use of projective techniques to provide cultural information, such investigations are small in number compared to the studies directed at an understanding of the psychological aspects of acculturation or the identification of personality types characteristic of particular cultures.

One may approach this question at a somewhat different level and reason that within these broad problem areas the likelihood that an investigator will derive assistance from projective techniques, or indeed that he will develop an initial interest in these instruments, will depend upon certain special aspects of his approach to these problems. For example, if he is strongly repelled by notions of unconscious motivation, it is unlikely that he will consider projective techniques seriously. Thus, the individual interested in national character is particularly likely to turn to projective techniques if he views the covert side of behavior as especially important. Moreover, the extent to which the investigator desires an uncontaminated or independent measure of personality factors is an index of the likelihood that projective techniques will have a special contribution to make to his research. If he is content to establish personality inferences on the basis of the same data used in describing the culture and the institutional structure of his subjects, he is not likely to look upon these tests as possessing any special merit for his purposes.

Thus, we may generalize that projective techniques have been used most often by workers concerned with the areas of acculturation and national character, and within these areas by those who emphasize covert aspects of personality and are concerned with developing measures of personality that are independent of ethnographic data.

If we ask what function or role the projective test may have in this setting, perhaps the most immediate and obvious answer is that it may be used to *test explicit hypotheses* or predictions. Such studies have a special appeal for they not only represent a particular kind of investigative ideal, but also they tend, in fortunate cases, to provide an antidote for some of the major doubts that exist concerning the validity of projective techniques. Let us assume that we have a reasonable prediction made on the basis of prior empirical findings, or firm theoretical derivation, and that this prediction is rationally linked to performance on a particular variety of test. If we then observe the predicted test performance, this not only serves as a confirmation of the prediction but also it provides some assurance that the test was, in fact, measuring what it was intended to measure. Negative results, of course, leave the investigator little advanced, for he has no means of telling whether the results indicate the infirmity of his measure or the vulnerability of his empirical prediction.

Those who have successfully digested the preceding survey of research will not have to be told that studies employing projective techniques to test explicit hypotheses are rare. Although there are a limited number of cases where a hypothesis is stated and projective-technique findings presented as relevant to the hypothesis (for example, Alexander & Anderson, 1957; Straus & Straus, 1957), careful examination reveals that the proposition is usually so general and the relation of the projective-technique data to the proposition so precarious that these studies possess little of the merit mentioned above. Thus, this function of projective tests remains largely a potential for the future rather than an accomplishment of the past.

Quite a different role may be assigned to the projective technique when it is expected to provide the basis for ideas, hunches, propositions, or even variables, for the analysis of other data. Thus, the analysis of projective-technique protocols may serve as a *source of suggestions for how to proceed with the treatment of interview or observational data*. In this case the ethnologist accepts the possibility that viewing these subjects from a different perspective may lead to ideas that he would not have encountered had he contented himself with customary anthropological data. This is clearly a rather unusual use of projective techniques, although one of the most interesting and rewarding studies that we discussed (Gladwin & Sarason, 1953) definitely involved this process.

More generally, it is possible to use the instruments as a "no-holds-barred" source of data that can be *subjectively embraced for whatever suggestions, convictions, generalizations, or enthusiasms can be empathically,* clinically, or intuitively *obtained.* Here the protocols are treated as a rich source of data, providing a diverse perspective or a new dimension of experience without regard for specific test validity or formal rules of analysis. In this case test responses are considered nothing more than another form of behavior that can be subjected to whatever scrutiny or analysis the investigator might choose to use with any other response data.

Undoubtedly the most typical of all functions assigned to the projective instrument in anthropological research is the simple role of providing *descriptive personality findings* for some specified group of subjects. Here the investigator uses the projective technique, alone or with other instruments, to achieve a set of findings that will permit him to attach particular personality statements to the group under study. In these studies there are no hypotheses being tested, nor are the findings of the projective test to be used as a criterion for assessing the accuracy of other inferences. There is no right or wrong, no acceptance or rejection; there is simply a class of objects and a measuring instrument used to permit appropriate description of the class of objects. A large proportion of the anthropological applications of these instruments have been of this variety.

Related to the simple descriptive use of projective techniques is the use of interpretations derived from the test for illustrating or *fleshing out generalizations* or hypotheses that the investigator has arrived at from other sources (for example, Honigmann, 1949). Here the test is used as a means of generating a wide variety of inferences or descriptive statements some of which may serve to illustrate or "confirm" generalizations that the ethnologist has arrived at on the basis of participant observation or interviews. As in the case of the descriptive study, there is no likelihood here of the projective technique being either right or wrong in any important sense of the word. The most it can do is provide vivid and compelling examples of the general relationships or classifications that the investigator is seeking to defend.

This particular use of the test may appear to many readers to border on the illicit or at least the trivial. Actually a great deal of the present use of projective techniques in their home territory (the individual clinical setting) is characterized by this same approach. The clinician uses the projective-technique protocols and their derived scores as a basis for defending or strengthening a diagnosis that has already been made, at least in broad terms, prior to the examination of the projective data. Frequency of use does not, of course, constitute a demonstration of significance, and most would agree that this is the least important of all the hypothetical functions that these devices may serve.

Quite the reverse is the role assigned to these instruments in studies where they are treated as the *criteria in appraising the results of analysis of other data sources.* Certainly one of the early reasons for enthusiasm over the potential contribution of the projective test to cross-cultural study was the possible contribution of these tests as a means of checking upon the loose personality inferences derived, with very little in the way of detailed specification, from general observation and interview. These somewhat imprecise generalizations constituted most of the field of culture and personality, and it was hoped that the projective technique would provide a means of judging the degree of confidence with which such findings should be accepted. Clearly this kind of analysis has seldom been carried out in any formal manner, although in an informal vein there has undoubtedly been a good deal of comparison of personality inferences derived from these two sources. As we shall see in a moment, most of these comparisons have led to congruent findings, but such results are not easy to interpret.

A final function that has very seldom been considered, although it is perfectly sound, is the application of the projective technique in the nonliterate society, or in multiple primitive societies, in order to *contribute to our understanding of processes involved in the projective test.* There is little doubt that our insight into these processes, as well as specific scoring procedures and interpretive rules, could benefit from an airing of these devices in a variety of different cultural settings. The relevant findings observed already in connection with such studies as those by Gladwin and Sarason (1953) and Kaplan (1955) suggest the potential merit of such an approach.

WHAT ARE THE FINDINGS?

We have seen something of the general purposes for which projective techniques have been used in cross-cultural research, and it remains for us to identify the specific empirical returns resulting.

First of all, let us ask what empirical generalizations can be dredged from this sea of studies? How many specific statements are there relating one variable to another, one condition to a particular range of values on a specified variable, or one event to another event? What is the nomothetic yield of all these thousands of man hours of investigation? Are there, in fact, dependable generalizations that have been achieved resulting from the use of projective techniques in anthropological research? Yes, there are a few.

One of the most obvious and important of these generalizations is the strong affirmation of individual differences in personality. *There is enormous variation in personality even within apparently homogeneous, nonliterate societies.* Anthropologists and psychologists alike agree that the findings of projective techniques point to greater diversity in personality variables among the members of particular cultures than has traditionally been acknowledged (Kaplan, 1955; Spindler, 1955; Wallace, 1952). The importance of individual differences has not been fully appreciated by most culture and personality investigators, and projective-technique findings have served to highlight this fact. Where relevant projective-technique data have been collected and analyzed, it appears that variation within cultures is much greater than that across or between cultures.

The persistent interest in psychological concomitants of acculturation, already commented upon, has resulted in a sufficient number of consistent findings to provide relatively firm support for the statement that *varying degrees or levels of acculturation are accompanied by varying personality attributes* and perhaps by variation in general level of adjustment (Hallowell, 1955; Spindler, 1955). Although virtually all the relevant studies display procedural shortcomings of varying degrees of severity, and although they certainly do not agree on the nature of these psychological differences, the existence of such psychological variations seems a matter of consensus.

A third generalization, uniformly supported, is that *individuals representative of different socialization practices and different cultural backgrounds respond differently to most projective techniques.* Although the precise meaning of these response differences may be a matter of debate, their existence is undeniable. These differences are not only apparent at the level of broad societal or cultural variation, but also in subcultural or within-culture groupings. It is obvious that this response variation is the raw material out of which might eventually be built a comprehensive picture of the relation between personality attributes and cultural variables. At present, it is difficult to be certain about much beyond the existence of group differences, for the extent to which they are a product of personality differences rather than differences in language, attitudes toward the test, or rapport is by no means clear.

A fourth generalization, which must be advanced very tentatively in view of the existing evidence, is that *personality inferences based upon the widely used projective techniques appear consistent with parallel inferences derived from ordinary field-work methods.* Although no single study is sufficiently well designed and executed to stand alone, the combined weight of a number of such studies (Du Bois, 1944; Gladwin & Sarason, 1953; W. E. Henry, 1947; Lessa & Spiegelman, 1954) suggests such congruence. In those cases where independent or semi-independent interpretations of projective techniques have been compared with data from life histories or ethnographers' reports, the findings generally show that the two sets of interpretations are consistent. We shall return to consider this point in more detail in a moment.

An empirical generalization is a delightfully tangible thing. The existence, the frequency, and even the importance of such statements is relatively easy to assess. But surely there are other forms in which an investigator utilizing a particular instrument might hope to make a contribution. In one sense there are, and it is here that we must become concerned with those less substantial and more difficult to identify and evaluate contributions that have to do with non-quantitative observations and frequently with the individual object rather than the general case. If we take the most permissive and tolerant of approaches, what can we say of the contribution of projective-technique findings to anthropological research and formulation?

To begin with, *a very large number of modal or typical personality descriptions for particular cultures have been derived from projective-test findings.* There are dozens of personality portraits written to describe individuals or groups who belong to specified nonliterate societies, and many of these were solely or partially dependent upon the findings derived from analysis of projective-technique protocols. Although these descriptions obviously vary enormously in quality, sensitivity, and accuracy, there are some that seem to achieve the highest standards of coherence, objectivity, logical consistency, and fit with independent data. Insofar as the student of culture and personality is necessarily dependent upon personality descriptions within particular cultural settings for the kinds of analyses that he proposes to carry out, it is obvious that whatever projective techniques may have done to enrich and improve the quality of these reports constitutes a worthwhile contribution.

For the individual with an idiographic or clinical inclination, it is very significant that *projective techniques have played an important role in the life-history records* published in recent years. When Kluckhohn's (1945) early analysis of the use of personal documents in anthropology was published, adequate case history information on nonliterate subjects was very scarce. This shortage may still exist, but the magnitude of the deficit has been materially reduced. In many of the studies we have examined, either as a central theme to the study or as a by-product, we found one or more case histories, and very often the personality inferences in these documents were heavily influenced by contributions from projective tests. In a few cases, such as Oberholzer's portraits of the Alorese, there are individual clinical portraits based solely upon projective-technique data. Thus, the development of adequate case histories for nonliterate subjects appears to have been stimulated by, or at least facilitated through, the use of projective-technique interpretations. One may note with approval, at this point, Kaplan's *Primary Records in Culture and Personality* (1956), which are microfilm records of the original data collected by many different investigators working in this area. This resource represents an important enrichment of existing cross-cultural life-history material.

Considerably less dramatic in its impact is the *influence that projective-technique data have had upon the analysis of other forms of ethnographic data*. This influence has been revealed most clearly in the study by Gladwin and Sarason (1953), but undoubtedly it is present, to a lesser and less explicit degree, in many other studies. We are referring here to the extent to which the treatment of interview and observation data has been colored by insights and generalizations, or even variables, suggested by projective-test results. Although such an outcome has seldom been an explicit part of the design or intent of investigators, the qualitative and complex nature of most of the data in such studies makes it likely that lines of influence will be mutually interactive, with ideas and hunches for analysis going in all directions, that is, from projective-technique data to cultural data, as well as the more conventional way.

The use of projective techniques by anthropologists has undoubtedly served to make many investigators *more aware of certain central research problems than they might otherwise have been*. The very vulnerability of these devices to sampling error, problems in quantitative and statistical analysis, their responsiveness to variation in situational factors, examiner effects, and such has served to make the anthropologist wary of their unrestrained use, and this caution must, to some extent, have been generalized to other techniques or procedures. It seems clear that these important matters of design, procedure, or method are more a matter of concern for the ethnologist today than they were a decade or so ago, and experience with projective techniques has perhaps made some contribution to this increased sophistication.

WHAT IS THE EVIDENCE FOR THE VALIDITY OF PROJECTIVE TECHNIQUES IN ALIEN CULTURAL SETTINGS?

In an important sense this question lies at the core of our entire discussion, and yet the attentive reader will surely have realized some time ago that there is no definitive evidence which can be used in answering this reasonable question. In our present discussion, let us first of all remind ourselves of the variety of uses for such an instrument, as well as the elusiveness of the notion of validity when applied to projective techniques. Having done this, we can survey the direct and indirect evidence that can be brought to bear upon the issue.

In addition to customary uses such as hypothesis testing, providing descriptive personality findings, or serving as a criterion for the evaluation of other data sources, projective techniques may, as we have already indicated, suggest to the anthropological investigator how to analyze other types of data. They also may serve to enlarge or illustrate generalizations derived from other data sources, or they may simply provide a novel perspective from which the behavior of a particular set of subjects can be viewed. It is quite possible for these devices to serve in these latter ways and yet possess little demonstrated validity in the ordinary sense of the word. Thus, although a deficiency in validity as conventionally assessed would certainly lessen the usefulness of these devices, it would not necessarily completely eliminate their usefulness to the cross-cultural investigator.

The phrase "ordinary sense of the word" is certain to evoke a snicker in many quarters, for *validity* is a term with many connotations and certainly no single meaning. Insofar as modern censensus can be stated, it is clear that the traditional meaning of validity as a test's success in measuring what it is supposed to measure has been expanded to include four different meanings. These are usually referred to as predictive validity, concurrent validity, content validity, and construct validity (Technical Recommendations, 1954; Cronbach & Meehl, 1955). Speaking in a quick and approximate manner, we may define the terms as follows: *Predictive validity* refers to the capacity of the test to predict correctly criterion measurements to be taken at a future point in time; for example, a measure of maladjustment would be said to possess predictive validity if its estimates were positively related to subsequent neurotic diagnosis. *Concurrent validity* refers to the same capacity to predict the criterion measure, except that this time the criterion measure is taken simultaneously with the test measure; for example, if the same measure of maladjustment successfully differentiated between normals and neurotics, it would be said to possess concurrent validity. *Content validity* refers to the extent to which the items included within the test accurately sample the domain of events the test is intended to assess and is most appropriate when applied to tests of achievement or aptitude rather than personality tests. *Construct validity* is used most appropriately where the test is intended to assess variables or dimensions that cannot be collapsed or mapped into any single index or cluster of indices. When the test is presumed to measure a hypothetical variable which in turn is related to a cluster of other variables or indices, none of which alone can be said to represent the underlying variable adequately and which may show little correlation with each other, the investigator must often be content to accept indirect evidence of validity. The investigator may say that if this test measures a particular variable (for example, ego strength) which theory or firm findings tell us is related to certain other variables (for example, permissive childhood experience, tolerance of frustration or persistence), then we may expect to find a particular association between performance on the test and these other variables (for example, the test measure of ego strength is positively related to degree of permissive experience in childhood). Observation of the predicted association would support the construct validity of the test.

The American Psychological Association publication dealing with technical recommendations concerning tests suggests: "Essentially in studies of construct validity we are validating the theory underlying the test. The validation procedure involves two steps. First, the investigator inquires: From this theory, what predictions would we make regarding the variation of scores from person to person or occasion to occasion? Second, he gathers data to confirm these predictions. . . . One tends to ask regarding construct validity just what is being validated—the test or the underlying hypothesis? The answer is, *both*, simultaneously." (Technical Recommendations, 1954, pp. 14-15).

Having made clear that there is more than one kind of validity, it remains only to indicate that the type of validity most relevant to projective techniques is construct validity, with all the consequent vagueness, complexity, and scarcity of simple coefficients. The link between projective techniques and complex, hypothetical variables (especially covert or latent dimensions) makes clear the difficulty, or impossibility, of identifying adequate criteria and the consequent necessity for resorting to indirect and complex inferential paths in the attempt to estimate validity. This close association between projective tests and construct validity has been noted in the past (Technical Recommendations, 1954; Cronbach & Meehl, 1955).

The major conclusion of this discussion is simply that any attempt to assess the validity of a particular projective technique, let alone the entire class of projective techniques, must involve a careful appraisal of a host of different kinds of evidence, much of it indirect and difficult to translate and summarize. Consequently, it is not surprising that there is little agreement concerning the over-all validity of projective techniques even within our own society and in restricted domains of application. From this statement it is an easy step to the conclusion that the evidence for or against the cross-cultural validity of these tests is far from what we would ideally wish and by no means sufficient to support conclusive generalizations.

Nevertheless, let us survey what evidence exists for the utility or lack of utility of these instruments in cross-cultural application. One of the earliest and best known of the studies providing relevant evidence is Du Bois' (1944) inquiry into the culture and personality of the Alorese. We have already discussed this study in considerable detail, and it is necessary here only to remind the reader that it includes findings based upon the Rorschach, interpreted by Oberholzer with a minimum of information concerning the culture, together with parallel findings based upon the ethnographer's observation, as interpreted by DuBois and by a psychoanalyst. Although no formal comparison of the Rorschach findings with those derived from the other sources was attempted, the general congruence between these sets of interpretations appears pronounced. The neutral observer examining the reported results would almost certainly conclude that the Rorschach test provided inferences that seemed at least compatible with, if not validated by, the findings based upon direct observation.

Perhaps the most careful attempt to assess the utility of projective techniques in an alien cultural setting is William Henry's (1947) application of the TAT in a study of the Hopi and Navaho. The findings we have already considered show that under relatively well-controlled circumstances the personality inferences derived from the TAT have considerable correspondence to similar inferences drawn from life-history information, observation, and the Rorschach. All in all, this study provides strong positive evidence for the utility of this instrument with American Indian subjects. The TAT study of Ulithian personality by Lessa and Spiegelman (1954) represents another careful and detailed comparison of projective-technique findings and ethnographic report, with results that generally affirm the accuracy or utility of the projective-test inferences. The reader will recall that in spite of the general excellence of the study, the investigators clearly failed to eliminate the possibility that their positive findings were produced, in part or whole, by bias or commitment on the part of the judges.

A further study that attempted to generalize concerning the merit of projective tests in this setting is the investigation in which Gladwin and Sarason (1953) compare Rorschach and TAT analyses with ethnographic findings. Their comparison was detailed and explicit but involved no empirical controls or quantification. The authors concluded that there is a high degree of consistency between the two domains of data. They also emphasized the value of projective-test findings as an aid in the analysis of ethnographic data. Employing TAT and Rorschach tests, Macgregor (1946) reported that findings derived from these instruments showed considerable correspondence to findings from other sources, including observation and nonprojective personality measures, although he does not mention the details of how he estimated this association. Likewise, Billig,

Gillin, and Davidson (1947, 1948) reported that blind analysis of Rorschachs secured from Indians and Ladinos of Guatemala led to results that ". . . agreed in almost all cases with the ethnologist's opinions" (p. 166), but they failed to indicate how this agreement was measured.

In the same vein, Hallowell (1955) surveyed his own experience and that of others in the cross-cultural use of the Rorschach test, focusing his analysis upon incidence of Movement responses and Popular responses, and concluded that although there are many problems in these applications of the Rorschach, the instrument appears to be a useful tool for the anthropologist. On the basis of the multiple interpretations of Unabelin's Rorschach protocols, Mead (1949) suggested that the test appears useful and worth inclusion among the instruments of the anthropologist, for it increases communication between anthropologist and psychologist and also might aid in identifying cultural elements of particular emotional significance.

To these studies might be added a large number of anthropological inquiries in which investigators have employed both projective techniques and other methods of observation and have arrived at generally favorable conclusions concerning the usefulness of the projective devices (for example, Barnouw, 1950; Caudill, 1952; Honigmann, 1949; Joseph & Murray, 1951; Kluckhohn & Rosenzweig, 1949; Spindler, 1955; Straus & Straus, 1957; and Wallace, 1952).

On the negative side is the study by Adcock and Ritchie (1958), who, on the basis of a factor analysis of Rorschach data collected from a number of Maori and white subjects, concluded that the use of this test in cross-cultural investigation is hazardous. They recommend searching for a more suitable instrument for personality assessment. The criticisms of this study outlined earlier make clear that this recommendation does not derive from trustworthy findings. A similar negative verdict resulted from a study in which the Draw-a-Person Test was applied to Eskimo and Cree Indian children. Honigmann and Carrera (1957) conclude that the test appears to have little usefulness for the person interested in assessing personality in a cross-cultural setting. Again, however, the procedural flaws in the study are sufficient to seriously impair one's confidence in this generalization. A further negative instance is provided by some of the publications by Jules Henry (Henry, 1955; Mensh & Henry, 1953) which are sharply critical of projective tests and were written following field experience with several of these instruments.

Thus, we find a considerable array of evidence pertinent to an evaluation of projective techniques in a cross-cultural setting. Furthermore, with only two or three somewhat frail exceptions, this evidence supports the actual or potential usefulness of these instruments for the anthropologist. It is essential to remember, however, that very few of these studies involved even minimal controls for ruling out the contribution of chance factors or observer bias. The vast majority of the evidence and opinion we have cited must be evaluated with a full awareness that these observers, raters, judges, and interpreters are persons who have committed large quantities of time and energy to research involving projective techniques. Most of them also had some faith or conviction in these instruments prior to embarking upon their research. Consequently it would not be easy for them to assert that such an activity was of little or no merit.

We may conclude then, that the generally positive attitude of those who have had experience with projective techniques in cross-cultural settings is not to be accepted alone as providing firm and unequivocal support for this use. On the other hand, one must admit that such evidence is worth something and, in the absence of contrary findings, it should be given some weight. Perhaps the most encouraging feature of this situation is that in those studies that have most successfully introduced the necessary empirical controls, the findings and opinions of the investigators are fully as positive as they are in studies with a minimum of such controls.

In summary, it is clear that (*a*) the process of assessing the cross-cultural validity of projective techniques is an enormously complex and demanding task; (*b*) we do not at present have adequate evidence upon which to base any confident generalizations; (*c*) what evidence we do have tends to support the utility of these tests in cross-cultural research, although this may be largely, or partially, a reflection of powerful biasing factors that have operated in most evaluations.

RORSCHACH OR TAT?

Although we have observed the application of a number of different projective techniques in anthropological research, it seems clear that general usage here is as concentrated upon Rorschach and TAT as it is in the psychiatric or clinical setting. Thus, if we are concerned with the relative merit of the various projective techniques for the anthropologist, it seems evident that the major question to be answered has to do with the differential effectiveness of these two instruments.

There are certain rational considerations that can be introduced meaningfully in our discussion without recourse to empirical data. For example, it is undeniable that language skills play a more important role in the production of TAT stories than in the identification of Rorschach percepts. It is also clear that cultural variation in regard to storytelling conventions would have a considerable effect upon TAT response and less influence upon Rorschach responses. What we know of Rorschach and TAT results in our own society suggests that the TAT is more vulnerable to age and education differences, so that this instrument would be expected to be more difficult to administer to very young subjects or to those with limited intelligence or education. The Rorschach stimulus material, at least on the surface, appears less culturally specific than TAT cards and consequently may be applicable in a much wider variety of cultural settings without extensive modification. The Rorschach test is accompanied by a much more elaborate and developed scheme for analysis than the TAT, and consequently there are a great many more specific Rorschach interpretive generalizations readily available than there are TAT generalizations. All of these considerations, and some of them are exceedingly important, point to the potential superiority of the Rorschach over the TAT in cross-cultural investigation.

On behalf of the TAT one may begin by pointing to the fact that it elicits much more profuse and varied response data than the Rorschach does. This more extensive array of data makes it possible to use the instrument to learn something about the culture which, although a minor goal for such an instrument, is largely closed to a test eliciting so few responses as the Rorschach. Furthermore, since the responses contain much more content, the investigator is better able in his analysis to test the reasonableness of his inferences against the range of responses themselves, that is, by their internal consistency. Perhaps most important of all is the fact that the person using the TAT is not nearly so likely to depend completely upon the cultural transitivity of specific interpretive rules as is the Rorschach interpreter. In some important respects, it seems much more defensible to link a particular response, the content of which manifests or reveals a particular interest or motive, to the existence of this motive in the subject than to take a particular type of classified Rorschach response and assume that its psychological significance in this nonliterate society will be the same as it is in Western Europe. More generally, one may reason that the lack of structure and prescription for interpretation of the TAT is likely to engender caution and respect for the complexity of cross-cultural interpretation, whereas the deceptive specificity of the scoring and analysis of the Rorschach may lead to a greater recklessness or willingness to plunge into interpretive generalizations. One must also remember that storytelling is almost a universal of human behavior and consequently the responses requested by the TAT examiner may appear relatively understandable and familiar even in quite diverse settings.

Thus, on a priori grounds it seems that each instrument offers certain strategic advantages in comparison to the others. However, it is difficult to be sure that the cumulative weight of these advantages clearly favors one instrument over the other, although some may feel that the scales are tipped slightly in favor of the Rorschach.

Have there been investigations in which both instruments were used and some effort made to compare their relative effectiveness? A few, but none of them offers the kind of definitive answer to this question that we are seeking. For example, Gladwin and Sarason (1953) used both tests and concluded that each had a unique contribution to make that warranted their dual application. However, if one looks closely at the analysis conducted by these authors, there seems little doubt that the Rorschach contributed more heavily to their psychological generalizations concerning the Trukese. This, of course, is not necessarily a decisive observation, for the prior preference and experience of the psychologist with the two instruments must have had some influence, and, furthermore, the readiness with which the Rorschach data can be interpreted (although granted that Sarason does not take the easy way out here) would also be expected to have some influence on the relative dependence upon each of the instruments. Joseph, Spicer, and Chesky (1949) used both TAT and Rorschach in their study of personality development among the Papago Indians and reported that the two tests led to highly consistent results, although they do not describe the empirical basis for this generalization. It is clear in this study also that the published report leans much more heavily upon Rorschach findings than upon TAT findings. Again the extensive experience of one of the authors with the Rorschach lessens the significance of this observation as a basis for judging the relative merit of the two instruments. Henry's

(1947) study of Navaho personality provides a more explicit comparison of the results derived from TAT and Rorschach, and he reports a high degree of consistency in the inferences derived from the two instruments.

In general, then, it seems that those who have used both the TAT and Rorschach in their cross-cultural studies have concluded that both tests possess merit, and there is little in these studies to suggest the clear superiority of either instrument over the other. Furthermore, there is some evidence indicating that the two tests provide congruent findings.

There seems little possibility of arriving at a general recommendation that will hold true for many different investigators and many different problems. Fortunately, the choice of instrument will often be settled automatically in the process of making arrangements for the collection and analysis of the personality data. If the person responsible for this phase of the research is enthusiastic about one instrument and indifferent about the other, it is obviously wise to select the test that evokes enthusiasm. Whatever differences there may be between the two instruments in their potential utility will surely be less than the difference between either instrument in the hands of a sophisticated, highly motivated analyst and the same instrument in the hands of a naïve or doubting analyst.

Lacking such an automatic basis for deciding between these instruments, perhaps the wisest course is to focus upon the matter of the specific, transcultural generality of Rorschach interpretive rules. If the investigator is willing to buy or accept this assumed generality, the Rorschach test is likely to prove the preferred instrument. However, if the anthropologist is unwilling to invest this much faith in the cultural flexibility of specific Rorschach scoring and interpretation, then the TAT will probably be favored.

One should not construe the fact that our discussion has dwelt upon the Rorschach and TAT as an endorsement of these two instruments for cross-cultural research. It is altogether possible that other avenues to the appraisal of personality, such as the interpretation of dreams, doll play, Chapple's Interaction Chronograph, a standardized interview, or perhaps approaches yet to be developed, will prove vastly superior to either the TAT or Rorschach. Here we are merely discussing status quo, and the existing state of culture and personality research is such that status quo may be anything but a stable image of the future.

WHAT IS THE OUTCOME OF THE PAST AND THE PROMISE OF THE FUTURE?

We now have a vivid picture of the great amount of effort that has been invested in cross-cultural research involving projective techniques, we have some idea of the kinds of problems that have been approached, we have seen something of the empirical findings that have resulted, and we have considered the evidence for the cross-cultural validity of these techniques. Does all of this permit us to arrive at an easy generalization concerning the merit of these devices in this setting?

In absolute terms, yes; in relative terms, no. By this I mean it is easy to look at the array of studies that have been conducted, their flaws, their resultant empirical findings and theoretical implications and conclude that what projective techniques have contributed to anthropology is slight. When we look for dependable empirical generalizations and find so few as we have just listed and, at the same time, consider the years of patient toil by capable investigators, it is not hard to arrive at a negative verdict. Although our discussion of the typical flaws in such research makes it clear that the instruments cannot be blamed alone for the failure of these studies to live up to any lofty ideal, these shortcomings in the research are not sufficient by themselves to account for so small a yield. If projective techniques were, in fact, sensitive, reliable instruments that enabled the skilled user to gain firm empirical control over important dimensions of behavior, there is little doubt that the results of the studies we have discussed would have been dramatically different, even without great changes in design and execution. Actually, the crucial importance of small deviations from the best possible procedure is largely a function of the precarious stability and sensitivity of the measures being employed. Things are already so bad that we can ill afford additional error variance! In brief, then, when compared to the ideal, projective techniques have proven themselves inefficient, and their empirical yield appears slight when contrasted with the enormous commitments of time, money, and talent to research in this area.

Regrettably it is seldom possible for the social scientist to indulge in the luxury of absolute judgments. Almost always he is faced with the necessity of choosing not what is a good or bad instrument but what is a better or a poorer instrument. If we apply this familiar perspective to the present scene and inquire what has been the contribution of studies employing projective techniques to this area of investigation in comparison to that of similar studies using other devices, there seems little doubt that our judgment of projective techniques must be more lenient. There are serious problems involved in the cross-cultural use of projective techniques (or, for that matter, in any use of these devices), but these are scarcely more serious than the comparable problems attached to the method of direct observation, participant observation, or the clinical interview. Although the firm empirical generalizations resulting from projective techniques are few, the study of culture and personality is not as a whole characterized by a high incidence of such generalizations. In fact, if we had conducted a similar survey of research findings involving the interview or participant observation, the empirical yield for these devices would undoubtedly have been similarly slight. Thus, we may conclude that if the investigator is determined to assess personality variables in a nonliterate culture, projective techniques, for all of their infirmities, may still be worth serious consideration.

In general, then, if we ask what has been the past contribution of the projective test in cross-cultural research, the answer must depend upon whether we adopt permissive or exacting standards. By any firm standards these tests do not have a distinguished record. Although the usefulness of these instruments and the number and significance of their findings are not compelling, it is evident that if we consider the relatively underdeveloped nature of cross-cultural research and the comparable contributions mediated by other personality instruments, projective techniques cannot be judged devoid of merit for the anthropologist.

What of the future? Clearly the extent to which these devices will be used in anthropological research is closely linked to the future development of projective techniques, particularly the Rorschach and TAT, as well as future developments in the domain of culture and personality.

At this point it is impossible to forecast accurately the ultimate fate of projective techniques in the hands of psychologists. We can say, however, that these instruments at present operate inefficiently, that they lack a firm theoretical underpinning, and that they are responsive to many factors in addition to those they are intended to assess. Thus, in the future these instruments will either have to be vastly improved or superseded. On the one hand, it is possible that with better understanding of the relevant parameters influencing test performance and perhaps with some modifications in the tests themselves, it will be possible to use these instruments with greater confidence and success. On the other hand, it may be that the focus of attention in the measurement of personality will shift to other instruments, to methods of biological assay, to refined techniques of objective observation, or to improved situational tests.

What we have said already concerning the link between projective techniques and psychoanalytic theory suggests that the future status of psychoanalysis may well have something to do with that of projective techniques. If social scientists in the future become disillusioned and abandon psychoanalytic concepts, undoubtedly their interest in projective techniques will become less intense.

Just as developments within psychology must play an important role in the future of these instruments in cultural research, so too events in anthropology must have a pronounced influence. The most obvious consideration here is the future expansion or contraction of interest in culture and personality. This area of cultural anthropology has undergone enormous development in the past several decades. If the interest in the relation between personal qualities and institutional and cultural events continues as the field of anthropology expands, undoubtedly the demand for personality measures that can be used outside our culture will continue unabated or even be enhanced. At present there seems no reason to expect any diminution of interest in problems concerned with national character or acculturation, and yet there is always the possibility of sudden shifts in empirical interest. If these topics should lose salience, the status of projective tests in anthropological research would be vastly changed.

Another relevant consideration is the extent to which anthropologists retain their interest in the individual and the particular. Current fascination with projective techniques has certainly been contributed to by the idiographers among psychologists and anthropologists. Our brief survey of the empirical findings derived from these instruments made clear the poverty of general findings and the relative wealth of individual or case-history findings. If anthropologists should become largely interested in general laws or nomothetic findings, there seems little doubt that their interest in projective techniques would diminish. Such a development does not seem likely.

One may note the informal belief of many anthropologists that interest in projective techniques has declined sharply among cultural anthropologists in the past five or ten years. Such a trend or shift in attitude may well exist, but it is not yet evident in the publication record. In observing anthropology graduate students during this same period, one also sees that although there may have been a decrease in fascination with these instruments, there remains a considerable degree of interest in them.

Although it is difficult to make specific and illuminating predictions for the future, there are certain generalizations about the present that can be made with confidence. First, projective techniques do not represent a magic door that opens easily to reveal the essential aspects of personality to the interested investigator. The problems posed by language differences, as well as many other non-personality correlates of culture that influence test performance, make it evident that only the most careful and sophisticated analysis of projective-test data is likely to provide valid and useful inferences concerning personality. In general, it seems a safe conclusion that *the present state of these instruments militates against important findings or empirical generalizations except when the instruments are applied with exceptional industry and caution by individuals of unusual competence.*

It is possible, however, for the investigator to eschew precision and firm empirical findings and to use these instruments with modest intent as nothing more than a source of data to be incorporated *descriptively* with the more conventional sources of ethnographic data. Here the projective-technique protocols are treated merely as an additional opportunity to observe subjects responding in a familiar situation. Such an approach will not result in secure empirical findings, dependable generalizations, or confirmation of predictions, but it may lead to new ideas or speculations of much the same sort that traditionally have comprised the field of culture and personality. The main consideration here is that the investigator be willing to treat the data in such a manner that their heuristic impact will be maximized. This suggests the advisability of not clinging tightly to conventional and formal methods of analysis.

It seems clear that future cultural research employing projective techniques would do well to *pay serious attention to the typical flaws or shortcomings* outlined in the previous chapter. Even a small number of studies carefully designed and executed to avoid these difficulties would make a much more substantial contribution to cultural anthropology, and to an understanding of projective techniques in this setting, than the extensive array of somewhat haphazard studies that have already been conducted.

One may argue that investigators thus far have shown altogether too little interest in re-examining the data and personality inferences embedded in the studies we have just discussed. Very little is known of *the extent to which personality inferences reported by one investigator* on the basis of projective-technique protocols, with or without other data, *can be reproduced by another investigator,* if he is given the opportunity to observe the same subjects or even the same raw data. We have already mentioned Kaplan's (1956) microfilm collection of various kinds of raw data, including projective techniques, and the existence of such a body of information makes it possible to conduct an extremely economical set of procedural studies. Such studies would at least tell us whether the personality inferences derived from projective-technique protocols collected in a cross-cultural setting can be independently reproduced by trained interpreters. It would be relatively easy to find out whether a skilled Rorschach analyst could examine Wallace's Tuscarora protocols and arrive at independent personality inferences corresponding to those reported by Wallace on the basis of a combination of ethnographic and projective-test data. Or we might ask whether Caudill's inferences concerning the Ojibwa could be essentially reproduced by a second analyst given only the TAT protocols with which Caudill worked. Would the Rorschach differences between Spindler's acculturation groups be sustained if the Rorschach protocols were independently analyzed by another investigator? The essential point here is that this is a type of study that would be of considerable importance in evaluating the contribution of projective techniques to anthropological research, that could be executed with relative ease, and yet remains to be executed.

Is there a general verdict concerning the use of projective techniques in anthropological research? It is a gray world in which we live! There are both good and bad aspects to the history of association between these instruments and this area of research. Although one may hope that research yet to be conducted will resolve many of the present ambiguities, one must, for the moment, leave the verdict to the individual observer. Those with high standards and a cathexis for rigor and empirical control will surely consider projective techniques guilty as charged and view them as possessing little or no demonstrated merit in this setting. Those who resonate to sensitive speculation and believe there is still a place for unadorned descriptive inquiry in the social sciences may well conclude that projective techniques have made defensible contributions to anthropological research and that their continued use is fully warranted.

My own impression is that studies involving the most sophisticated use of these instruments in this setting (for example, Gladwin & Sarason, 1953; Spindler, 1955; Wallace, 1952) provide a clear justification for the anthropologist displaying renewed interest in projective techniques. Unfortunately, I must add that such studies at present are vastly outnumbered by those in which these devices do not appear to have made a legitimate investigative contribution.

REFERENCES

ADCOCK, C. J., & RITCHIE, J. E. Intercultural use of Rorschach. *Amer. Anthrop.*, 1958, 60, 881-892.

ALEXANDER, T. & ANDERSON, R. Children in a society under stress. *Behav. Sci.*, 1957, 2, 46-55.

BARNOUW, V. Acculturation and personality among the Wisconsin Chippewa. *Amer. Anthrop. Assoc. Memoir*, 1950, No. 72.

BILLIG, O., GILLIN, J., & DAVIDSON, W. Aspects of personality and culture in a Guatemalan community: ethnological and Rorschach approaches. Part I. *J. Pers.*, 1947, 16, 153-187.

BILLIG, O., GILLIN, J., & DAVIDSON, W. Aspects of personality and culture in a Guatemalan community: ethnological and Rorschach approaches. Part II. *J. Pers.*, 1948, 16, 326-368.

CAUDILL, W. Japanese-American personality and acculturation. *Genet. Psychol. Monogr.*, 1952, 45, 3-102.

CRONBACH, L. J., & MEEHL, P. E. Construct validity in psychological tests. *Psychol. Bull.*, 1955, 52, 281-302.

DU BOIS, Cora. *The People of Alor*. Minneapolis: Univer. Minnesota Press, 1944.

GLADWIN, T., & SARASON, S. B. *Truk: man in paradise*. New York: Wenner-Gren Foundation, 1953.

HALLOWELL, A. I. *Culture and experience*. Philadelphia: Univer. Pennsylvania Press, 1955.

HENRY, J. Symposium: Projective testing in ethnography. *Am. Anthrop.*, 1955, 57, 245-247, 264-269.

HENRY, W. E. The Thematic Apperception Technique in the study of culture-personality relations. *Genet. Psychol. Monogr.*, 1947, 35, 3-135.

HONIGMANN, J. J. Culture and ethos of Kaska society. *Yale University Publications in Anthropology*, 1949, No. 40.

HONIGMANN, J. J., & CARRERA, R. N. Cross-cultural use of Machover's figure drawing test. *Am. Anthrop.*, 1957, 59, 650-654.

JOSEPH, Alice, & MURRAY, Veronica F. *Chamorros and Carolinians of Saipan: personality studies.* Cambridge: Harvard Univer. Press, 1951.

JOSEPH, Alice, SPICER, Rosamund B., & CHESKY, Jane. *The desert people: A study of the Papago Indians.* Chicago: Univer. Chicago Press, 1949.

KAPLAN, B. A study of Rorschach responses in four cultures. *Peabody Museum of Harvard University Papers*, 1955, 42, No. 2.

KAPLAN, B., (Ed.) *Primary records in culture and personality*, Vol. I. Madison, Wisconsin: The Microcard Foundation, 1956.

KLUCKHOHN, C. The personal document in anthropological science. In L. Gottschalk, C. Kluckhohn, & R. Angell, The use of personal documents in history, anthropology, and sociology. *Soc. Sci. Res. Council Bull.*, 1945, No. 53, 79-173.

KLUCKHOHN, C., & ROSENZWEIG, Janine C. Two Navaho children over a five-year period. *Amer. J. Othopsychiat.*, 1949, 19, 266-278.

LESSA, W. A., & SPIEGELMAN, M. Ulithian personality as seen through ethnological materials and thematic test analysis. *University of California Publications in Culture and Society*, 1954, 2, 243-301.

MACGREGOR, G. *Warriors without weapons: A study of the society and personality development of the Pine Ridge Sioux.* Chicago: Univer. Chicago Press, 1946.

MEAD, Margaret. The Mountain Arapesh, V. The record of Unabelin with Rorschach analysis. *Anthrop. Papers Amer. Museum Nat. Hist.*, 1949.

MENSH, I., & HENRY, J. Direct observation and psychological tests in anthropological field work. *Amer. Anthrop.*, 1953, 55, 461-480.

SPINDLER, G. D. Sociocultural and psychological processes in Menomini acculturation. *University of California Publications in Culture and Society*, 1955, 5.

STRAUS, M. A., & STRAUS, Jacqueline H. Personal insecurity and Sinhalese social structure: Rorschach evidence for primary school children. *East. Anthrop.*, 1957, 10, 97-111.

Technical recommendations for psychological tests and diagnostic techniques. *Psychol. Bull. Supplement*, 1954, 51, 2, Part 2, 1-38.

WALLACE, A. F. C. The modal personality structure of the Tuscarora Indians as revealed by the Rorschach Test. *Bull. Bur. Amer. Ethnol.*, 1952, No. 150.

Author Index

331

Subject Index

Acculturation, 307, 311, 325; and adjustment, 14-15, 226-230, 232-239, 242, 245, 248-249, 255-256; projective tests and study of, 208, 226-257, 267; sex differences, 14-15, 236-238, 239-241

Achievement motive, 69, 71; in Japanese-Americans, 249

Adaptation-level theory, 110

Adjustment, 53, 265-266, 277; and acculturation, 14-15, 226-230, 232-239, 242, 245, 248-249, 255-256

Affect: and Rorschach test, 59-60; temporary, 147, 162, 163-164, 167

Affiliation, TAT measure of, 70

Age: effects on projective-test response, 247-249, 299; and personality in Saipanese, 207-209; and personality in Utes, 292-294

Aggression, 131-132, 161; in Algerians, 255-257; in Eskimo and Cree children, 294-296; fantasy vs. overt, 135-139; in Hopi, 259-260; in Japanese-Americans, 245; in Ojibwa, 227, 229-230; play technique, 16, 89; Rorschach, 61; TAT, 69; in Tepoztecans, 204; in Tuscarora, 211

Algeria, 254-257

Algonkians. See Ojibwa

Alorese, 196-200, 313, 316

Ambivalence, 27

American Indian TAT, 70

Antecedent events and projective tests, 181, 243-244

Anxiety, 27, 130; and aggression, 138; in Algerians, 255; in Chinese, 217; in Guatemalans, 265; in Hopi, 259; in Menomini, 235; Rorschach, 61; in Saipanese, 208-209; in Sinhalese, 214; in Sioux, 260; in Trukese, 273; TAT, 69

Arab, 254-257

Arapesh, 280-283

Arthur Point Performance Scale, 258

Association techniques, 51-66

Assumptions underlying projective tests, 145-152, 154, 161

Auditory projective test, general description of, 65-66

Banias, 223

Bavelas' Moral Ideology Test, 258, 293

Bender Gestalt Test, 209

Berens River. See Ojibwa

Bhilinese, 223

Blacky Pictures: general description of, 73-75; and psychoanalytic theory, 127-128

Blind interpretation, 171, 188-189, 200, 213, 217, 265, 268, 283-284, 296-297

Body image of Hindu, 222

Body-Word Association Test, 293

Brahmins, 222

Carolinians, 206-210, 290-293

Caroline Islands, TAT study, 290-293

Ceylon, 213-216

Chamorros, 206-210

Cheyenne, 251-252

Children's Apperception Test, 70

Chinese, 216-218, 239-241

Chippewa. See Ojibwa

Choice techniques, 82-88

Clinical tradition, 31-32

Cloud pictures, general description of, 64-65

Cognitive style, 147

Color response, 15, 57-58, 61, 144, 204, 219, 231, 250, 261, 265-267

Completion techniques, 75-82

Conflict, 111, 114-115, 163-165; in Navaho, 241

Conflict, sexual: in Eskimo and Cree children, 294-296; in Trukese, 271

Constriction, 59, 161, 204, 214, 216, 235, 260-261, 265-267

Construction techniques, 66-75

Contamination of data, 188-189, 274-275

Content analysis, 57, 59, 68, 161

Projective tests: anthropologist's interest in, 2-11; classification of, 49-51; contributions to anthropological research, 306-328; criticism of cross-cultural use of, 18-22, 177-193; cross-cultural applications, 194-305; cross-cultural validity of, 191-192, 275-296, 314-319; definition of, 38-46; early cross-cultural use, 11-17; effects on analysis of ethnographic data, 272-273, 313-314; and field-work data, 188-189, 312; interpretation of, 160-176, 185-186; origins of, 31-38; results isolated from ethnographic data, 300; statistical problems, 185; theoretical foundations of, 108-159; varieties of, 49-107

Psychiatric interview *vs.* projective tests, 183-184

Psychoanalytic theory: and concept of projection, 25-31; and interest in projective test, 5, 7, 325; and origins of projective tests, 32-38; and projective tests, 75, 110, 117-128, 131, 152-155; and Sinhalese culture and personality, 216

Psychobiology, 222

Psychocultural synthesis of the Alorese, 196-200

Psychodrama, 93-94

Psychological theory and projective tests, 108-159

Psychometric tradition, 32

Psychosis and projective test with Saipanese, 207

Purpose of cross-cultural use of projective tests, 306-310

Quantification of projective-test data, 63, 162-163, 170-171, 185, 210, 228, 283-284, 314

Quckchi, 16

Rajputs, 222

Random factors and projective tests, 162-163

Rapport, effects on Rorschach, 286-287

Raven Progressive Matrices test of intelligence, 222

Reaction formation, 114-115, 120

Receptor-orienting responses, 113

Regression in service of the ego, 118, 121

Reliability, 327; of Micronesian TAT, 290-291; of Rorschach, 281, 284-287; of TAT, 70, 278-279, 290-291

Response-produced stimuli, 113

Response set, 147, 162, 165-167

Rigidity: in Algerians, 255-256; in Guatemalans, 267; in Hopi, 269; in Japanese-Americans, 248-249; in Menomini, 235-236

Role-playing, 92-93

Rorschach test, 3-4, 6, 11, 18-21, 52, 64, 67, 69, 72, 77, 79, 82, 109, 117, 119-120, 122, 126-127, 131-135, 140-143, 151, 184-186, 190, 196-199, 264-265, 267-268, 288-290, 295-296, 300, 316-318; with Algerians, 254-257; with Algonkian, 226-229; with Alorese, 196-200; with Arapesh, 280-283; with Carolinians, 206-210; with Chamorros, 206-210; with Cheyenne, 251-252; with Chinese, 216-218, 239-241; cross-cultural validity of, 275-277; early applications, 11-16; general description of, 55-63; with Hindu, 222-224; with Hopi, 258-260; with Japanese, 200; with Japanese-Americans, 247-249; with Kaska, 200-202; with Menomini, 232-239; with Mormons, 218-222; with Moroccans, 12-14; with Navaho, 218-222, 241-244, 249-251, 258, 262-263, 284-287; with Ojibwa, 14-15, 210-213, 226-229, 230-231, 276-277; origins of, 33-34; with Papago, 258, 262-263; with Pilaga, 15-16; reliability of, 281, 284-287; with Sinhalese, 213-216; with Sioux, 258, 260; with Spanish-Americans, 218-222, 249-251; with Swiss, 12; and TAT, 272-273, 278-280, 319-322; with Tepoztecans, 203-210; with Trukese, 269-275; with Tuscarora, 210-213; with Utes, 293-294; with Zuni, 218-222, 249-251

Rotter Incomplete Sentences Blank, 76-78

Sacks Sentence Completion Test, 77

Saipan, 206-210

Salteux. *See* Ojibwa

Sampling error, 186-187, 314

Schizophrenics *vs.* normals: neurotics and Algerians, 254-256; neurotics and Japanese-Americans, 247-249

Sensory-tonic theory and Movement response, 141-142, 144-145

Sentence completion test, 81; origins of, 34-35; general description of, 76-79; with Navaho, 241